Law and Politics under the Abbasids

Abu Ma'ali al-Juwayni (d. 478/1085) lived in a politically tumultuous period. The rise of powerful dynastic families forced the Abbasid Caliph into a position of titular power and created instability. He also witnessed intellectual upheavals living amid great theological and legal diversity. Collectively, these experiences led him to consider questions of religious certainty and social and political continuity. He questioned that if political elites are constantly changing, paralleled with shifting intellectual allegiances, what ensures the continuity of religion? He concluded that continuity of society is contingent on knowledge and practice of the Shari'a. Here, Sohaira Z. M. Siddiqui explores how scholars grappled with questions of human reason and knowledge, and how their answers to these questions often led them to challenge dominant ideas of what the Shari'a is. By doing this, she highlights the interconnections between al-Juwayni's discussions on theology, law, and politics and the sociopolitical intellectual landscapes that forged them.

Sohaira Z. M. Siddiqui is an assistant professor at Georgetown University Qatar. She has published articles in the *Journal of Islamic Studies*, *Islamic Law and Society*, the *Journal of the American Oriental Society*, and *Middle East Law and Governance*. She is also the editor of a forthcoming volume entitled *Locating the Shari'a: Legal Fluidity in Theory, History and Practice*. She has held fellowships at the University of Cambridge and Harvard Law School and is a series editor for *Sapientia Islamica*.

Cambridge Studies in Islamic Civilization

Other titles in the series are listed at the back of the book.

Law and Politics under the Abbasids

An Intellectual Portrait of al-Juwayni

SOHAIRA Z. M. SIDDIQUI
Georgetown University Qatar

CAMBRIDGE
UNIVERSITY PRESS

CAMBRIDGE
UNIVERSITY PRESS

University Printing House, Cambridge CB2 8BS, United Kingdom

One Liberty Plaza, 20th Floor, New York, NY 10006, USA

477 Williamstown Road, Port Melbourne, VIC 3207, Australia

314–321, 3rd Floor, Plot 3, Splendor Forum, Jasola District Centre,
New Delhi – 110025, India

79 Anson Road, #06–04/06, Singapore 079906

Cambridge University Press is part of the University of Cambridge.

It furthers the University's mission by disseminating knowledge in the pursuit of education, learning, and research at the highest international levels of excellence.

www.cambridge.org
Information on this title: www.cambridge.org/9781108496780
DOI: 10.1017/9781108654784

First published 2019

Printed and bound in Great Britain by Clays Ltd, Elcograf S.p.A.

A catalogue record for this publication is available from the British Library.

Library of Congress Cataloging-in-Publication Data
Names: Siddiqui, Sohaira Zahid, author.
Title: Law and politics under the Abbasids : an intellectual portrait of al-Juwayni / Sohaira Z. M. Siddiqui.
Description: Cambridge, United Kingdom ; New York, NY : Cambridge University Press, 2019. | Series: Cambridge studies in Islamic civilization | Includes bibliographical references and index.
Identifiers: LCCN 2018061699 | ISBN 9781108496780 (hardback : alk. paper)
Subjects: LCSH: Imām al-Ḥaramayn al-Juwaynī, ʻAbd al-Malik ibn ʻAbd Allāh, 1028-1085. | Islamic law–History–To 1500. | Islamic law–Methodology. | Muslim scholars–Biography. | Abbasids
Classification: LCC KBP330.I43 S55 2019 | DDC 340.5/9–dc23
LC record available at https://lccn.loc.gov/2018061699

ISBN 978-1-108-49678-0 Hardback

To

All those who are certain of their doubt,

And doubtful of their certainty.

Contents

Acknowledgments

> The requisites of knowledge: a quick mind, zeal, poverty, foreign land, a teacher's inspiration, and of life a long span.
>
> – al-Juwaynī (quoted in George Makdisi, *The Rise of Colleges*, 1981)

After many iterations of these pages I realized that striving for perfectly complete acknowledgments is akin to chasing a receding horizon. A project that has been in gestation for the past ten years is inevitably inspired, informed, and assisted by more individuals than can be adequately acknowledged in a few pages. What follows is a mere attempt at recognizing the confluence of forces, individuals, and prayers that facilitated the completion of this project.

I must begin by thanking God, who created human beings with reason. Curiosity, ingenuity, invention, and knowledge are but outworkings of this basic faculty of reason. Though scholars have long debated its limits and form, none has contested its existence.

This project started off as a simple question on human reason and legal knowledge that I posed to my PhD supervisor and mentor, Ahmad Atif Ahmad. Instead of giving me a direct answer, he asked me whether I had read al-Juwaynī's discussion on the matter. My answer in the negative brought on his suggestion to do so. Dr. Ahmad's refusal to provide me with immediate satisfaction resulted in this project, and his unparalleled dedication and mentorship has left an indelible mark on this work and on my entire approach to the discipline of Islamic law. He graciously sat with me for countless hours reading classical treatises in *uṣūl al-fiqh*, guiding me toward nuanced arguments not immediately intelligible to an apprentice's eye. His intellectual curiosity, uncanny ability to recall texts with great accuracy, and emphasis on the interconnectivity of seemingly distinct inquiries and disciplines has continued to inspire me. This project would have been simply impossible without him. I thank him most for teaching me the value of not giving simple answers to complex questions.

I was also fortunate to have the direct academic guidance of Juan Campo, who pushed me to investigate the implications of al-Juwaynī's scholarship both during his time and beyond to ours. Racha El Omari also served as an invaluable advisor and inspiration with her keen insight into the development of early Islamic thought. Her attention to detail encouraged me to trace the intellectual debates in *uṣūl al-fiqh* to their earliest articulations, which are often found in books of *kalām*. Going back further, I am indebted to Jonathan Brown and Clark Lombardi for introducing me to the intellectual playground of *uṣūl al-fiqh* and the implications of classical Islamic legal thought in the modern world. The first primary text I read in Islamic legal theory was with Jonathan, and it was al-Juwaynī's *Waraqāt fī uṣūl al-fiqh*. Neither he nor I had any premonition at the time that al-Juwaynī would become such a long-standing intellectual companion.

In the formulation of this project I benefited greatly from the institutional support of the Asian and Middle Eastern Studies Faculty at Cambridge University, the Islamic Legal Studies Program at Harvard Law School, the University of Tübingen, and, most of all, Georgetown University in Qatar. The support I found in Qatar for the past few years has been especially important. In particular I would like to thank Rory and Michelle Miller, Mahveen Azam, Mateen Quraishi, Sophie Khan, and Billal Riaz – their unending words of encouragement, friendship, and ceaselessly open table spreads saw this project through to its completion. Conversations with mentors, colleagues, and friends who took the time to engage with this project have also been invaluable, and for this I would like to thank Asma Afsaruddin, Asifa Quraishi-Landes, Ovamir Anjum, Anver Emon, Lejla Demiri, Dale Correa, Samy Ayoub, Sohail Hanif, Heba Sewliman, Rosabel Martin-Ross, Munther al-Sabbagh, Samaneh Oladi, Nathan French, Ahmet Temel, Elliott Bazzano, Rico Monge, Martin Becker, and Dusty Hoesly. Special gratitude is due to my closest confidants who, beyond encouraging my academic development, were pillars of emotional and spiritual support. They taught me that few things cannot be resolved through long walks, thoughtful conversation, and true companionship – to Amina Nawaz, Arsalan Ghani, Nabila Winter, and Layla El-Wafi, I am truly indebted.

It is standard in academia to recognize one's students, as they are usually the most consistent interlocutors for one's ideas and writings. Though this is certainly the case with my students, their role goes beyond that: they pushed me to personalize this project and my study of Islamic law in a way I had previously neglected. Perhaps most important, they made me realize that the community I speak of within this book is in fact the community both they and I inhabit – a community with a continually evolving set of challenges and circumstances that must be addressed in a way that is both methodologically robust and religiously honest. For their curiosity, questions, and insight, I specifically thank Nada Abdelhay, Salman Ahad, Sherif el Gindi, Hisham Hassan, Aya Makki, and Abdurrehman Naveed.

My parents deserve the most gratitude, for contrary to their better judgment and cultural mores, they simply set me free to explore. Everything they taught me before that moment informed everything that happened after it. My sister and brother have been my most cherished friends throughout this entire project. My sister, Fareeha Siddiqui, deserves particular mention, as the burden of sacrificing her own dreams early in her life led her to fearlessly defend mine. At all the pivotal crossroads in life, she was my most important signpost. My brother and oldest companion, Waqaas Siddiqui, is the archetypal elder brother – never have I encountered a brother with such generosity, an entrepreneur with such humility, or a man with so many bow ties. Our conversations have always been a source of insight, and his dedication to his vocation has served as an inspiration. But what I thank them for most are my nieces, Maysoun and Maysaan, born during the final stages of this project. Together they perfected the art of distraction with smiles and syllable-based talk, providing a constant source of joy and welcome distraction. I enjoyed writing the most when they were cradled in my arms or bouncing on my knees.

When the ebbs and flows of this project, and academia more broadly, could have easily derailed me, I always found myself guided and grounded by my husband, Rizwan Rahman. He has been my most consistent interlocutor, my most cherished confidant, my most sympathetic critic, and my most beloved companion. This project has been enriched by his ceaseless support, and my life by his love.

Finally, I would like to thank al-Juwaynī for his thoughts, his students for transmitting them, scribes for writing them, and the generations of scholars who kept his ideas alive by teaching them. I am continuously humbled and amazed by the breath and ingenuity of Islamic thought. It is my sincere prayer that this book provides accurate reflection of a man in whose shadow I have stood for many years. Inasmuch as I can call this project my own, it is the product of the support I received and the erudition of centuries of scholars before me, and that has made all the difference.

Introduction

Imagine, if you will, the two Persian luminaries, Abū Isḥāq al-Shīrāzī (d. 476/1083) and Abū Ma'ālī al-Juwaynī (d. 478/1085), sitting with knees crossed and brows tightened as they fervently debate whether it is the consideration of time or direction that is more integral to the performance of obligatory prayers, after which they turn their attention to the proper scope of marital agency on the part of the adult virgin. Beyond sharing an affinity for the law, al-Shīrāzī[1] and al-Juwaynī were at the helm of the newly established Niẓāmiyya madrassas in Baghdad and Nishapur, respectively. Readers who stumble on these debates in al-Subkī's *Ṭabaqāt al-Shāfi'iyya* can almost visualize the two scholars perched in a miniature.[2] In the background would appear the towering madrassa of Nishapur and a vibrant market; in the foreground would be an eclectic audience of devoted students and passers-by, with books delicately balanced atop one another in the corner.

In the first debate, al-Juwaynī asserts that facing the correct direction is more important to fulfilling one's duty of prayer, while al-Shīrāzī argues instead that it is praying at the proper time. To support his claim, the latter invokes the permission granted for one to pray while mounted on

1 Abū Isḥāq Ibrāhīm b. 'Alī b. Yūsuf al-Fīrūzābādī al-Shīrāzī lived the majority of his life in Baghdad, where he was the preeminent student of Qāḍī Abū al-Ṭayyib al-Ṭabarī (d. 450/1058) before being appointed in 459/1066 by Niẓām al-Mulk as the head of the Niẓāmiyya in Baghdad. For his full biography, see Tāj al-Dīn al-Subkī, *Ṭabaqāt al-Shāfi'iyya al-kubrā*, ed. Maḥmūd Muḥammad al-Ṭaḥānī and 'Abd al-Fattāḥ Muḥammad al-Ḥilw (Cairo: 'Īsā al-Bābī al-Ḥalabī, 1965), 4:215, and Ḥasan Hītū, *al-Imām al-Shīrāzī* (Damascus: Dār al-Fikr, 1980).

2 Al-Subkī, *Ṭabaqāt al-Shāfi'iyya*, 5:209–18.

an animal, which ignores the direction of the *qibla*, as does the prayer of fear (*khawf*) in wartime. In both scenarios, the direction of the *qibla* may be disregarded, but the designated prayer time may not. Al-Juwaynī rebuts these examples with his own, pointing to the permission to join prayers while traveling, ignoring the prescribed prayer times but not the direction. Both scholars accept that in certain circumstances obligations with respect to prayer direction or time can be abandoned without invalidating the prayer.[3] The debate is thus not about validity, but rather about which element is *intrinsically* more important to prayer in the mind of the Lawgiver.

In spite of the ardor of the discussion, the absence of legal consequence for either position may lead the reader to conclude that the issue is inconsequential. What is the point of two great scholars debating which element of prayer is *more* important when both elements can be forfeited? Is this just another example of the pedantic nature of legal sparring, or does it reveal something deeper about how Islamic law was conceptualized by two of the greatest legal minds of the fifth/eleventh century? Indeed, far from a mere exercise, the exchange between al-Juwaynī and al-Shīrāzī encapsulates the core guiding principle of the juristic vocation in Islam – that God's law is enclosed within the mind of the Lawgiver and that jurists, while seeking to capture it, must accept the fallibility of their own opinion and, as a corollary, the possibility of the veracity of their opponent's. The debate between the two scholars ends on this note, with each defending his position while conceding the potential correctness of the other's view. Scholars of Islamic law have referred to this guiding legal principle in a variety of ways – such as "the valorization of uncertainty," "legal indeterminacy," and "self-conscious epistemology" – all of which emphasize the acceptance on the part of jurists of the gulf that exists between the law as reasoned and the law as dictated by God.

Yet while the domain of Islamic law accepts legal uncertainty in many circumstances, this principle is not extended to the realm of theology (*kalām*). Theologians – the *mutakallimūn* – have, in fact, been adamant that the soundness of one's belief in God is contingent on the certainty of rational proofs,[4] which lead one to accept the truth of the Prophetic message and all that it entails. This axiom has motivated theologians to expend great effort in providing logically sound proofs for belief so as to

[3] Ibid., 5:209–14.

[4] Richard Frank, "Knowledge and *Taqlīd*: The Foundations of Religious Belief in Classical Ashʿarism," *Journal of the American Oriental Society* 109, no. 1 (1989): 37–62.

assuage the doubts of laypersons and withstand the critiques of skeptics of belief. Once the veracity of the Prophetic message has been established, reason no longer functions as an independent tool of inquiry for the acquisition of knowledge, but now takes its place alongside revelation. This is not to say that revelation trumps reason, a topic of great debate;[5] rather, revelation comes both to guide and to assist the human intellect.

On a theoretical level, the differentiation between the acceptance of legal uncertainty and the drive for theological certainty is reflected in theological and legal works. On a more practical level, however, scholars have more often than not been both jurists and theologians, constantly straddling the competing epistemological paradigms of these two disciplines. As a scholar, al-Juwaynī was lauded both as an Ashʿarī theologian and as a renowned Shāfiʿī jurist. Although he recognized, as had others before him, the distinct epistemological paradigms in theological versus legal discourse, al-Juwaynī came to emphasize the theme of certainty – and this preoccupation can be identified not just in his theological works but also across his entire oeuvre.

The aim of this book is to present the shared intellectual threads that connect al-Juwaynī's theological, legal, and political writings. Rather than evaluate his major texts as discrete units, I start with the assertion that al-Juwaynī was a syncretic thinker with a specific intellectual project that can be identified regardless of which texts of his are analyzed. This intellectual project, which both informed and molded al-Juwaynī's intellectual concerns, was not formulated in a vacuum but rather emerged within a sociopolitical environment that left an indelible mark on him. On the intellectual scene, al-Juwaynī observed his Ashʿarī comrades embroiled in debates with their rivals, the Muʿtazila, who confidently asserted that one could arrive at certainty in both legal and theological matters. On a very basic level, the tension produced within al-Juwaynī by the conflicting epistemologies of these two schools gave rise to his profound concern with certainty.

However, it was not his intellectual environment alone that had such a profound and permanent effect on al-Juwaynī. He lived in a politically tumultuous period, in which the rise of powerful dynastic families forced

[5] For additional analysis, see A. J. Arberry, *Revelation and Reason in Islam* (New York: Routledge, 1957); Franz Rosenthal, *Knowledge Triumphant* (Leiden: Brill, 2007), 19–142; and Kevin Reinhart, *Before Revelation: The Boundaries of Muslim Moral Thought* (Albany: State University of New York Press, 1995). The first two works focus on the contexts of the reason versus revelation debate, whereas the last work details how the Muʿtazila, more specifically, addressed the issue.

the ʿAbbasid caliph into a position of merely titular power. Witnessing upheavals and the rise of countercaliphates, the most prominent of these being the Fatimids,[6] al-Juwaynī also became preoccupied with the question of continuity – both of social mores and of religious doctrine. If political elites, and along with them intellectual allegiances, are constantly changing, al-Juwaynī worried, what ensures the continuity of religion? Just in his short lifetime, al-Juwaynī experienced, at the hands of a singular dynastic power, the Seljuks, both the persecution and the adulation of the Ashʿarī-Shāfiʿīs. If the Seljuks could adopt such contrasting policies toward the Ashʿarī-Shāfiʿīs within the space of only a few decades, he ruminated that religious thought must be maintained and safeguarded by forces more powerful than just political affiliations and allegiances. His own lived political reality thus encouraged him to rethink the role of the imam in preserving order, and the role of the *ʿulamāʾ* in preserving religion. This process ultimately led him to reconceptualize the nature of the Sharīʿa and its relationship to the individuals who practice it.

To respond to his dual concerns of certainty and continuity, al-Juwaynī made foundational changes to the Ashʿarī epistemology he had inherited in order to enlarge the scope of knowledge individuals can achieve certainty in. This departure facilitated the creation of a dialectical relationship between certainty and continuity in which the continuity of religion and society is possible only through the epistemically certain knowledge attained by individuals, and this epistemically certain knowledge is in turn preserved by the continuity of the society these individuals inhabit. As we explore al-Juwaynī's theological, legal, and political texts in the course of this book, this dialectical relationship, along with its tensions and implications, will become evident.

Although al-Juwaynī has long been recognized as a seminal figure within Islamic intellectual history, there is a striking absence of comprehensive scholarship addressing his thought. By approaching al-Juwaynī not merely as a Shāfiʿī jurist or an Ashʿarī theologian but also as an intellectual figure with a historically informed project that is manifested throughout his works, this book brings some of al-Juwaynī's most influential texts together into a single conversation, providing insight into a complex thinker and laying the foundation for future research.

[6] Marshall Hodgson, "The Ismāʿīlī State," in *The Cambridge History of Iran*, vol. 5 (Cambridge: Cambridge University Press, 1968), 422–82.

A BRIEF GLIMPSE INTO NISHAPUR

Ideas rarely form in a vacuum – they are produced through a natural engagement with one's socioreligious context, intellectual inheritance, and political circumstances. The politically strategic and rapidly developing social environment of Nishapur lent itself to the attraction of religious groups vying for political and social authority. Nishapur, alongside Marw, Herat, and Balkh, was one of the four great cities of Khurasan, itself among the important provinces in the ʿAbbasid Empire. In the century before al-Juwaynī's birth, political power in Nishapur passed from the ʿAbbasids to the Samanids and then to the Ghaznavids, with each transition of power ushering in new intellectual trends.[7] The rulers of these dynasties quickly realized that while they held political authority, social and religious authority was also integral to legitimacy. Because of the flourishing system of patronage, intellectual trends often reflected changing political circumstances. Shams al-Dīn al-Muqaddasī (ca. 946–91), the lauded geographer, noted during his travels to Nishapur that it was fraught with factionalism along theological lines between the Karrāmiyya and the Shīʿa; however, by the time of the Ghaznavids, the lines of tension had been redrawn.[8]

The most significant intellectual cleavage in Nishapur before and during the time of al-Juwaynī was that between the Ḥanafī and Shafiʿī legal schools. The Ghaznavids, whose rule began in the fourth/tenth century, preferred the Ḥanafīs, meaning that patronage and politically appointed religious positions, such as the post of the chief *qāḍī* (judge) and other prominent judgeships, were almost always conferred on Ḥanafī jurists. Beyond showering direct patronage on individual legal scholars, the Ghaznavids supported the construction of madrassas for prominent Ḥanafī scholars. But despite the institutional support afforded to the Ḥanafīs, they could not easily eclipse the Shāfiʿīs. As Richard Bulliet has argued, what the Shāfiʿīs lacked in formal political support they made up for through the support of wealthy private families who established systems of patronage and funded the building of madrassas.[9] The divide between the Ḥanafīs and

[7] For the transition of power between these dynasties and their relationship to the ʿAbbasid caliphate, see Clifford Edmund Bosworth, *The Ghaznavids* (Edinburgh: Edinburgh University Press, 1963), and Bosworth, "The Early Ghaznavids," in *The Cambridge History of Iran*, vol. 4 (Cambridge: Cambridge University Press, 1975), 162–98.

[8] Muḥammad b. Aḥmad Shams al-Dīn al-Muqaddasī, *Aḥsan al-taqāsīm fī maʿrifat al-aqālīm*, ed. M. J. de Goeje (Leiden: E. J. Brill, 1967), 336.

[9] Richard Bulliet, *The Patricians of Nishapur* (Cambridge: Cambridge University Press, 1972), 7, 38–46.

the Shāfiʿīs in Nishapur, however, was not merely a sociopolitical one, nor one over substantive matters of law; rather, it was a widening cleft between emerging theologies that would eventually split fully open.

Both the Ḥanafīs and the Shāfiʿīs were widely recognized as representatives of legitimate legal schools in Nishapur and throughout the ʿAbbasid Empire. Scholars tracing the historical development of the *madhhab*s largely agree that by the fourth/tenth century, the legal schools had concretized, and by the fifth/eleventh century, they were an unremarkable part of daily life.[10] Given the widespread influence of the legal schools over Islamic societies, leaders of new religious trends sought legitimacy through political patronage. They could also turn to these legal institutions for validation. To the extent that new religious trends or theologies were adopted by the intellectual flagbearers of the legal schools, they could claim orthodoxy by affiliation. This argument was first forwarded by George Makdisi in relation to the Ashʿarī theological school, which strategically aligned itself with the Shāfiʿī legal school in the fourth/tenth century in order to attain the status of orthodoxy. The locus of this newfound alliance was Nishapur.

Between 290/902 and 343/955, prominent Ashʿarī scholars such as Abū Bakr Muḥammad Ibn Fūrak (d. 406/1015), Abū Isḥāq al-Isfarāyīnī (d. 418/1027), Abū Bakr al-Bāqillānī (d. 403/1013), and Abū Manṣūr ʿAbd al-Qāhir al-Baghdādī (d. 429/1037) responded to the call of Abū Sahl al-Ṣuʿlukī (d. 369/980) to come and settle in Nishapur. This newly forming Shāfiʿī-Ashʿarī synthesis became the catalyst for further tension between the two legal schools, as the Ḥanafīs did not forge the same alliance with the Ashʿarīs. Prior to the Ashʿarīs' arrival in Nishapur, many Ḥanafī scholars had supported the Basran Muʿtazilī school, a rival theological school. Tensions increased after 408/1017, when Maḥmūd of Ghazna (d. 421/1030), a prominent Ghaznavid ruler, expelled all of the Muʿtazilī scholars to Khurasan, with many settling in Nishapur. The relationship between the Ḥanafīs and the Muʿtazila allowed the latter to flourish in Nishapur, with prominent Muʿtazilī scholars being granted judgeships there. This fueled tensions with the Ashʿarīs, who had entered the intellectual milieu in Nishapur just a few decades earlier.

[10] See Christopher Melchert, *The Formation of the Sunni Schools of Law, 9th–10th Centuries C.E.* (Leiden: Brill, 1997); Wael Hallaq, *The Origins and Evolution of Islamic Law* (Cambridge: Cambridge University Press, 2005); and, more recently, Ahmed El Shamsy, *The Canonization of Islamic Law: A Social and Intellectual History* (Cambridge: Cambridge University Press, 2015).

The strained relationships between the various schools continued under the Ghaznavids, but with the capture of Nishapur in 429/1037 by the Seljuks, a potential spark for change appeared on the horizon. Knowing that they would likely lose political power with the rise of the Seljuks, prominent Ḥanafīs within the city were reluctant to welcome their new rulers. It was thus the Shāfiʿīs, under the leadership of Ibn al-Muwaffaq (d. 440/1048), who brokered the formal entrance of the Seljuks into Nishapur.[11] While this earned the Shāfiʿīs temporary favor, Ṭughril Beg, the Seljuk sultan, eventually came to favor the Ḥanafīs because of his own personal adherence to the Ḥanafī school. The political reascendance of the Ḥanafīs highlighted the political impotence of the Ashʿarī-Shāfiʿīs, and in 440/1048 intellectual persecution of the Ashʿarī-Shāfiʿīs began. This persecution culminated in 446/1054, when Ṭughril Beg commanded the arrest of four prominent Ashʿarī-Shāfiʿī scholars, among them al-Juwaynī. Though he narrowly escaped arrest by having earlier absconded, al-Juwaynī was forced to abandon the city, undertaking travels that would eventually bring him to the Hejaz.[12]

Al-Juwaynī would return to Nishapur in 451/1059 at the behest of the Seljuk vizier, Niẓām al-Mulk (d. 485/1092), who appointed him the head of the newly minted Niẓāmiyya madrassa. However, his turbulent formative years amid shifting political powers and allegiances made addressing the question of social and religious continuity inescapable for him. The pendulous nature of intellectual-political affiliations served to impress on him all the more the need to contemplate the challenge of continuity – a theme most salient in his political writings. Yet the continual political rearrangements notwithstanding, the intellectual and theological lines that divided groups were not simply the outcome of practical decision-making on the basis of social power within the city; they also reflected substantive issues that demarcated the competing factions. These substantive issues, alongside political instability, formed the backdrop against which al-Juwaynī's second primary concern, certainty, was born.

[11] In his monograph *The Ghaznavids*, Bosworth provides an account related by Abū al-Faḍl al-Bayhaqī (d. 470/1077) in his *Tārīkh al-Bayhaqī*. For an analysis of this account, see Paul Jurgen, "The Seljuk Conquest(s) of Nishapur: A Reappraisal," *Iranian Studies* 38, no. 4 (2005): 575–77.

[12] For accounts of this incident, see Shams al-Dīn Muḥammad b. Aḥmad al-Dhahabī, *Tārīkh al-Islām wa-wafayāt al-mashāhīr wa-l-aʿlām*, ed. ʿUmar ʿAbd al-Salām Tadmurī (Beirut: Dār al-Kitāb al-ʿArabī, 1990), 30:122–23, and ʿAlī b. al-Ḥasan Ibn ʿAsākir, *Tārīkh madīnat Dimashq*, ed. ʿAlī Shīrī (Beirut: Dār al-Fikr, 1995), 5:204–5.

The Ashʿarīs and the Muʿtazila can be distinguished from one another in a variety of ways, but for al-Juwaynī their most important intellectual conflict was an epistemological one. As noted earlier, although Sunnī legal theorists of all schools were generally amenable to the notion of legal uncertainty, theologians were adamant that belief had to have an epistemically certain foundation based on rational proofs. In this schema, the intellect is assumed to be a judicious tool capable of reasoning from rational proofs to arrive at knowledge. Curiously, however, Ashʿarī theologians argued that once an individual arrives at sound belief and receives revelation, further guidance for his or her affairs is derived from revelation, raising the question of why the human intellect is in need of such assistance. If the intellect is able to arrive, with certainty, in belief in God, why, then, can it not reason in other matters? And what does the dependence of reason on revelation entail for law?

Given that revelation is the source of guidance for believers, the Ashʿarīs argued that human beings are not accountable for their actions before they receive revelation. Such individuals behave in the world according to what they deem beneficial, but their actions bear no otherworldly legal consequences. With the onset of revelation – the source of morality and guidance – this situation changes. At that point individuals become obligated to act in accordance with God's dictates and are rewarded and punished accordingly.[13] With revelation as the reservoir of guidance, individuals must derive from it a legal and moral code. This derivation is primarily the duty of prophets and messengers, but with their temporal demise, the mantle of scriptural interpretation passes to jurists. These jurists turn first to the Quran and the *ḥadīth* in order to deduce the law, but given the hermeneutical complexity of the Quran, the absence of the Prophet, and the fallibility of human reason, rulings issued by jurists are epistemically only probable and cannot be certain. This fact is the foundation of the epistemic uncertainty pervading Islamic law.

By contrast, the Basran Muʿtazila afforded reason a wider scope both before and after revelation. As they saw it, morality is not simply legislated through scripture; on the contrary, people can achieve knowledge of what is good and bad through reason – the argument being that each action is either objectively good or objectively bad based on the circumstance of its

[13] Richard Frank, *Early Islamic Theology: The Muʿtazilites and al-Ashʿarī*, vol. 2 of *Texts and Studies on the Development and History of Kalām*, ed. Dimitri Gutas (London: Routledge, 2007); and W. Montgomery Watt, *Free Will and Predestination in Early Islam* (London: Luzac, 1948), 135–50.

occurrence.[14] This doctrine, known as *taḥsīn wa-taqbīḥ*, means that individuals are responsible for their actions whether or not they have received revelation. Revelation thus comes to affirm what the intellect has already determined or to provide particularities for generalities already deduced. In the realm of law, the Muʿtazila, like the Ashʿarīs, acknowledged the hermeneutical complexity of scripture and the difficulty entailed by the absence of the Prophet. But given their belief in the independence of the intellect, the law for them was not burdened to the same extent with legal uncertainty. The Muʿtazila, though relying on scriptural sources, stressed the importance of the intellect when scriptural sources were silent and believed in the epistemological equivalence of rulings deduced from scripture and rulings deduced through the intellect.

Given the diverging epistemologies of the Ashʿarīs and the Muʿtazila and the ramifications of their respective theories for the epistemological value of legal rulings, the two schools' coexistence in Nishapur was bound to cause tension and conflict as well as synthesis. In the early part of al-Juwaynī's life, before his sojourn in the Hejaz, the intellectual conflicts between the Ashʿarīs and the Muʿtazila and between the Ḥanafīs and the Shāfiʿīs punctuated his life and career. And although he emerged triumphant, returning to Nishapur to assume a position at the prestigious Niẓāmiyya, these early conflicts had an enduring impact on his prodigious production. On the political front, the precarious nature of politics during his lifetime ushered in his concern for stability, and on the intellectual front, the legal and theological factionalism resulted in his desire to provide rationally sound and epistemically certain arguments for both belief and legal action.

AL-JUWAYNĪ: BETWEEN CERTAINTY AND CONTINUITY

Al-Juwaynī's intellectual work is best read as his response to, and means of coping with, the most pressing intellectual and political challenges of his time. The parallel themes of theological and legal certainty, on the one hand, and social and religious continuity, on the other, emerge directly from his environment. It is, however, important to note that it was not simply the socioreligious politics of Nishapur that produced al-Juwaynī's

[14] Ayman Shihadeh, "Theories of Ethical Value in Kalām: A New Interpretation," in *Oxford Handbook of Islamic Theology*, ed. Sabine Schmidtke (Oxford: Oxford University Press, 2016), 384–407, and George F. Hourani, "Two Theories of Value in Medieval Islam," *Muslim World* 50, no. 4 (1969): 269.

dual concerns. As Paul Heck has recently elaborated in *Skepticism in Islam*, from the third/ninth to fifth/eleventh centuries, Muslim scholars were concerned with skepticism and its corollary, certainty. The hub of this movement in the third/ninth century was Baghdad, where diverse intellectual interlocutors were forced to defend their positions and contend with opposing ones. With its political stability and patronage, Baghdad became the center of intellectual inquiry, allowing scholars to employ a variety of intellectual strategies, including skepticism. However, these scholars were not skeptics in the traditional sense of denying the possibility of knowledge; rather, they employed skepticism as a "constitutive element of religious reasoning."[15] Their goal was to "question assumptions about the way in which knowledge, in this case religious knowledge, can be established as certain."[16] The epistemological desire for certainty and invocation of skepticism was thus not unique to al-Juwaynī but was very much in the intellectual air. What is unique about al-Juwaynī is the manner in which he resolved his quest for certainty and the extent to which a desire for continuity is imbricated in his quest for certainty.

To achieve a basis for certainty, al-Juwaynī moves beyond the legal and theological constraints he inherited from the Ashʿarīs to construct a new epistemology, broadening the scope of human reason. In doing so, he is concerned not merely with epistemic certainty but also with *practical certainty* for both individuals and jurists in legal matters. Certainty, for al-Juwaynī, is contingent on whether individuals can assert true knowledge of something or confidence in their conclusion. Whereas knowledge for al-Juwaynī's Ashʿarī predecessors was the product of either reason or revelation, he, by contrast, argues that knowledge can also be acquired through custom or repetition. That is, to the extent that a certain practice is habitual for an individual, it can be said to be *practically* certain from that individual's perspective, whether or not it is epistemically certain from an objective perspective. This means that al-Juwaynī addresses certainty not just through an objective epistemological lens but also through a subjective, personal one.

In applying his epistemology to legal thought, al-Juwaynī has two goals: (1) establishing a definitive basis of authority for the primary sources of legal derivation and (2) achieving epistemic certainty in rulings. While he is easily able to accomplish the former, he is frustrated in the latter, given that epistemic certainty in the domain of Islamic law is

[15] Paul Heck, *Skepticism in Classical Islam* (London: Routledge, 2013), 13.
[16] Ibid., 10.

contingent on both the accurate transmission of scriptural sources and their clear signification – considerably narrowing the realm of legal norms that are truly epistemically certain. Recognizing the impossibility of arriving at objective epistemic certainty in all legal affairs, al-Juwaynī consequently elevates his desire for societal and religious continuity over his desire for legal certainty. Societal continuity for al-Juwaynī is tied to the idea of legal universality – the belief that for every human action there is a specific legal ruling – which means that the continuity of society is contingent on knowledge and practice of the Sharīʿa. This is best exemplified in his political thought, where he emphasizes the imam's duty to safeguard and propagate the faith. But given his own fragile political context, marred by the weakness of the caliphate, he recognizes that the imamate could deteriorate. Consequently, he philosophizes about the mechanisms through which the security and continuity of society might be guaranteed. He concludes that social continuity in this situation is contingent on the practical certainty that individuals or society have in legal knowledge. In this way, the continuity of society is bound to the certain knowledge of the individual, not the continued existence of a specific political structure, revealing that the two concerns stand in a dialectical relationship and can never be invoked singularly.

AL-JUWAYNĪ AND THEMES IN ISLAMIC STUDIES

In setting out to write this book, I faced a choice between two predominant modes of approaching the study of Islamic intellectual history. The first traces the evolution of an idea or concept to illuminate its development over time, whereas the second studies an individual in order to demonstrate that person's contributions to a broader intellectual discourse. The former approach affords scholars a coherent bird's-eye view of perennial themes and trends that traverse temporal and locational constraints, imparting a sense of cohesiveness to an intellectual project that may span centuries. The latter approach adds a layer of nuance to thematic discussions by pointing to the intellectual diversity that exists within sustained discussions. This book, through the lens of studying al-Juwaynī, aims to achieve the second of these tasks. Usually recounted in contemporary discourse as an archetypal Ashʿarī-Shāfiʿī scholar, al-Juwaynī, in following his dual preoccupation with certainty and continuity, departs from the dominant opinions put forward by Sunnī scholars before him. In tracing al-Juwaynī's divergences, I necessarily engage with themes and concepts identified by scholars of Islamic intellectual thought who have employed the first of the two scholarly approaches mentioned above. Of these issues, the most prominent in this work are reason and revelation, legal uncertainty, and the role of the caliph. These themes are woven throughout al-Juwaynī's work and his conclusions, and often his departures from the positions of his predecessors with regard to each of the themes can contribute to a fuller and more nuanced understanding of the development of Islamic intellectual thought, especially in the fifth/eleventh century.

In Speculative Theology: Reason and Revelation

Al-Juwaynī's concern with certainty entails a corollary investigation into the sources of knowledge and the mechanisms of knowledge creation. While al-Juwaynī's fixation on certainty constituted a central element of his thinking, his engagement with the sources of knowledge harks back to perennial questions in the history of Islamic intellectual life. During the time of the Prophet, the centrality of revelation as a source of knowledge was established, and reason acted as an instrument for comprehension. The Prophet's role as the divine vessel precluded conflicts between these two cardinal sources, but following the death of the Prophet, scholars questioned whether such conflict had now become possible.[17] According to A. J. Wensinck, these early debates on the potential tension between reason and revelation intensified in the fourth/tenth century, when systematic Ashʿarī theology emerged as a rebuttal to Muʿtazilī arguments.[18] A central point of contention between the two groups was whether conflict between reason and revelation is possible and, if so, which source of knowledge should prevail. For the Muʿtazila, the answer was straightforward: revelation merely affirms what can be concluded through the use of reason, and therefore conflict cannot exist – both humans and God are bound by the laws of reason. By contrast, the Ashʿarīs asserted the omnipotence of God: while God may act in accordance with human reason, He is not bound to do so. Thus, on the surface, for the Muʿtazila, a conflict between reason and revelation was impossible. For the Ashʿarīs, it was improbable but possible.

[17] W. Montgomery Watt, *Islamic Philosophy and Theology* (Edinburgh: Edinburgh University Press, 1979), parts 1 and 2; Tilman Nagel, *History of Islamic Theology* (Princeton, NJ: Markus Wiener, 2009), chapter 2.

[18] According to A. J. Wensinck, the first systematic Ashʿarī thought emerged with al-Bāqillānī; see Wensinck, *The Muslim Creed* (New York: Routledge, 2013), chapter 8. However, debates between the Ashʿarīs and the Muʿtazila existed before al-Bāqillānī. See Frank, *Early Islamic Theology*.

Although the question of conflict between reason and revelation was introduced through the quarrel between the Ashʿarīs and the Muʿtazila, it was not resolved by these two schools. Early Ashʿarīs, despite recognizing the centrality of epistemology, did not present a robust enough epistemological framework to address this issue fully. They were more concerned, as Josef van Ess has argued, with answering foundational questions regarding the existence of God and His attributes.[19] In surveying the texts of al-Ashʿarī, Wensinck goes as far as to say that al-Ashʿarī put forward no clear epistemological doctrine. For Wensinck, the first scholar to address epistemology properly was Abū Manṣūr al-Baghdādī in his *Uṣūl al-dīn*, and to him should be added the name of Abū Bakr al-Bāqillānī. Al-Bāqillānī and al-Baghdādī, students of al-Ashʿarī's own students, penned some of the earliest systematic books on Ashʿarī *kalām*, which were later studied by al-Juwaynī. Yet despite the citation of these thinkers as early progenitors of theories of epistemology, Frank Griffel argues that the most comprehensive examination of the potential conflict between reason and revelation – and its resolution – took place at the hands of al-Ghazālī, due primarily to a synthesis forged between the Ashʿarīs and the *falāsifa* (philosophers).

Abū Ḥāmid al-Ghazālī (d. 505/1111), who passed away almost a full century after al-Bāqillānī and al-Baghdādī, is credited with providing a robust theoretical apparatus to resolve the potential conflict between reason and revelation by incorporating philosophical tools of reasoning – the most important being logic – into Ashʿarī *kalām*.[20] Griffel argues that al-Ghazālī saw reason and revelation as emanating from a single source, namely, God, which entails that they work in tandem, not in tension. At the same time, it is conceivable that human beings misapprehend revelation, resulting in an apparent conflict between reason and revelation and leading them to conclusions involving heterodox interpretations. To avoid such outcomes, al-Ghazālī articulates the *qānūn al-taʾwīl* (rules of interpretation): a literal interpretation of scriptural sources is preferred, but a nonliteral interpretation is permitted in certain circumstances. The *qānūn* further details when a nonliteral interpretation is permissible, along with the extent of its application.[21]

[19] Josef van Ess, "Early Islamic Theologians on the Existence of God," in *Islam and the Medieval West*, ed. Khalil I. Semaan (Albany: State University of New York Press, 1980), 64–81.

[20] See note 18.

[21] Frank Griffel, *Al-Ghazālī's Philosophical Theology* (Oxford: Oxford University Press, 2009), 111–20.

According to Ovamir Anjum, the relationship between the *qānūn* and the conflict between reason and revelation is predicated on al-Ghazālī's notion of demonstration (*burhān*). For al-Ghazālī, if rational demonstration can establish a proposition beyond doubt, revelation cannot be interpreted in a way that conflicts with it. If a conflict arises, the *qanūn* dictates that a nonliteral interpretation be invoked in order to unify the two propositions.[22] Al-Ghazālī's trepidation regarding conflict stems from the implications of calling reason into question, since both the assertion of faith and the recognition of revelation are results of reason. By arguing for sound knowledge through demonstration, al-Ghazālī elevates human reason to the level of revelation. In his view, any conflict between the two must be due either to incorrect reasoning or to a failure to interpret figuratively when necessary – both being methodological errors rather than indicators of an intrinsic conflict between reason and revelation.

Ashʿarī scholars accepted al-Ghazālī's doctrine of *qānūn al-taʾwīl* and his demonstration as a resolution of the issue, and later scholars built on al-Ghazālī's theories to continue to expand the scope of human reason. If al-Ghazālī was the catalyst for the *kalām–falsafa* synthesis, Fakhr al-Dīn al-Rāzī (d. 544/1149) represents its apex. Ayman Shihadeh argues that al-Rāzī's thought, especially toward the end of his life, offered, "for the first time, an 'Islamic philosophy.'"[23] Al-Rāzī gives an even more dominant role to reason than did al-Ghazālī, averring that reason can give an individual sound knowledge of things not accounted for in revelation. This is because "the human psyche seeks pleasure and avoids pain"[24] and "the measure of moral value becomes the subjective interests of the individual agent, though Revealed Law is reinstated as an objective source for normative judgement."[25] In al-Rāzī's conception, though scripture remains a source of normative judgments, reason itself is an independent judicious tool that can provide individuals with certitude in matters not directly addressed in revelation.

But while al-Ghazālī is credited with setting in motion the synthesis between reason and revelation and al-Rāzī with extending reason beyond the realm of revelation, it was al-Juwaynī who laid the groundwork for

22 Ovamir Anjum, *Politics, Law, and Community in Islamic Thought: The Taymiyyan Moment* (Cambridge: Cambridge University Press, 2012), 147–53.

23 Ayman Shihadeh, "From al-Ghazālī to al-Rāzī: 6th/12th Century Developments in Muslim Philosophical Theology," *Arabic Sciences and Philosophy* 15 (2015): 178.

24 Ayman Shihadeh, *The Teleological Ethics of Fakhr al-Dīn al-Rāzī* (Leiden: Brill, 2006), 67.

25 Ibid., 68.

both innovations. Al-Juwaynī affirmed the centrality of revelation while emphasizing that reasoning (*naẓar*) can produce sound conclusions that accord with revelation. Like al-Ghazālī, who recognized the singular source of reason and revelation, al-Juwaynī asserted that sound reason should not conflict with what is conveyed in revelation. If a conflict emerges, it is likely due either to unsound reasoning (*al-naẓar al-fāsid*) brought about by incorrect proofs or to the absence of convincing demonstrations. Al-Juwaynī does not go further, however – as al-Ghazālī does – to argue that scriptural interpretation can be the source of the apparent conflict between reason and revelation, thereby necessitating the *qānūn*. Yet despite the fact that it overlooks the interpretational problems that can be engendered by revelation, al-Juwaynī's equalization of reason and revelation as sources of knowledge demonstrates that Ashʿarī epistemology, though previously articulated by al-Baghdādī and al-Bāqillānī, was still changing in fundamental ways. And although al-Ghazālī's scholarship may have marked a definitive turn within Ashʿarī *kalām*, this turn was likely precipitated by al-Juwaynī.

In Legal Theory: Legal Uncertainty

Al-Juwaynī's emphasis on reason was integral to theological mediation, as he saw reason as the only mechanism through which the individual could assent to faith with certainty. For al-Juwaynī, uncertain or probable faith was not simply weak but unacceptable. In law, however, both certainty and probability were accepted and, in fact, necessary. Aron Zysow, in his seminal work *The Economy of Certainty*, asserts that "certainty and probability were the fundamental categories with which [jurists] approached every question of law."[26] These categories of certainty and probability were applied to legal rulings, but before that they were applied most fundamentally to legal sources. The main distinction in *uṣūl al-fiqh*, according to Zysow, is between formalist and materialist jurists. The former were more preoccupied with the sources of the law, believing that the validity of legal norms "is ensured by the fact that the framework within which [the jurist] practices is known with certainty."[27] Probability enters the formalist system of law in legal rulings themselves: although the sources of the law are certain, the actual laws derived from

[26] Aron Zysow, *The Economy of Certainty: An Introduction to the Typology of Islamic Legal Theory*, (Atlanta: Lockwood Press, 2013), 1.
[27] Ibid., 4.

them are not. Opposite the formalists stood the materialists, who afforded no place to probability within the law. For them, both the scriptural sources of the law and the legal framework had to be epistemically certain, resulting in a body of epistemically certain rulings only. In Zysow's classification, the Shāfiʿīs were thoroughgoing formalists. Focusing on the framework of the law, they sought to ensure an epistemically certain foundation for each source of the law but were willing to entertain probability in legal outcomes. But how exactly was probability introduced to the domain of legal interpretation?

Uncertainty, from the formalist viewpoint, seeped into the law via two sources: scriptural interpretation and scriptural limitation. Despite the exhaustive hermeneutical discussions undertaken by jurists to ensure the accurate interpretation of scriptural sources, scriptural interpretation was recognized as susceptible to the inescapably fallible nature of human reason in interpreting the injunctions of God. For Baber Johansen, the potential fallibility of human reasoning has three repercussions within the realm of law: (1) the legitimization of "normative pluralism," allowing for multiple schools of *fiqh* and normative systems; (2) "the peaceful co-existence" of conflicting yet legitimate normative systems; and (3) the protection of the judiciary from "ethical and cognitive" attacks.[28] Taken together, these features give rise to what Johansen labels the "contingency of the law." Of the three, the most important is the acceptance of normative pluralism within the law, something academics have noted to be the sine qua non of Islamic law. In Johansen's mind, the foundation of normative pluralism relates directly to the "ontological difference between the knowledge as revealed by God in the Koranic texts ... and the knowledge which human beings acquire through their own reasoning."[29] Once jurists accept the ontological distinction between knowledge produced by reason and knowledge conveyed by the Lawgiver, they are forced to concede the existence of legal uncertainty.

The other mechanism by which legal uncertainty is introduced, scriptural limitation, delimits the realm from which legal norms can be generated to scripture alone. Given the paucity of scriptural commands, jurists were compelled to derive rulings on the basis either of analogies to scriptural rulings or of broad objectives (*maqāṣid*) that could be extracted from scripture. Sherman Jackson labels this the "hegemonic propensity of

[28] Baber Johansen, *Contingency in a Sacred Law: Legal and Ethical Norms in the Muslim Fiqh* (Leiden: Brill, 1999), 39.
[29] Johansen, *Contingency in a Sacred Law*, 39.

the religious law," wherein "the only sound judgements are those rooted in scripture."[30] This notion of scripturalism meant that jurists sought to attach their derived norms to scriptural sources, even if only tangentially, and as the gulf between generated rulings and scriptural sources widened, probability permeated the legal realm. As Jackson notes, "the authority of an interpretation could not, therefore, inhere in the interpretation itself, since no interpretation could claim to be objectively true, at least not in any way that its truth could be objectively known and verified."[31] The ability of jurists to derive rulings only tangentially connected to scriptural sources is a product of what David Vishanoff calls the "law-oriented hermeneutical paradigm":

> The triumph of the law-oriented paradigm ... guaranteed that scholars of law would always be able to imagine their systems of legal rules as revealed and thus divinely authoritative, even as they continued to adapt those laws to changing social contexts. The law-oriented hermeneutical paradigm did this because it maximized both interpretive power and interpretive flexibility. That is, it maximized in theory the ability of an imagined interpreter to ascribe a strong and definite legal significance to a text, while simultaneously maximizing his ability to depart from that definitive meaning as needed.[32]

While the law-oriented paradigm and its corollary of interpretative flexibility afforded jurists the benefit of norm generation beyond the plain meaning of the text, the resultant rulings could not escape a probabilistic character.

The paradox generative of legal probability thus centers on scripture: jurists hold steadfast to the belief that scripture is the font of norm generation, but its limited nature, coupled with the fallibility of human reason, forces them to acquiesce to the existence of probability.[33] On this

30 Sherman Jackson, *Islamic Law and the State: The Constitutional Jurisprudence of Shihāb al-Dīn al-Qarāfī* (Leiden: Brill, 1996), 22.

31 Ibid., 31.

32 David Vishanoff, *The Formation of Islamic Hermeneutics: How Sunnī Legal Theorists Imagined a Revealed Law* (New Haven, CT: American Oriental Society, 2011), 2–3.

33 The emphasis on differentiating the rulings obtained through juristic interpretation from the rulings intended by the Lawgiver is what has prompted scholars to distinguish the terms Sharīʿa and *fiqh*, with the former denoting God's law and the latter juristic law. Bernard Weiss notes: "We thus, according to the Muslim view, do not receive the law considered as a body of fully articulated and implantable rules directly from God; we receive it rather from great jurists. But the law expounded by the jurists – the jurists' law – has validity only by virtue of its claim to being the closest approximation to the ideal law of God that the jurists are capable of producing." Weiss, *The Spirit of Islamic Law* (Atlanta: University of Georgia Press, 2006), 15. For more on this larger debate, see Chapters 3 and 4.

basis, the meta-principle guiding the juristic vocation and human behavior is that overwhelming probability (*ghalabat al-ẓann*) necessitates action. The *mujtahid* who seeks legal rulings is, therefore, not pursuing an objectively correct answer (normative plurality is accepted); instead, the search is for an answer that prevails in the jurist's mind. And though the four Sunnī schools differed as to whether they considered that an objectively correct answer exists in the mind of the Lawgiver, they all upheld the basic validity of legal plurality and legal uncertainty.

Al-Juwaynī inherited the juristic concession to legal uncertainty. However, given his intellectual context, shaped by debates with the Muʿtazila, who touted the ability of their epistemology to provide certainty in legal norms, the acceptance of legal uncertainty seemed to him to leave the Shāfiʿī-Ashʿarīs in a precarious position in relation to their intellectual rivals. As Johansen observes, underlying the acceptance of legal uncertainty is a theological postulate that asserts an ontological difference between the knowledge God has as Lawgiver and the knowledge humans acquire of legal norms through the fallible medium of human reason.[34] While al-Juwaynī does not reject this ontological differentiation, he circumvents it by expanding the sources of knowledge and focusing on the ability of individuals to reach certainty in their personal affairs. The former he achieves by incorporating custom as a legitimate source of knowledge alongside reason and revelation, and the latter he accomplishes by asserting that habitual practice that becomes customary to an individual can result in *practical* certainty, even though it remains epistemically uncertain.

By advocating for the possibility of practical certainty in human affairs through customary practice, al-Juwaynī is not rejecting the ontological differentiation between human knowledge and God's knowledge but separating the two to accommodate the existence of a realm of such practical certainty. Though this reliance on custom does not bridge the epistemic gulf between a norm conceived by a jurist and a norm articulated by God, it does create a basis for certainty in individual action. In terms of rulings derived by jurists, since al-Juwaynī contends that sound reasoning can enable one to arrive at true knowledge, overwhelming probability predominating in the mind of a jurist when searching for a legal norm is therefore tantamount to subjective certainty. In such a situation, jurists in their reasoning, like lay people in their practice, attain practical certainty in their conclusions, despite the ontological fact that

[34] Johansen, *Contingency in a Sacred Law*, 39.

their opinions are only probable. And though this distinction does not substantively weaken the position of the Muʿtazila, it does open up a theoretical realm of practical certainty within Islamic law.

The connection between epistemology and legal theory in al-Juwaynī's work is not itself new, as scholars had long recognized the interconnection between *kalām* and *uṣūl al-fiqh*, with epistemology serving as the nexus.[35] However, al-Juwaynī's reformulated epistemology does suggest that Ashʿarī epistemology was still subject to debate in the fifth/eleventh century, which means that one ought not presuppose the epistemology of any scholar when delving into his or her legal thought. In the case of al-Juwaynī, his epistemology fashions new proofs for the cardinal sources of the law and allows for the potential of legal certainty for individuals. Al-Juwaynī's approach to epistemology also challenges the neat division proposed by Zysow that distinguishes between formalistic legal systems, which tie epistemic certainty to process and procedure, and materialist legal systems, which tie epistemic certainty to the sources of the law.[36] For al-Juwaynī, epistemic certainty is about the material sources of the law, the process through which the laws are derived, and the individual enactment of the law. This perspective augments our conception of how acceptable uncertainty was within a formalistic legal paradigm and demonstrates that while the cardinal sources of the law were agreed on in the fifth/eleventh century, contestation around the foundations of their legitimacy and the epistemic value of the resultant rulings continued.

Al-Juwaynī's concern for certainty not only gives nuance to our scholarly understanding of legal uncertainty and the debate of reason versus revelation but also sheds light on the development of the Shāfiʿī school and the scholars whom Kevin Reinhart labels the "speculative Shāfiʿīs."[37] The connection between the Shāfiʿī school and theological inquiry was first articulated by George Makdisi, who argues that al-Shāfiʿī's legal theory was an attempt to provide an alternative to speculative theology (*kalām*), which often dominated early intellectual discourse.[38] Citing him as the first true "traditionalist," Makdisi argues that not only did al-Shāfiʿī seek to

[35] After this book went to press, recent publications have come to light that are relevant to this issue: Muhamed Eissa, *The Jurist and the Theologian: Speculative Theology in Shāfiʿī Legal Theory* (Piscataway, NJ: Gorgias Press, 2017), and Omar Farahat, *The Foundation of Norms in Islamic Jurisprudence and Theology* (Cambridge: Cambridge University Press, 2019).

[36] Zysow, *Economy of Certainty*, 1–3.

[37] Reinhart, *Before Revelation*, 15.

[38] George Makdisi, "The Juridical Theology of Shāfiʿī: Origins and Significance of *Uṣūl al-Fiqh*," *Studia Islamica*, no. 59 (1984): 40–43.

establish the centrality of *ḥadīth* in legal reasoning, but he also sought to create a science that could "be used as an antidote to *kalām*."[39] Ahmed El Shamsy notes that al-Shāfiʿī's disdain for *kalām* resulted in his engagement in certain theoretical-theological discussions that were then expanded on by later Shāfiʿīs, marking an increasing turn toward *kalām*. Presenting the hitherto unstudied texts of Ibn Surayj (d. 306/918) and al-Khaffāf (first half of the fourth/tenth century), El Shamsy argues that these two scholars furthered theoretical inquiry and "[a]s part of this process ... introduced a keen attention to delineating the relationship between reason and revelation, reflecting an influx of theological concerns, particularly ethics and natural philosophy, as well as theories of language."[40] Ibn Surayj is an important figure not only for El Shamsy but also for Reinhart, who traces a unique brand of Shāfiʿī-Muʿtazilī thought back to him. Unfortunately, no major legal-theoretical works by Ibn Surayj or others whom Reinhart places in this camp, such as ʿAbd Allāh al-Ṣayrafī (d. 330/342) and al-Qaffāl al-Shāshī al-Kabīr (d. 365/976), have survived.[41] El Shamsy notes, "The most likely reason for the disappearance of these works lies in the theological attitudes that they displayed – attitudes rooted in Muʿtazilī ethics, which came to be considered unacceptable by later generations of Shāfiʿī jurists."[42] Reinhart and El Shamsy identify two discussions that were heavily influenced by the Muʿtazila: the status of human action prior to revelation and the connection between the rationality of the law and human benefit (*maṣlaḥa*). Surveying the short surviving works of al-Khaffāf and al-Qaffāl al-Kabīr, El Shamsy argues that both believed in a "double rationality of the law" that returns to ideas espoused by the Muʿtazilīs of Baghdad.[43] Though El Shamsy argues for some continuities in Shāfiʿī

[39] Ibid., 12.

[40] Ahmed El Shamsy, "Bridging the Gap: Two Early Texts of Islamic Legal Theory," *Journal of the American Oriental Society* 137, no. 3 (2017): 515.

[41] Reinhart, *Before Revelation*, 15–18.

[42] Ahmed El Shamsy, "The Wisdom of God's Law: Two Theories," in *Islamic Law in Theory: Studies on Jurisprudence in Honor of Bernard Weiss*, ed. Robert Gleave and Kevin Reinhart (Leiden: Brill, 2014), 19–37. To make his argument, El Shamsy looks at the introduction to al-Khaffāf's *al-Aqsām wa-l-khiṣāl* and the *Maḥāsin al-sharīʿa* of al-Qaffāl, which has recently been edited.

[43] El Shamsy, "Wisdom of God's Law," 24–25. El Shamsy defines the double rationality as follows: "The first kind of rationality relates to necessary truths that are intelligible independently of divine revelation; these are few in number. Within the vast realm of the rationally possible, a second type of rationality exists, namely a means–ends rationality: God's wisdom gives rise to laws that serve the benefit of His creatures." Ibid., 25.

thought from the eponym of the school to the scholars of the late fourth/tenth century, given the paucity of extant texts available, a comprehensive history of the middle centuries is currently unlikely. Given that the present work focuses on a scholar of the fifth/eleventh century, I will make no attempt to construct arguments for the middle centuries or to project al-Juwaynī's ideas back to scholars who may be his intellectual forebears; however, since al-Juwaynī's epistemology was likely influenced by the Basran Muʿtazilīs, the brand of "speculative Shāfiʿism" highlighted by Reinhart may not be limited to the middle centuries of early Shāfiʿīs. Though al-Juwaynī's positions on the issues outlined by El Shamsy and Reinhart are unremarkable, his departure from traditional Shāfiʿī and Ashʿarī positions on other issues indicates that legal-theological cross-pollination in the fifth/eleventh century would be a worthy subject of further inquiry.

In Political Thought: The Role of the Caliph

Beyond the legal and epistemological connection apparent in the discussion of legal uncertainty, there is a further connection between epistemology and political thought, one that, I argue in this work, was first forged by al-Juwaynī. Islamic political thought, as a disciplinary field within Islamic studies, has not aroused widespread interest among contemporary academics. In part, this dearth of interest is due to the fact that writings on Islamic political thought fall into three distinct categories: (1) juridical treatises bearing the influence of early theological debates; (2) mirrors for princes, focusing mostly on issues of statecraft; and (3) Islamic philosophical-political treatises deeply influenced by the Greek tradition and concerned with the ideal of politics.[44] The first of these, Islamic political thought in juridical treatises, will be the focus of analysis here, as al-Juwaynī wrote squarely within this genre.

Juridical treatises are often critiqued as overlooking fundamental questions of authority and instead directing attention to the legitimization of the caliphate and the political struggles of the nascent Muslim community after the death of the Prophet. This critique has been most forcefully articulated by Andrew Hess, who declares that "[w]ith the exception of the Prophet's time, Islamic civilization failed to provide a satisfactory political system." Hess asks: "How have the governments of Islamic

[44] This tripartite division was presented by Ann Lambton in *State and Government in Medieval Islam* (Oxford: Oxford University Press, 1981), xvi.

civilization, so laden with political instabilities, so devoid of legitimation, and so incapable of lasting success, been able to maintain a political identity for over a millennium?"[45] For Hess, the absence of a satisfactory political system *in reality* meant that Islamic political thinkers were not in the business of articulating an ideal political doctrine based on thick notions of authority and legitimacy but were merely coping with the challenging political realities surrounding them.

Hess's position echoes the earlier sentiment of Hamilton Gibb, who notes the preoccupation of Islamic political thinkers with the caliph as the source of stability and order, leading them to neglect other important facets of political thought.[46] Most egregious for Gibb is the retrospective nature of Sunnī political thought, that is, its focus on prior political circumstances in the history of the Muslim community. This leads him to claim that "Sunni political theory was, in fact, only the rationalization of the history of the community ... and all the imposing fabric of interpretation of the sources is merely the *post eventum* justification of the precedents which have been ratified by *ijma*."[47]

The notion that Islamic political thought is merely the justification of historical contingencies, however, neglects certain lines of inquiry within this thought that demonstrate the extent to which Muslim scholars grappled with evolving political realities. One of the first modern scholars to assess the development of Islamic political thought systematically through an analysis of the most significant treatises in the juridico-theological tradition was Ann Lambton. In *State and Government in Islam*, she analyzes treatises that span the second/eighth to ninth/fifteenth centuries, seeking to address broader questions such as the relationship between the Sharīʿa and the state, between the community and the state, and between jurists and the state. She finds that the thread binding the seemingly disparate inquiries together is "the divine nature of ultimate sovereignty," which presupposes "the existence of a state within which the early life of the community runs its course and whose function is to guarantee the maintenance of Islam, the application of the Sharīʿa, and the defense of orthodoxy against heresy. All tend to concentrate on the position of the ruler."[48]

45 Andrew Hess, "Islamic Civilization and the Legend of Political Failure," *Journal of Near Eastern Studies* 44, no. 1 (1985): 28.
46 Hamilton Gibb, "The Heritage of Islam in the Modern World (1)," *International Journal of Middle East Studies* 1, no. 1 (1970): 11.
47 Hamilton Gibb, "Al-Māwardī's Theory of the Caliphate," in Gibb, *Studies on Islamic Civilization*, ed. Stanford Shaw and William Polk (Boston: Beacon Press, 1968), 162.
48 Lambton, *State and Government*, xvi.

Lambton does recognize numerous inquiries, but they all seem to coalesce around a single central figure, the caliph. Thus, beyond the differences in the approaches and arguments of Hess, Gibb, and Lambton, all three agree on the overwhelming emphasis placed by Islamic political thinkers on the figure of the caliph and on the necessity of order within society.

Anjum has made the most recent contribution to the discussion of Islamic political thought, likewise bemoaning the ubiquitous focus on the power of the caliph in juridical treatises. For Anjum, the early Muslim political model was a community-centered vision of rule, which was replaced by a rule-centered vision of politics as dynastic powers took root. The redeeming figure in his eyes is Ibn Taymiyya (d. 728/1328), whose political thought reasserted the early community-centered mode of politics as an ideal. Unlike Hess and Gibb, who contend that the ruler-centered vision is simply the result of political thinkers yielding to political realities, Anjum believes that

> [t]he foundations of the classical caliphate theory, namely a ritualistic understanding of the caliphate and depoliticization of the Community, were underpinned by theological cynicism toward reason in postrevelational life on the one hand and elitism on the other, both of which deepened as the Sunni *kalām* doctrine matured in the classical period. Both elitism and cynicism toward reason militated against the other option, that of resurrecting and reimagining a Community-centered vision of Islam.[49]

For Anjum, the cause of the juridical compromise with political rulers and elitism is not simply an unconscious acceptance of new political realities, but the materialization of an epistemology that is cynical toward reason, thereby restricting the political agency of both the individual and the community.[50] This means that when Ibn Taymiyya comes to reorient political thought toward a focus on the community, he does so by first challenging the inherited epistemology underlying it.[51] In addition to excavating the political thought of Ibn Taymiyya, Anjum's work uncovers a previously unrecognized connection – that between epistemology and political thought.

Indebted to Anjum's insights, I similarly argue that al-Juwaynī's political thought was impacted by his epistemology; however, I do not believe that al-Juwaynī subscribed to the same ruler-centered vision of politics as al-Mawardī or al-Bāqillānī did before him. Al-Juwaynī's epistemology is primarily influenced by his desire for certainty, but enmeshed within his legal

[49] Anjum, *Politics, Law, and Community*, 168–69. [50] Ibid., 128–36.
[51] Ibid., 196–227.

thought are concerns for both legal certainty and societal and religious continuity. Ultimately, the desire for continuity trumps the desire for certainty in his legal thought. The implications of this priority are then fully realized in his political thought, where he forgoes a ruler-centered vision of politics to ensure the continuity of society. In doing so, al-Juwaynī becomes an example that stands at odds with characterizations of Islamic political thought as centered on elite power, as he offers a new vision of the Sharīʿa that recognizes its centrality to the question of continuity.

Taken together, al-Juwaynī's synthesis of reason and revelation through a reformed epistemology, his reconceptualization of the proofs for legal sources, and his theorization of structures of power beyond the caliph are all illustrative of the diversity that exists in Islamic intellectual history. Moreover, as will be seen throughout the course of this book, al-Juwaynī's divergence from his predecessors not only enhances scholarly understandings of the fifth/eleventh century but also augments it in important ways.

BEYOND THEMES

Beyond themes in Islamic studies, al-Juwaynī's epistemology and its ramifications in the realms of law and politics have broader implications with regard to the scholarly conception of human knowledge and the relationship of that knowledge to the Sharīʿa. As this book demonstrates, one of al-Juwaynī's central aims was to carve out a realm of practical certainty for individuals regardless of the ontological reality of their knowledge. The effect of this epistemological argument is manifest in al-Juwaynī's political thought, where he argues that the continuity of society, and indeed the Sharīʿa, is guaranteed only to the extent that individuals retain practical certainty in specific matters of the law. In this way, religious continuity comes to be predicated on human knowledge. While the full contours of this argument will be explored in subsequent chapters, especially in Chapter 10, a few introductory remarks are pertinent at this point.

Traditionally, the study of epistemology, as a subset of analytical philosophy, has focused on evaluating the doxastic decision-making of individuals. The individual is placed at the center as the "knowing subject," and knowledge is acquired by the individual through self-reliance. Knowledge is not defined as what is epistemically certain, but as what is *justified* according to the individual. This definition leads to an evaluation of the basic sources of knowledge, as knowledge is justified on the basis of sources alone. The four main sources of knowledge are perception, memory, consciousness, and reason. In this paradigm, the sources of knowledge and the parameters of justified belief are centered on the individual.[52] This "internalist" paradigm has increasingly been challenged by an "externalist"[53] paradigm that, broadly speaking,[54] argues for an understanding of knowledge that is not entirely self-referential. Early externalists noted that doxastic justification of belief does not merely occur within an individual but rather is spread across an entire "epistemic community."[55] This realization led to the birth of a subdiscipline within epistemology, social epistemology. Social epistemology starts from the premise that while cognitive processes are suited to producing justified belief, both cognitive processes and justified belief are impacted by the external environment in which an individual operates.[56] Social epistemologists argue that because of the individual's situatedness within a specific context and environment, knowledge is not merely the result of justified belief on the basis of self-referential sources of knowledge but rather emerges in a dialectical relationship between the individual and society. Therefore, instead of focusing on the justified belief of singular individuals, social epistemologists are more concerned with the collective epistemic products of doxastic agents who inhabit a similar context.

While there are many collective epistemic communities that can be analyzed from the perspective of social epistemology, the most salient for

[52] Robert Audi, "The Sources of Knowledge," in *The Oxford Handbook of Epistemology*, ed. Paul K. Moser (Oxford: Oxford University Press, 2002), 71–94.

[53] The debate between traditional epistemology and social epistemology is characterized within the field as the "internalism–externalism debate." In this debate, the social epistemologists are supported by others who also identify sources of knowledge, or justifications for belief, outside the individual. For more on the debate, see Laurence BonJour, "Recent Work on the Internalism–Externalism Controversy," in *The Blackwell Companion to Epistemology*, ed. Jonathan Dancy, Ernest Sosa, and Matthias Setup (Chichester: Wiley-Blackwell, 2010), 33–43, and Hamid Vahid, "Externalism/Internalism," in *The Routledge Companion to Epistemology*, ed. Sven Bernecker and Duncan Pritchard (London: Routledge, 2011), 144–55.

[54] Social anthropologists are not in complete agreement regarding how useful internalist paradigms of epistemology continue to be. There are three main positions: revisionism, which rejects traditional epistemology entirely; preservationism, which accepts the parameters of inquiry set by traditional epistemology while seeking to incorporate within it externalist elements; and expansionism, which seeks to expand the parameters of inquiry set by traditional epistemology while also incorporating externalist elements into it. For more on these three positions and social epistemology, see Alvin Goldman, "Why Social Epistemology Is Real Epistemology," in *Social Epistemology*, ed. Adrian Haddock, Alan Millar, and Duncan Pritchard (Oxford: Oxford University Press, 2010), 1–28.

[55] Miranda Fricker, "Skepticism and the Genealogy of Knowledge: Situating Epistemology in Time," in *Social Epistemology*, ed. Adrian Haddock, Alan Millar, and Duncan Pritchard (Oxford: Oxford University Press, 2010), 51.

[56] Goldman, "Why Social Epistemology," 1–3, 14–16.

this study are religious communities with a sociolegal core. Though social epistemologists have largely not yet begun evaluating religious communities as epistemic communities, Robert Cover, in his article "Nomos and Narrative," makes the argument that individuals inhabit a *nomos*, or normative universe, within which they acquire knowledge and reason. Though he focuses on religious communities with strong legal traditions, he argues that all communities aim to create normative behavior and that "the intelligibility of normative behavior inheres in the communal character of the narratives that provide the context of the behavior."[57] While social anthropologists point out that knowledge construction has an external element rooted in the context that individuals inhabit, Cover goes a step further to define that context as *nomos*. For Cover, in order for a *nomos* to exist, there must be a communally identifiable narrative that makes it significant, as well as a commitment to that narrative. When a *nomos* is constituted, the creation of legal meaning is possible.[58] Widening this argument to the realm of social epistemology, once a *nomos* is fashioned by a community, reasoning is no longer doxastic reasoning but the collective reasoning of an epistemic community.

Applying the insights of social anthropologists and Cover to al-Juwaynī's understanding of practical certainty and the continuity of society, we can see the practical certainty of individuals as supported by communal norms within society. In this manner, the knowledge of the individual and the knowledge present in society stand in a dialectical relationship in which the two are continually imbricated. In al-Juwaynī's political thought, this knowledge present in society is knowledge of the Sharīʿa, and to this extent, the Sharīʿa is not simply a set of rules and regulations but a *nomos* that supports individual knowledge, provides a meaningful paradigm of reasoning, and helps govern society. This broader understanding of the Sharīʿa as *nomos* is contingent on the epistemology that al-Juwaynī constructs, which envisions individuals not merely as individuals who enact the law but as members of an epistemic community that preserve it.

THE SCOPE OF THE BOOK

Given that the aim of this volume is to present the interconnectivity of al-Juwaynī's discussions on the themes of certainty and continuity across his

[57] Robert Cover, "The Supreme Court, 1982 Term – Foreword: Nomos and Narrative," *Harvard Law Review* 4, no. 28 (1983): 4–64.

[58] Ibid., 64–86.

intellectual production, it will rely on an array of texts from his oeuvre. The difficulty inherent in this approach is rooted in the fact that he not only wrote texts that fall within multiple disciplines but also authored numerous texts within each discipline. Therefore, I have chosen to focus on the foundational elements of his thought as presented in his theological, legal, and political writings. Though each text explored in this study is replete with subsidiary discussions that are all worthy of study, I have chosen recurrent themes that frame al-Juwaynī's overall intellectual project. In the realm of theology, I rely predominantly on the various editions of the *Shāmil* and the *Irshād*. While the *Shāmil* is undoubtedly a more exhaustive *kalām* text, the absence of a complete manuscript or edition[59] has led me to read it alongside the *Irshād*.[60] In law, I rely primarily on al-Juwaynī's *uṣūl al-fiqh* through a reading of his *Burhān* and *Talkhīṣ*. Focusing on al-Juwaynī's *uṣūl al-fiqh*, I have not engaged heavily with his texts on *fiqh*, most obviously his *Nihāyat al-maṭlab*,[61]

[59] The main preserved portions of the *Shāmil* have been published. See al-Juwaynī, *al-Shāmil fī uṣūl al-dīn*, ed. ʿAlī al-Nashshār, Fayṣal ʿAwn, and Suhayr Mukhtār (Alexandria: Munshaʾāt al-Maʿārif, 1969). Additional portions of the *Shāmil* were edited and published by Richard Frank. See al-Juwaynī, *al-Shāmil fī Uṣūl al-Dīn: The Exposition of al-Bāqillānī's Commentary on the Kitāb al-Lumaʿ; Some Additional Portions of the Text*, ed. Richard Frank (Tehran: McGill University/Tehran University, 1981). More recently, see the commentary on al-Juwaynī's *Shāmil* by Ibn al-Amīr (d. 735/1335): Ibn al-Amīr al-Ḥājj, *al-Kāmil fī ikhtiṣār al-Shāmil*, ed. ʿAbd al-Nāṣir ʿAbd al-Munʿim (Cairo: Dār al-Salām, 2010). A manuscript of the *Shāmil* is also preserved in al-Jāmiʿa al-ʿArabiyya (ms. 188, *ʿilm al-kalām*).

[60] The most commonly cited edition of the *Irshād ilā qawāṭiʿ al-adilla fī uṣūl al-iʿtiqād* is that by Dr. Muḥammad Yusūf Mūsā and Shaykh ʿAlī ʿAbd al-Munʿim ʿAbd al-Ḥamīd (Cairo: Maktabat al-Khānjī, 1950). A published translation into English is also available: *A Guide to the Conclusive Proofs for the Principles of Belief*, ed. Paul Walker (Reading: Garnet, 2001). (A French translation from 1938 by Jean-Dominique Luciani also exists.) In addition, there are three manuscript commentaries on the *Irshād*: (1) *Nukat al-Irshād*, a five-volume commentary by Abū Isḥāq b. Yūsuf housed at Dār al-Kutub (ms. 22888); (2) *al-Rashād fī sharḥ al-Irshād*, by ʿAbd al-Raḥmān b. Aḥmad b. ʿUmar, which is an original manuscript by the author and is also housed at Dār al-Kutub (ms. 20709); and (3) an untitled commentary by Abū Bakr Ibn Maymūn, housed at Jāmiʿat al-Duwal al-ʿArabiyya (ms. 143). There are also two published commentaries on the *Irshād*: (1) Muẓaffar b. ʿAbd Allāh al-Muqtaraḥ (d. 612/1215–16), *Sharḥ al-Irshād fī uṣūl al-iʿtiqād*, ed. Nazīha Maʿārij, 2 vols. (Tetouan: Markaz Abī al-Ḥasan al-Ashʿarī, in press); and (2) Abū Bakr Ibn Maymūn, *Sharḥ al-Irshād*, ed. Aḥmad Ḥijāzī Aḥmad al-Saqqā (Cairo: Maktabat al-Anjilū al-Miṣriyya, 1987).

[61] The *Nihāya* was especially important, as it represents one of the first attempts by a Shāfiʿī scholar to systematize the doctrines of the school. Demonstrative of its importance is the fact that al-Ghazālī produced four abridgments of it: *al-Basīṭ*, *al-Wasīṭ*, *al-Wajīz*, and *al-Khulāṣa*. The most definitive edition of the text is *Nihāyat al-maṭlab fī dirāyat al-madhhab*, ed. ʿAbd al-ʿAẓīm al-Dīb (Doha: Dār al-Minhāj/Wizārat al-Awqāf al-Qaṭariyya, 2007).

nor with his texts on comparative Ḥanafī and Shafi'ī *fiqh*[62] or juristic disputation (*jadal*).[63] While all of these legal texts merit study, they are beyond the scope of the present work. Finally, in the realm of political thought, I shift the gaze to al-Juwaynī's sole treatise on politics, *Ghiyāth al-umam* (*Ghiyāthī*). While this book does not claim to put all of al-Juwaynī's works in conversation with one another, it does bring together some of his most important output, affording the reader a better understanding of al-Juwaynī's intellectual project and laying the foundation for future research on this seminal figure.

My decision to read al-Juwaynī's above-mentioned texts in conjunction with one another is informed largely by the manner in which scholars have approached his work so far as well as by the insights provided by these scholars. The most recent monograph in English[64] dedicated solely to the study of al-Juwaynī is Mohammad Saflo's dissertation, published as *Al-Juwaynī's Thought and Methodology, with a Translation and Commentary on "Luma' al-Adilla."*[65] The dissertation attempts to demonstrate the full extent of al-Juwaynī's contribution to Islamic theology by providing a thoroughgoing analysis of his *Luma' al-adilla*.[66] Critics of Saflo's work, such as Frank Griffel,[67] have cast doubt on its utility,

62 The most important in this genre is his *Mughīth al-khalq fī tarjīḥ al-qawl al-ḥaqq* (Cairo: al-Maṭba'a al-Miṣriyya, 1934). There is another manuscript, entitled *al-Durra al-muḍiyya fīmā waqa'a min khilāf bayna al-Shāfi'iyya wa-l-Ḥanafiyya*, one version of which can be found in the British Library (ms. 7574) and the other in al-Jāmi'a al-'Arabiyya (ms. 23, *ikhtilāf al-fuqahā'*).

63 Al-Juwaynī, *al-Kāfiya fī al-jadal*, ed. Fawqiyya Ḥusayn Maḥmūd (Cairo: 'Isā al-Bābī al-Ḥalabī, 1979).

64 The only other monograph solely devoted to al-Juwaynī is Helmut Klopfer's dissertation, published as *Das Dogma des Imam al-Haramain al-Juwayni und sein Werk al-Aqidat an-Nizamiya* (Wiesbaden: Harrassowitz, 1958). However, since Klopfer's work is concerned only with al-Juwaynī's theology and does not address his legal thought at all, I will not focus on it in this book.

65 Mohammad Saflo, *Al-Juwaynī's Thought and Methodology, with a Translation and Commentary on "Luma' al-Adilla"* (Berlin: Schwarz, 2000).

66 Al-Juwaynī wrote a series of theological texts, so it is important to place the *Luma'* in connection to his other works. His lengthiest theological text, *al-Shāmil fī uṣūl al-dīn*, was a commentary on al-Bāqillānī's commentary on al-Ash'arī's *al-Luma' fī al-adilla*. The *Shāmil* was abridged into a shorter work known as *al-Irshād ilā qawāṭi' al-adilla fī uṣūl al-i'tiqād*. The *Irshād* was then itself abridged into *al-Luma' fī qawā'id ahl al-sunna wa-l-jamā'a*. The final theological text al-Juwaynī penned was *al-'Aqīda al-Niẓāmiyya*. Written at the end of his life, it was intended as a primer for students beginning their study of theology.

67 Frank Griffel, Review of *Al-Juwaynī's Thought and Methodology, with a Translation and Commentary on "Luma' al-Adilla,"* by Mohamed Moslem Adel Saflo, *Journal of the American Oriental Society* 122 (2002): 858–59.

arguing that Saflo does not provide an accurate historical or theological exposition on al-Juwaynī and his works and that the thesis lacks rigorous research. In part, this weakness can be attributed to Saflo's singular textual focus on the *Luma*ʿ and his neglect of al-Juwaynī's more comprehensive works on theology, such as the *Irshād* and the *Shāmil*. This shortcoming, in addition to Saflo's scant historical research into the sociopolitical milieu of al-Juwaynī's time, results in only a partial depiction of al-Juwaynī's scholarship.

Following in a similar vein is the unpublished dissertation of Ismail Haji Abdullah, entitled "The Influence of Imam al-Juwaynī on the Theology of Imam al-Ghazālī."[68] Like Saflo, Abdullah focuses solely on the theology of al-Juwaynī with an eye to comparing it with that of al-Juwaynī's extolled student, al-Ghazālī. Abdullah undertakes a systematic analysis of key issues (such as the origin of the world, the existence of God, the attributes of God, free will, and prophecy) and notes moments of convergence and divergence between the two scholars. He argues that al-Ghazālī's scholarly inclinations in *kalām*, philosophy, and Sufism were an imitation and extension of al-Juwaynī's intellectual trajectory. Although Abdullah does not, in my opinion, convincingly demonstrate al-Juwaynī's proclivities toward Sufism, he does uncover some individual examples of Sufi inclination. For Abdullah, the intellectual stature of al-Ghazālī is indisputable, but he shows al-Ghazālī's indebtedness to al-Juwaynī and calls into question those elements of al-Ghazālī's scholarship for which he is credited as a trailblazer, arguing that they often find their nascent forms in al-Juwaynī. But what is missing in both Saflo's and Abdullah's studies is a focus on al-Juwaynī's most seminal texts and a placement of his intellectual trajectory within his sociopolitical and intellectual context.

The most useful study to date on al-Juwaynī is Tilman Nagel's *Die Festung des Glaubens: Triumph und Scheitern des islamischen Rationalismus im 11. Jahrhundert* (Consolidation of the Faith: Triumph and Failure of Muslim Rationalism in the Eleventh Century).[69] As Nagel's study is motivated by an interest in the notion of decline and rationalism in Islamic thought, al-Juwaynī features centrally in it. Nagel's discussion of al-Juwaynī starts by depicting the direct bearing that al-Juwaynī's

68 Ismail Haji Abdullah, "The Influence of Imam al-Juwaynī on the Theology of Imam al-Ghazālī" (PhD diss., University of St. Andrews, 1996).

69 I am relying on the summary in French of the German text by Claude Gilliot. See Gilliot, "Quand la théologie s'allié à l'histoire: Triomphe et échec du rationalisme musulman à travers l'oeuvre d'al-Juwaynī," *Arabica* 39, no. 2 (1992): 241–60.

political, social, and religious context had on his intellectual preoccupations, especially his more apocalyptic tendencies. For Nagel, al-Juwaynī stands at the nexus between the early *kalām* of al-Ashʿarī (d. 324/936) and the later *kalām* of al-Ghazālī, the latter applauded for its synthetic nature.[70] Griffel similarly identifies both al-Juwaynī's adoption of philosophy and his deep understanding of it, something that Griffel believes subsequently informed al-Ghazālī's scholarly inclinations.[71]

Al-Juwaynī's syncretism in terms of disciplines has been further noted by Heck, who states that al-Juwaynī adopted doctrines from the philosophers and the Muʿtazila alike.[72] The more tangible elements of this intellectual pluralism are underscored by Robert Wisnovsky, who demonstrates al-Juwaynī's adoption of some of Ibn Sīnā's terminology regarding the necessity of God's existence and the contingency of the remainder of the world.[73] Richard Frank has also contributed to the presentation of al-Juwaynī's more novel ideas by elaborating on al-Juwaynī's argument regarding the knowledge one must have of God. Frank shows that al-Juwaynī was keen to introduce an element of rationality into belief: although he begrudgingly accepts superficial belief, he asserts that for those who desire true knowledge of God above and beyond mere platitudes of faith, rational apprehension is a prerequisite.[74]

All of these scholarly inquiries note in al-Juwaynī both his nascent development of a philosophical turn and his focus on the rational comprehensibility of matters of personal faith. In this book, I will focus more on the latter, arguing that it is informed by debates between the Muʿtazila and the Ashʿarīs. Moreover, al-Juwaynī's concern with rational comprehensibility can be taken as part and parcel of his concern with certainty ab initio, a concern identifiable not merely in his theological treatises but also, as I will demonstrate, in his legal and political works. By shedding

[70] Ibid. [71] Griffel, *Al-Ghazālī's Philosophical Theology*, 29–30.

[72] Paul Heck, "Jovayni, Emām-al-Ḥaramayn," in *Encyclopaedia Iranica* (New York, 1996–), www.iranicaonline.org/articles/jovayni-emam-al-haramayn. Heck argues that al-Juwaynī's borrowing from the Muʿtazila and from philosophers is most apparent in his theological works, but he also characterizes al-Juwaynī's overall intellectual project in terms of a search for certainty in religious matters. This search encompasses both theological and legal matters, which explains al-Juwaynī's overwhelming concern with certainty. Heck also claims that al-Juwaynī was concerned with establishing a righteous community and that this desire formed the backdrop of his discussions in the *Ghiyāthī*.

[73] Robert Wisnovsky, "One Aspect of the Avicennian Turn in Sunni Theology," in *Arabic Sciences and Philosophy* 14 (2004): 91–95.

[74] Richard Frank, "Knowledge and *Taqlīd*," 53–57.

light on al-Juwaynī's epistemology and its relationship to the rest of his thought, I unearth one element of al-Juwaynī's intellectual output; yet many fruitful areas of inquiry remain, such as his incorporation of philosophy into his theological works, his theory of dialectical disputation (*jadal*), and the consequences of his epistemology on *fiqh*. All of these are beyond the scope of the present study.

This book presents al-Juwaynī's intellectual project through a reading of his texts in distinct disciplines. Chapters 1 and 2 provide the historical background for al-Juwaynī's life as well as his intellectual accomplishments. The remainder of the book is divided into three additional parts: (1) epistemology, (2) legal theory and (3) political thought. Part II begins with Chapter 3, which focuses on the theological debates between the Muʿtazila and the Ashʿarīs and outlines the epistemologies of the competing schools. Building on previous scholarship, I demonstrate the impact of the two schools' theological conclusions on Islamic jurisprudence. Chapter 4 discusses al-Juwaynī's epistemology and his emphasis on certainty. I highlight moments both of convergence with his Ashʿarī predecessors and of divergence from them, as well as concessions that he makes to his Muʿtazilī interlocutors.

Part III comprises Chapters 5 through 8. Chapters 5 and 6 are dedicated to two sources of the law, *ḥadīth* and *ijmāʿ*, respectively, and they demonstrate how al-Juwaynī's concern with certainty forces him to rethink the method of establishing the validity of both sources of law. Chapters 7 and 8 discuss the two major types of *qiyās* – *qiyās al-maʿnā* and *qiyās al-shabah*, respectively. I argue that al-Juwaynī's desire for certainty is challenged in this context, as rulings derived through *qiyās* cannot rise above epistemic probability. I show how al-Juwaynī copes with the rise of legal uncertainty and argue that his acceptance of legal uncertainty signals the triumph of his desire for continuity.

In Part IV, which treats al-Juwaynī's political thought, Chapter 9 presents al-Juwaynī's political thought in connection with his desire for continuity, and Chapter 10 explores al-Juwaynī's argument for the absence of the imam and the continuity of society. In Chapter 9, I argue that al-Juwaynī's willingness to make political concessions is not a result of his simply yielding to political realities; rather, he is seeking a theory that will ensure societal continuity. In Chapter 10, I show that this continuity, for al-Juwaynī, is predicated on the ability of the individual to acquire and recall basic religious knowledge. In this manner, continuity is contingent on certainty, which emphasizes once again the foundational nature of epistemology.

Before proceeding, it is important to address the fact that al-Juwaynī is often depicted in biographical dictionaries as having rejected *kalām* and more advanced intellectual thought at the end of his life. Both al-Subkī and al-Dhahabī note that near the time of his death, he especially regretted his engagement with *kalām* and prayed that he be permitted to reach the end of his life with the simple faith a woman of Nishapur.[75] A similar sentiment is heard when he praises the belief of the *salaf* (predecessors) in the *Niẓāmiyya*, one of his last works.[76] On this note, a reminder that al-Juwaynī was fully embroiled in theological debates against the Muʿtazila in defense of the newly rising Ashʿarī school is germane. Whether in the early stages of his life, when the Ashʿarīs faced persecution, or in the latter part of his life, after he had assumed his chair at the Niẓāmiyya madrassa, al-Juwaynī was front and center in the most contentious theological debates of his time, many of which remained unresolved. It is thus not surprising that at the end of his life, al-Juwaynī preferred to distance himself from *kalām*. However, his works on law, and specifically the *Burhān* – a late text of al-Juwaynī's – contain no similar sentiments of regret.

Irrespective of whether al-Juwaynī regretted his intellectual explorations in the world of *kalām*, his *kalām* had a profound impact on later Ashʿarī scholars – most obviously on his famed student al-Ghazālī – and offers great insight into the theological debates of the fifth/eleventh century. Perhaps most importantly, al-Juwaynī's *kalām* and its relationship, through his epistemological framework, to his legal and political thought reveal interconnections between disciplines that are often evaluated discretely. It is true that tensions and contradictions in al-Juwaynī's thought cannot be ignored, but his ideas and works remain foundational to the development of Islamic intellectual thought.

[75] Al-Subkī, *Ṭabaqāt al-Shāfiʿiyya*, 5:191, and al-Dhahabī, *Siyar aʿlām al-nubalāʾ*, ed. Muḥibb al-Dīn Abū Saʿīd ʿUmar b. Gharāma al-ʿAmrawi (Beirut: Dār al-Fikr, 1997), 18:473–74.

[76] Al-Juwaynī, *al-ʿAqīda al-Niẓāmiyya*, ed. Muḥammad Zāhid al-Kawtharī (Cairo: Maktabat al-Khānjī, 1948), 21.

PART I

HISTORICAL BACKGROUND

1

Politics, Patronage, and Scholarship in Nishapur

From the death of the Prophet in CE 632 through the fourth/tenth century, intense political, theological, and legal debates divided the Muslim community. And though debates continued long after, the fourth/tenth and fifth/eleventh centuries are recalled as the period in which the theological and legal identity of Sunnī Islam was cemented through the consolidation of the four schools of law: the Ḥanafī, the Mālikī, the Shāfiʿī, and the Ḥanbalī,[1] and the two schools of theology: the Ashʿarī and the Māturīdī. The creation of this identity, however, should not be confused with strength, as scholars writing during these centuries continued to respond to threats, both internal and external, perceived and actual. It was these actual threats that faced al-Juwaynī in his hometown of Nishapur.

Nishapur, alongside the three other great cities of the intellectually fertile province of Khurasan in northeastern Persia, namely, Marw, Herat, and Balkh, was the regional capital for politics, scholarship, and commerce starting in the third/ninth century.[2] Despite being located in

[1] For the development of the legal schools, see Melchert, *Formation of the Sunni Schools*, and El Shamsy, *Canonization of Islamic Law*.

[2] I reconstruct the history of Nishapur during this time primarily from biographical dictionaries that have survived. The *Kitāb al-Siyāq li-tārīkh Nīsābūr*, composed by Abū al-Ḥasan al-Fārisī (d. 529/1135), is preserved in facsimile form in *Histories of Nishapur*, ed. Richard Frye (Cambridge, MA: Harvard University Press, 1965). This is the principal text used by Richard Bulliet for the argument he advances in his *Patricians of Nishapur* regarding the social and intellectual elites in Nishapur. See Richard Frye (ed.), *Histories of Nishapur* (Cambridge, MA: Harvard University Press, 1965), and Richard Bulliet, *The Patricians of Nishapur* (Cambridge: Cambridge University Press, 1972).

Persia, the city itself had a large Arab population dating from the time of the early conquests, when wealthy families migrated and permanently settled there.[3] The mingling of Arab settlers, indigenous Persians, a vibrant trade culture, and Islamic scholars created a social and religious elite centered on prominent families within the city. These patrician families were typically connected to the scholarly class and were divided in their adherence to particular legal schools, the most prominent at that time being the Ḥanafī and Shāfiʿī schools.

The intellectual cleavages within the city between rival theological and legal groups ultimately led to al-Juwaynī's concern with certainty. However, intellectual diversity was not the only factor that had an indelible impact on al-Juwaynī's intellectual production. Al-Juwaynī witnessed the gradual weakening of the ʿAbbasid caliphate and the rise of competing dynastic authorities that would often clash violently in Nishapur. The precarious nature of politics during his lifetime naturally gave rise to his second concern – that of continuity. Al-Juwaynī's intellectual preoccupations throughout his works can be better understood when examined against this backdrop of competing political factions and intellectual groups.

AL-JUWAYNĪ'S TIME AND HIS SCHOLARSHIP

In order to sketch an intellectual portrait of al-Juwaynī, the story must begin with his context, as the tumultuous political, intellectual, and social environment contributed to his articulation of novel ideas in the realms of speculative theology, jurisprudence, and political theory. Though the immediate context for al-Juwaynī's intellectual growth was Nishapur, between the third/ninth and fourth/eleventh centuries, as Paul Heck has recently argued, scholars across the Islamic lands were embroiled in difficult theological debates, leading them to employ new methods of inquiry. Heck focuses on skeptical reasoning, which, according to him, was employed by Muslim theoreticians in various disciplines in order to provide a foundation for religious knowledge that was epistemically certain. Instead of representing an end to intellectual inquiry, skepticism provided Muslim theoreticians with a way to arrive at rationally compelling arguments for religious doctrines. To show the breadth of skeptical arguments in the period under study, Heck devotes each chapter of his

[3] Bulliet, *Patricians of Nishapur*, 20.

book to a different scholar, writing in a different era and on a different issue. While most of the issues are theological in nature, the surveyed scholars are scattered across the Muslim lands. Heck's inquiry begins with Abū ʿUthmān ʿAmr al-Jāḥiẓ (d. 255/869) who set out to respond to growing anthropomorphic tendencies among scholars in Baghdad, and it ends with the Damascene scholar Taqī al-Dīn Ibn Taymiyya (d. 728/1328), who elaborated on the nature of the relationship between finite human beings and an infinite God. Between these two figures, Heck focuses on two scholars from Nishapur, Abū al-Ḥasan al-ʿAmīrī (d. 383/993) and Abū Ḥāmid al-Ghazālī (d. 505/1111). Though the intellectual trend to employ skepticism as a means of developing rationally compelling arguments started in Baghdad, the epicenter of ʿAbbasid intellectual life, such trends spread from Baghdad across what Hugh Kennedy has called the "Muslim commonwealth"[4] to satellite cities within the ʿAbbasid Empire such as Nishapur. The general concern with rationally convincing arguments was then further shaped by the sociopolitical currents of each city. As I will argue later, the intellectual environment of Nishapur in al-Juwaynī's lifetime fostered his insistence on epistemically sound knowledge, and the political environment, marked by upheaval and instability, ushered in his other concern, that of continuity.

Tilman Nagel also links al-Juwaynī's historical moment with his scholarly production in his work.[5] Nagel investigates the notion of the decline of Islam and the fate of religious thought vis-à-vis the production of scholars, especially that of al-Juwaynī. Nagel's monograph touches on various elements of al-Juwaynī's thought, ranging from his understanding of *kalām* and law to his view of the caliphate and the structure of society. But Nagel's most important contribution is his illumination of the connection between al-Juwaynī's political, social, and religious context and his scholarship. For Nagel, al-Juwaynī's life under a weak ʿAbbasid caliphate that had divested its authoritative power to the Seljuk sultans was a politically unpredictable one at best. Closer to home, in Nishapur the intellectual environment was increasingly fractured because of the Shīʿī intellectual threat posed by the Fatimids and because of mounting suspicions against the Ashʿarīs, the Shāfiʿīs, and the Sufis. These factors had

[4] Hugh Kennedy, *The Prophet and the Age of the Caliphates* (London: Longman, 1986), 200. The term was also invoked by Dimitri Gutas in *Greek Thought, Arabic Culture: The Graeco-Arabic Translation Movement in Baghdad and Early ʿAbbasid Society* (London: Routledge, 1998), 154.

[5] I am relying on Claude Gilliot's French summary of the German text. See Gilliot, "Quand la théologie s'allié à l'histoire," 241–60.

a cumulative effect on al-Juwaynī's intellectual concerns, and their results can be identified in his writings.

With respect to theology, Nagel finds that al-Juwaynī's key concern in *kalām* is to resolve all uncertainty and ambiguity in order to ensure definitive answers to all theological questions. In the realm of law, al-Juwaynī's aims are similar: Nagel notes that he seeks to limit legal possibilities and to focus on what is obligatory so that individuals can submit completely to God. Submission becomes the central force behind the law, and when it is not possible to ascertain a legal ruling exactly, the individual willingly submits to the most likely ruling as an act of obedience. With regard to al-Juwaynī's political thought, according to Nagel al-Juwaynī legitimizes a new political structure that entails a bifurcation between the powerful seat of the sultan and the figurehead seat of the caliphate.[6] In this new model, the formal office of the imam is limited, and the concerns and needs of the community are addressed by the de facto leaders.

For the most part, I agree with Nagel's assessment of al-Juwaynī's scholarship and concerns. However, I would further argue that al-Juwaynī's desire for certainty, mentioned explicitly in his *kalām* texts, underpins the entirety of his legal and political thought. Moreover, despite his preoccupation with certainty, he is also deeply concerned with social stability and continuity. This concern is manifest in his political thought, where he is forced to reckon with a political reality that is starkly different from his theoretical ideal. Seen from this vantage point, beyond simply responding to the political and intellectual realities of his day, al-Juwaynī is trying to come to terms with them within his own intellectual framework so that both he and the average Muslim can transcend them. For al-Juwaynī, the method of transcending uncertainty and other difficulties is the identification of epistemically certain knowledge in both religious and mundane affairs. This knowledge then becomes the touchstone for the believer in situations in which certainty and theoretical ideals are unavailable, thereby guaranteeing the continuity of society and religious knowledge. Analyzing al-Juwaynī's intellectual production in this way demonstrates that he was a syncretic thinker not overly concerned with

[6] Nagel's discussion of al-Juwaynī's theory of government forms the final part of his indispensable analysis of the life and thought of al-Juwaynī, with the two other sections focusing on his historical situation and his overall thought. My project differs from Nagel's study in that it specifically traces al-Juwaynī's epistemology through his legal and political thought to demonstrate that his framework for resolving political, theological, and legal issues is an epistemological one.

discrete questions but more focused on developing a framework that could be invoked in a variety of sociopolitical and religious crises. To understand his specific moment of crisis, we turn to the city of his birth and life, Nishapur.

NISHAPUR: A CITY DIVIDED

With the weakening of the ʿAbbasid caliphate from the end of the second/eighth century onward, territories near the capital, Baghdad, slowly came under the dominion of various dynastic families vying for power and resources. By the time of al-Juwaynī in the fifth/eleventh century, power had transferred from the ʿAbbasids first to the Samanids and then to the Ghaznavids,[7] who continued to rule until they were militarily overpowered by the Seljuk Turks in 429/1037. The continuous flux of political power left the social and intellectual realms open to cultivation, ushering in a notable diversity of views. This diversity, however, resulted in increasing sectarianism, which was easily identified by onlookers. Muḥammad Shams al-Dīn al-Muqaddasī (ca. 946–91), the famed geographer, noted on his visit to Nishapur that factionalism (*ʿasabiyya*) was rampant, especially between the Karrāmiyya[8] and the

[7] To understand the transition of power between these various dynasties and their relationship to the ʿAbbasid caliphate, see Bosworth, *Ghaznavids*. For a shorter exposition of their rise to power by the same author, see Bosworth, "Early Ghaznavids."

[8] The Karrāmiyya are historically remembered as a heterodox sect that championed literalist and anthropomorphic interpretations of scriptural sources. Despite their theological divergence from mainstream Sunnīs, scholars have argued that the Karrāmiyya should be situated between the Muʿtazila and the *ahl al-ḥadīth*. Their inclusion within Sunnism is in part due to the ascetic and pietistic beliefs that formed the cornerstone of the teachings of Abū ʿAbd Allāh b. Karrām (ca. 190–225/806–68), the eponym of the school. This pietism enabled the popularization of the sect's beliefs in Nishapur, where devotional trends were emerging within Sunnī thought. After the death of ʿAbd Allāh b. Karrām, adherents of Karrāmī beliefs in Nishapur were under the leadership of Abū Bakr Muḥammad b. Iṣḥāq b. Maḥmūdshadh (d. 421/1030), who received patronage both from the founder of the Ghaznavid dynasty, Sabuktigin (r. 367–87/977–97), and from his son, Sultan Mahmūd (r. 388–421/998–1030). Having gained the patronage of the Ghaznavids, Karrāmī beliefs proliferated, especially through debate, angering the Ḥanafī and Shāfiʿī inhabitants of the city. When Sultan Maḥmūd withdrew his patronage in 402/1011–12, Abū Bakr took up a life of seclusion. Margaret Malamud notes that when Sultan Maḥmūd conquered Ghur in 411/1010–11, Karrāmī teachings were allowed to continue until 595/1199 when Ghurid kings finally renounced Karrāmī beliefs. The dearth of surviving Karrāmī texts means that the bulk of their thought can only be reconstructed through the eyes of their opponents, which, needless to say, provide an unfavorable account of their doctrines. There is one surviving Karrāmī text – an anonymous collection of ethical

Shīʿa.[9] He traced the roots of this factionalism to the intense internal solidarity within each faction; yet according to Richard Bulliet and, more recently, Martin Nguyen, the factionalism between the Karrāmiyya and the Shīʿa gave way to a deeper cleavage between the Ḥanafīs and the Shāfiʿīs,[10] which emerged during the rule of the Ghaznavids and widened with the rise of the Seljuks.

Relating the tensions between the Ḥanafīs and the Shāfiʿīs to an earlier division in the third/ninth century when the two groups had adhered to rival regional legal schools, Bulliet argues that the rift between the two moved beyond formalistic methodological differences and gave rise to two competing visions of the world. According to this account, the Ḥanafīs held a rational worldview rooted in the aim of creating a society modeled on an older Prophetic one, whereas the vision of the Shāfiʿīs was more forward-looking, progressive, and willing to adopt new tendencies, especially pietistic ones embodied in Sufism.[11] The notion that the Shāfiʿīs had a particular proclivity toward Sufism is supported by Bulliet's statistical survey of biographies of Nishapuri individuals: of the twenty-eight figures who self-identified as Sufi, twenty-three were also Shāfiʿī.[12] As Nguyen demonstrates, the connection between the Shāfiʿīs and the Sufis was the product of their intertwined intellectual heritage.[13] This shared intellectual genealogy was strengthened by theological affiliations, marriages, and even political ambitions. The continued connection between the Shāfiʿīs and the Sufis deepened the fissure with the Ḥanafīs, but it was by no means the only cause of the divergence between the groups. Both Bulliet and Wilferd Madelung acknowledge Sufism as a key point of tension, but they also

and mystical traditions – in the British Museum, ms. Or. 8049. Louis Massignon, in his *Essai sur les origines du lexique technique de la mystique musulmane* (Paris: Librairie Orientaliste, 1954), 267–68, tentatively attributes this text to the Karrāmī leader of Nishapur, Abū Bakr Maḥmūdshadh. See Clifford Bosworth, "Karrāmiyya," in *Encyclopaedia of Islam*, 2nd edn., ed. P. Bearman, T. Bianquis, C. E. Bosworth, E. van Donzel, and W. P. Heinrichs (Brill Online, 2014). For an important article that notes the relationship between the Karrāmiyya and the political elite in Nishapur, as well as the inclusion of Karrāmī piety into Sufism, see Margaret Malamud, "The Politics of Heresy in Medieval Khurasan: The Karramiyya in Nishapur," *Iranian Studies* 27, nos. 1–4 (1994): 37–51.

[9] Al-Muqaddasī, *Aḥsan al-taqāsīm*, 336.

[10] Bulliet, *Patricians of Nishapur*, 21, 38–46. See also Martin Nguyen, "The Confluence and Construction of Traditions: Al-Qushayrī and the Intersection of Qurʾānic Exegesis, Theology and Sufism" (PhD diss., Harvard University, 2009), chapter 2.

[11] Bulliet, *Patricians of Nishapur*, 39.

[12] Ibid., 42. Of the other five Sufis, two were Ẓāhirīs, two were Mālikīs, and one was a Ḥanafī.

[13] Nguyen, "Confluence and Construction," 101–2.

recognize the contribution of other political, social, and theological factors.[14] These various differences were exacerbated by the institution of the legal school, *madhhab*, which, beyond representing a reservoir of legal knowledge and a distinct jurisprudential procedure, created a social structure that commanded adherence and allegiance from its members, resulting in the very *ʿasabiyya* that al-Muqaddasī recognized.

The mounting rivalry between the Ḥanafīs and the Shāfiʿīs reached its apex after the transition of power from the Ghaznavids to the Seljuks. When the Ghaznavids had begun their rule in the fourth/tenth century, they had altered some of the political practices of the Samanids but retained their predecessors' preference for the Ḥanafī legal school, which meant that at the time of al-Juwaynī's birth the chief *qāḍī* was the Ḥanafī Abū al-ʿAlāʾ Ṣāʿid (d. 431/1040).[15] Naṣr, the brother of Sultan Maḥmūd of Ghazna, not only maintained Qāḍī Ṣāʿid's position but also constructed a madrassa for him, providing the Ḥanafīs with a way to disseminate their thought easily.[16] The institutionalized presence of the Ḥanafīs, however, did not detract from the prominence of Shāfiʿī scholars and their families. An example is the Basṭāmī family, led by Abū ʿAmr Muḥammad al-Basṭāmī (d. 408/1017). Al-Basṭāmī himself served as the *raʾīs* of the Shāfiʿīs in Nishapur around the year 370/981 and as the interim chief *qāḍī* in 388/998 during a rebellion, after which the position was returned to the Ḥanafīs.[17] With the Ḥanafīs occupying the position of the chief *qāḍī* and prominent Shāfiʿī families promoting education through patronage, the delicate balance between the two factions could easily be fractured, as it was in the reign of the Seljuk Turks.

As the Seljuk Turks pursued their relentless advance into Ghaznavid lands, it became clear that the Ghaznavid stronghold in Nishapur was weakening, and by 429/1038 the Seljuks had arrived at the borders of the city.[18] Inside the city, leaders such as Qāḍī Ṣāʿid and the son of al-Basṭāmī, Ibn al-Muwaffaq (d. 440/1048), were at a political crossroads, charged with the decision of whether or not to surrender. They were compelled to

[14] Wilferd Madelung, *Religious Trends in Early Iran* (Albany: State University of New York Press, 1988), 27, and Bulliet, *Patricians of Nishapur*, 33.

[15] ʿAbd al-Qādir b. Muḥammad, *al-Jawāhir al-muḍiyya fī ṭabaqāt al-Ḥanafiyya* (Hyderabad: Majlis Dāʾirat al-Maʿārif al-Niẓāmiyya, 1914), 1:261–62.

[16] Bosworth, *Ghaznavids*, 175.

[17] This date is cited by Bulliet in *Patricians of Nishapur*, 118. See also al-Subkī, *Ṭabaqāt al-Shāfiʿiyya*, 4:140–43. Al-Basṭāmī's son, Ibn al-Muwaffaq (d. 440/1048), was also a prominent scholar and a contemporary of al-Juwaynī. See al-Subkī, *Ṭabaqāt al-Shāfiʿiyya*, 4:271–92.

[18] The date of the occupation of Nishapur is from Bulliet, *Patricians of Nishapur*, 204.

make this decision themselves, as the Ghaznavid sultan was abroad and consulting him was an impossibility.[19] The Ḥanafīs were reluctant to abandon their patrons in a moment of crisis and tarried in making a definitive decision. The Shāfiʿīs, on the other hand, are reported to have actively arranged the surrender through Ibn al-Muwaffaq, the *raʾīs* of the city at the time. To formalize the surrender, Ibn al-Muwaffaq, along with other unnamed scholars, exited the city to welcome the Seljuk commander, despite the obvious abstention of key Ḥanafī scholars such as Qāḍī Ṣāʿid. Three days later, when the famed Seljuk leader Ṭughril Beg arrived in the city, Qāḍī Ṣāʿid, along with other prominent Ḥanafīs, formally accepted the surrender.[20] The scholars' surrender of the city did not prevent attempts by the Ghaznavids to reassert control, but in 431/1040 the Seljuks won a decisive battle at Dandaqan and the Ghaznavids were forced to relinquish their position in Nishapur permanently.

Under Seljuk rule, the prominence of Nishapur grew exponentially, as Ṭughril Beg declared the city his capital, prompting an influx of people into the city, especially those of Seljuk Turkic descent. With the growth in population and the firm establishment of the new rulers, a natural assumption would be that the religio-political contours of the city shifted in favor of the Shāfiʿīs, who had directly facilitated the transition of power. Surprisingly, however, early Shāfiʿī support for Seljuk rule was not rewarded and the Ḥanafīs retained their dominant share of official patronage, deepening the tensions between the two groups. But the breaking point in the tense relationship between the two legal schools in Nishapur was the result not of legal or political preferences but of theological ones.

Recall that the Shāfiʿīs inhabiting Nishapur were, according to Bulliet, progressive in their acceptance of the new pietistic Sufi trends that were gaining prominence.[21] The Shāfiʿī affiliation with Sufism was accompanied by a new theological alliance with the school of Abū al-Ḥasan al-Ashʿarī (d. 324/936). The rise of Ashʿarism[22] in Nishapur during this

[19] In *The Ghaznavids*, Bosworth provides an account related by Abū al-Faḍl al-Bayhaqī (d. 470/1077) in the latter's *Tārīkh al-Bayhaqī*. For an analysis of this account, see Jurgen, "Seljuk Conquest(s) of Nishapur," 575–77.

[20] Bosworth, *Ghaznavids*, 256.

[21] For more details on the Sufi scholars living in Nishapur during the time of al-Juwaynī and the connections between these scholars, see Nguyen, "Confluence and Construction," chapter 1; Bulliet, *Patricians of Nishapur*, chapters 2 and 3; and Margaret Malamud, "Sufi Organizations and Structures of Authority in Medieval Nishapur," *International Journal of Middle East Studies* 26, no. 3 (1994): 427–42.

[22] Here, it is important to note that Ashʿarism is often associated with theological orthodoxy, but during this period in Nishapur Ashʿarism was still relatively nascent and did not possess

time is credited to ʿAbd Allāh al-Juwaynī's teacher, Abū Sahl al-Ṣuʿlukī (d. 369/980), who was one of the first scholars in Nishapur to represent a combination of Shāfiʿī and Ashʿarī views; thanks to al-Ṣuʿlukī's prolific teaching, the Shāfiʿī-Ashʿarī synthesis began to flourish, with an influx of Ashʿarīs into Nishapur between 290/902 and 343/955.[23] Four prominent scholars[24] who would later greatly influence al-Juwaynī arrived in Nishapur as part of this migration: Abū Bakr Ibn Fūrak (d. 406/1015),[25] Abū Isḥāq al-Isfarāyīnī (d. 418/1027),[26] Abū Bakr al-Bāqillānī (d. 403/1013),[27] and Abū Manṣūr ʿAbd al-Qāhir al-Baghdādī (d. 429/1037).[28] According

such a status. George Makdisi noted in 1962 that the understanding of Ashʿarism in Western academic circles was based on an exclusive reliance on Ashʿarī sources, namely, al-Shahrastānī's *al-Milal wa-l-nihal*, Ibn ʿAsākir's *Tabyīn kadhib al-muftarī*, and al-Subkī's *al-Ṭabaqāt al-Shāfiʿiyya*. These works, according to Makdisi, are apologetic in nature and were designed to defend the right of Ashʿarism to exist alongside the Shāfiʿī legal school. See George Makdisi, "Ashʿarī and the Ashʿarites in Islamic Religious History, Part 1," *Studia Islamica*, no. 17 (1962): 37–80; and Makdisi, "Ashʿarī and the Ashʿarites in Islamic Religious History, Part 2," *Studia Islamica*, no. 18 (1963): 19–39. Makdisi makes a similar argument in his later monograph, *The Rise of Colleges: Institutions of Learning in Islam and the West* (Edinburgh: Edinburgh University Press, 1981).

23 Bulliet, *Patricians of Nishapur*, 116, and Bulliet, "A Quantitative Approach to Medieval Muslim Biographical Dictionaries," *Journal of the Economic and Social History of the Orient* 13 (1970): 195–211. See also Michel Allard, *Le Problème des attributs divins dans la doctrine d'al-Ashari et ses premiers grands disciples* (Beirut: Imprimerie Catholique, 1965), 75–77, 312–55; Heinz Halm, *Die Ausbreitung der šāfiʿitischen Rechtsschule von den Anfängen bis zum 8./14. Jahrhundert* (Wiesbaden: Ludwig Reichert, 1974), 32–41; and George Makdisi, "Ashʿarī and the Ashʿarites, Part 1," 37–80, and "Ashʿarī and the Ashʿarites, Part 2," 19–39.

24 Three of the four scholars mentioned – Ibn Fūrak, al-Isfarāyīnī, and al-Bāqillānī – studied under Abū al-Ḥasan al-Bāhilī, who himself was a renowned pupil of Abū al-Ḥasan al-Ashʿarī.

25 Abū Bakr Muḥammad b. al-Ḥasan b. Fūrak al-Anṣārī al-Isfahānī is known as Ibn Fūrak. For his biography, see al-Subkī, *Ṭabaqāt al-Shāfiʿiyya*, 4:127–35; Ibn ʿAsākir, *Tabyīn kadhib al-muftarī fī-mā nusiba ilā al-imām Abī al-Ḥasan al-Ashʿarī*, ed. Muḥammad Zāhid al-Kawtharī (Damascus: al-Qudsī, 1928), 232–33; Ibn Khallikān, *Wafayāt al-aʿyān wa-anbāʾ abnāʾ al-zamān*, ed. Iḥsān ʿAbbās, Wadād Qāḍī, and Mūsā ʿIzz al-Dīn ʿUmar Aḥmad (Beirut: Dār Ṣādir, 1977), 4:272–73; and al-Dhahabī, *Siyar aʿlām al-nubalāʾ*, 13:130–31.

26 Abū Isḥāq Ibrāhīm b. Muḥammad b. Ibrāhīm b. Mirhān al-Isfarāyīnī. For his biography, see al-Subkī, *Ṭabaqāt al-Shāfiʿiyya*, 4:256–62; Ibn ʿAsākir, *Tabyīn kadhib al-muftarī*, 243–44; Ibn Khallikān, *Wafayāt al-aʿyān*, 1:28; and al-Dhahabī, *Siyar aʿlām al-nubalāʾ*, 13:225–27.

27 Al-Qāḍī Abū Bakr Muḥammad b. al-Tayyib b. Muḥammad al-Bāqillānī. For his biography, see Ibn ʿAsākir, *Tabyīn kadhib al-muftarī*, 218–26, and Ibn al-ʿImād, *Shadharāt al-dhahab fī akhbār man dhahab* (Beirut: al-Maktab al-Tijārī li-l-Ṭibāʿa wa-l-Nashr wa-l-Tawzīʿ, 1966), 3:168–70.

28 Abū Manṣūr ʿAbd al-Qāhir b. Ṭāhir b. Muḥammad b. Tamīmī al-Baghdādī. For his biography, see al-Subkī, *Ṭabaqāt al-Shāfiʿiyya*, 5:136–48.

to Massignon, both Ibn Fūrak and al-Isfarāyīnī undertook the journey at the insistence of Abū ʿAlī al-Daqqāq (d. 405/1015)[29] and the latter's teacher, al-Naṣrābādhī (d. 367/977–78), a prominent Sufi scholar who was at the time living in Nishapur.[30]

Instead of ameliorating some of the tensions between the Shāfiʿīs and other groups, the arrival of the Ashʿarīs in Nishapur only exacerbated them. Although the Ashʿarī school eventually became synonymous with Sunnī orthodoxy, at that time it faced the dominance of Muʿtazilī rationalism, which was associated with the Ḥanafī school. The Muʿtazilī school, divided into the Baghdadi and Basran branches, had an adherent of the Ḥanafī *madhhab* as the leader of each branch. In Basra, this was Abū ʿAlī al-Jubbāʾī (d. 303/915–16), the teacher of al-Ashʿarī, followed by Abū ʿAbd Allāh al-Baṣrī (d. 369/979–80) and then Abū al-Ḥasan al-Baṣrī (d. 426/1044). At the helm of the Baghdadi school was the Ḥanafī Abū al-Qāsim al-Balkhī (d. 319/931). That is not to say that no Muʿtazilīs were adherents of the Shāfiʿī school – in fact, one of the most famous late Muʿtazilī scholars, Qāḍī ʿAbd al-Jabbār (d. 415/1025), was a Shāfiʿī. But at the time when Ashʿarism arrived in Khurasan at the end of the third/ninth and beginning of the fourth/tenth century, it was introduced through the Shāfiʿī school, whereas the Ḥanafī school was more strongly

[29] Abū ʿAlī al-Ḥasan b. ʿAlī b. Muḥammad al-Daqqāq. For his biography, see al-Subkī, *Ṭabaqāt al-Shāfiʿiyya*, 4:329–31, and Ibn ʿAsākir, *Tabyīn kadhib al-muftarī*, 226–27.

[30] This connection led Massignon to argue that relationships were beginning to form between Sufi scholars in Nishapur and Ashʿarī theologians elsewhere in Khurasan and the ʿAbbasid Empire. As these scholars relocated to Nishapur, they attracted adherents, most often through madrassas built for them, such as the one built for Ibn Fūrak, who also had one in his previous home in Baghdad. Later biographers such as al-Subkī and Ibn ʿAsākir acknowledge that Ibn Fūrak, al-Isfarāyīnī, and al-Bāqillānī were instrumental in bringing Ashʿarī ideas to Khurasan and especially Nishapur. Given that these new scholars came at the behest of various Shāfiʿī scholars, the Ashʿarī newcomers were quickly affiliated with the Shāfiʿī school of law and by extension drawn into the mounting tensions between the Ḥanafīs and the Shāfiʿīs. On Abū ʿAlī al-Ḥasan b. ʿAlī b. Muḥammad al-Daqqāq, see al-Subkī, *Ṭabaqāt al-Shāfiʿiyya*, 4:329–31, and Ibn ʿAsākir, *Tabyīn kadhib al-muftarī*, 226–27, 232–33. On the development of Sufism, see Louis Massignon, *The Passion of al-Hallāj* (Princeton: Princeton University Press, 1982), 1:172–75 and 2:69. After Massignon, Tilman Nagel pointed to a trend he labeled "New Piety," representing a synthesis of Shāfiʿism, Sufism, and Ashʿarism. See Nagel, *Die Festung des Glaubens: Triumph und Scheitern des islamischen Rationalismus im 11. Jahrhundert* (Munich: Beck, 1988), 95–120. These arguments have not gone without criticism. See Wilferd Madelung, Review of *Die Festung des Glaubens*, *Bulletin of the School of Oriental and African Studies* 53, no. 1 (1990): 130–31, and Josef van Ess, "Sufism and Its Opponents: Reflections on Topoi, Tribulations and Transformations," in *Islamic Mysticism Contested: Thirteen Centuries of Controversies and Polemics*, ed. Frederick de Jong and Bernd Radtke (Leiden: Brill, 1999), 33.

linked to Muʿtazilism.[31] Creating a bond between the Ashʿarīs and the Shāfiʿīs, according to George Makdisi, was a strategic move on the part of the former. Struggling to gain status as an orthodox theological school, Makdisi notes, the Ashʿarīs realized that the "most practical means of determining orthodoxy was membership in one of the Sunnite schools of law. To be a member of a school of law, one had only to adhere to its juridical system. These schools were the guardians of the divine positive law (Sharīʿa) which embraced the civil as well as the religious life of the faithful."[32] Thus, the aspiring Ashʿarī newcomers affiliated themselves with the Shāfiʿī school of law and were thus drawn into the mounting antagonism between the Ḥanafīs and the Shāfiʿīs.

Under the Ghaznavids, the factionalism that divided the Ḥanafīs and the Shāfiʿīs continued to worsen with no signs of amelioration, finally culminating in the persecution of the Ashʿarīs, who were seen as the newcomers. As Nguyen describes it:

> The politics of the city's new rulers, the Seljuks, would shift matters drastically, turning the *fitna* into a *miḥna*, a period of outright persecution and suppression in which the victims, the Ashʿarīs, were made to suffer. And it appears, on the surface of things, that what lay at the core of this suppression was nothing more than the erudite disputations of theology. But percolating just underneath this veneer of bookish discussions were political maneuvers for power and legitimacy on all sides.[33]

Nguyen's assertion that political maneuverings lay at the core of the intellectual unrest echoes Bulliet's early sentiments regarding the patrician families of Nishapur, whom he depicts as "politicians without policy."[34] However, for Nguyen, it was the rise of Seljuk power that eventually caused the imbalance between the two factions, leading to widespread persecution within Nishapur and the self-imposed exile of the scholarly elite.

The Seljuks' arrival in the newly conquered town of Nishapur disrupted a carefully constructed balance of power, one in which the Ḥanafīs occupied the seat of formal power in the position of the chief *qāḍī* and the Shāfiʿīs were represented by a growing group of elite scholars at

31 Melchert, *Formation*, 83–85. Kevin Reinhart has identified early Shāfiʿī scholars with Muʿtazilī influences such as Ibn Surayj (d. 306/918), al-Khaffāf (fl. first half of the fourth/tenth century), ʿAbd Allāh al-Ṣayrafī (d. 330/342), and al-Qaffāl al-Shāshī (d. 365/976). See Reinhart, *Before Revelation*, 15–18, and El Shamsy, "Wisdom of God's Law," 20–22.

32 Makdisi, "Ashʿarī and the Ashʿarites, Part 1," 45.

33 Nguyen, "Confluence and Construction," 141.

34 Bulliet, *Patricians of Nishapur*, 58–66.

institutions from which they could disseminate their doctrines. The Shāfiʿīs' assistance in the transfer of power from the Ghaznavids to the Seljuks earned the *raʾīs* of the Shāfiʿīs, Ibn al-Muwaffaq, the role of an advisor to the new sultan, Ṭughril Beg. However, on the death of Ibn al-Muwaffaq in 440/1048, a contest over which faction would acquire the ear of the sultan ensued. Ṭughril Beg's personal affiliation with the Ḥanafī school tipped the scale in favor of the Ḥanafīs, and after Ibn al-Muwaffaq, the sultan's patronage was bestowed solely on the Ḥanafīs. Thus, not only was the chief *qāḍī* a Ḥanafī, but so were provincial *qāḍīs* and the *khaṭībs* who gave the weekly sermons in mosques.[35] In fact, Abū ʿUthmān al-Ṣabūnī, the long-standing Shāfiʿī *khaṭīb*, was also replaced by a Ḥanafī.[36] With the Ḥanafīs occupying the judgeships, delivering sermons, and advising the sultan, the Shāfiʿīs were rendered politically impotent and irrelevant. This political marginalization eventually translated into intellectual persecution: in 440/1048[37] Sultan Ṭughril Beg announced that Abū al-Ḥasan al-Ashʿarī, along with the Shīʿa, should be cursed from the pulpits by the Ḥanafī *khaṭībs*.[38] Because it had been prominent Shāfiʿī jurists who had originally extended an invitation to the Ashʿarīs and also adopted their doctrines, the Shāfiʿīs were likewise condemned.

To respond to the persecution, petitions were drawn up, the most important of which was *Shikāyat ahl-al-Sunna bi-ḥikāya mā nālahum min al-miḥna* (The Complaint of the Sunnī Community through an Account of the Tribulation Afflicted on Them),[39] written by Imam al-Qushayrī in 446/1054–55. In the document, al-Qushayrī defends Ashʿarī doctrines and assigns blame to the Ḥanafīs, who, he notes, were spearheading the defamation of Abū al-Ḥasan al-Ashʿarī and his doctrinal followers in Nishapur. Invoking the *miḥna*, or inquisition, instituted by

35 Wilferd Madelung, *The Spread of Māturīdism and the Turks*; reprinted in Madelung, *Religious Schools and Sects in Medieval Islam* (London: Variorum, 1985), 109–68, 126–27.

36 Ngyuen, "Confluence and Construction," 143. The replacement is reported by ʿAbd al-Ghaffār al-Fārisī but not related in other biographical or historical works.

37 I am adopting the revised dating of these events that Martin Nguyen has proposed. See his "Confluence and Construction," 163.

38 The most exhaustive account of these events is provided by al-Subkī in his *Ṭabaqāt*, where he refers to them as a *miḥna*, probably in order to evoke the first *miḥna*, which took place from 218/833 until 234/848. See al-Subkī, *Ṭabaqāt al-Shāfiʿiyya*, 3:390–405.

39 The text of this document has been preserved by al-Subkī in *Ṭabaqāt al-Shāfiʿiyya*, 3:400–422. For the complete account of the preservation of this text, see appendix A to Ngyuen, "Confluence and Construction," and pp. 135–37.

the ʿAbbasid caliph al-Maʾmūn in 218/833, al-Qushayrī refers to the situation in Nishapur as a second *miḥna*[40] to highlight the gross injustice of the new policy of intellectual persecution.[41]

Al-Qushayrī's bold attempt fell on deaf ears, and the persecution worsened to the point that in 446/1054 Ṭughril Beg ordered the arrest of four prominent Ashʿarī-Shāfiʿī: Abū al-Maʿālī al-Juwaynī, Abū Sahl Ibn al-Muwaffaq, Abū al-Faḍl Aḥmad al-Furātī, and Abū al-Qāsim al-Qushayrī.[42] However, predicting the intensification of the persecution, al-Juwaynī had already surreptitiously left the city. He traveled in the direction of Baghdad and then continued onward to the Hejaz, where he would remain for four years before returning to his home in Nishapur. Ibn al-Muwaffaq, too, was fortuitously already outside Nishapur when the decree was issued; however, al-Qushayrī and al-Furātī were both imprisoned. Ibn al-Muwaffaq, determined to negotiate the release of the two scholars, returned to Nishapur bearing arms. Eventually, fighting broke out in the night, and, with the Seljuk commander wounded, the escape of al-Furātī and al-Qushayrī was orchestrated. However, things did not end well for Ibn al-Muwaffaq, who was later imprisoned by Ṭughril Beg for what was seen as obstinate actions against the power of the Seljuk sultan.

After the issuance of the arrest decree, scholars and nonscholars alike realized that leaving Nishapur and other areas under Seljuk control was urgent. More than four hundred residents fled the city, seeking refuge either in Iraq or in the Hejaz, much as al-Juwaynī and his Ashʿarī-Shāfiʿī comrades had done. The departure of key Shāfiʿī-Ashʿarī scholars did not undermine the importance of Nishapur as one of the intellectual and cultural centers of the ʿAbbasid caliphate and the Seljuk sultanate. Historically, however, this particular moment in the intellectual and political history of Nishapur, a moment that would come to be called a *fitna* (tribulation), has been fraught with contestation. While Ḥanafī and Shāfiʿī factionalism and Ḥanafī political patronage have been identified as contributors to the intellectual hardship that began in 440/1048, definitive identification of the central figures responsible for championing the intellectual persecution has been the subject of extensive debate.

[40] He does this in both the title and the text of the letter.

[41] Al-Qushayrī's plea also had a secondary, but important, objective, which was to illustrate that the Ashʿarīs are distinct from the Muʿtazila, whom he deems heretical. For more details on the contents and objectives of the letter, see note 39.

[42] The account of this has been given in various biographical sources. See al-Dhahabī, *Tārīkh al-Islām*, 30:122–23, and ʿAlī b. al-Ḥasan Ibn ʿAsākir, *Tārīkh madīnat Dimashq*, ed. ʿAlī Shīrī (Beirut: Dār al-Fikr, 1995), 5:204–5.

THE *FITNA* IN NISHAPUR: WHO WAS TO BLAME?

In addition to Ṭughril Beg, two individuals are implicated as key actors in the turbulence of the time: the vizier of Ṭughril Beg, al-Kundurī, and the main *khaṭīb* of Nishapur at the time, Abū al-Ḥasan al-Ṣandalī (d. 484/1091). But before detailing the role that each of these individuals played, it is important to note the impossibility of attaching sole blame to either, as any narrative we might produce must be gleaned from historical accounts that were undoubtedly shaped by the intellectual proclivities of their authors and the political exigencies of the time in which the account was composed. Therefore, though historical sources provide us with important insights into the time period under question, their limitations must always be acknowledged ab initio.

It was Ṭughril Beg who ordered the proverbial guillotine to come down on the Ashʿarī-Shāfiʿī faction in Nishapur, but it was his vizier ʿAmīd al-Mulk al-Kundurī[43] who is most frequently recalled as the mastermind behind the intellectual manhunt. Al-Kundurī served Ṭughril Beg from 431/1040 until 455/1063, and the sources describe him as continually preoccupied with gaining influence over the sultan and other powerful factions within society.[44] Indicative of al-Kundurī's obsession with political power is his early connection and affinity with Shāfiʿī jurists such as al-Juwaynī and Ibn al-Muwaffaq, which subsequently gave way to a strict intellectual allegiance to the Ḥanafīs.[45] This change likely reflected al-Kundurī's realization, on attaining political influence as the vizier of the sultan, that since Ṭughril Beg favored the Ḥanafīs, he had much to gain by adapting his loyalties to those of the sultan.

The notion that al-Kundurī[46] was primarily responsible for the persecution of the Ashʿarīs and the Shāfiʿīs during this time is conveyed in a variety of accounts, such as Ibn ʿAsākir's *Tabyīn kadhib al-muftarī*, al-

[43] His full name is Muḥammad b. Manṣūr b. Muḥammad Abū Naṣr al-Kundurī (d. 457/1064). For more on him, see al-Fārisī, *Siyāq li-tārīkh Nīsābūr* in Frye, *Histories of Nishapur*, 88; Ibrāhīm b. Muḥammad al-Ṣarīfīnī, *al-Muntakhab min kitāb al-Siyāq li-tārīkh Nīsābūr*, in Frye, *Histories of Nishapur*, 481; and Ibn Khallikān, *Wafayāt al-aʿyān*, 5:138–43.

[44] George Makdisi, "Al-Kundurī," in *Encyclopaedia of Islam*, 2nd edn.

[45] Ngyuen, "Confluence and Construction," 154–55.

[46] For the political tactics of al-Kundurī during this time, see Richard Bulliet, "The Political-Religious History of Nishapur in the Eleventh Century," in *Islamic Civilization 950–1150*, ed. D. S. Richards (Oxford: Bruno Cassirer, 1973), 71–91; Heinz Halm, "Der Wesir al-Kunduri und die Fitna von Nishapur," *Die Welt des Orients* 6 (1971): 205–33; and Allard, *Le Problème des attributs divins*, 75–77.

Subkī's *Ṭabaqāt al-Shāfiʿiyya al-kubrā*, and al-Bākharzī's *Dumyat al-qaṣr*.[47] Al-Bākharzī is probably the most interesting source because he was counted among the Shāfiʿīs of Nishapur and actually kept company with al-Kundurī in his youth.[48] Nguyen notes that he is probably the most objective source, because on the one hand he was a Shāfiʿī, while on the other he was indebted to al-Kundurī, who gave him a secretarial position in the Seljuk administration. It was also al-Bākharzī who, on al-Kundurī's death, composed a eulogy for him. Despite this almost filial connection, spanning the years from their youth to their time in the administration, al-Bākharzī includes in his account a poem by al-Qushayrī that maligns the defeated al-Kundurī after the failure of the latter's campaign of persecution in Nishapur.[49] Given al-Bākharzī's close personal relationship with al-Kundurī, his transmission of the poem by al-Qushayrī lends credence to the claim that al-Kundurī played a pivotal role in the tribulations of the Shāfiʿī-Ashʿarīs of Nishapur.

As Wilferd Madelung has pointed out, Ibn ʿAsākir's *Tabyīn kadhib al-muftarī* is a defense of Ashʿarī doctrine, and given the political context in which it was written,[50] the author treads carefully so as not to incriminate the Seljuks in any anti-Ashʿarī sentiments; therefore, instead of censuring Ṭughril Beg, Ibn ʿAsākir shifts blame to his vizier.[51] Ibn ʿAsākir's account relies on a treatise by Abū Bakr al-Bayhaqī (d. 458/1066), an Ashʿarī living in Nishapur during the time of the *fitna*. In Ibn ʿAsākir's revised narrative of the events, both Ṭughril Beg and al-Kundurī played active roles, though the former merely commanded that heretical innovators (*mubtadiʿa*) be censured during sermons, whereas the latter, acting out of his own volition and desire for political supremacy, ordered the Ashʿarīs to be included as heretical innovators, thereby earning the favor

47 His full name is Abū al-Ḥasan ʿAlī b. al-Ḥasan b. ʿAlī al-Bākharzī. For biographical information, see Ibn Khallikān, *Wafayāt al-aʿyān*, 3:387–89, and al-Dhahabī, *Siyar aʿlām al-nubalāʾ*, 13:642.

48 A full account of al-Bākharzī's relation to al-Kundurī is given in Nguyen, "Confluence and Construction," 154. See also ʿAlī b. al-Ḥasan al-Bākharzī, *Dumyat al-qaṣr wa-ʿuṣrat ahl al-ʿaṣr* (Kuwait: Dār al-ʿUrūba, 1985), 2:138.

49 See Nguyen, "Confluence and Construction," 156, and al-Bākharzī, *Dumyat al-Qaṣr*, 2:246.

50 Ibn ʿAsākir wrote the text under the patronage of Nūr al-Dīn Abū al-Qāsim Zangī (d. 569/1174), known principally as Nūr al-Dīn, a Seljuk sultan who ruled from 541/1146 to 569/1174, first over Aleppo and then over Damascus.

51 Wilferd Madelung, "The Spread of Maturidism and the Turks," in Madelung, *Religious Schools and Sects in Medieval Islam* (London: Valorium Reprints, 1985), 129 n. 49.

of their opponents, the Ḥanafīs.[52] According to Ibn ʿAsākir, the command to curse heretical innovators referred to the Shīʿa and others residing in Nishapur during the time and was in no way meant to encompass the Ashʿarīs or the Shāfiʿīs. The attack against the latter, he claims, was thus orchestrated solely by al-Kundurī. In fact, Ibn ʿAsākir distances Ṭughril Beg from the *fitna* even more by praising him as a leader and protector of the Sunnī community. Accounts after Ibn ʿAsākir's such as those of Ibn al-Athīr (d. 630/1233),[53] Ibn Khallikān (d. 681/1282),[54] and al-Subkī all mirror his in lifting culpability from Ṭughril Beg and assigning it to al-Kundurī. In these narratives, al-Kundurī is depicted as a staunch Muʿtazilī-Shīʿī who harbored doctrinal and political hatred toward the Ashʿarīs, the Sunnīs, and the Shāfiʿīs alike.[55]

Among the sources that implicate Ṭughril Beg, the earliest is Ibn al-Jawzī's (d. 597/100) *Muntaẓam*. Al-Jawzī relates that when the condemnation of the Ashʿarīs was pronounced, al-Qushayrī responded by composing his *Shikāya*[56] in defense of Ashʿarī doctrine. Afterward, Ibn al-Jawzī reports that al-Qushayrī, along with a band of unnamed Shāfiʿīs, went to the sultan to defend the doctrine of the Ashʿarīs. Their rejoinder was dismissed and the sultan continued steadfastly to charge the Ashʿarīs as deviant innovators.[57] Some later accounts, such as al-Dhahabī's (d. 748/1348) *Tārīkh al-Islām* and Ibn Kathīr's (d. 774/1371) *al-Bidāya wa-l-nihāya*, echo that of Ibn al-Jawzī in fully implicating the sultan in the *fitna*.[58]

The last figure maligned as responsible for the *fitna* is the Ḥanafī *khaṭīb* of Nishapur, Abū al-Ḥasan al-Ṣandalī (d. 484/1091),[59] who is

52 Ibn ʿAsākir, *Tabyīn kadhib al-muftarī*, 108.

53 ʿIzz al-Dīn Ibn al-Athīr, *al-Kāmil fī al-tārīkh*, ed. ʿUmar ʿAbd al-Salām Tadmurī (Beirut: Dār al-Kitāb al-ʿArabī, 1997), 8:190. For the English translation, see D. S. Richards, *The Annals of the Saljuk Turks: Selections from al-Kāmil fi'l Tārīkh of ʿIzz al-Dīn b. al-Athīr* (New York: Routledge, 2002), 148.

54 Ibn Khallikān, *Wafayāt al-aʿyān*, 5:138.

55 Ibn ʿAsākir, *Tabyīn kadhib al-muftarī*, 108; al-Subkī, *Ṭabaqāt al-Shāfiʿiyya*, 3:390.

56 See note 39.

57 ʿAbd al-Raḥmān b. ʿAlī Ibn al-Jawzī, *al-Muntaẓam fī tārīkh al-mulūk wa-l-umam*, ed. Muḥammad ʿAbd al-Qādir ʿAṭā and Ibrāhīm Shams al-Dīn (Beirut: Dār al-Kutub al-ʿIlmiyya, 1992), 15:340.

58 Al-Dhahabī, *Tārīkh al-Islām*, 30:13–14, and Ismāʿīl b. ʿUmar Ibn Kathīr, *al-Bidāya wa-l-nihāya*, ed. Aḥmad ʿAbd al-Wahhāb al-Futayḥ (Cairo: Dār al-Ḥadīth, 1992), 11:71.

59 Bulliet notes that although al-Ṣandalī acquired the honorable position of the *khaṭīb*, he did not come from one of the prominent families in Nishapur. See Bulliet, *Patricians of Nishapur*, 234–36. Most interestingly, Bulliet points out that his daughter married into a family that was connected to both the Ḥanafīs and the Shāfiʿīs.

portrayed as actively cursing the Ashʿarīs from the pulpit during his sermons.[60] The account provided by ʿAbd al-Ghāfir al-Fārisī is of particular interest, since al-Fārisī was from Nishapur and witnessed many of the events he describes. His objectivity is questionable, however, since he was not only a Shāfiʿī but also al-Juwaynī's student and the grandson of ʿAbd al-Karīm al-Qushayrī. In view of these affiliations, his lack of censure of Ṭughril Beg could reflect the fact that al-Fārisī and his family remained in Nishapur and were politically subject to Seljuk rule.

Comparison of the abovementioned accounts yields no consensus on the main instigator of the *fitna*. For if one source blames al-Kundurī, another absolves him, and the same is true for Ṭughril Beg and al-Ṣandalī. What can plausibly be said is that all three figures were important in both the design and the implementation of the policies that affected the Shāfiʿī-Ashʿarīs at the time. It is not possible that al-Kundurī would have implemented these policies without at least the implicit or tacit approval of Ṭughril Beg, and it is not possible that the negative views regarding the Ashʿarīs would have spread without the influence of al-Ṣandalī's pulpit. As such, while no individual can be singled out because of the variant assessments of the narratives, all three figures did contribute in some way to the *fitna* that led to the flight of prominent Ashʿarī-Shāfiʿī scholars from Nishapur.

It is in the intellectual and political environment portrayed in this chapter that al-Juwaynī was born and spent the formative years of his life. As Chapter 2 will show, despite the factionalism and political upheavals in Nishapur, al-Juwaynī's adolescence and early adult life were consumed with studying with the foremost scholars of Nishapur and Khurasan more broadly. Though al-Juwaynī's studies in the early period of his life were uninterrupted by political events, the politics of the city, and his eventual expulsion from it, left a lasting intellectual imprint.

CONCLUSION

Nishapur was a cosmopolitan town with a diverse and interwoven intellectual and political history. The intellectual factionalism and antagonism between various theological and legal schools was further exacerbated by shifting political tides, which made the inhabitants of the city acutely aware of the waning power of the ʿAbbasid caliphate and the increasing

60 For a detailed account of al-Ṣandalī's involvement, see Nguyen, "Confluence and Construction," 150–53.

need to rely on strong local dynastic authorities. Given the diversity of his intellectual environment, al-Juwaynī's insistence on articulating religious doctrine in an epistemically sound manner is not surprising. Nor is his emphasis on the need for political stability in a historical context marked by political transitions of power from the Samanids to the Ghaznavids and then from the latter to the Seljuks. However, Nishapur's endurance despite all of its upheavals showed him that the continuity of society was not necessarily tied only to a stable political power.

2

Al-Juwaynī

Life of a Scholar

Al-Juwaynī was born in Nishapur, in the province of Khurasan, and lived the majority of his life there. The previous chapter described the great intellectual and political diversity of the city, which created both challenges and opportunities for its inhabitants. Al-Juwaynī benefited from his birth into a scholarly family, receiving his education from his father and other prominent scholars in the area. He was forced to leave Nishapur in the middle of his life but returned at the behest of Niẓām al-Mulk to teach at the prestigious Niẓāmiyya, where he continued his studies, educated some of the foremost scholars of the following generation, and penned his most famous works.

AL-JUWAYNĪ: EARLY LIFE AND EDUCATION

ʿAbd al-Mālik b. ʿAbd Allāh b. Yūsuf al-Juwaynī,[1] also known as Abū al-Maʿālī al-Juwaynī and Imām al-Ḥaramayn,[2] was born into a scholarly

[1] All biographers refer to him as al-Juwaynī with the exception of al-Subkī, who calls him al-Nīsābūrī because he spent the majority of his life there. Although there is no disagreement regarding his name or those of his father and grandfather, there is some confusion about the names of his earlier ancestors. According to al-Subkī, his full name was ʿAbd al-Malik b. ʿAbd Allāh b. Yūsuf b. Muḥammad b. ʿAbd Allāh b. Ḥayyūya, whereas according to Ibn Khallikān and Ibn al-ʿImād, it was ʿAbd al-Malik b. ʿAbd Allāh b. Yūsuf b. ʿAbd Allāh b. Yūsuf b. Muḥammad al-Ḥayyūya. See al-Subkī, *Ṭabaqāt al-Shāfiʿiyya*, 5:165; Ibn Khallikān, *Wafayāt al-aʿyān*, 1:361; Ibn al-ʿImād, *Shadharāt al-dhahab*, 3:357; Ibn al-Jawzī, *al-Muntaẓam*, 9:18; Abū al-Maḥāsin Yūsuf Ibn Taghrībardī, *al-Nujūm al-zāhira fī mulūk Miṣr wa-l-Qāhira* (Cairo: al-Muʾassasa al-Miṣriyya al-ʿĀmma li-l-Taʾlīf wa-l-Ṭibāʿa wa-l-Nashr, 1963), 5:121.

[2] The bulk of al-Juwaynī's biography has been reconstructed from biographical dictionaries and historical accounts, though some secondary sources have been invaluable. Richard

family on the eighteenth day of Muḥarram in the year 419/February 17, 1028[3] in Nishapur.[4] His father, ʿAbd Allāh b. Yūsuf b. ʿAbd Allāh b. Yūsuf b. Muḥammad b. Ḥayyūya, had been born in the Khurasanian town of Juwayn,[5] which he left as a youth for Nishapur to seek the tutelage of Abū Sahl al-Ṣuʿlukī (d. 369/980),[6] subsequently moving to Marw to study with Abū Bakr al-Qaffāl al-Marwazī (d. 417/1026–27).[7] Finally returning to Nishapur in the year 407, the father taught and partook in scholarly debate until the end of his life in 438/1047.[8] In addition to teaching and debating, al-Juwaynī senior imparted the knowledge he had acquired from the foremost scholars of his age to his son ʿAbd al-Malik, instilling in him a love of knowledge from a young age.

Bulliet's seminal work *The Patricians of Nishapur* has been particularly important for understanding the sociopolitical context of al-Juwaynī's life. Similarly, the first two chapters of Martin Nguyen's doctoral dissertation on the life of al-Qushayrī, a contemporary of al-Juwaynī, provide important insights into the intellectual setting of al-Juwaynī's life. Finally, two books in Arabic have been particularly useful: Fawqiyya Ḥusayn Maḥmūd, *al-Juwaynī: Imām al-Ḥaramayn* (Cairo: al-Dār al-Miṣriyya, 1964), and ʿAbd al-ʿAẓīm al-Dīb, *Imām al-Ḥaramayn* (Kuwait: Dār al-Qalam, 1981). Another important contemporary biography of al-Juwaynī is Muḥammad al-Zuḥaylī, *al-Imām al-Juwaynī: Imām al-Ḥaramayn* (Damascus: Dār al-Qalam, 1992).

3 Early historians agree on the date. See al-Subkī, *Ṭabaqāt al-Shāfiʿiyya*, 3:251; Ibn Khallikān, *Wafayāt al-aʿyān*, 1:362; Ibn Kathīr, *al-Bidāya wa-l-nihāya*, 7:129; and Ibn ʿAsākir, *Tabyīn kadhib al-muftarī*, 285. However, later historians such as Ibn al-Jawzī and Ibn Taghrībardī state that he was born in the year 417. See Ibn al-Jawzī, *al-Muntaẓam*, 9:18, and Ibn Taghrībardī, *al-Nujūm al-ẓāhira*, 5:121.

4 All of the sources, except for Carl Brockelmann in *Geschichte der arabischen Litteratur*, agree that al-Juwaynī was born in Nishapur. Brockelmann claims that he was born in Bushtinqan, which is on the outskirts of Nishapur; however, that is the city in which al-Juwaynī died, not where he was born. For details on the sociointellectual landscape during the time of al-Juwaynī, see Bulliet, *Patricians*, chapters 1 through 3.

5 It was his father's relationship to the town of Juwayn that gave al-Juwaynī his last name; however, al-Juwaynī himself was not directly connected to the town, and there is no official account of him visiting it.

6 Al-Subkī, *Ṭabaqāt al-Shāfiʿiyya*, 3:167–73.

7 Two Qaffāls are commonly mentioned in the sources: Abū Bakr al-Qaffāl al-Marwazī and the older Abū Bakr al-Qaffāl al-Shāshī al-Kabīr (d. 336/947). Typically, when al-Juwaynī and other Shāfiʿī scholars refer to "al-Qaffāl," they mean al-Marwazī unless they specify "al-Qaffāl al-Kabīr." For the biography of the latter, see al-Subkī, *Ṭabaqāt al-Shāfiʿiyya*, 3:220–22, and for the former, see al-Subkī, *Ṭabaqāt al-Shāfiʿiyya*, 5:53–62.

8 Al-Subkī, *Ṭabaqāt al-Shāfiʿiyya*, 3:207–10. There is a difference of opinion regarding the year of death of al-Juwaynī's father, with some citing 434 and others 438. Al-Subkī, in his *Ṭabaqāt*, states that al-Juwaynī assumed the teaching position of his father around the age of twenty; since he took up the position immediately after his father's death, and based on al-Juwaynī's date of birth in 419, it is more likely that his father died in the year 438. Little is known about al-Juwaynī's uncle, but mention of him is made in various genealogical trees. See Bulliet, *Patricians*, 121.

This affinity for knowledge was reinforced by al-Juwaynī's uncle, Abū al-Ḥasan ʿAlī b. Yūsuf al-Juwaynī (d. 463/1071), a prominent Sufi scholar known as Shaykh al-Ḥijāz,[9] and by the scholarly environment that surrounded him in Nishapur.[10]

Al-Juwaynī's intense early study of various Islamic disciplines made him well placed to inherit his father's teaching position on the latter's death. Through teaching, al-Juwaynī acquired a reputation as an erudite scholar with mastery of the Quran, *ḥadīth*, and *uṣūl al-fiqh*. He was also known for his commitment to reason and his willingness to critique earlier scholars, even his father.[11] Al-Juwaynī maintained his teaching position in Nishapur until he decided to continue his quest for knowledge by seeking the instruction of other scholars in Khurasan. His hiatus from teaching began with study under the most renowned Ashʿarī and Shāfiʿī scholar of the age, Abū al-Qāsim ʿAbd al-Jabbār al-Isqāf al-Isfarāyīnī (d. 452/1060),[12] who was teaching in the madrassa of al-Bayhaqī at the time.[13] Al-Isfarāyīnī was lauded for his disputational skills and his adoption of the early ascetic practices that were then flourishing in Nishapur.[14] Under al-Isfarāyīnī, al-Juwaynī studied numerous subjects, but his focus was on *kalām* (dialectical theology). Although al-Isfarāyīnī was his chief *kalām* teacher, al-Juwaynī also studied independently the oeuvre of earlier

9 See al-Subkī, *Ṭabaqāt al-Shāfiʿiyya*, 5:289–90, and Yāqūt al-Ḥamawī, *Muʿjam al-buldān* (Beirut: Dār Ṣādir, 1955), 5:181–82.

10 Beyond the scholars connected to al-Juwaynī's family, scholarly activity was increasing throughout the Islamic empire. For a more detailed look at the intellectual trends current in the time of al-Juwaynī, see Seyyed Hossein Nasr, "The Religious Sciences," "Philosophy and Cosmology," and "Sufism," in *Cambridge History of Iran*, vol. 4. Although Nishapur was one of the most important centers of intellectual activity at the time, the capital city of the ʿAbbasids, Baghdad, surpassed it as the epicenter of erudition and scholarship in the Islamic world. For a general overview of Baghdad and its role in the empire in al-Juwaynī's time, see Hugh Kennedy's *When Baghdad Ruled the Muslim World: The Rise and Fall of Islam's Greatest Dynasty* (Boston: De Capo Press, 2006), and Jonathan Berkey's *The Formation of Islam: Religion and Society in the Near East, 600–1800* (Cambridge: Cambridge University Press, 2002). On the intellectual culture of Baghdad in particular, see Gutas, *Greek Thought, Arabic Culture*, which includes an invaluable bibliography of prominent articles and monographs on the topic.

11 Al-Subkī, *Ṭabaqāt al-Shāfiʿiyya*, 3:258. When he would criticize his father, he would follow it up by saying, "This is an error committed by the Shaykh, God save his soul." See al-Subkī, *Ṭabaqāt al-Shāfiʿiyya*, 5:169.

12 Al-Subkī, *Ṭabaqāt al-Shāfiʿiyya*, 5:99.

13 Abū Bakr al-Bayhaqī (d. 458/1066) was a famous Shāfiʿī jurist and Ashʿarī theologian at the time. He had been a student of Abū al-Fatḥ Nāṣir b. Muḥammad al-ʿUmrī al-Marwazī (d. 444/1052), Abū Bakr Ibn Fūrak, ʿAbd al-Qāhir al-Baghdādī, and al-Ḥākim al-Nīsābūrī (d. 405/1014).

14 Ibn ʿAsākir, *Tabyīn kadhib al-muftarī*, 265.

scholars such as al-Qāḍī Abū Bakr al-Bāqillānī. In fact, al-Juwaynī is quoted as saying, "I would never utter a single word about *ʿilm al-kalām* until I had memorized twelve thousand pages of the words of al-Qāḍī Abū Bakr."[15] Biographical scholars such al-Subkī note that al-Juwaynī also studied other subjects such as philosophy (*falsafa*) on his own; however, the nature of his study of philosophy is uncertain, since biographical sources do not indicate that he pursued a formal course of study in the subject.[16]

In addition to specializing in *kalām*, al-Juwaynī continued his study of the Quran and *ḥadīth*. With respect to the former, he studied Quranic recitation with Abū ʿAbd Allāh Muḥammad b. ʿAlī b. Muḥammad al-Naysābūrī al-Khabbāzī (d. 447/1055),[17] a renowned reciter of that time. As for *ḥadīth*, he studied with Abū Bakr Aḥmad b. Muḥammad b. Ḥārith al-Iṣbahānī al-Yamanī, Abū Saʿīd ʿAbd al-Raḥmān b. Ḥamdānī al-Nīsābūrī, Abū al-Ḥasan Muḥammad b. Aḥmad al-Mazkī, Abū ʿAbd Allāh Muḥammad b. Ibrāhīm Yaḥyā al-Mazkī, and al-Ḥāfiẓ Abū Nuʿaym al-Iṣbahānī.[18] Later, during his travels to Baghdad, he also studied *ḥadīth* under Abū Muḥammad al-Jawharī (d. 454/1062). Of the disciplines in which he attained mastery, the study of *ḥadīth* was criticized as his weakest. The main critic of his *ḥadīth* knowledge is al-Dhahabī, who faults al-Juwaynī's use of certain weak *ḥadīth* in his legal arguments.[19]

15 Al-Subkī, *Ṭabaqāt al-Shāfiʿiyya*, 5:193.

16 I will return to this topic later in the chapter when speaking of al-Juwaynī's scholarly influences.

17 Ibn ʿAsākir, *Tabyīn kadhib al-muftarī*, 279; al-Subkī, *Ṭabaqāt al-Shāfiʿiyya*, 5:170; and al-Dhahabī, *Siyar aʿlām al-nubalāʾ*, 11:159.

18 Al-Subkī, *Ṭabaqāt al-Shāfiʿiyya*, 5:193; al-Ḥamawī, *Muʿjam al-buldān*, 11:255.

19 Al-Dhahabī criticizes al-Juwaynī's use of the *ḥadīth* of Muʿādh b. Jabal in his *Burhān*, noting that although al-Juwaynī characterizes the *ḥadīth* as reliable (*ṣaḥīḥ*), al-Bukhārī and al-Tirmidhī both deem it unreliable. Al-Subkī, however, disagrees with al-Dhahabī on this point, observing that the *ḥadīth* that al-Juwaynī uses is in fact included in al-Tirmidhī's collection. Al-Subkī's observation does not, however, address al-Juwaynī's claim that al-Bukhārī had also accepted the *ḥadīth*. See al-Subkī, *Ṭabaqāt al-Shāfiʿiyya*, 5:187–88; al-Dhahabī, *Siyar aʿlām al-nubalāʾ*, 18:471–72; and Abū al-Maʿālī ʿAbd al-Malik al-Juwaynī, *al-Burhān fī uṣūl al-fiqh*, ed. ʿAbd al-ʿAẓīm al-Dīb (Cairo: Dār al-Anṣār, 1979; reprint, Doha: Wizārat al-Awqāf wa-l-Shuʾūn al-Islāmiyya, 1997), 2:882. Moreover, Jonathan Brown has noted that al-Subkī was incorrect with respect to al-Tirmidhī, because although the latter relates the report, he criticizes it for lacking a continuous *isnād*. As for al-Bukhārī, according to Brown, he deems the *ḥadīth* weak because one of the narrators, al-Ḥārith b. ʿAmr al-Thaqāfī, is considered a weak (*majhūl*) transmitter. See Jonathan Brown, *The Canonization of al-Bukhārī and Muslim* (Leiden: Brill, 2007), 196–205.

Sufism was also gaining prominence in this period. The precise extent of al-Juwaynī's engagement with Sufism is not known, but we know that he was introduced to it either by his uncle, a famous Sufi, or through the friendship his father maintained with Imam al-Qushayrī, with whom he undertook Ḥajj.[20] Despite al-Juwaynī's lack of formal study of Sufism, al-Subkī notes that his proclivity toward it was particularly pronounced during his later stay in Mecca. According to al-Subkī, "In the course of his classes he would launch into an account of Sufi states (*aḥwāl*) and delve into the science of Sufism. He would reduce those present to tears by his own weeping, making their eyes bleed by his crying."[21] Moreover, among his known writings is a work entitled *Kitāb al-Nafs*, which may have been a spiritual didactic inquiry; however, this text has not survived.

LEAVING NISHAPUR AND LIFE IN THE HEJAZ

On completion of his extensive studies, al-Juwaynī resumed his teaching position and participated in disputational circles with scholars of various intellectual leanings, bolstering his intellectual reputation. However, his career in Nishapur was abruptly interrupted by the command for his arrest by Ṭughril Beg in 446/1054. Narrowly escaping the fate of imprisonment, al-Juwaynī had left town earlier. Biographical sources disagree on the impetus for his departure. Did he leave to meet and study with scholars elsewhere? Or had he predicted further turbulence and decided that absconding would be the wisest course of action?

According to al-Subkī, Ibn al-ʿImād, and ʿAbd al-Ghāfir al-Fārisī (d. 529/1135), al-Juwaynī fled Nishapur because he anticipated that the political-intellectual harassment of the Ashʿarī-Shāfiʿīs would intensify.[22] However, according to Ibn Khallikān[23] and Ibn al-Jawzī, he left in order to further his studies with scholars outside Nishapur. In fact, Ibn al-Jawzī specifically states that al-Juwaynī went to Baghdad seeking the tutelage of

[20] ʿAbd Allāh b. Yūsuf al-Juwaynī and al-Qushayrī were also accompanied on the Ḥajj by Abū Bakr al-Bayhaqī. No date is given for this event in the various biographical and historical sources, but since al-Juwaynī senior was the first of the three to die, in 438/1047, the journey must have taken place before that.

[21] Al-Subkī, *Ṭabaqāt al-Shāfiʿiyya*, 5:179.

[22] Al-Subkī, *Ṭabaqāt al-Shāfiʿiyya*, 3:358, and Ibn al-ʿImād, *Shadharāt al-dhahab*, 3:357. The account of al-Fārisī is provided in al-Subkī, *Ṭabaqāt al-Shāfiʿiyya*, 3:254–55, and Ibn ʿAsākir, *Tabyīn kadhib al-muftarī*, 280.

[23] Ibn Khallikān, *Wafayāt al-aʿyān*, 1:361.

Abū Muḥammad al-Jawharī (d. 454/1064).[24] Finally, Ibn Taghrībardī speaks of al-Juwaynī's travels to the Hejaz without reference to either an impulse for knowledge or a fear of persecution.[25] Given the conflicting views, a definitive explanation for al-Juwaynī's departure is not possible. However, of the sources mentioned, al-Fārisī's account (related also by al-Subkī and Ibn ʿAsākir) probably stands closest to the truth, because al-Fārisī was a student of al-Juwaynī's for four years[26] and the only narrator who had direct contact with al-Juwaynī.

The roughly five-year phase of al-Juwaynī's life that he spent outside Nishapur is shrouded in mystery. Biographical sources recount the early and late periods of his life in detail, but information on his middle years is scanty, leaving an important element of his scholarly story untold. Among the few details known about this phase are the dates of his departure and return. Ṭughril Beg issued the order for al-Juwaynī's arrest in 446/1054, but al-Juwaynī had left Nishapur a short time earlier in the same year. That he left in 446/1054 is corroborated by Ibn al-Jawzī, who states that al-Juwaynī arrived in Baghdad at the same time as Ṭughril Beg in the year 447/1055.[27] However, Ibn al-Jawzī does not indicate how long al-Juwaynī spent in Baghdad or how he occupied his time there beyond noting that he studied with some of the city's foremost scholars.[28] Other biographical accounts are similarly silent on al-Juwaynī's time in Baghdad, though al-Subkī and Ibn Khallikān do claim that he spent some time

[24] Ibn al-Jawzī, *al-Muntaẓam*, 18. [25] Ibn Taghrībardī, *al-Nujūm al-zāhira*, 5:121.

[26] Al-Ṣarīfīnī, *al-Muntakhab*, 542–43.

[27] Ṭughril Beg entered Baghdad on two separate occasions. The first was in Ramaḍān 447/December 1055, after he had assembled his troops at Hamadhan, Dinawar, Kirmanshah, and Hulwan. This first entrance was intended to display Ṭughril Beg's power to the ʿAbbasid caliph, al-Qāʾim (r. 422–47/1031–75), who lived in the city. It is this first Baghdad visit that al-Juwaynī attended. Ṭughril Beg's second visit occurred at the end of 449/beginning of 1058. On this occasion, in contrast to the first visit, the caliph met with Ṭughril Beg. The caliph also bestowed on Ṭughril Beg various honorific titles, such as *rukn al-dawla* and *mālik al-mashriq wa-l-maghrib*, and further allowed him to be referred to as the sultan. This, however, does not mean that the relationship between the caliph and the sultan was henceforth a good one, for the caliph remained apprehensive of the Seljuk Turks' power. The frailty of the relationship is illustrated by al-Qāʾim's reluctance to wed his daughter to Ṭughril Beg, even though the caliph himself had previously married a Turkic woman, one of Chagrī Beg's daughters. For two years al-Qāʾim procrastinated, until he was finally coerced into permitting the union. See George Makdisi, "The Marriage of Tughril Beg," *International Journal of Middle East Studies* 1 (1970): 259–75.

[28] Ibn al-Jawzī, *al-Muntaẓam*, 19. For a chronological history of the events in Ṭughril Beg's life, see C. E. Bosworth, "The Political and Dynastic History of the Iranian World," in *Cambridge History of Iran*, 5:18–23, 38–49.

there engaging in scholarly disputation and teaching, along with learning from prominent scholars of the day.[29] Despite the sparseness of the details available regarding this time in al-Juwaynī's life, his travels to the intellectual epicenter of the ʿAbbasid Empire and engagement with prominent scholars no doubt further raised his stature and recognition within the Muslim community. Though his intellectual reputation likely preceded him thanks to the status of Nishapur and the command issued for his arrest, his time in the capital of the caliphate would have extended his reputation beyond Nishapur and connected him with scholars whom he would not have encountered otherwise.

After a brief stay in Baghdad, al-Juwaynī – along with other scholars – continued on to the Hejaz, where he resided for four years until 451/1058, when he returned to Nishapur at the behest of Niẓām al-Mulk, the venerated vizier of Alp Arslān. As in the case of al-Juwaynī's time in Baghdad, we have little information on his sojourn in the Hejaz. Al-Subkī states that he first performed the pilgrimage and then settled in Mecca, and Ibn Khallikān reports that he taught in both cities, which is what earned him the appellation Imam al-Ḥaramayn, referring to the two sanctuaries of Mecca and Medina, even though his stay in the latter was quite brief. Details beyond these facts are scarce, but al-Subkī notes that al-Juwaynī's pietistic inclinations were particularly prominent during the time he spent in the Hejaz, as he divided his time primarily between teaching and extensive worship. It is in the context of these lessons that al-Subkī describes him as at times becoming so impassioned when speaking about spiritual topics that he would be reduced to tears.[30]

Through his teaching in the sacred sanctuary and his steadfastness in his intellectual convictions despite the ill treatment he had faced in Nishapur, al-Juwaynī became a renowned scholar, extolled for his understanding of *kalām* and *uṣūl al-fiqh* as well as for his piety. The reverence he was accorded was due to a combination of factors, ranging from his scholarly family and his exhaustive education to his intellectual honesty regardless of repercussions and the time he had spent in two great centers of Islamic civilization, Baghdad and Mecca. Thus, when the political, social, and intellectual turmoil in Nishapur subsided with the rise of Alp Arslān, it

[29] Al-Subkī, *Ṭabaqāt al-Shāfiʿiyya*, 5:180. Al-Subkī's account also includes the description of al-Fārisī, which supports al-Subkī's claim that al-Juwaynī briefly studied and engaged with other scholars in Baghdad. See al-Subkī, *Ṭabaqāt al-Shāfiʿiyya*, 5:173; see also Ibn Khallikān, *Wafayāt al-aʿyān*, 1:361; Ibn al-ʿImād, *Shadharāt al-dhahab*, 3:357; and Ibn Taghrībardī, *al-Nujūm al-zāhira*, 5:121.

[30] Al-Subkī, *Ṭabaqāt al-Shāfiʿiyya*, 5:183.

was no surprise that Alp Arslān's vizier, Niẓām al-Mulk (d. 485/1092),[31] requested that al-Juwaynī return to Nishapur to chair a new institutionalized model of Islamic education, the Niẓāmiyya madrassa.

AL-JUWAYNĪ'S RETURN TO NISHAPUR

Al-Juwaynī's return to Nishapur, much like his departure, was tied to sociopolitical developments that were reshaping the intellectual landscape of his hometown. The tensions that had driven al-Juwaynī out of Nishapur were, as recounted earlier, an outgrowth of the political situation created by the rule of Ṭughril Beg and his vizier, al-Kundurī. Ṭughril Beg and his brother Chaghrī Beg (d. 451/1059), cofounder of the Seljuk dynasty,[32] became the unexpected de facto rulers over the ʿAbbasid lands in 426/1035, when Khurasan passed from the Ghaznavids to the Seljuk Turks. Using Khurasan as his base, Ṭughril Beg was successful in steadily expanding territory under his control, amassing unprecedented amounts of wealth that would secure future generations of Seljuk sultans long after his death. When he died childless in Ramaḍān 455/September 1063, he designated Chaghrī Beg's son Sulaymān as his heir. Sulaymān was the son of a Khwarizmian princess who, on being widowed by the death of Chaghrī Beg, married his brother, Ṭughril Beg. In this way, Sulaymān was not only Ṭughril's nephew but also his stepson. However, Sulaymān's political inexperience led to the seizure of power by Alp Arslān, his half-brother and a son of Chaghrī Beg from another wife. Unlike Sulaymān, Alp Arslān had already earned acclaim through his military accomplishments against the Ghaznavids and was able to easily marshal support and gain recognition by the ʿAbbasid caliph al-Qāʾim as the rightful successor

31 Niẓām al-Mulk is lauded as one of the most skilled and perceptive viziers to serve under the Seljuks. In addition to providing political guidance, Niẓām al-Mulk introduced policies directed at the social and intellectual betterment of the Muslim empire, such as his creation of the Niẓāmiyya madrassas. For a complete biography of Niẓām al-Mulk, see H. Bowen and C. E. Bosworth, "Niẓām al-Mulk," in *Encyclopaedia of Islam*, 2nd edn. For a more extensive biography, see Sajid Rizvi, *Niẓām al-Mulk: His Contribution to Statecraft, Political Theory and the Art of Government* (Lahore: Sheikh Muhammad Ashraf, 1978).

32 For the relationship between the two brothers, see Richard Bulliet, "Numismatic Evidence for the Relationship between Ṭughril Beg and Chaghrī Beg," in *Near Eastern Numismatics, Iconography, Epigraphy and History: Studies in Honor of George C. Miles*, ed. Dickran K. Kouymjian (Beirut: American University of Beirut, 1974), 289–96.

to both his uncle and his father.[33] On assuming power, Alp Arslān continued the Seljuks' military expansion with an eye to establishing Turkic power against the Byzantines and responding to the growing Fatimid heresy.[34] On the first of these fronts, Alp Arslān continued to carry out military expeditions into Syria, fighting a decisive battle against the Byzantines at Manzikert in 463/1071 that resulted in victory for the Muslims and the imprisonment of the Byzantine emperor. In addition, he planned military campaigns into Transoxania while keeping abreast of developments in Egypt and elsewhere. Alp Arslān's increasing fixation on military expansion and on securing the borders of the ʿAbbasid and Seljuk territories meant that administrative affairs were largely under the control of his vizier, Niẓām al-Mulk.

Abū ʿAlī al-Ḥasan b. ʿAlī b. Isḥāq al-Ṭūsī, famously known as Niẓām al-Mulk, was the most celebrated vizier of the Seljuk sultans Alp Arslān and his son Malikshāh. His career in service to the Seljuk sultans began in 445/1053–54, when he served Chaghrī Beg in Marw. Shortly after that, he left for Khurasan, where he served under Alp Arslān's vizier Abū ʿAlī Aḥad b. Shādhān. Following the death of Ibn Shādhān, he was appointed the vizier of Alp Arslān and remained in this role until the latter's death. He honed his skills as an administrator under Alp Arslān in Khurasan, but the true test of his abilities and prowess took place in the period between the death of Chaghrī Beg in 451/1059 and that of Ṭughril Beg in 455/1063, when he assumed virtual control over all administrative affairs in

33 Alp Arslān did face some internal resistance from his brother, Kawurt of Kirman, who also aspired to share in the succession of his father. For more on this, see Claude Cahen, "The Historiography of the Seljuqid Period," in *Historians of the Middle East*, ed. Bernard Lewis and Peter Holt (London: Oxford University Press, 1962), and K. A. Luther's entry on Alp Arslān in *Encyclopaedia Iranica*, 1 (8–9): 895–98.

34 The Fatimid dynasty's reign began in North Africa and subsequently spread outward within Africa. Their rule lasted from 297/909 until 575/1171. The dynasty was based on the Shīʿī doctrine of Imāʿīlism, which was not only a religious doctrine but a highly political one. Without delving into details on the Fatimid caliphate, which is beyond the scope of this biographical account of al-Juwaynī's life, we should note that the Fatimids were particularly important to Alp Arslān and al-Juwaynī for two reasons. First, they established a countercaliphate to the ʿAbbasids, resulting in the existence of two caliphates at the same time. Although a similar situation had occurred during the reign of the Umayyads because of the presence of another caliphate in Cordoba, the Fatimid caliphate was particularly troublesome to its rival because of its Shīʿī beliefs. Second, the Ismāʿīlī nature of the Fatimid dynasty was of concern to Alp Arslān and others, who saw the Fatimids as heretics and emphasized the need to establish orthodox belief. For a more detailed history of the rise of the Fatimids, their beliefs, and their institutions, see the in-text citations and bibliography in M. Canard's article "Fāṭimids," in *Encyclopaedia of Islam*, 2nd edn. See also Hodgson, "Ismāʿīlī State."

Khurasan. It was during this time, when Khurasan was under the control of Niẓām al-Mulk, that al-Juwaynī returned to his home in Nishapur.

The exact date of al-Juwaynī's return to Nishapur is not given in the biographical accounts, but other, circumstantial information indicates that he returned in the year 451/1059. We know that al-Juwaynī left Nishapur in the year 446/1054 and went to Baghdad, where he stayed for a short time before continuing to and finally settling in the Hejaz. Though there is no information regarding how long he spent in Baghdad, it is likely – given that he taught, sat with scholars, and engaged in disputations – that he stayed for at least a few months before departing for the Hejaz. The year 451/1059, therefore, seems the likely date of his return to Nishapur. This date is also supported by al-Subkī and Ibn Khallikān,[35] both of whom say that he returned at the bidding of Niẓām al-Mulk, who assumed power in Khurasan at approximately the same time, after the death of Chagrī Beg in 451/1059.

Beyond being a distinguished administrator, Niẓām al-Mulk was known for his religiosity and his adherence to the Ashʿarī school of *kalām* and the Shāfiʿī school of law. These intellectual predilections contrasted starkly with those of al-Kundurī, the previous vizier of Ṭughril Beg. When Alp Arslān assumed power, he dismissed al-Kundurī within a month and banished him to Marw, where he was beheaded ten months later. Al-Kundurī's removal as a political and intellectual force in Khurasan meant that Niẓām al-Mulk could now mold the province according to his own inclinations. However, Niẓām al-Mulk's support for the Ashʿarīs and the Shāfiʿīs stemmed from more than just a personal desire to promote views that he deemed correct. The establishment of the Fatimid caliphate in North Africa and Egypt had made Shīʿī Ismāʿīlism a growing threat to the ʿAbbasid caliphate and Sunnī thought in the fourth/tenth century. Given the vast territorial distance between the two caliphates, doctrinal proselytizing was seen as a greater danger than was military engagement. This view arose from the Fatimids' interest in education, marked by their construction of what was to become the famed al-Azhar mosque and madrassa,[36] inaugurated in Ramaḍān

35 Al-Subkī, *Ṭabaqāt al-Shāfiʿiyya*, 5:170; Ibn Khallikān, *Wafayāt al-aʿyān*, 1:361; Ibn al-ʿImād, *Shadharāt al-dhahab*, 3:357; Ibn al-Jawzī, *al-Muntaẓam*, 9:18; and Ibn Taghrībardī, *al-Nujūm al-zāhira*, 5:121.

36 For an overview of Fatimid educational institutions, see Paul Walker, "Faṭimid Institutions of Learning," *Journal of the American Research Center in Egypt* 34 (1997): 197–200. For more on the establishment of al-Azhar and its use up to the modern period, see Bayard Dodge, *Al-Azhar: A Millennium of Muslim Learning* (Washington, DC: Middle East Institute, 1974).

361/June 972. Furthermore, although they represented a minority community within the Islamic empire as a whole, the Fatimids made a point of welcoming individuals with differing doctrinal beliefs.

In some sense, therefore, Niẓām al-Mulk was responding to increasing doctrinal diversity when he began, on assuming the de facto governorship of Khurasan, to erect educational institutions that came to be known as the Niẓāmiyya madrassas. Beyond the desire to create orthodox institutions, Niẓām al-Mulk was an ambitious administrator who sought to leave behind a legacy, and there could be no nobler marker of his memory than the foundation of institutions of learning. However, Niẓām al-Mulk was not breaking new ground by establishing these institutions,[37] as madrassas had existed in both Shīʿī and Sunnī lands long before the creation of the Niẓāmiyya.[38] Closer to the time of al-Juwaynī, the most prominent school established in Nishapur was the Bayhaqiyya madrassa, founded by al-Bayhaqī (d. 458/1066) when he moved to Nishapur in 441/1049–50. Thanks to the prominence of its founder, the school attracted many students from around Khurasan, including al-Juwaynī himself. There were three other significant madrassas in Nishapur in al-Juwaynī's time. The oldest was the Ṣāʿidiyya madrassa, founded in 389/999 by Amīr Naṣr b. Sebuktigin, the governor of Nishapur; the other two had been established for Abū Saʿd Ismāʿīl al-Astarābādī and Abū Isḥāq al-Isfarāyīnī, respectively.[39] Heinz Halm notes that the presence of a patrician

[37] In addition to madrassas established by patrician families, madrassas were also founded for specific scholars by their patrons. For example, the Simurids built a madrassa for Ibn Fūrak and the Ghaznavids built the Ṣāʿidiyya madrassa for Abū al-ʿAlāʾ Ṣāʿid.

[38] As George Makdisi notes in his seminal study *The Rise of Colleges*, there were three discrete stages in the development of madrassas from small teaching circles *(ḥalaqas)* to fully fledged "madrasa colleges of law." These phases marked intellectual shifts from the informal study of the Quran to the systematic study of Islamic jurisprudence. See Makdisi, *The Rise of Colleges*.

[39] This brief history of these madrassas is based on Hillenbrand's entry "Madrasa" in the *Encyclopaedia of Islam* (2nd edn.), which contains extensive information regarding the early development of education in the Muslim world. For more detailed information on madrassas in Nishapur, see Bulliet, *Patricians of Nishapur*, appendixes 1 and 2. For later educational developments and the systemization of education, George Makdisi's *The Rise of Colleges* is an invaluable resource. See also Makdisi, "Madrasa and University in the Middle Ages," *Studia Islamica*, no. 32 (1970): 255–64; Makdisi, "Muslim Institutions of Learning in Eleventh Century Baghdād," *Bulletin of the School of Oriental and African Studies* 24 (1960): 1–56; J. Pedersen, "Some Aspects of the History of the Madrassa," *Islamic Culture* 3 (1929): 525–37; and Michael Chamberlain, *Knowledge and Social Practice in Medieval Damascus, 1190–1350* (Cambridge: Cambridge University Press, 2002), chapter 2 ("Madrasas, the Production of Knowledge, and the Reproduction of Elites"). See also the extensive bibliography in Hillenbrand, "Madrasa."

class in Khurasan, and more specifically in Nishapur, facilitated the flourishing of so many independent madrassas in northern Persia. In addition to commanding political weight, these families had substantial landholdings and *waqf*s (endowed properties), giving them the financial resources necessary for institution-building. The patrician families sponsored the construction of madrassas and assigned them to prominent scholars or to scholars among their own kin.[40] Said Arjomand, building on Halm's work, argues that the governors of the patrimonial state were influenced and inspired by the early example of these patrician families and established their own madrassas in a similar fashion, relying on prominent scholars and the creation of endowments to support the new institutions.[41]

The first Niẓāmiyya madrassa was built in Nishapur, one of the centers of Islamic learning at the time. Bulliet has argued that Niẓām al-Mulk most likely commissioned the Niẓāmiyya in Nishapur immediately after Alp Arslān's assumption of power in 450/1058 or, at the latest, in 451/1059. Subsequently, other Niẓāmiyya madrassas were established in Amul, Mosul, Herat, Damascus, Jazirat Ibn ʿUmar, Balkh, Ghazna, Marw, Basra, and, most famously, in the intellectual and political epicenter of the Seljuk-ʿAbbasid world, Baghdad.[42] Unlike the existing madrassas in Nishapur, which had been founded for specific scholars, the new Niẓāmiyya madrassa was not earmarked for a particular individual, and Niẓām al-Mulk thus had to find an illustrious figurehead for his new institution. His eye fell on al-Juwaynī, who was both a native of Nishapur and a scholar of considerable repute throughout Khurasan. The biographical accounts of al-Juwaynī's life link his return to Nishapur with Niẓām al-Mulk's offer of a position at the Niẓāmiyya, but they do not say whether he had been inclined to return home anyway. In any case, on his return to Nishapur al-Juwaynī immediately assumed his position at the Niẓāmiyya and continued to occupy the highest institutional seat there until his death. The remainder of his life in Nishapur, and specifically at the Niẓāmiyya, thus marks the last important phase of his intellectual life.

[40] Heinz Halm, "Die Anfänge der Madrasa," *Zeitschrift der deutschen morgenländischen Gesellschaft* 19 (1977): 438–48.

[41] See Said Amir Arjomand, "The Law, Agency and Policy in Medieval Islamic Society: Development of the Institutions of Learning from the Tenth to the Fifteenth Century," *Comparative Studies in Society and History* 41, no. 2 (1999): 262–93.

[42] The Niẓāmiyya madrassa in Baghdad opened in 459/1067, construction of the building having started two years earlier in 457/1065. For more details on the various Niẓāmiyya madrassas, see Ann Lambton, "The Internal Structure of the Saljuk Empire," in *Cambridge History of Iran*, 5:203–83. See also al-Subkī, *Ṭabaqāt al-Shāfiʿiyya*, 3:137.

TEACHING AT THE NIẒĀMIYYA

Biographical and historical sources provide few details on al-Juwaynī's tenure at the Niẓāmiyya, but the available information permits three important observations. First, al-Juwaynī dedicated a substantial amount of time to teaching. Second, as he continued to pursue his scholarly interests, he spent extended periods of time sitting with other scholars and engaging in debate with them. And third, he wrote prolifically, penning some of his greatest works in *uṣūl al-fiqh* and *kalām*.

Al-Juwaynī's tenure as the head of the Niẓāmiyya, lasting nearly three decades, was a period of significant intellectual growth for him, his students, and the inhabitants of the city. Nishapur, already a flourishing intellectual center replete with madrassas and prominent scholars, began to attract even more students with the opening of the Niẓāmiyya. Al-Subkī notes that on average al-Juwaynī's lectures were attended by some three hundred students, many of whom were not natives of Nishapur.[43] The backgrounds of these students were most likely diverse, given the culture of traveling for the sake of knowledge.

Of the multitude of al-Juwaynī's students, three were particularly important and became scholars of considerable repute: al-Kiyā al-Harrāsī (d. 504/1110–11),[44] Abū Ḥāmid al-Ghazālī (d. 505/1111), and Abū al-Qāsim al-Anṣārī (d. 512/1118). Al-Kiyā al-Harrāsī was born in 450/1058 and began his studies at a young age in Tabaristan. At the age of twenty, he moved from Tabaristan to Nishapur to study with al-Juwaynī, and he remained a student there until the latter's death. His intellectual inclinations were toward *uṣūl al-fiqh* and disputation (*jadal*), proclivities he most likely inherited from al-Juwaynī himself. Although al-Kiyā al-Harrāsī was one of al-Juwaynī's foremost disciples, he did not inherit his teacher's position, which instead went to al-Juwaynī's son, Abū al-Qāsim.[45] At that time, it is most likely that al-Kiyā al-Harrāsī moved to

[43] Al-Subkī, *Ṭabaqāt al-Shāfiʿiyya*, 5:172.

[44] His full name was Shams al-Islām ʿImād al-Dīn Abū al-Ḥasan ʿAlī b. Muḥammad b. ʿAlī al-Ṭabarī al-Kiyā al-Harrāsī.

[45] The full name of al-Juwaynī's son was Abū al-Qāsim al-Muẓaffar b. ʿAbd al-Malik b. ʿAbd Allāh al-Juwaynī. He was born in Rayy in the year 445/1053, during his father's exile from Nishapur, and saw Nishapur for the first time on his father's return to the city. His main teacher was his father, and he learned all of the disciplines his father taught; however, he did not achieve the stature of his father's other students. Thus, when his father died, he was not immediately given the latter's position and instead taught classes at the Muṭarriz Mosque. It is not clear who assumed al-Juwaynī's post immediately after his death, but Abū al-Qasīm objected to the appointment, going to Niẓām al-Mulk to

the town of Bayhaq to teach but, on the murder of Abū al-Qāsim in 493/1099, he assumed al-Juwaynī's position until 498/1105, when he moved to Baghdad to become chair of the Niẓāmiyya madrassa there. He retained his position in Baghdad until his death approximately six years later in 504/1110–11.[46]

Al-Kiyā al-Harrāsī's classmate, al-Ghazālī,[47] is by far the most prolific and widely remembered student of al-Juwaynī. Born in the year 450/1058 in Tabaran, in the district of Tus, he began his education there before moving to Nishapur, just slightly to the south. In Nishapur, he studied with al-Juwaynī until the latter's death; however, the available information regarding al-Ghazālī's time in Nishapur and his studies with al-Juwaynī is sparse. As Frank Griffel notes, ʿAbd al-Ghāfir al-Fārisī, another classmate of al-Ghazālī's and a famous historian of the period, makes little mention of al-Ghazālī's activities in Nishapur aside from his tutelage under al-Juwaynī. After al-Juwaynī's death, al-Ghazālī accompanied Niẓām al-Mulk as part of the latter's scholarly entourage[48] until 484/1091, when he was appointed head of the Niẓāmiyya madrassa in Baghdad. This position was even more prestigious than his teacher's post had been, since Baghdad was the capital of the ʿAbbasid Empire and as such the heart of Islamic intellectual life. This new public role, as al-Ghazālī famously relates in his own autobiography, caused him a considerable amount of stress,[49] leading him to abandon his post in 488/1095,

assert his right to his father's position. Even though Abū al-Qasīm was eventually installed as the head of the Niẓāmiyya, difficulties remained because of the political situation in Nishapur, involving Karrāmī and Khārijī uprisings. During one such uprising, in 493/1099, Abū al-Qāsim was poisoned and killed. For more details on his life, see Bulliet, *Patricians of Nishapur*, 126, and al-Subkī, *Ṭabaqāt al-Shāfiʿiyya*, 5:330.

46 Among the most famous works of al-Kiyā al-Harrāsī are his *Shifāʾ al-murshidīn* and his *Naqd al-mufradāt al-Imām Aḥmad*, both of which are books on *khilāf* and most likely born out of his interest in *jadal*. He also produced two other works that are extant in manuscript form. One is his book on *uṣūl*, entitled *Taʿlīq fī uṣūl al-fiqh*; it is held in the library of the University of Ankara, where it was found by George Makdisi. The other is a book on *kalām* entitled *Uṣūl al-dīn*. A manuscript of this work, according to Brockelmann, is available at the National Library of Cairo. For details, see Makdisi, "Al-Kiyā al-Harrāsī, S̲h̲ams al-Islām ʿImād ad-Dīn Abu'l-Ḥasan ʿAlī," in *Encyclopaedia of Islam*, 2nd edn.

47 Detailed biographies of al-Ghazāli's life are plentiful in English. For one of the latest and most comprehensive, see Griffel, *Al-Ghazālī's Philosophical Theology*, chapters 1 and 2.

48 Al-Subkī, *Ṭabaqāt al-Shāfiʿiyya*, 6:208.

49 This stress was due not merely to the position he held but also to the politically difficult time. During his tenure, his lifelong patron Niẓām al-Mulk was assassinated in 485/1092, and Malikshāh, the new sultan, decided to transfer the capital of the ʿAbbasid Empire from Baghdad to a new city of his choice. However, within a month of Niẓām al-Mulk's

in his fourth year of teaching.[50] After leaving Baghdad, al-Ghazālī traveled to Syria and the Hejaz before finally returning to his home province of Khurasan, where he died in Tabaran in 505/1111.

The internal turmoil often associated with al-Ghazālī's life did not impede his intellectual prowess, and he is remembered as a scholar with vast interests who left an indelible mark on Islamic intellectual history. Recalling the entirety of his oeuvre is beyond the scope of this work, but one of his earlier texts, *al-Mankhūl min taʿlīqāt al-uṣūl*, which Griffel dates to around 471/1078, merits particular mention. This text was written during the life of al-Juwaynī and is understood to represent a summary of al-Juwaynī's curriculum in *uṣūl al-fiqh*.[51] In addition to providing insight into al-Juwaynī's teaching, the text allows for comparison of al-Juwaynī's thought with that of al-Ghazālī, highlighting instances of disagreement between the two scholars.

The last of al-Juwaynī's three famous students is Abū al-Qāsim al-Anṣārī.[52] Born in Arghiyan near Nishapur, al-Anṣārī spent the majority of his life in Nishapur and nearby towns, acquiring knowledge from the foremost scholars of the day. Of his teachers, he became most attached to Abū Qāsim al-Qushayrī (d. 465/1072), the pilgrimage companion of al-Juwaynī's father as well as a contemporary of al-Juwaynī. Al-Anṣārī's

death, Malikshāh also died, triggering a struggle for succession among his six underage sons. All of these various changes within the power structure of the empire had a bearing on al-Ghazālī, who was both financially and personally deeply connected with the Seljuks. For more, see Griffel, *Al-Ghazālī's Philosophical Theology*, 36–40.

50 The reasons for al-Ghazālī's departure are numerous. See Griffel, *Al-Ghazālī's Philosophical Theology*, 40–50. See also al-Ghazālī's autobiography, *Deliverance from Error*, trans. Richard McCarthy (Louisville, KY: Fons Vitae, 2001). An early biography of al-Ghazālī is Duncan B. Macdonald, "The Life of al-Ghazālī," *Journal of Arabic and Oriental Studies* 20 (1899): 71–132. Since the publication of Macdonald's article, a great deal of research on al-Ghazālī has been published, including works by Griffel and others that should be read in addition to the early article. See also Kenneth Garden, *The First Islamic Reviver* (Oxford: Oxford University Press, 2014). W. Montgomery Watt's article on al-Ghazālī in the *Encyclopaedia of Islam* (2nd edn.) is also useful, along with its bibliographic citations.

51 See Griffel, *Al-Ghazālī's Philosophical Theology*, 32–34. Ibn al-Jawzī claims that al-Juwaynī was frustrated with al-Ghazālī's text because he considered it disrespectful toward himself; however, Griffel argues that Ibn al-Jawzī's claim could be due in part to Ibn al-Jawzī's own antagonism to al-Ghazālī. However, the report of tension between al-Ghazālī and al-Juwaynī is supported by the account of their contemporary, al-Fārisī, who states that while al-Juwaynī praised his student, he secretly did not have a good opinion of him. See Ibn al-Jawzī, *al-Muntaẓam*, 9:168–69; and, for the account of al-Fārisī, al-Subkī, *Ṭabaqāt al-Shāfiʿiyya*, 6:205.

52 His full name was Abū al-Qāsim Salmān b. Nāṣir b. ʿImrān al-Arghiyānī al-Nīsābūrī al-Anṣārī.

connection with al-Qushayrī was born of the former's inclination toward Sufism and the pietistic trends taking root in Nishapur. His studies with al-Juwaynī began before al-Juwaynī's departure from Nishapur, making al-Anṣārī one of the pupils who studied the longest with al-Juwaynī, as he subsequently accompanied al-Juwaynī and al-Qushayrī to the Hejaz. Al-Anṣārī's trajectory of return was, however, different from al-Juwaynī's, as the former traveled first to Baghdad and then to Syria, seeking out various scholars before returning to Nishapur and resuming his studies with al-Juwaynī at the Niẓāmiyya.[53] In addition to his interest in Sufism, al-Anṣārī studied *kalām* and wrote a commentary, *Sharḥ al-Irshād*,[54] on al-Juwaynī's *kalām* compendium, *al-Irshād*. Al-Anṣārī also wrote an independent treatise in *kalām*, *Kitāb al-Ghunya fī ʿilm al-kalām*.[55] As he was a devoted pupil of al-Juwaynī, most of al-Anṣārī's theological positions mirror those of his teacher, though he is keen to point out inconsistencies in al-Juwaynī's statements, especially regarding the source of human actions.[56] Later in his life, al-Anṣārī became a teacher at the Bayhaqiyya madrassa, the second most prestigious madrassa in Nishapur in his day. The sources also mention that he taught at the Niẓāmiyya after al-Ghazālī, but it is not clear what position he held, if any.[57] Although his early studies were with al-Qushayrī, he is remembered mainly as an Ashʿarī theologian because the majority of his writings concerned the science of *kalām*.

Beyond teaching, al-Juwaynī continued to further his own education, engaging with other scholars and studying independently. Despite attaining one of the highest formal positions within the educational institutions of the time, al-Juwaynī was keen to pursue his scholarly interests. Being based in Nishapur was helpful, as traveling scholars frequented the city. Al-Subkī notes that in 469/1076 Abū al-Ḥasan ʿAlī b. Faḍḍāl b. ʿAlī al-Mujāshiʿī,[58]

53 See al-Subkī, *Ṭabaqāt al-Shāfiʿiyya*, 7:96–99. Also see Claude Gilliot's entry on al-Anṣārī, "Al-Anṣārī, Abū l-Qāsim," in *Encyclopaedia of Islam*, 3rd edn., ed. Kate Fleet, Gudrun Krämer, Denis Matringe, John Nawas, and Everett Rowson (Brill Online, 2017).

54 An extant manuscript of this commentary is available in the Princeton University Library, ELS, no. 634.

55 An extant manuscript of this text is available in Istanbul (Istanbul, Ahmet III, 1916). It has been edited and published as part of a master's thesis. See Abū al-Qāsim al-Anṣārī, *al-Ghunya fī ʿilm al-kalām*, ed. Muṣṭafā Ḥasnayn ʿAbd al-Hādī (Cairo: Dār al-Salām, 2010).

56 Richard Frank, *Al-Ghazālī and the Ashʿarite School* (Durham, NC: Duke University Press, 1994), 115 n. 2.

57 See Griffel, *Al-Ghazālī's Philosophical Theology*, 304 n. 252. Nūr Allāh al-Kasāʾī mentions that he taught there, but this information is not corroborated by other biographical accounts.

58 See Ibn al-ʿImād, *Shadharāt al-dhahab*, 3:357, 360.

one of the great grammarians of the time, visited Nishapur. Al-Juwaynī met with him and read aloud one of his works on grammar, entitled *Aksīr al-dhahab*. In another instance, Abū Isḥāq al-Shīrāzī (d. 476/1083),[59] the head of the Niẓāmiyya in Baghdad, visited Nishapur, where he was hosted by al-Juwaynī. This visit is documented by al-Subkī, who records the scholarly debate between the two over matters of *fiqh*.[60] Given that both were heads of Niẓāmiyya madrassas and renowned Shāfiʿī jurists interested in *jadal*,[61] their engagement is no surprise and also demonstrates that the Niẓāmiyya institutions, beyond being connected by a shared patron, Niẓām al-Mulk, maintained cordial relations with one another.

In addition to studying formally with scholars such as al-Mujāshiʿī and engaging in scholarly disputation with others such as al-Shīrāzī, al-Juwaynī also continued his studies of certain disciplines independently. This is the murkiest element of al-Juwaynī's intellectual trajectory, yet one of considerable importance because it had a direct bearing on his intellectual production. As al-Juwaynī's early education shows, he focused on the foundational disciplines in his time, including *kalām*, *uṣūl al-fiqh*, *tafsīr*, and *ḥadīth*. It has also been noted that he was influenced by the discipline of Sufism, given the prominence of Sufi scholars in Nishapur and his personal connections to some of them. Biographical sources also refer to al-Juwaynī's knowledge and, at times, appropriation of Greek philosophy. However, the relatively few details available about

[59] His full name was Abū Isḥāq Ibrāhīm b. ʿAlī b. Yusūf al-Fīrūzābādī al-Shīrāzī. He undertook the majority of his education in Baghdad, where he was the preeminent student of Qāḍī Abū al-Ṭayyib al-Ṭabarī (d. 450/1058). After completing his education, he taught at various mosques and madrassas in Baghdad before Niẓām al-Mulk appointed him the head of the Niẓāmiyya in Baghdad in 459/1066. For his full biography, see al-Subkī, *Ṭabaqāt al-Shāfiʿiyya*, 4:215, and also Hītū, *al-Imām al-Shirāzī*.

[60] The dialogue between al-Juwaynī and al-Shīrāzī is preserved by al-Subkī in his *Ṭabaqāt al-Shāfiʿiyya*, 5:209–18. The first point of difference, as mentioned in the Introduction to the present work, concerns the question of whether the timing of prayer is more important than its direction. In the second debate, the two disagree over whether an adult female virgin (*al-bikr al-bāligha*) can be married without her consent, like a prepubescent *bikr* can.

[61] The fact that both scholars were interested in *jadal* can be established from biographical sources and the works they penned. According to al-Subkī, al-Shīrāzī was "a lion of disputation (*munāẓara*)" and wrote many works on the topic, including *al-Mulakhkhaṣ fī al-jadal* and *Kitāb al-Maʿūna fī al-jadal*. Al-Juwaynī, too, wrote works on *jadal*, the most prominent being *al-Kāfiya fī al-jadal*. For a complete list of al-Shīrāzī's books on *jadal* and where their manuscripts can be found, see Eric Chaumont, "Al-S̲h̲īrāzī," in *Encyclopaedia of Islam*, 2nd edn. For more on the development of *jadal* and al-Shīrāzī's thought, see Walter Edward Young, *The Dialectical Forge: Juridical Disputation and the Evolution of Islamic Law* (Cham: Springer, 2017).

the latter part of his life make the contours of al-Juwaynī's activity in this area difficult to ascertain.

That said, the influence of Greek philosophy on al-Juwaynī is in many ways not surprising. As Dimitri Gutas notes in his seminal work, *Greek Thought, Arabic Culture*, translations of philosophical works from Greek and Syriac into Arabic began appearing in the Islamic world already during the reign of the Umayyads.[62] With the shift of power to the ʿAbbasids, this movement gained further strength, with pervasive ramifications for the social and intellectual milieu of the time. The early ʿAbbasid caliphs, particularly al-Manṣūr (r. 136–58/754–75) and his son and heir al-Mahdī (r. 158–69/775–85), promoted the translation movement with policies of intellectual patronage that would become virtually synonymous with early ʿAbbasid rule. The importance of translating key texts, recognized by al-Manṣūr, was likewise endorsed by later ʿAbbasid caliphs, and the official support for scholars and the translation of texts continued, especially under Hārūn al-Rashīd (r. 170–93/786–809) and al-Maʾmūn (r. 199–218/813–33). The early translation movement did not discriminate between languages, and thus Persian and Pahlavi texts were translated into Arabic alongside Greek and Syriac ones. One of the earliest complete Greek texts to be translated, under the command of the Caliph al-Mahdī, was Aristotle's *Topics*.[63]

The translation of texts from Greek, Syriac, and other languages continued until the end of the Buyid period in 447/1055, when Greek texts were no longer seen as providing a fertile ground for further scholarship. This does not mean that the zeal for scholarship diminished;

[62] Gutas notes that the translation movement did not reach its zenith until the time of the ʿAbbasids, though it began during the Umayyads' reign. Gutas complicates the notion that the translation movement commenced at one particular time, thanks to efforts of one particular caliph; he shows that it was a process that started early on under the Umayyads and was to some degree transformed by each caliph in power, also in part in response to the social and political context in which each caliph found himself. Although Gutas accepts that the caliphs' individual propensities may have influenced what texts were translated (for example, al-Mahdī, who enjoyed falconry, had a book commissioned on it), much of the movement's development was shaped by external influences. See Gutas, *Greek Thought, Arabic Culture*, chapters 1 and 2.

[63] Ibid., 65–71. According to Gutas, the *Topics* of Aristotle was particularly important because it introduced Aristotle's style of dialectic, which was subsequently adopted as the normative method for both theological and legal debates in Islamic circles. The methodology provided by the *Topics* was so valuable that it led to a preference for Greek translations into Arabic over translations from other languages. Consequently, after the *Topics*, translators turned to Aristotle's *Physics* for its theological and cosmological debates, from which Muslim theologians benefited.

rather, patrons shifted their financial support from the translation of texts to the composition of original works in Arabic. As Gutas observes: "From this vantage point, the translation movement stopped or came to an end because the Arabic philosophical and scientific enterprise which had created the need for it from the very beginning became autonomous."[64]

Although the Greek translation movement had waned by the time of al-Juwaynī's birth,[65] it shaped the intellectual and social milieu in which he lived and had a direct bearing on his scholarship. One of its general consequences was the spread of intellectual currents from Baghdad throughout the Islamic empire. This meant that although Baghdad remained the epicenter of Islamic intellectual activity, satellite intellectual cities such as Nishapur sprang up across the ʿAbbasid Empire. There is evidence that philosophy was an active field in Nishapur, but scholars before al-Juwaynī were divided over its value.[66]

So where did al-Juwaynī obtain his knowledge of philosophy? In support of al-Juwaynī's familiarity with philosophy, al-Subkī notes that both his *kalām* and his *uṣūl al-fiqh* works reveal philosophical influences. One of the most famous commentators on the *Burhān*, al-Māzarī (d. 536/1141),[67] supports al-Subkī's assertion, stating that al-Juwaynī deviates

64 Gutas, *Greek Thought, Arabic Culture*, 152.

65 There is an impressive list of philosophers who lived before al-Juwaynī, many of whom had patrons from the ʿAbbasid family. They include Abū Yūsuf al-Kindī (d. 260/873), Ibn al-Rāwandī (d. ca. 245/910), Abū Bakr Zakariyyā al-Rāzī (dc. 320/932), al-Fārābī (d. 339/950), Yaḥyā b. ʿAdī (d. 363/974), Abū Sulaymān al-Sijistānī al-Manṭiqī (d. 390/1000), Abū al-Ḥasan al-Tawhīdī (d. 414/1023), Ibn Miskawayh (d. 421/1030), and Ibn Sīnā (d. 429/1037). Given the cosmopolitan nature of the ʿAbbasid Empire and the norm of traveling in search of knowledge, it is unlikely that the philosophical ideas of the aforementioned scholars were confined to their hometowns and did not reach Nishapur. In fact, as W. Montgomery Watt has argued, Nishapur did not lag behind Baghdad in terms of status as one of the foremost cities of Islamic thought at the time; rather, the main difference between the two was that Baghdad was a metropolitan city and the seat of the ʿAbbasid caliph, whereas Nishapur was smaller – although, as mentioned previously, it was later the base of Seljuk power. See Watt, *Islamic Philosophy and Theology*, 79. For a deeper understanding of the development of philosophy before the time of al-Juwaynī, see Majid Fakhry's introductory work, *A History of Islamic Philosophy*, 3rd edn. (New York: Columbia University Press, 2004). Chapters 3, 4, 6, and 7 are particularly valuable for understanding the early development of philosophy and its subsequent integration into other disciplines. For a study focused on the late integration of philosophy and theology, especially in the work of al-Juwaynī's student al-Ghazālī, see Oliver Leaman, *An Introduction to Classical Islamic Philosophy* (Cambridge: Cambridge University Press, 2001).

66 Gutas, *Greek Thought, Arabic Culture*, 160.

67 Abū ʿAbd Allāh Muḥammad b. ʿAlī b. ʿUmar b. Muḥammad al-Tamīmī al-Māzarī, *Īḍāḥ al-maḥsūl min Burhān al-uṣūl* (Beirut: Dār al-Gharb al-Islāmī, 2001), 38–45.

from certain opinions accepted within the Shāfiʿī and Ashʿarī schools because of philosophical ideas he had adopted. This sentiment is also echoed by a later commentator on al-Juwaynī's *Shāmil*, Ibn al-Amīr (d. 736/1336), who likewise testifies to the impact of philosophy on al-Juwaynī's work.[68] Though both commentators affirm al-Juwaynī's philosophical inclinations, neither identifies when or how al-Juwaynī was exposed to philosophy or which philosopher had the greatest influence on him. That al-Juwaynī did not undertake any formal study of philosophy is indicated by the lack of evidence adduced by later biographers and by the absence of any mention of such study in the contemporaneous account of his student al-Fārisī. But this does not preclude the possibility of independent systematic study. Indeed, it seems most probable that he studied philosophy independently and that his studies were facilitated by his travels to Baghdad and by the library connected to the Niẓāmiyya in Nishapur.

Baghdad was of particular importance for al-Juwaynī's exploration of philosophy, because by the time he arrived there in the year 447/1055, the translation movement had largely dwindled. This means that al-Juwaynī did not personally witness the heyday of the movement but was likely exposed to it during his visit. Although the brevity of his stay in Baghdad and the dearth of available information on it render any conclusions speculative, his general thirst for knowledge and intellectual curiosity make it likely that he encountered philosophical discussions during his stay. After this exposure to philosophical ideas in Baghdad, al-Juwaynī probably continued his independent study in Nishapur at the Niẓāmiyya. The translation movement had led to the circulation and preservation of books in libraries around Baghdad, the most important of which was the Bayt al-Ḥikma ("House of Wisdom"),[69] and like other aspects of the

Unfortunately, only a part of the commentary is extant, but in his introduction al-Māzarī lists various points on which al-Juwaynī has changed his position between his earlier works and his later ones, such as the *Burhān*. It is on these points that he thinks al-Juwaynī was most influenced by the philosophers.

68 See Mūsā b. Muḥammad al-Tabrīzī Ibn al-Amīr al-Ḥājj, *al-Kāmil fī uṣūl al-dīn fī ikhtiṣār al-Shāmil fī uṣūl al-dīn li-Imām al-Ḥaramayn al-Juwaynī*, ed. Jamāl ʿAbd al-Nāṣir ʿAbd al-Munʿim (Cairo: Dār al-Salām, 2009). Ibn al-Amīr mentions al-Juwaynī's various borrowings from the philosophers and also his arguments with them in the sections regarding knowledge (specifically, *naẓar*) and the createdness of the world.

69 Gutas argues against the notion that Bayt al-Ḥikma was a formal institution in which translations were undertaken. He suggests that it was most likely a library, returning to the original Sasanian word for library, *bayt al-ḥikma*. The ʿAbbasids adopted many Sasanian administrative elements into their system of governance, and it is likely that

city's intellectual culture, libraries, too, spread to the empire's satellite cities. These included the library built adjacent to the Niẓāmiyya madrassa in Nishapur. That library, known as the Khizānat al-Kutub,[70] likely housed books on all the important disciplines of the era, including philosophy. This conclusion is supported by al-Subkī's biography of al-Ghazālī, which says that al-Ghazālī likewise read *falsafa* during his time in Nishapur but does not mention a teacher, indicating that al-Ghazālī studied the subject on his own.[71] It is thus no surprise that Griffel argues that the "Niẓāmiyya madrasa in Nishapur became the cradle of Avicenna's lasting influence on Ashʿarite theology."[72]

Reconstructing the details of the arguments or methods that al-Juwaynī may have derived from philosophers is beyond the scope of the present work; I will limit myself to some brief preliminary remarks.[73] Of the various arguments of the philosophers that al-Juwaynī addresses, the one he discusses in most detail is the argument for the eternity of the world. In his theological magnum opus, *al-Shāmil*, al-Juwaynī allocates extensive space both to presenting and to rebutting the philosopher's argument on the issue before laying out his own argument for the createdness of the world.[74] According to Griffel,

the notion of *bayt al-ḥikma* had a similar origin. See Gutas, *Greek Thought, Arabic Culture*, 53–60. This theory is supported by Makdisi's study *Rise of Colleges*, in which he identifies three terms that were used to refer to the structure of a library – *bayt* (room), *khizāna* (closet), and *dār* (house) – and three distinct words used for the contents of the library – *ḥikma* (wisdom), *ʿilm* (knowledge), and *kutub* (books). Makdisi concludes that seven different terms were variously used to denote a library: *bayt al-ḥikma*, *khizānat al-ḥ ikma*, *dār al-ḥikma*, *dār al-ʿilm*, *dār al-kutub*, *khizānat al-kutub*, and *bayt al-kutub*. See Makdisi, *Rise of Colleges*, 24. This portion of his findings relies on the earlier work of Y. Eche, *Les Bibliotheques arabes publiques et semi-publiques en Mesopotamie, en Syria et en Egypte au moyen âge* (Damascus: Institut français de Damas, 1967).

70 Makdisi, *Rise of Colleges*, 25.

71 Al-Subkī, *Ṭabaqāt al-Shāfiʿiyya*, 6:196–97. In discussing the functions of these different libraries, Makdisi notes that while they were utilized by the scholars and students of the institution with which they were associated, they were also open to the general public and to travelers. In addition to this primary function, moreover, they served as a venue for the copying of texts, a function that was especially important for travelers who came to the city for short periods of time in search of specific texts. Makdisi, *Rise of Colleges*, 25–26.

72 Griffel, *Al-Ghazālī's Philosophical Theology*, 30.

73 The points that follow are based on al-Juwaynī's writings in *kalām* and do not touch on his *uṣūl al-fiqh*. The latter offers a potentially fruitful line of inquiry, and I hope to pursue it in future writings; however, an investigation both of al-Juwaynī's ideas in the *Burhān* and of all of the various potential influences on these is well beyond the scope of the present book.

74 Al-Juwaynī, *al-Shāmil*, 123–342.

al-Juwaynī was the first Muslim theologian who seriously studied Avicenna's books. On the one hand, al-Juwaynī fully realized the methodological challenge of the Aristotelian methods of demonstration (*apodeixis/burhān*) as used by Avicenna. The Muslim philosophers (*falāsifa*) claimed, for instance, that through a chain of conclusive arguments, one can prove demonstrably that the world is pre-eternal (*qadīm*), and one can thus disprove the claim of the theologians that the world is created in time (*ḥādith*). On the other hand, al-Juwaynī also understood that the works of Avicenna and other *falāsifa* contained solutions to many theological problems the Ashʿarī school had wrestled with for centuries.[75]

Though al-Juwaynī staunchly rejected the argument put forth by the philosophers for the pre-eternity of the world, he realized that certain philosophical methods and terms were useful. Robert Wisnovsky argues, for example, that al-Juwaynī was the first Ashʿarī scholar to accept fully Ibn Sīnā's distinction between the being that is necessary by virtue of itself (*wājib al-wujūd*) and that which by itself is only contingent (*mumkin al-wujūd*).[76] Al-Juwaynī employs these concepts in the greatest detail in his *Shāmil*[77] as a means of proving the existence of God, but they are also found in his shorter works, including *al-Irshād*,[78] *al-Lumaʿ fī al-adilla*,[79] and *al-ʿAqīda al-Niẓāmiyya*.[80] For Griffel, while al-Ghazālī may have been the first scholar to appropriate Ibn Sīnā's philosophy and to

[75] Griffel, *Al-Ghazālī's Philosophical Theology*, 29–30. One of the earliest scholars to note the influence of philosophy on al-Juwaynī was Richard Frank in his study of al-Ghazālī's appropriation of Ibn Sīnā. See Frank, *Creation and the Cosmic System: Al-Ghazālī and Avicenna* (Heidelberg: Winter, 1992), 10 n. 2, 17, 66.

[76] Robert Wisnovsky translates al-Juwaynī's statement in the *Shāmil* in his very useful article, "One Aspect of the Avicennian Turn," 91. He argues that the turn in Sunnī *kalām* occurred not with al-Ghazālī and his appropriation of Ibn Sīnā, but rather with Ibn Sīnā himself; he also claims that the first scholar to adopt completely Ibn Sīnā's terminology was al-Juwaynī. For Ibn Sīnā's use of the *wājib al-wujūd/mumkin al-wujūd* distinction in providing a proof for God, see Herbert Davidson, *Proofs for Eternity, Creation and the Existence of God in Medieval Islamic and Jewish Philosophy* (New York: Oxford University Press, 1987), chapter 6. For an overview of how scholars after Ibn Sīnā used this theory of necessary existence and his distinction between essence and existence, see Wisnovky, "Avicenna and the Avicennian Tradition," in *The Cambridge Companion to Arabic Philosophy*, ed. Peter Adamson and R. Taylor (Cambridge: Cambridge University Press, 2004), 92–136.

[77] Al-Juwaynī, *al-Shāmil*, 82, 196–97, 540–41, 618.

[78] Al-Juwaynī, *al-Irshād*, 59, 84.

[79] Al-Juwaynī, *al-Lumaʿ fī al-qawāʿid ahl al-sunna wa-l-jamāʿa*, 137.

[80] Al-Juwaynī, *al-ʿAqīda al-Niẓamiyya*, 23. The passages in which al-Juwaynī draws on Ibn Sīnā have all been translated by Wisnovsky in "One Aspect of the Avicennian Turn."

comment on it extensively, it was al-Juwaynī who established the intellectual parameters by which a full engagement with philosophy was possible.

In addition to teaching and studying, al-Juwaynī's third area of activity during his years at the Niẓāmiyya was the writing of treatises on the various Islamic disciplines that piqued his interest. The entirety of al-Juwaynī's oeuvre can be divided into four categories: texts on *uṣūl al-fiqh*, texts on *kalām*, texts on *fiqh*, and texts on differences (*khilāf*) between the *madhhab*s (especially between the Shāfiʿī and Ḥanafī schools). These works reflect not only al-Juwaynī's scholarly interests but also the exigencies of the time. One of the notable elements of al-Juwaynī's biography, as we have seen, is that he lived amid great political, intellectual, and social flux. Because of this context, aspects of his scholarship can be understood as responses to some of the intellectual challenges that were current in his lifetime.

DEATH

Al-Juwaynī's illustrious career came to an end at the relatively young age of fifty-eight. He was first afflicted with jaundice, marking the beginning of the decline of his health, and despite a brief recovery he fell ill again. On this second illness, he was taken to the neighboring town of Bushtinqan, which was known for the purity of its air, thought to aid patients in their recovery. But his stay there did not reverse the illness, and he passed away in 478/1085.[81] He was buried on the grounds of his house in Nishapur.[82] Al-Fārisī provides more details on these events, recalling that al-Juwaynī's illness worsened in the early evening of the fifteenth of Rabīʿ al-Thānī. Al-Fārisī reports that after his death, he was taken

[81] Al-Subkī relates that al-Juwaynī is claimed to have made two statements before his death: "I preoccupied myself with *kalām*, but if I had known that *kalām* would have brought me to where I am, I would have not been preoccupied with it" and "I testify that I abandon all of my positions that oppose the *salaf* and I die upon what the elderly of Nishapur die upon [in terms of faith]." While al-Subkī rejects the authenticity of these claimed statements, and others have agreed that they are fabrications, in combination they have been taken by some as evidence that al-Juwaynī renounced the discipline of *kalām* at the end of his life. Al-Subkī also relates other statements to this effect, including one that was heard by al-Qushayrī in a lesson of al-Juwaynī's and another that al-Juwaynī reportedly made close to the time of his death. Al-Subkī, *Ṭabaqāt al-Shāfiʿiyya*, 5:185–87.

[82] Al-Subkī, *Ṭabaqāt al-Shāfiʿiyya*, 5:181; Ibn al-ʿImād, *Shadharāt al-dhahab*, 3:360; Ibn Taghrībardī, *al-Nujūm al-zāhira*, 1:121; Ibn al-Jawzī, *al-Muntaẓam*, 9:20; and Ibn Khallikān, *Wafayāt al-aʿyān*, 1:362.

back to Nishapur, where his son Abū al-Qāsim led the funeral prayer and he was laid to rest.[83]

CONCLUSION

The portrait of al-Juwaynī that emerges from his biography is that of a reflective and responsive scholar. His reflective tendencies are evident in his continual desire to accumulate knowledge, irrespective of his stature and the surrounding political conditions; his responsiveness can be seen in his writings, which engage with the social and political realities in an attempt to transcend them. The response he ultimately formulates reflects al-Juwaynī's twin objectives of certainty and continuity. Given the polyvalent political and intellectual environment he inhabited, his preoccupations are not surprising. As seen throughout this book, while al-Juwaynī's desire for certainty and continuity dictates much of his legal and theological work and leads him to novel arguments not made by other Shāfiʿī-Ashʿarīs of his time, he is not always successful in his attempts to ensure both simultaneously, revealing an intellectual negotiation and tension that remains unresolved.

[83] Al-Subkī, *Ṭabaqāt al-Shāfiʿiyya*, 5:182 (for al-Fārisī's account). There is some confusion regarding al-Juwaynī's final resting-place. Al-Subkī states that he was buried on the grounds of his home but that his body was later transferred to be laid to rest next to the burial ground of Imam al-Ḥusayn. As Fawqiyya Maḥmūd points out, this is a strange statement for several reasons. First, there are no reports of Imam al-Ḥusayn's being buried in Nishapur, and second, it would be strange for al-Juwaynī's body to be excavated and reinterred elsewhere. She does note, however, that there is a mosque in Cairo by the name of al-Juwaynī. A plaque in the mosque gives the year of its construction as 627/1230, and it bears the full names of al-Juwaynī, his father, and his son. However, as Maḥmūd notes, there is no way to verify this information. She also observes that other members of al-Juwaynī's family could have settled in Cairo and died there, so the mosque may mark a relative of al-Juwaynī's rather than the man himself.

PART II

EPISTEMOLOGY

3

Intellectual Fissures

The Ashʿarīs and the Muʿtazila

> We cannot hope to understand the nomocracy of Islam if we study the theology of Islam without its relation to law.
>
> – George Makdisi[1]

As the preceding chapters have shown, Nishapur in al-Juwaynī's lifetime was intellectually divided along two main axes – in law, between the Ḥanafīs and the Shāfiʿīs, and in theology, between the Ashʿarīs and the Muʿtazila. Though the initial division was that of legal perspective, what eventually precipitated the exodus of Shāfiʿī scholars from Nishapur was their theological adherence to the Ashʿarī school. It is thus no surprise that in al-Juwaynī's writings, whether legal, theological, or political, his primary interlocutors are the Muʿtazila. Not only were Muʿtazilī ideas circulating in Nishapur, but key Muʿtazilī scholars sought refuge in the city during al-Juwaynī's youth, stoking intellectual discourse and rivalry between the two schools.

At the heart of the debates between the Muʿtazila and the Ashʿarīs lay disagreements about human reason, the possibility of true knowledge, and the role of revelation. The stances that the two groups took on these questions had not only pervasive theological ramifications but legal and political ones as well. In fact, it would not be an exaggeration to say that the entire vocation of the jurist was built on the theological assertions inherent in the answers given to these fundamental theological and epistemological questions.

[1] Makdisi, "Ashʿarī and the Ashʿarites," part 1, 39.

THE MUʿTAZILĪ SCHOOL IN NISHAPUR

The Muʿtazilī theological school was founded in the first half of the second/eighth century by Wāṣil b. ʿAtāʾ (d. 131/748) and ʿAmr b. ʿUbayd (d. 144/761), who had been diligent students of Ḥasan al-Baṣrī (d. 110/728) before parting ways with their teacher over a purported theological disagreement on the legal status of a sinner.[2] Like other intellectual movements within Islam, the school developed over a long period of time, with varying relationships to other intellectual and political movements. The two most important early figures in the school, credited with systemizing the school's doctrine, were Bishr al-Muʿtamir (d. 210/825) in Baghdad and Abū al-Hudhayl al-ʿAllāf (d. 235/849) in Basra. Eventually the Basran school eclipsed the Baghdadi one in terms of size, and the majority of the Muʿtazilī texts extant today are from the former. In addition, the development of the two branches of the school indicates that the Muʿtazilī ideas present in Nishapur reflected the Basran school, making it the most relevant branch for the present purposes.[3]

From its inception, the Muʿtazilī school enjoyed steady ascendance among intellectual and, perhaps more importantly, political elites until the fourth/tenth century. But the latter success began to work against the school's adherents during the infamous fifteen-year *miḥna* of the ʿAbbasid caliph al-Maʾmūn (r. 199–218/813–33), who sought to force scholars across the empire to adopt Muʿtazilī views, most importantly the Muʿtazilī dogma regarding the createdness of the Quran. His policies were continued

[2] The origins of the Muʿtazilī school have been subject to much scholarly debate. For the different approaches, see Racha El Omari, "The Muʿtazilite Movement (I): The Origins of the Muʿtazila," in Schmidtke, *Oxford Handbook of Islamic Theology*, 131–41. The veracity of this story has been challenged by W. Montgomery Watt, who claims that it is a later invention. See Watt, *Islamic Philosophy and Theology*, 46–47. For a more extensive discussion, see Margaretha T. Heemskerk, *Suffering in Muʿtazilite Theology* (Leiden: Brill, 2000), 15.

[3] These are the two largest Muʿtazilī branches, but historically scholars have described many more. For example, ʿAbd al-Qāhir al-Baghdādī (d. 429/1037) notes that there are twenty-two Muʿtazilī groupings, and al-Shahrastānī (d. 548/1153) identifies twelve. The overwhelming majority of Western scholars focus on the Basran school, but recently attention has been extended to the Baghdadi school. See Racha El Omari, *The Theology of Abū l-Qāsim al-Balkhī/al-Kaʿbī (d. 319/931)* (Leiden: Brill, 2015). For the various schools, see Muḥammad b. ʿAbd al-Karīm al-Shahrastānī, *Al-Milal wa-l-nihal: Book of Religious and Philosophical Sects*, ed. William Cureton (London: Society for the Publication of Oriental Texts, 1842–46), 1:46–85, and ʿAbd al-Qāhir b. Ṭāhir al-Tamīmī al-Baghdādī, *Al-Farq bayna al-firaq: Moslem Schisms and Sects*, trans. Kate C. Seelye (New York: Columbia University Press, 1966).

by his successors, al-Mu'tasim (r. 218–27/833–42) and al-Wāthiq (r. 227–32/842–47), until they were finally reversed by al-Mutawakkil (r. 232–47/847–61) in 234/848. The intellectual participation of the Mu'tazila in the *miḥna* led to the weakening of the school and to what has been termed the triumph of traditionalism. However, this view is slightly misleading, as the Mu'tazilī school continued to attract adherents despite its fall from political grace. In fact, two of the most lauded figures in the Basran school, Abū 'Alī al-Jubbā'ī (d. 303/915–16) and his son Abū Hāshim al-Jubbā'ī (d. 321/933), lived well after the *miḥna*.[4]

With the death of Abū 'Alī, the Basran school faced the difficult question of intellectual succession. While it seemed natural that his son Abū Hāshim would become the leader of the school, senior scholars within the school felt that Abū Hāshim was too young, being only twenty-five at the time. More importantly, they noted that he disagreed with his father on central tenets of the school and thus could not be considered a true intellectual successor to his father. Although it is not entirely clear on what doctrines the two differed,[5] many of the school's adherents deemed the disagreements drastic enough to reject Abū Hāshim's succession and even, in some cases, to brand him a disbeliever, thus creating another division within the Mu'tazilī school. The Mu'tazilīs who rejected Abū Hāshim coalesced around Abū 'Abd Allāh Muḥammad b. 'Umarī al-Ṣaymarī (d. 315/927) and eventually left for Baghdad. In his *Fihrist*, Ibn al-Nadīm identifies al-Ṣaymarī as the new leader of the Basran Mu'tazila;[6] however, Abū Hāshim came to be recognized as the principal successor to his father. Those who followed Abū Hāshim were eventually known as the Bahshamiyya, and those who departed with al-Ṣaymarī took the name Ikhshīdiyya, after al-Ṣaymarī's main student, Abū Bakr Aḥmad b. 'Alī b. Ma'jūr al-Ikhshīd (d. 326/938). The enmity between the two groups grew steadily, probably reflecting disagreement over specific

4 According to Richard Frank, although early Mu'tazilī scholars such as al-Naẓẓām (d. 231/845) and Abū al-Hudhayl played an important role, the school itself did not acquire a coherent structure until the third/ninth century when discussions centered on the issue of *qudra* (the power to realize an act, or efficient causality) and the possibility of being. See Frank, "Remarks on the Early Development of Kalām," in *Atti del III Congresso di Studi Arabi e Islamici* (Naples, 1967), 315–29.

5 'Abd al-Jabbār claimed that the differences between the father and the son are similar to the differences between Abū Ḥanīfa and his disciples – i.e., the differences in their characteristic features are not extreme enough to place the scholars in distinct schools. See Heemskerk, *Suffering in Mu'tazilite Theology*, 22.

6 Muḥammad Isḥāq Ibn al-Nadīm, *Kitāb al-Fihrist*, ed. Gustav Flügel (Beirut: Khayat, 1964), 219.

doctrinal points, despite the fact that the Ikhshīdiyya were stationed in Baghdad, at a good distance away from the Bahshamiyya.[7]

There is some confusion with regard to who took the reins of the Bahshamiyya after Abū Hāshim's death. Margaretha Heemskerk identifies a variety of possibilities but concludes that eventually Abū al-Ḥasan ʿAbd al-Jabbār al-Asadābādī (d. 415/1025) became the leader of the school.[8] ʿAbd al-Jabbār lived in the town of Asadabad, in the province of Jibal, which was ruled at the time by Rukn al-Dawla, one of the three Buyid brothers who had taken control in the East. The other two brothers, Muʿizz al-Dawla and ʿImād al-Dawla, ruled Iraq and Fars, respectively. The three brothers had no predispositions toward the Muʿtazila, but things changed when Rukn al-Dawla died in 366/976. He had planned to divide his lands between two of his sons, Muʾayyid al-Dawla and Fakhr al-Dawla, but when Fakhr al-Dawla subsequently tried to seize the territory of Muʾayyid al-Dawla, a third son, ʿAḍud al-Dawla, intervened, giving all of the land to Muʾayyid al-Dawla and driving Fakhr al-Dawla away to Nishapur.[9] Shortly after taking power, Muʾayyid al-Dawla replaced his father's vizier with al-Ṣāḥib b. ʿAbbād (d. 385/925). Al-Ṣāḥib b. ʿAbbād's appointment gave the Muʿtazilī school a boost, because the vizier preferred it to other theological schools and accordingly appointed ʿAbd al-Jabbār as the chief judge.[10]

Beginning his tenure in 367/977, ʿAbd al-Jabbār supervised the judges in Jibal, dictated his magnum opus, *al-Mughnī*, and taught a great number of students.[11] He held the position until the death of al-Ṣāḥib b.

[7] The Ikhshīdiyya remained prominent in Baghdad until the fourth/tenth century. After that, Heemskerk notes, it is not clear whether they continued to be considered a distinct school, and although the name of the group can be located in the work of later Basran Muʿtazilīs such as ʿAbd al-Jabbār, Ibn Mattawayh, and Ibn al-Murtaḍā, it is not readily found in heresiographical works from the same time. See Heemskerk, *Suffering in Muʿtazilite Theology*, 27–28.

[8] See Heemskerk, *Suffering in Muʿtazilite Theology*, 29–36. For a full biography of ʿAbd al-Jabbār, see Heemskerk's "ʿAbd al-Jabbār b. Aḥmad al-Hamadhānī," in *Encyclopaedia of Islam*, 3rd edn.

[9] On the death of Muʾayyid al-Dawla in 373/983, Fakhr al-Dawla returned to power as the ruler of Jibal. See Ḥasan-i Fasāʾī, *History of Persia under Qajar Rule*, trans. Heribert Busse (New York: Columbia University Press, 1972), 289–90.

[10] In addition to serving as a vizier, al-Ṣāḥib b. ʿAbbād also wrote theological treatises promoting Muʿtazilī positions. Two have recently been found in the Geniza collection and have been published. See *Al-Ṣāḥib Ibn ʿAbbād: Promoter of Rational Theology*, ed. Wilferd Madelung and Sabine Schmidtke (Leiden: Brill, 2016).

[11] For a full list of the works he completed during this time, see Heemskerk, *Suffering in Muʿtazilite Theology*, 39–48, 51–53.

ʿAbbād in 385/995, after which he spent the next thirty years teaching students both in Rayy and in Baghdad until his death in 415/1025. The political situation in these decades was particularly complex because Fakhr al-Dawla, who had taken over after the death of Muʾayyid al-Dawla in 373/983, died two years after the death of al-Ṣāḥib b. ʿAbbād. The two sons of Fakhr al-Dawla were too young and inexperienced to rule, so his widow al-Sayyida Shīrīn assumed power. When she died in 419/1028, shortly after ʿAbd al-Jabbār, her sons inherited the empire but had no political experience. One son, Majd al-Dawla, not knowing what to do, beseeched Maḥmūd of Ghazna, a neighboring ruler, for help; but Maḥmūd took advantage of the situation and seized Majd al-Dawla's lands.[12] The caliph at the time, al-Qādir (r. 381–433/991–1031), desired to strengthen the intellectual and political situation of the Sunnīs, and thus in 408/1017, capitalizing on the political unrest in the eastern regions, he forbade the teaching and spreading of Muʿtazilī and Imāmī Shīʿī doctrines. To secure his position in the caliph's eyes, the ambitious Maḥmūd of Ghazna expelled all Muʿtazilīs from his realm to Khurasan.[13]

During these politically volatile times, the leadership of the Bahshamiyya passed from ʿAbd al-Jabbār to Abū Rashīd Saʿīd al-Nīsābūrī (d. ca. 460/1068),[14] a native of Nishapur who had traveled to Rayy to study with ʿAbd al-Jabbār but returned to his hometown to spread Muʿtazilī teachings.[15] In spite of the ban on Muʿtazilism issued by Caliph al-Qādir and upheld by his son al-Qāʾim in 433/1041, Muʿtazilī ideas continued to circulate in Khurasan, where the ʿAbbasid caliph had little regulatory power. Moreover, by the time of al-Qāʾim's reign, the Seljuks under Ṭughril Beg were ruling Khurasan, and given Ṭughril Beg's personal preference for the Ḥanafī school and the standing alliance between the Ḥanafīs and the Muʿtazila at the time, the Muʿtazilī school was given freedom to develop.[16] The Seljuks not only allowed the Muʿtazilīs to propagate their teachings in Nishapur but also appointed Muʿtazilī

12 C. E. Bosworth, "The Political and Dynastic History of the Iranian World (A.D. 1000–1217)," in *Cambridge History of Iran*, 5:128.

13 Heemskerk, *Suffering in Muʿtazilite Theology*, 53–54.

14 The dates of both his birth and his death are contested, but it is known that he was born before 360/970 and lived beyond the death of ʿAbd al-Jabbār in 415/1025. See Heemskerk, *Suffering in Muʿtazilite Theology*, 55–56.

15 For more on the development of the Bahshamiyya, see Sabine Schmitdke, "The Muʿtazilite Movement (III): The Scholastic Phase," in Schmidtke, *Oxford Handbook of Islamic Theology*, 167.

16 Madelung, *Religious Schools and Sects*, 129–30.

scholars as judges. For example, Abū Bakr Muḥammad al-Nāṣiḥī (d. 484/1091), a Ḥanafī Muʿtazilī, was appointed as a judge in Nishapur and later in Rayy.[17] Al-Juwaynī, in the early years of his life before his self-imposed exile from Nishapur, was thus continually confronted with Muʿtazilī ideology, which was both supported by the early Seljuks and propagated by key Muʿtazilī figures.

MUʿTAZILĪ EPISTEMOLOGY AND ITS LEGAL CONSEQUENCES

Despite the spatial and temporal spread of the Muʿtazilī school, it is likely that the primary strand of Muʿtazilī thought encountered by al-Juwaynī was the Bahshamī branch, as inherited by ʿAbd al-Jabbār. My focus here will thus be on the late Basran Muʿtazilī school.[18] In order for the Muʿtazila to be considered cohesive and independent from other theological schools, they had to articulate fundamental principles that could serve as distinguishing markers. This was achieved through their "five principles" (*al-uṣūl al-khamsa*), first enumerated explicitly by the Baghdadi Muʿtazilī Abū al-Ḥasan al-Khayyāṭ (d. ca. 300/913) in his *Kitāb al-Intiṣār*. These principles are unity (*tawḥīd*), justice (*ʿadl*), the promise and the threat (*al-waʿd wa-l-waʿīd*), the intermediate position (*al-manzala bayna al-manzalatayn*), and commanding the right and forbidding the wrong (*al-amr bi-l-maʿrūf wa-l-nahy ʿan al-munkar*).[19] Though these were the five defining features of the school's thought, shared by the Baghdadi and Basran branches, the school as a whole is most often characterized by its intense rationalism, which stems from the belief in

[17] Ibid., 206.

[18] For an overview of the central tenets of the school, see Richard Frank, "Several Fundamental Assumptions of the Baṣran School of the Muʿtazila," *Studia Islamica*, no. 3 (1971): 5–18.

[19] ʿAbd al-Jabbār also wrote a work on the five principles entitled *Kitāb al-Uṣūl al-khamsa* and dictated a commentary for it entitled *Sharḥ al-Uṣūl al-khamsa*, which is not extant. What is available now is Mānkdīm Shashdīw's book *Taʿlīq Sharḥ al-Uṣūl al-khamsa*, a commentary on ʿAbd al-Jabbār's commentary. See Heemskerk, *Suffering in Muʿtazilite Theology*, 60–62. Sophia Vasalou provides a translation of these five principles as articulated by the Baghdadi Muʿtazilī al-Balkhī, the primary student of al-Khayyāṭ, in her *Moral Agents and Their Deserts: The Character of Muʿtazilite Ethics* (Princeton: Princeton University Press, 2008), 2. ʿAbd al-Jabbār's commentary was published as *Sharḥ al-Uṣūl al-khamsa*, ed. ʿAbd al-Karīm ʿUthmān (Cairo: Maktabat Wahba, 1965). But this text has been identified by Daniel Gimaret as *Taʿlīq Sharḥ al-Uṣūl al-khamsa*, and it is now attributed to Mānkdim Shashdīw.

divine justice.[20] It is here that one of the most significant fissures between the Ashʿarīs and the Muʿtazila is located, and it is also here that law and theology most obviously collide.

Known popularly as the people of unity and justice (*ahl al-ʿadl wa-l-tawḥīd*), the Muʿtazila were most concerned with God's unity and justice among their five fundamental principles. The emphasis on the unity of God, although not directly related to the larger discussion of Muʿtazilī epistemology, reveals an important element of the Muʿtazilī understanding of reason in relation to scripture. Regardless of theological affiliations, all Muslim scholars affirmed the unity of God (*tawḥīd*) and His utterly unique nature in comparison to creation. The Muʿtazila were particularly concerned with this latter element, leading them to reject any plain-sense interpretation of a Quranic verse that would allow for potentially anthropomorphic conclusions. Verses referring to body parts in relation to God (such as the hands of God or God's sitting upon a throne) were interpreted allegorically using the method of *taʾwīl*, enabling denial of any interpretation of God that limited Him to a physical form.

More important than unity in terms of practical ramifications, as Sophia Vasalou has observed, was the way in which the Muʿtazilī principle of God's justice "percolated into seminal streams of Islamic thought and practice to a greater extent than did the theological discussions of divine unity." She explains: "This was in great part a function of the relations these topics bore to legal thought, in which the values of acts were theorized, making works on legal theory (*uṣūl al-fiqh*) and often substantive law (*fiqh*) vehicles for the expression of theological commitments."[21] The multidimensional nature of the principle of divine justice naturally affected discussions of law, because the discussion of God's justice incorporated inquiries into human action and agency, the nature of good and evil, and, perhaps most importantly, the role of human reason. The foundation of these discussions was Quranic verses in which God declares Himself to be just.[22]

Interpreting these verses literally, the Muʿtazila argued that God's justice means that it is impossible for Him to perform a bad act or to omit an obligation. In relation to human beings, this position entails that

[20] For a more detailed overview of their foundational tenets, see David Bennett, "The Muʿtazilite Movement (II): The Early Muʿtazilites," in Schmidtke, *Oxford Handbook of Islamic Theology*, 142–58.

[21] Vasalou, *Moral Agents and Their Deserts*, 4.

[22] Quran 6:115, 16:90, 21:47, and 57:25.

God judges human beings solely on the basis of their actions, since to do anything else would be "bad." Consequently, God cannot be willfully merciful to an undeserving disbeliever; instead, He is obligated by His justice to punish the disbeliever. In the Muʿtazilī framework, God's obligation to reward and punish, beyond being a simple consequence of the principle of God's justice, became one of the five fundamental doctrines of the school itself – the promise and the threat (*al-waʿd wa-l-waʿīd*). God promises in the Quran to reward those who do good, and therefore He must do so; similarly, God threatens in the Quran to punish wrongdoers, and therefore He must do so. Although the Muʿtazila were criticized for limiting both God's will and God's power by adopting this position, it enabled them to accomplish what many before them had tried:[23] to affirm the absolute free will of individuals.

The doctrine of radical human free will[24] and reason espoused by the Muʿtazila was an outgrowth of their doctrine of divine justice, because it would be unjust of God to to punish individuals who are unable to understand His commands or to act in accordance with them. To affirm free will and reason, the Muʿtazila had to construct an epistemology centered on the human being and on humans' ability to comprehend reality and to formulate accurate knowledge of it. If the capacity of human rationality was limited, there would be no defensible way in which the Muʿtazila could uphold their principle of divine justice. Therefore, free will and the entire epistemological system constructed by the Muʿtazila are paradoxically both a natural consequence and a prerequisite of their interpretation of God's justice. According to Ayman Shihadeh, the Muʿtazilī adoption of the "metaethics" of God's justice within the realm of human activity has six implications: (1) human beings, much like God, are understood to be autonomous agents with autonomous volition; (2) God imposes obligations (*taklīf*), through which humans seek advantage; (3) obligations imposed on humans are in accordance to their capacity as autonomous actors; (4) God is obligated to motivate humans to fulfill their obligations through the promise of reward and the threat of

[23] The earliest known group to assert the complete free will of individuals was the Qadariyya, which existed from approximately 70/690 until the early third/ninth century. For more on the development of the school, its doctrinal assimilation into the Muʿtazilī school, and its relationship with politics, see Josef van Ess, "Ḳadariyya," in *Encyclopaedia of Islam*, 2nd edn.

[24] I am denoting the Muʿtazilī doctrine one of "radical" free will so as to differentiate it from the doctrine of free will espoused by the Ashʿarīs, which assigns a central role to God as the enabler of human action.

punishment; (5) undeserved suffering in the worldly life of an autonomous agent will be compensated in the hereafter; and (6) humans obtain knowledge of the promise of God's reward and the threat of His punishment first by reason and then by revelation.[25] Since the impact of the Muʿtazilī notion of God's justice in human affairs hinges on the autonomous nature of human beings and their ability to understand and act on obligations imposed on them by God, the primary duty of autonomous individuals must be to *know* the obligations of God.[26]

Let us turn now to the specifics of Muʿtazilī thought in Nishapur. Since a critical edition of the work of Abū Rashīd al-Nīsābūrī, ʿAbd al-Jabbār's representative and successor, has not yet been published,[27] I will rely primarily on ʿAbd al-Jabbār's magnum opus, *al-Mughnī fī abwāb al-tawḥīd wa-l-ʿadl*, to explicate the epistemology of the Muʿtazila.[28] As a starting point, it should be noted that the Muʿtazilī emphasis on individual rationalism is often characterized as *radical* because human beings are equally morally responsible whether or not they have received the revelatory message of God through a prophet or a scripture. This means that

25 Shihadeh, "Theories of Ethical Value."

26 Frank, in various articles, analyzes the various consequences of Basran Muʿtazila in relation to human agency. See Richard Frank, "Remarks on the Early Development of Kalām"; Frank, "Two Islamic Views of Agency," in *La Notion de liberté au Moyen Âge: Islam, Byzance, Occident* (Paris: Les Belles Lettres, 1983), 37–49; Frank, "Reason and Revealed Law: A Sample of Parallels and Divergences in Kalām and Falsafa," *Recherches d'Islamologie: Recueil d'articles offerts à Georges C. Anawati et Louis Gardet* (Louvain: Peeters, 1978), 123–38; and Frank, "Currents and Countercurrents in the Muʿtazila, Ashʿarites and al-Ghazālī," in *Islam: Essays on Scripture, Thought and Society; A Festschrift in Honour of Anthony Johns*, ed. P. G. Riddell and T. Street (Leiden: Brill, 1997), 113–34.

27 I have learned since writing this chapter that a critical edition of Abū Rashīd al-Nīsābūrī's text *Kitāb Masāʾil al-khilāf fī al-uṣūl* is being prepared by Hassan Ansari and Sabine Schmidtke. Schmidtke also notes another work of his, *Kitāb Masāʾil fī al-khilāf bayna al-Baṣriyyīn wa-l-Baghdādiyyīn*. See also Daniel Gimaret, "Pour servir à la lecture des *Masāʾil* d'Abū Rašīd al-Nīsābūrī," *Bulletin d'études orientales* 60 (2011): 11–38.

28 Abū al-Ḥasan ʿAbd al-Jabbār, *al-Mughnī fī abwāb al-tawḥīd wa-l-ʿadl*, ed. Muḥammad Muṣṭafā Ḥilmī et al. (Cairo: al-Dār al-Miṣriyya li-l-Taʾlīf wa-l-Nashr, 1960–69). In addition to ʿAbd al-Jabbār's *Mughnī*, another important text is his *al-Muḥīṭ bi-l-taklīf*, for which the commentary of his student Ibn Mattawayh is available: *Kitāb al-Majmūʿ fī al-Muḥīṭ bi-l-taklīf*, ed. J. J. Houben (Beirut: Imprimerie Catholique, 1965). For a list of ʿAbd al-Jabbār's works, see Johannes Maria Peters, *God's Created Speech: A Study in the Speculative Theology of ʿAbd al-Jabbār* (Leiden: Brill, 1976), 11–14. The earliest noteworthy expositions of ʿAbd al-Jabbār's epistemology in English are Peters, *God's Created Speech*, and George Hourani, *Reason and Tradition in Islamic Ethics* (Cambridge: Cambridge University Press, 1985). The former has been instrumental for the present study in navigating the epistemological contours of ʿAbd al-Jabbār's thought.

individuals have the rational capability to recognize truth, and good and evil, regardless of revelation.

On the most fundamental level, ʿAbd al-Jabbār casts the acquisition of knowledge as an inquiry into a thing (*shayʾ*) with the express purpose of affirmation (*ithbāt*) or negation (*nafi*). The former entails either affirmation of the existence of a thing or affirmation that it is in a true state of affairs.[29] The latter entails negating the existence of a thing or the assertion that it is in an untrue state of affairs. After the individual has either negated or affirmed the subject of their inquiry, the knowledge (*ʿilm*) resulting from this inquiry may be divided into two categories – necessary (*ḍarūrī*) or acquired/speculative (*muktasab/naẓarī*).[30] The first of these is further subdivided into *direct* or *indirect* knowledge, with the first occurring without any preconditions[31] and referring to any state (*ḥāl*) in which individuals find themselves as a result of either experience or nonexperience. According to ʿAbd al-Jabbār, knowledge that is the result of experience includes rules of logic and argumentation that the human being acquires solely through experience. Knowledge obtained through nonexperience includes knowledge of basic ethical postulates of good and evil. Indirect necessary knowledge, by contrast, is knowledge generated (*tawallud*) through something else, the primary example being knowledge produced through sensory apprehension. Since the senses are technically "generating" this knowledge, it is not considered direct but rather indirect.

It may seem odd that knowledge of logic, argumentation, and ethics is classified as direct and necessary knowledge whereas sensory knowledge is considered indirect, so it is useful to pause to gain a deeper understanding of what ʿAbd al-Jabbār means by necessary knowledge more broadly. He describes it as "the knowledge which occurs in us, not from ourselves"

[29] For a thing (*shayʾ*) to be in a true state of affairs means that it corresponds (*muṭābiq*) to reality. If it corresponds to reality and knowledge of it is reached through sound reason, it is classified as knowledge (*ʿilm*). If, on the other hand, the thing is determined not to correspond to reality, it is classified as falsehood or ignorance (*jahl*). For more, see Ayman Shihadeh, "The Argument from Ignorance and Its Critics in Medieval Arabic Thought," *Arabic Sciences and Philosophy* 23 (2013): 175–76.

[30] Here I utilize Peters's classification of ʿAbd al-Jabbār's system in his *God's Created Speech*, which differs from Hourani's in *Reason and Tradition*. There are a variety of ways to translate the terms *ḍarūrī*, *muktasab*, and *naẓarī*. Shihadeh suggests "immediate" (*ḍarūrī*), "acquired" (*muktasab*), and "discursive" (*naẓarī*). However, for reasons that will become clear in the course of my comparison of the Muʿtazilī and Ashʿarī epistemological frameworks, the above translation of the terms is most fitting.

[31] ʿAbd al-Jabbār, *Sharḥ al-Uṣūl al-khamsa*, 50.

and "the knowledge we cannot in any way banish from our soul."[32] In other words, it is knowledge occurring in the individual not by virtue of independent reflection, but through God. While at first glance it may seem as if knowledge of argumentation and ethics is derived through reason and reflection, 'Abd al-Jabbār maintains that the foundational elements of both are supplied to the intellect *directly* by God. These basic foundations, then, become the basis for all subsequent reflection the individual undertakes. Sensory knowledge, by contrast, is not given *directly* by God but rather is created by the senses, and it is therefore considered indirect. The directness or indirectness of knowledge is thus a function of how the knowledge is produced in the individual's mind in relation to God.

As for the second type of knowledge, speculative (*naẓarī*) or acquired (*muktasab*) knowledge, this is "drawn from other knowledge-items already present in the knower's mind through the process of speculative reasoning (*naẓar*) or cognition (*fikr*). If it reflects soundly, the mind must rely on proper evidence (*dalīl*), be it either rational (*'aqlī*) or scriptural (*samī'*), and by this means arrive at a new knowledge-item, referred to as 'what is evidenced' (*madlūl*, *madlūl 'alayhī*)."[33] Broadly speaking, speculative knowledge is any knowledge resulting from individual intellectual efforts to apprehend the reality of a given thing. However, this knowledge, too, relies on divine assistance. The basic process of attaining knowledge through speculation consists of isolating an indication (*dalīl*) that guides the individual toward the thing indicated (*madlūl*), producing knowledge. If the individual's process of reasoning is correct, it is understood that God has placed the indications in such a way that sound reasoning will naturally generate (*tawallud*) real knowledge.[34] The consequence of this theory is that ultimately all knowledge is given to human beings by God. Peters summarizes this conclusion in an important passage:

> Hence, in the eyes of 'Abd al-Jabbār there is no purely human knowledge; the only thing man can do and even has to do (because it belongs to the duties imposed upon him) is to reflect (*naẓar*) upon the knowledge God gave to him, and to acquire in this way further knowledge, which is as certain as the knowledge God gave to him; this reflection is always based upon an indication (*dalīl*) which God has placed for mankind. By way of conclusion, we say that God gives knowledge

32 Peters, *God's Created Speech*, 54. 33 Shihadeh, "Argument from Ignorance," 174.

34 'Abd al-Jabbār, *al-Mughnī*, 12:11–15, 69–70, 100–102. 'Abd al-Jabbār notes that there are four types of connections between the indication (*dalīl*) and the thing indicated (*madlūl*). See the discussion in Peters, *God's Created Speech*, 66–69, and 'Abd al-Jabbār, *al-Mughnī*, 12:48–51.

to mankind in two ways: either directly in the heart of every single individual – and we call this intuition or *ʿaql* – or through His prophets and the community of believers – and this we call revelation or *samʿ* – but ultimately all knowledge is divine.[35]

If all human knowledge can be attributed to God, either by direct bestowal or through the natural causation present between indications and knowledge, what are the implications for human responsibility? The notion that all human knowledge is in some sense given by God reduces the importance of revelation as God's communication, since every instance of sound or true knowledge acquired by the human being is technically equivalent to revelation. Consequently, contrary to the Ashʿarīs, who argue that human beings have no legal responsibility before they receive divine revelation, ʿAbd al-Jabbār and the Muʿtazila hold that legal responsibility begins as soon as an individual is able to reason properly. At the point of intellectual maturity, the individual is necessarily able to evaluate all actions and assign to them ethical value judgments independent of the actions themselves. Recall that the Muʿtazila consider basic ethical principles *ḍarūrī* knowledge, and thus every human being is naturally endowed with them. This means that human beings will universally and immediately know the goodness of certain actions, such as thanking a benefactor (*shukr al-munʿim*). Knowledge of the ethical value of other acts, which do not fall in the necessary realm, can be attained through reflection. In addition to endorsing ethical inquiry independent of revelation, the Muʿtazila took a step further by arguing that independent ethical value judgments of actions in their circumstances are objective; therefore, individuals are obligated to reason and then act in accordance with their reasoning, and God, because He is just, is obligated to reward and punish individuals on the basis of their actions.

If the object of all knowledge inquiry is either affirmation or negation, then the object of inquiry into human action is to determine which actions are bad (*qabīḥ*) and thus deserve censure (*dhamm*) and which actions are good (*ḥasan*) and thus deserving of praise.[36] If an action is considered good, one of three judgments is applied to it: (1) it is permissible (*mubāḥ*), and therefore the individual can perform it or abstain from it without consequence; (2) it is recommended (*mandūb*) and attracts praise if performed, but no blame if omitted; and (3) it is obligatory (*fardh/wājib*),

[35] Peters, *God's Created Speech*, 92.

[36] For these general definitions, see ʿAbd al-Jabbār, *al-Mughnī*, 12:14. For a more detailed view, see Peters, *God's Created Speech*, 87–88.

entailing praise if it is performed and censure if it is omitted. If an act is considered bad, an individual who performs it is censured. The link between the typology of human action and the epistemology described earlier lies in the nature of human knowledge of the value of actions. For Muʿtazilīs, the basic "goodness" or "badness" of actions falls within the realm of necessary knowledge granted by God. This means that these values are objective, existing beyond the subjective evaluations of the individual. What, then, is the place of human subjectivity and the diversity of human reasoning in this equation?

Subjective human reasoning enters the Muʿtazilī framework in the form of moral axioms that are not part of necessary knowledge. Such axioms are considered acquired and are the product of human reflection. The Muʿtazila thus distinguish between self-evident moral axioms that constitute necessary knowledge and other, acquired moral axioms that are the result of reasoning and reflection on foundational moral axioms. Early scholars of Muʿtazilī ethics such as George Hourani interpreted this system as ethical or moral objectivism. According to Hourani, moral objectivism is "any theory which affirms that value has a real existence in particular things or acts, regardless of the wishes or opinions of any judge or observer as such."[37] As Hourani sees it, not only do values such as goodness and badness have real existence from the Muʿtazilī perspective, but they inhere in acts – regardless of circumstances. Later scholars such as Shihadeh have argued convincingly that this view of Muʿtazilism is not entirely correct and that it is more accurate to understand the Muʿtazilī system of moral reasoning as supporting a form of "ethical realism" in which acts do not have essences but rather possess attributes.[38] This distinction relates to the Muʿtazilī definition of an action or act as an "accident" (*ʿaraḍ*). As such, an act or action cannot have an ethical value in its essence; rather, it is accompanied by a "configuration" (*wajh*)[39] that imbues it with an attribute (*ḥukm* or *ṣifa*) that gives it a moral value. Given that the action itself does not have an essence, it is its occurrence that endows it with an ethical value, meaning that "all acts without exception can occur upon a certain *wajh* and be good, and upon

[37] Hourani, "Two Theories of Value," 269. [38] Shihadeh, "Theories of Ethical Value."

[39] Vasalou notes that *wajh* is a particularly difficult term to translate because of the issue of causality. She translates it as "act-description" or "ground" depending on the context, whereas I have adopted "configuration," the translation used by Shihadeh. Vasalou also notes various other translations of the term, such as "ground" by George Hourani and "aspect" and "way" by Jan Peters. For the full discussion, see Vasalou, *Moral Agents and Their Deserts*, 200.

a different *wajh* and be bad."[40] The goodness or badness of an action is thus not essential to the act but rather the cause of specific configurations accompanying it. The terminology of moral objectivism misses the subtlety of the Muʿtazilī view that acts are objectively good or bad in specific circumstances, but a change in circumstances will bring about a change in the ethical value of the action. This means that ethical properties, instead of being connected to actions, are connected to distinct attributes: "'bad' [is connected] to badness, or the act's 'being bad,' 'good' to goodness, 'recommended' to recommendedness and 'obligatory' to obligatoriness," with each attribute conditioned on the circumstances of the action.[41]

The implication of the Muʿtazilī belief in ethical realism is that individuals should be able to ascertain the attribute and the legal value of an action through sound reasoning. Consequently, legal obligation (*taklīf*) vis-à-vis God is not subject to revelation; rather, once individuals are capable of reasoning, they are legally responsible in the eyes of God. Revelation, however, is still useful because it serves human beings' welfare (*maṣlaḥa*), and some Muʿtazilīs went as far as to say that it is obligatory for God to provide revelation even though it does not establish the moral value of an action – the purpose of revelation is to assist the human being in apprehending truths rationally, to bolster conclusions that the human being has already reached, or to provide particulars for norms already understood in their general form.[42] Abū Hāshim argued that the best way to understand the role of revelation is through the concept of *lutf* (assistance), defined by Vasalou as "the acts by which God provided human beings with the assistance necessary for them to fulfill the obligations imposed on them."[43] She continues, "Revelation then was considered to be good (and indeed obligatory for God to provide) by way of conferring assistance to and serving the welfare (*maṣlaḥa*) of human beings in their fulfillment of the rationally known truths."[44]

[40] Shihadeh, "Theories of Ethical Value," 392. [41] Ibid., 392.

[42] Vasalou, *Moral Agents and Their Deserts*, 50. Vasalou notes that there was also a difference between the Basran and Baghdadi Muʿtazila with regard to the role of God more broadly: the Basrans held that by providing human beings with revelation, God was maximizing their ability to attain otherworldly benefit, but God was not required to benefit their worldly affairs in a more active manner. The Baghdadis disagreed and claimed that God plays an assistive role vis-à-vis human beings in both worldly and otherworldly matters. See ibid., 39.

[43] Ibid., 49. [44] Ibid., 49.

In this manner, the function of revealed injunctions is instrumental: "they are obligatory insofar as they are a means for one's performing acts that are intrinsically obligatory, and eschewing acts intrinsically evil, and thus do not themselves constitute independent grounds for reward and punishment."[45] Being instrumental, revelation is not seen as the repository of objective moral truths – that role is played by the intellect. As a corollary, because revelation in general is aimed at the welfare of individuals, it is necessarily conditioned by circumstances, as what may support people's welfare in one context may not do so in another. Revealed injunctions thus emerge as particular and relative, supporting the notion that revealed norms do not possess the same universal status as do self-evident moral axioms. Accordingly, Mu'tazilī scholars distinguish between rationally derived responsibility (*taklīf 'aqliyya*), which is universal, and responsibility resulting from revealed injunctions, which is particular. This view is summarized in the following statement by 'Abd al-Jabbār:

> The special character of revealed laws (*sharā'i'*) is founded on variations in the situations of the subjects of the Law, and variations in time, place, and the conditions of acts ... So how could it be proved through reason [alone] that prayer without purification does not lead a person to perform what is obligatory but rather leads him to do what is evil, whereas when it occurs in a state of purification, it leads one to do what is obligatory and leads one to refrain from shameful and unjust deeds?[46]

The Basran stance on the particularity of revelation is especially salient in this passage, as 'Abd al-Jabbār notes that revealed injunctions can differ based on circumstance. As a result, revealed prescriptions cannot be seen as uniform moral truths, since they are always conditioned by the circumstances of their revelation.

In the Mu'tazilī conceptualization of moral values, law, and revelation, individuals have a dual responsibility – first, to use reason to know the law, and second, to follow it. This raises the important question of what happens if people fail to fulfill one of these responsibilities or, more importantly, if they use reason incorrectly. If God's justice is intimately connected to His punishment and reward of individuals on the basis of their fulfillment or nonfulfillment of their obligations, does this, by extension, entail that God must punish individuals for faulty reasoning? And if rational moral judgments, as opposed to revealed prescriptions, are deemed objective, is there any way that people can disagree on them?

[45] Ibid., 49. [46] Ibid., 50.

As noted earlier, for the Muʿtazila there are two main moral values: goodness (*ḥusn*) and evil (*qubḥ*). The former applies to all actions deemed obligatory (*wājib*), recommended (*mandūb*), or permissible (*mubāh*), whereas the latter pertains only to evil actions from which it is necessary to abstain. Vasalou argues that this typology of moral values represents only one-half of the structural scheme of values constructed by the Muʿtazila. The other half, she maintains, is centered on rights (*ḥuqūq*) and is both more instructive with regard to the Muʿtazilī theory of value and more illustrative of the relationship between revelation, reason, and law.

Vasalou's assertion is based on conclusions derived from a close reading of ʿAbd al-Jabbār's *Mughnī*, where legal discussions often arise amid discussions of repentance (*tawba*), defined not simply as regret over an evil action committed and a resolve not to repeat it but also as a "restoration of the normative order of the world, and in particular, the order dictated by the crucial normative currency of *ḥuqūq* (rights)."[47] The basic idea here is that it is not enough to feel internal repentance for one's action – remorse must be coupled with external action to rectify any harm caused to other actors. This notion of external restoration is based on the premise that an individual actor either has a right or claim to something or someone (*ḥaqq lahu*) or is the subject of a claim or an obligation owed to someone else (*ḥaqq ʿalayhī*). If a person's action leads to a violation of another person, part of the actor's repentance must involve redressing the perpetrated wrong. The claims of individual actors in the world (*ḥuqūq ādamī* or *ḥuqūq li-l-ʿibād*) are obligations, and according to ʿAbd al-Jabbār, they constitute necessary or self-evident knowledge (*ʿilm ḍarūrī*). The example that ʿAbd al-Jabbār uses throughout his *Mughnī* is theft – if an individual wrongfully takes the property of another, then by virtue of reason the thief must know that the action was evil, that he or she has violated the rights of another, and that the property must be returned. Therefore, every action is evaluated both from the perspective of its moral value as good or evil and from the perspective of rights, whether the rights of others have been violated or not; if they have been, what needs to be done is to redress the wrong. Crucially, it is the violation of the rights of others that entails punishment, not the moral value of the act per se.[48] And although there may be some disagreement between rational actors with regard to the moral value of an act (that is, its classification as

[47] Ibid., 41. [48] Ibid., 61.

obligatory, recommended, or permissible), there should be no disagreement over the violation of rights, since recognition of such violations is considered part of necessary knowledge, unlike the specific classification of actions, which is acquired (*muktasab*).

In sum, the Mu'tazila divide knowledge broadly into necessary knowledge and acquired knowledge. The former consists of axiomatic moral principles and knowledge of the rights (*ḥuqūq*) of individuals. This knowledge enables the individual to uncover the basic moral value of an action as either good or evil. These moral values are objective and form the basis of all other moral conclusions that the individual may reach. The second category of knowledge, acquired knowledge, consists of moral values discovered through reasoned reflection on axiomatic moral knowledge or the notion of rights. The legal and moral values derived through the intellect are epistemically certain, as they are the result of indications God has placed on Earth for the judicious intellect to reason from, but they are not intrinsic to the action; therefore, in undertaking an action, the individual must take into consideration the circumstances (*wajh*) of the action and, importantly, whether it violates another's right or claim. In the Mu'tazilī system, therefore, all legal and moral values relate to the intellect and are epistemically certain, but they differ in their classification as necessary knowledge (and therefore reflective of intrinsic moral values) or acquired knowledge (reflective of circumstantial moral values or considerations). Since all moral values, and by extension all legal values, lie within the domain of rational reflection, the importance of revelation is truncated. Revelation is aimed at supporting human welfare (*maṣlaḥa*) by providing psychological incentives for action through the promise of reward and the threat of punishment or by supplying details regarding moral actions already identified by reason.

For the Mu'tazila's Ash'arī interlocutors, this circumscribed and limited conception of revelation was unacceptable, as it rendered revelation almost entirely superfluous. In the realm of law, in particular, Mu'tazilī epistemology had a series of important, interrelated implications:

(1) The centrality of human reason makes legal responsibility contingent on a well-functioning intellect as opposed to clear revelatory injunctions. By extension, law is a matter of universal recognition rather than of Godly creation.
(2) The elevated status of reason entails a moral universalism in which every action has a moral value that can be ascertained rationally, though moral values can differ as circumstances vary.

(3) The moral and legal values ascertained by individuals are epistemically certain, since they are the result of either necessary knowledge, given by God, or acquired knowledge, reached on the basis of indications God has placed in the world that engender (*tawallud*) specific judgments.
(4) Given that the moral values of actions can be attained with epistemic certainty without recourse to revelation, revelation simply serves the benefit of believers by supporting the conclusions of a judicious intellect.

The epistemology of the Muʿtazila, and especially its ramifications with respect to law, was squarely rejected by the Ashʿarīs. While the latter maintained the Muʿtazila's broad categories of knowledge in their counterepistemology, the Ashʿarīs emphasized the power of God over His creation, resulting in an epistemology in which the law is ultimately contingent on revelation and God rather than human reason.

ASHʿARĪ EPISTEMOLOGY AND ITS LEGAL CONSEQUENCES

Unlike the Muʿtazila, who traveled the well-trodden road to Nishapur after being forced into exile elsewhere, the Ashʿarīs enjoyed a more organic relationship with both the land and its people. As noted in Chapter 1, Ashʿarī scholars moved to Nishapur between 290/902 and 343/955 at the invitation of Abū Sahl al-Ṣuʿlukī (d. 369/980). The influx of Ashʿarīs into Nishapur included four important scholars: Abū Bakr Ibn Fūrak (d. 406/1015), Abū Isḥāq al-Isfarāyīnī (d. 418/1027), Abū Bakr al-Bāqillānī (d. 403/1013), and Abū Manṣūr ʿAbd al-Qāhir al-Baghdādī (d. 429/1037). Of these scholars, al-Bāqillānī would have the greatest influence on al-Juwaynī. The migration of Ashʿarīs into Nishapur took place during the lifetime of al-Ashʿarī (d. 324/936) himself and can be seen as an attempt by early Ashʿarīs to create an Ashʿarī stronghold in the east while the Basran Muʿtazilī school was gaining strength under the leadership of Abū ʿAlī al-Jubbāʾī, and subsequently his son Abū Hāshim, in the west.

Abū al-Ḥasan ʿAlī b. Ismāʿīl al-Ashʿarī was born in 260/873 in Basra, the epicenter of Muʿtazilism.[49] Exposed to Muʿtazilī thought from

[49] For more on al-Ashʿarī's thought, see Richard McCarthy, *The Theology of al-Ashʿarī* (Beirut: Imprimerie Catholique, 1953); Frank, *Early Islamic Theology*; and Watt, *Free Will and Predestination*, 135–50.

a young age, he rose to become Abū ʿAlī's top student alongside Abū Hāshim. However, three years before the death of his teacher in 303/915,[50] al-Ashʿarī abandoned Muʿtazilī teachings and began to articulate a theological vision that gave priority to revelation and God's power over all elements of creation. Although the primacy of revelation and God's majesty had been emphasized before, most prominently by Aḥmad Ibn Ḥanbal (d. 241/855),[51] al-Ashʿarī's synthesis of reason and revelation eventually came to constitute an independent theological vision. By rejecting Muʿtazilī epistemology and giving a central role to revelation, Ashʿarī scholars had to articulate an alternative epistemology reflecting their own conclusions regarding the place of reason within a schema dominated by revelation. Like the framework articulated by the Muʿtazila, the Ashʿarī epistemological framework had pervasive implications within the realm of law.

Given that the bulk of al-Juwaynī's education took place in Nishapur, the best avenue for gaining insight into the epistemology he inherited is through the works of Ashʿarīs in Nishapur that were written before and during his lifetime, such as those of Abū Bakr Muḥammad b. al-Ṭayyib al-Bāqillānī (d. 403/1013),[52] whom al-Juwaynī himself praises as his intellectual predecessor. Abū Bakr al-Bāqillānī, who is counted among one of the

[50] Several different reasons are proposed for al-Ashʿarī's abrupt departure from his teacher. Most popular is the story of the three brothers, but the veracity of this account has been disputed by Rosalind Gwynne. See Gwynne, "Al-Jubbāʾī, al-Ashʿarī and the Three Brothers: The Uses of Fiction," *Muslim World* 75, nos. 3–4 (2007): 132–61. According to Watt, al-Ashʿarī parted ways with the Muʿtazila after having three dreams in which the Prophet exhorted him to defend the true teachings of Islam. For this narrative of events, see Watt, *Islamic Philosophy and Theology*, 65.

[51] For Ibn Ḥanbal's understanding of revelation and its relationship to law, see Susan A. Spectorsky, "Aḥmad Ibn Ḥanbal's Fiqh," *Journal of the American Oriental Society* 102, no. 3 (1982): 461–65; Yasir Qadhi, "Salafī-Ashʿarī Polemics of the 3rd and 4th Islamic Centuries," *Muslim World* 106, no. 3 (2016): 433–47; and Christopher Melchert, "Aḥmad ibn Ḥanbal and the Qur'an," *Journal of Qur'anic Studies* 6, no. 2 (2004): 22–34.

[52] The selection of al-Bāqillānī as a representative is by no means random, as he was an immediate predecessor of al-Juwaynī and carried tremendous intellectual weight. Perhaps most importantly, al-Juwaynī's first legal treatise, *al-Talkhīs*, was actually a commentary on and abridgment of al-Bāqillānī's magnum opus, the *Taqrīb*. Al-Juwaynī is also quoted as saying, "I would never utter a single word about *ʿilm al-kalām* until I had memorized twelve thousand pages of the words of al-Qāḍī Abū Bakr." See al-Subkī, *Ṭabaqāt al-Shāfiʿiyya*, 5:193. For more on al-Bāqillānī, see Yusuf Ibish, *The Political Doctrine of al-Bāqillānī* (Beirut: American University of Beirut, 1966), and Ibish, "Life and Works of al-Bāqillānī," *Islamic Studies* 4, no. 3 (1965): 225–236. See also the works of Eric Chaumont, available primarily in French.

central scholars of early Islamic intellectual thought, began his life in Basra and then relocated to Baghdad, where the intellectual environment was ripe for the cultivation of scholarship. He remained in Baghdad until his death. It was there, under the tutelage of senior disciples of al-Ashʿarī, that al-Bāqillānī quickly rose to prominence, attracting an independent following and becoming known as one of the first Ashʿarī scholars to provide a systematic articulation of the doctrines of the school.[53] Of the fifty-two works he penned, as enumerated by al-Qāḍī ʿIyād b. Mūsā al-Yaḥṣubī (d. 544/1123), six are extant in toto and some others in part.[54] The most advanced of the intact works are *al-Tamhīd* and *al-Taqrīb wa-l-irshād*.[55] In presenting al-Bāqillānī's epistemology, I will rely primarily on the *Tamhīd*, with some additions taken from the *Taqrīb*. The *Tamhīd* is divided into seven sections, each focusing on a distinct inquiry: (1) the reality of knowledge, (2) the types of knowledge, (3) necessary knowledge, (4) reason-based knowledge, (5) the means of perception of knowledge (*madārik*), (6) deduction (*al-istidlāl*), and (7) the types of intelligible things (*al-maʿlūmāt*).

After the standard salutatory introduction and brief description of the contents of the text, al-Bāqillānī commences with the section on the reality of knowledge. In this first inquiry, al-Bāqillānī defines knowledge (*ʿilm*) as "the knowing of something knowable (*al-maʿlūm*) as it truly is."[56] He

[53] Rosenthal, *Knowledge Triumphant*, 103.

[54] Al-Qāḍī ʿIyād presents a biography of al-Bāqillānī as well as a list of his writings in his book on preeminent Mālikī scholars, entitled *Tartīb al-madārik wa-taqrīb al-masālik li-maʿrifat aʿlām madhhab Mālik* (Beirut: Dār al-Kutub al-ʿIlmiyya, 1998). Al-Bāqillānī's largest work of *kalām* is his *Hidāyat al-mustarshidīn*, which is said to have comprised at least sixteen volumes, though only four have survived. For more on this important work, see Sabine Schmidtke, "Early Ashʿarī Theology: Abū Bakr al-Bāqillānī (d. 403/1013) and His *Hidayāt al-Mustarshidīn*," *Bulletin d'études orientales* 60 (2011): 39–71.

[55] Abū Bakr Muḥammad b. al-Ṭayyib b. al-Bāqillānī, *Kitāb Tamhīd al-awāʾil wa-talkhīṣ al-dalāʾil* (Beirut: al-Maktaba al-Sharqiyya, 1957); al-Bāqillānī, *al-Taqrīb wa-l-irshād* (Beirut: al-Risāla, 1993). Before proceeding, it should be noted that although I am portraying this as al-Bāqillānī's epistemology, little is known about the systems of his predecessors, such as Abū Ḥamīd al-Isfarāyīnī or the eponym of the school, al-Ashʿarī himself. Because of the paltry number of surviving sources from this early period, it is quite plausible that some of al-Bāqillānī's ideas actually originate with his predecessors or are products of contemporary cross-fertilization. With this disclaimer, my discussion of al-Bāqillānī should be understood as a limited synopsis. For more on early Ashʿarī thought, see Richard Frank, *Classical Islamic Theology: The Ashʿarites*, vol. 3 of *Texts and Studies on the Development and History of Kalām*, ed. Dimitri Gutas (Aldershot: Ashgate, 2008).

[56] Al-Bāqillānī, *al-Tamhīd*, 6, and *al-Taqrīb*, 174. He provides the same definition in both texts; however, in the *Taqrīb* he also accepts the use of other words aside from *maʿlūm* as long as they emphasize the idea of knowing.

defends this conceptualization against the competing definition of the Muʿtazila, "the knowing of a thing (*shay*ʾ) as it truly is." The Ashʿarīs took issue with the Muʿtazilī definition because "thing" can refer to anything in existence regardless of its substance or essence. The problem emerges because God's knowledge is considered eternal, so if the objects of God's knowledge are "things," then these things must be eternal with him. For the Ashʿarīs, only God is eternal, necessitating a rejection of any definition of knowing that includes the knowing of a "thing." In addition to the problem of coeternity that thinghood produces, al-Bāqillānī notes that the word *shay*ʾ fails to cover the impossible (*muḥāl*) as a possible object of cognition.[57] The terminology is of paramount importance because al-Bāqillānī's phrasing allows the individual to have knowledge of something that lacks a material form, whereas the usage of the word *shay*ʾ limits knowledge to material, perceivable objects.[58] By acknowledging the potential immateriality of the object of knowledge, al-Bāqillānī provides a more expansive definition of "knowing" that is able to move beyond the world of sensory perception. This seemingly broad definition, encapsulating material and immaterial existence, the finite and the infinite, is constrained by the final part of the definition, which states that knowledge must correspond to reality or, in al-Bāqillānī's words, that knowledge of something consists of knowing it "as it really is."

After providing a definition of knowledge, al-Bāqillānī divides knowledge into what is eternal (*qadīm*) and what is created (*muḥdath*). Eternal knowledge is limited to God's knowledge, as it is ever-present and encompasses all knowledge of the created world. Conversely, created knowledge belongs to the realm of created beings, be they humans or animals, and is drastically restricted in comparison to God's knowledge. Created knowledge is then further subdivided into necessary knowledge (*ʿilm ḍarūrī*) and speculative and deductive knowledge (*ʿilm al-naẓar wa-l-istidlāl*).[59]

[57] For more on the knowledge of possible things, see Richard Frank, "The Non-Existent and the Possible in Classical Ashʿarite Thinking," *Mélanges de l'Institut dominicain d'études orientales* 24 (2000): 1–37.

[58] In the *Taqrīb*, he similarly debunks other definitions he finds faulty. See al-Bāqillānī, *al-Taqrīb*, 174–78.

[59] Although al-Bāqillānī states that there are two subcategories of created knowledge, immediately afterward he refers to three types of knowledge, so it is not clear whether *naẓar* and *istidlāl* represent one type of knowledge or two. I am treating them as a single type of knowledge following al-Bāqillānī's usage in the *Taqrīb*. He also delves deeper into the types of knowledge in the *Taqrīb*, illustrating the difference between God's knowledge, the knowledge of angels, and the knowledge of human beings. Al-Bāqillānī, *al-Taqrīb*, 183–85.

Al-Bāqillānī defines the former, much as the Muʿtazila did, as knowledge that is self-evident and imposed on an individual so that it is impossible for him or her to be ignorant of it unless extenuating circumstances such as insanity or temporary unconsciousness impede the individual's basic cognitive capacity. Because this type of knowledge occupies a privileged position in al-Bāqillānī's schema, it is fixed by conditions and parameters delineated later in his text.

In Section 5, al-Bāqillānī expands on the notion of necessary knowledge, starting with the assertion that the most basic and apparent type of necessary knowledge is that obtained through the five senses.[60] Following sensory knowledge, other forms of necessary knowledge include knowledge of the self, of internal states, and of bodily pain. Encapsulated in the idea of internal states are two other types of knowledge: knowledge from intentionality, including any resolve the human being has, whether executed or not, and knowledge of external emotional states exhibited by others and apprehended by an onlooker through, for example, the facial expressions a person displays when angry, sad, or brave.[61] Beyond the realm of internal knowledge is the fifth and final form of necessary knowledge – knowledge gained from reports transmitted by large numbers of people (*al-akhbār al-mutawātir*), which I will call simply concurrent reports. These include, for example, knowledge of lands not visited and of the existence of bygone historical figures, especially prophets.[62] Though this knowledge differs substantively from the other types of necessary knowledge in that it is not derived from the senses or internal understanding, al-Bāqillānī argues for its equivalence because one cannot doubt the veracity of knowledge attested to by masses of people.[63] Any knowledge obtained outside these five avenues, then, inhabits the second division in al-Bāqillānī's schema, namely, speculative and deductive knowledge (*ʿilm al-naẓar wa-l-istidlāl*).

Up to this point in the *Tamhīd*, al-Bāqillānī has largely bypassed any discussion of the intellect or reason (*al-ʿaql*) in his presentation of necessary knowledge, even though reason forms the basis of many of his assertions. By contrast, his larger work, *al-Taqrīb*, does contain an elaborate discussion of the intellect as forming the basis of the classification of

[60] Al-Bāqillānī, *al-Tamhīd*, 9. A parallel discussion can be found in the *Taqrīb*, 188.
[61] Al-Bāqillānī, *al-Tamhīd*, 10. [62] Ibid.
[63] Al-Bāqillānī gives a similar treatment of historical reports in his *Taqrīb*, but he digresses within this treatment to discuss his position on the debate regarding the intrinsic goodness or badness of actions. See al-Bāqillānī, *al-Taqrīb*, 193.

knowledge that he proposes in the *Tamhīd*. In the *Taqrīb*, al-Bāqillānī argues that the intellect, rather than being a mere tool for reasoning, is actually a constitutive element of necessary knowledge.[64] This does not mean that the intellect encompasses *all* necessary knowledge, as some types of necessary knowledge, especially historical knowledge, continue to accrue throughout one's life; but the intellect can never be devoid of all knowledge. Knowledge is therefore always imbricated in the individual by virtue of his or her existence, and it accumulates further as the individual continues to reason.

However, knowledge innate to the individual and knowledge acquired by the individual are not epistemically equivalent, and this difference is reflected in the terminological distinction between necessary knowledge and acquired knowledge. Al-Bāqillānī argues that knowledge classified as necessary is epistemically certain because it cannot be divorced from the intellect, partly because elements of it are always contained within the intellect and partly because the intellect is unable to accept doubt, suspicion, or suspension regarding it. The impenetrable nature of this knowledge results in its classification as certain (*qaṭʿī*), and once it settles in the intellect, it becomes part of it. Such knowledge thus possesses an epistemic primacy not afforded to speculative knowledge.

If necessary knowledge is innately present in the individual or naturally attained without reflection, then speculative and deductive knowledge stands in contrast to it, being the result of formalized proofs, significant reflection, or interpretation. Al-Bāqillānī states that this type of knowledge is synonymous with acquired knowledge (*al-ʿilm al-kasbī*),[65] as the prerequisite for both is the presence of reason; however, his terminology of *ʿilm al-naẓar wa-l-istidlāl* is more accurate because it indicates the central processes necessary to attain this knowledge – reasoning and deduction. Asserting that the processes of reasoning are innumerable, al-Bāqillānī limits himself to presenting two: clear reasoning and oblique reasoning. Clear reasoning takes place when the knowledge sought can be ascertained through a simple process of categorization wherein premises

64 Before providing his definition of the intellect, al-Bāqillānī presents definitions put forward by others, such as the idea of the intellect as an atom (*jawhar*) or as matter (*mādda*); he then systematically rebuts these definitions. He supports his own definition by noting that it is agreed upon by the majority of theologians. Ibid., 195.

65 In the *Taqrīb*, al-Bāqillānī goes into greater detail regarding the equivalence of *ʿilm al-naẓar wa-l-istidlāl* and *ʿilm kasbī*. He also states that *kasbī* knowledge is divided into two types, though the second category seems to overlap with *ʿilm ḍarūrī*. See al-Bāqillānī, *al-Taqrīb*, 185–87.

are either dismissed as false or accepted as true on the basis of proofs (*dalāʾil*). The individual in this case does not struggle or tarry in either affirmation or negation of the various premises and is swiftly able to affirm one or the other conclusion.[66] By way of example, al-Bāqillānī argues that the investigation into the createdness of the world is simple because there are only two possibilities: either the world is created or it is not created. Through reasoning, an individual will recognize that everything in nature is created and, by extension, that the world must be created, too. By rejecting the assertion that the world is eternal, one confirms the assertion that it is created.[67] Such binary situations contrast with propositions that do not accept simple categorization and require more mental exertion from the reasoner. Al-Bāqillānī describes three problems that may arise given the complexity involved in such cases: (1) the overwhelming abundance of proofs (*dalāʾil*) may cause the intellect to waver between various options; (2) the plentitude of propositions may prevent easy categorization; and (3) the proofs may be only tangentially related to the propositions at hand and thus do not aid affirmation or negation.[68] Two of the three problems are connected to proofs, which can either simplify or complicate the process of categorization. For al-Bāqillānī, proofs are of central importance to speculative knowledge because he conceptualizes them as indications that are not established but rather recognized by the senses and that help the reasoner arrive at conclusions that are not easily apparent. If the proofs are unclear, it will be difficult for the individual to reflect sufficiently and accurately on the propositions being evaluated.[69]

Proofs in this sense are utilized only for speculative knowledge and provide another way of distinguishing between speculative knowledge and necessary knowledge. By using proofs, the reasoner is able not only to assess various premises but also to abate doubt, suspicion, and confusion. However, speculative knowledge, unlike necessary knowledge, nonetheless remains open to the possibility of doubt, which impacts its epistemic strength: whereas necessary knowledge is immune to doubt and therefore epistemically certain, speculative knowledge is epistemically only probable. Though al-Bāqillānī does not use any consistent terminology to differentiate the epistemic value of speculative knowledge from

[66] Al-Bāqillānī, *al-Tamhīd*, 11. A parallel discussion can be found in the *Taqrīb*, 211.
[67] Al-Bāqillānī, *al-Tamhīd*, 11; *al-Taqrīb*, 217.
[68] Al-Bāqillānī, *al-Tamhīd*, 13; *al-Taqrīb*, 219.
[69] Al-Bāqillānī, *al-Tamhīd*, 13; *al-Taqrīb*, 202.

that of necessary knowledge, he does distinguish between the two on the basis of the mechanisms used to create the knowledge, the resultant knowledge's relationship to doubt, and the final epistemic value of the knowledge created.

The opening sections of al-Bāqillānī's *Tamhīd* provide the reader with the basic elements of his epistemology, which are then fully applied in subsequent investigations. Throughout these discussions, al-Bāqillānī highlights a series of dichotomies. The primary one, between necessary and speculative knowledge, has already been addressed, but this dichotomy stands on a deeper one between God's knowledge, which is eternal, and human knowledge, which is created. Human knowledge is created because it is contingent on reasoning, and although some things are known intuitively, most are comprehended only after a struggle to discover proofs and eliminate doubts. This understanding of knowledge and reason affirms the creative power of the intellect, but the degree of individual comprehension is contingent on the mode of apprehension: knowledge arrived at without the aid of reason is considered necessary and epistemically certain, whereas knowledge ascertained through mechanisms of reasoning is deemed epistemically probable. Since human knowledge is reliant on reason, all human knowledge is also temporal, as it can diminish alongside the cognitive capabilities of an individual.

The legal ramifications of al-Bāqillānī's epistemological framework are not addressed in his *Tamhīd*, but they appear clearly in the *Taqrīb*. Al-Bāqillānī intended the book primarily as a work of jurisprudence (*uṣūl al-fiqh*), and its first major section, which comprises more than a hundred and fifty pages, is dedicated to a discussion of knowledge and its implications for law. Al-Bāqillānī begins by presenting the epistemological framework found in the *Tamhīd*, but subsequently he undertakes a series of secondary investigations, revealing the tangible implications of his epistemology for law. The various discussions can be distilled down to three main questions: (1) What can the individual know with the aid of reason alone, and thus without revelation? (2) What can the individual know only through revelation? (3) What can be known through both reason and revelation?[70] Recall that for the Muʿtazila, the individual, through sound reason, can and should determine the moral and legal values of actions without needing to turn to revelation; revelation merely provides

[70] Al-Bāqillānī brings up these questions later in this section, but they serve as the most direct way to address the main inquiries in this opening section.

the motive for action or details on conclusions already reached by a judicious intellect. In the Muʿtazilī framework, human beings are endowed with legal responsibility (*taklīf ʿaqlī*) prior to receiving revelation. By contrast, the Ashʿarī al-Bāqillānī argues that although people are capable of reasoning before they receive revelation, they have no legal responsibility at that point; and although they may come to certain conclusions regarding their behavior, their actual actions have no otherworldly consequences. In matters of religion, al-Bāqillānī asserts that the only thing an individual *can* know without revelation is that the world is created. That being said, the simple fact that an individual is *capable* of arriving at this conclusion does not make doing so obligatory. The individual, therefore, has no legal or religious responsibility, and any action he or she undertakes, whether in accordance with or in contradiction to later revealed religious dictates, has no consequences in the afterlife.[71]

Since, al-Bāqillānī argues, the intellect is unable to establish the legal value of actions, only revelation can provide the individual with this information. Al-Bāqillānī thus squarely rejects the Muʿtazilī belief that goodness and evil (*taḥsīn wa-taqbīḥ*) can be ascertained independently of revelation. Instead, revelation constitutes the sole repository of legal and moral values.[72] Al-Bāqillānī goes on to define "good" (*ḥasan*) actions as those that the Lawgiver requires the legally responsible individual (*mukallaf*) to perform and "bad" (*qabīḥ*) actions as those that the Lawgiver requires the legally responsible individual to avoid.[73] He concludes: "We condemn the notion that the *ʿaql* by itself can lead to knowledge of the goodness or badness of an act, or its prohibition, permissibility, or obligatoriness. We assert that these rulings are proven only by revelation (*al-sharʿ*), without any consideration given to the *ʿaql*."[74] On this basis, al-Bāqillānī argues that legal values as decided by the Lawgiver also represent moral values. Unlike the Muʿtazila, who uphold the independence of moral values, al-Bāqillānī, and the Ashʿarīs more broadly, claim that what is good and bad is ordained by God and by God alone. George Hourani has labeled this stance theistic subjectivism, since the moral

[71] Al-Bāqillānī, *al-Taqrīb*, 228–30.

[72] Al-Bāqillānī addresses the notion of *taḥsīn wa taqbīh* in various passages; see *Al-Taqrīb*, 120, 123, 202.

[73] Al-Bāqillānī, *al-Taqrīb*, 278–89. [74] Ibid., 105.

values of acts are determined only by God, contrasting it with moral objectivism, the position advocated by the Mu'tazila.[75]

Despite the limitations that al-Bāqillānī and the Ash'arīs place on human reason, they do not altogether exclude it from the process of lawmaking. In answering the final question, namely, what can be known through both reason and revelation, al-Bāqillānī notes that most legal rulings are a result of reason and revelation working in tandem. He states that "knowledge of the rulings for the legally responsible individual is obtained through speculative reasoning (*naẓar*),"[76] but this reasoning is built on revelation. He then goes on to assert, "Know that knowledge of these rulings is reached only by reasoning about certain proofs and foundations (*adilla qāṭi'a wa-amārāt*) that facilitate reflection [in order] to arrive at knowledge of the rulings for legally responsible individuals."[77] Knowledge of legal rulings, therefore, is the product of reasoning from revelation, ultimately making God the sole legislator of the legal as well as the moral value of actions. Al-Bāqillānī goes on to qualify this statement by saying that the process of legal reflection and legal derivation is a specific intellectual endeavor that ought to be undertaken only by those qualified in the science of jurisprudence (*uṣūl al-fiqh*). So, although everyone has the mental capacity to reason alongside taking recourse to revelation, not everyone possesses the technical skills to engage in legal reasoning.

Individuals who engage in legal derivation, according to al-Bāqillānī, arrive at legal rulings in one of two ways: through clear revelatory proofs or, if clear revelatory proofs are unavailable, through reason and analogy from such clear proofs. Rulings derived from clear revelatory proofs, al-Bāqillānī asserts, yield true knowledge (*'ilm*), whereas rulings based on reason and analogy provide probable knowledge (*ghalabat al-ẓann*). From an epistemological perspective, rulings of the first type are legally certain (*qāṭi'*), whereas rulings obtained through indications are only probable (*ẓannī*).[78] Here the question arises of whether an individual is obligated to follow epistemically probable rulings. According to al-Bāqillānī, once revelation is received, all actions on the part of legally responsible individuals are governed by the sacred law, and this principle is unambiguously certain. Therefore, all legal rulings, whether epistemically

[75] Hourani, "Two Theories of Value." As noted earlier, Shihadeh has argued that the Mu'tazilī opinion is more akin to ethical realism than to moral objectivism; see Shihadeh, "Theories of Ethical Value."

[76] Al-Bāqillānī, *al-Taqrīb*, 172. [77] Ibid. [78] Ibid., 227.

certain or not, must be followed in recognition of the expansive domain of the sacred law and of God's commands.

With respect to al-Bāqillānī's original epistemological framework, which divides knowledge into necessary (*ḍarūrī*) and speculative/deductive (*naẓarī/istidlālī*), all human knowledge regarding moral and legal values, to the extent that it is mediated through reason, is acquired and therefore speculative. This means that moral and legal values are excluded from the realm of individual necessary knowledge (*ʿilm ḍarūrī*), supporting the Ashʿarī notion that moral values are instituted by God. The only exception to this general rule is legal rulings classified as historical reports (*akhbār mutawātir*) or derived through the consensus (*ijmāʿ*) of legal scholars, though they, too, relate to clear revelatory sources.[79]

Just as the epistemological paradigm of the Muʿtazila had a wide-reaching impact on law, the primacy given to revelation in the epistemological framework of the Ashʿarīs had certain legal ramifications: (1) a focus on the centrality of revelation, such that individuals have no legal responsibility (*taklīf*) prior to revelation; (2) a belief in scriptural universalism, which entails that every action has a legal and moral value derived directly from scripture or through reasoning on the basis of scripture; (3) the acceptance of legal indeterminacy due to the limited nature of direct scriptural injunctions and the reliance on human reason; and (4) the marginalization of the individual and the valorization of the jurist as a consequence of the notion that deriving legal rulings is not something that may be done by anyone who can reason, but rather is the exclusive province of legal scholars trained in the methods of legal interpretation.

Comparing these four points with the legal ramifications of Muʿtazilī epistemology presented earlier in this chapter, we see that they are almost diametrically opposed. Whereas the Muʿtazila emphasize the centrality of reason, the Ashʿarīs emphasize the centrality of revelation. Whereas the Muʿtazila embrace moral universalism, the Ashʿarīs endorse scriptural universalism. Whereas the Muʿtazila endow the individual with moral and legal certainty even in the absence of revelation, the Ashʿarīs accept legal indeterminacy. And finally, whereas the Muʿtazila extol the individual's capacity to reason independently, the Ashʿarīs consider jurists uniquely capable of legal reasoning, with laypeople obligated to follow them. Looking at the comparison from another angle, we can say that whereas the Ashʿarīs emphasize God's power and domain as the

[79] For more on the connection between *mutawātir* reports, *ijmāʿ*, and revelatory texts, see Chapters 5 and 6 in the present work.

Lawgiver and the position of humans as His obedient servants, the Mu'tazila emphasize God's endowment of the individual with reason and His divine justice, which together enable individuals to make, and guide them toward, correct moral and legal decisions. In this sense, beyond legal and epistemological divergences, the Mu'tazila and the Ash'arīs differ fundamentally on God's involvement in the world and His role as Lawgiver.[80]

Each of these two starkly opposed epistemologies, legal views, and understandings of God had ardent supporters throughout the Islamic empire between the third/ninth and fifth/eleventh centuries, and especially so in Nishapur in al-Juwaynī's lifetime. Even though al-Bāqillānī opposed the epistemology espoused by the Mu'tazila, Jan Thiele has argued that he nonetheless adopted certain terms and principles from the Mu'tazila, such as his theory of states (*aḥwāl*), the manner in which he argues for the existence of God, and his understanding of human action.[81] These appropriations demonstrate the intellectual cross-pollination that was taking place in Nishapur, in which al-Juwaynī would also participate.

CONCLUSION

Between the third/ninth and fifth/eleventh centuries, the Mu'tazila and the Ash'arīs constructed two opposing epistemological systems, connected only by a common agreement that reason and revelation comprise the primary sources of guidance. The primary difference between the two frameworks lies in the fact that while the Mu'tazila considered it possible for an individual to have certain knowledge of most legal and moral matters both before and after recourse to revelation, the Ash'arīs limited the epistemic certainty an individual could acquire and emphasized the centrality of revelation. Even though the Ash'arīs saw revelation as the font of guidance, because of limitations on human reason and the unclear nature of linguistic indications, human beings are not, in their view, continually provided with epistemically certain legal guidance, although

80 Bernard Weiss, in *The Spirit of Islamic Law*, analyzes the specific understanding of Islamic law to which Ash'arī theology gives rise. For Weiss, the emphasis on "divine sovereignty" leads to "human subordination," with people constantly turning to God for legal and moral guidance. Mediating this relationship are the scriptural sources that jurists turn to when attempting to discover the divine intent.

81 Jan Thiele, "Between Cordoba and Nīsābūr: The Emergence and Consolidation of Ash'arism (Fourth–Fifth/Tenth–Eleventh Century)," in Schmidtke, *Oxford Handbook of Islamic Theology*, 231.

they are obligated to follow the merely probable guidance that is available to them. These debates took place during al-Juwaynī's lifetime, and although he is remembered as a prototypical Ashʿarī, his exposure to and observation of the various epistemological paradigms led him to develop an epistemological system aimed at achieving certainty – a significant departure from the standard Ashʿarī epistemological framework.

4

The Epistemology of al-Juwaynī

Al-Juwaynī's writing is situated between two competing epistemologies: of the Ashʿarīs and of the Muʿtazila. As described in the previous chapter, the two differ most starkly on the notion of scriptural and legal universalism and on the epistemological status of moral and legal values ascertained through human reason. For the Ashʿarīs, who adhered to the doctrine of scriptural universalism, all human actions after the advent of the Prophet were endowed with values determined by scripture. However, given the fallible nature of human reasoning as a tool of discovery, rulings produced by human reasoning were epistemically only probable. Therefore, the Ashʿarīs' scriptural universalism was coupled with an acceptance of legal indeterminacy. In opposition to the Ashʿarīs stood the Muʿtazila, who argued for moral universalism, asserting that each action has a moral value independent of revelation. The moral value of any action can be ascertained through human reason. God, in His unwavering justice, has placed indications in the world to guide human beings toward the right conclusions. As long as human beings grasp the correct indications, they will ascertain the correct moral value in each instance. The Muʿtazila's confidence in this process endowed their moral universalism with a degree of epistemic certainty that escaped their Ashʿarī counterparts.

In his writings, al-Juwaynī maintains the Ashʿarīs' scriptural universalism, but he also departs from them in important ways. These departures allow him to carve out a realm in which legal rulings can achieve *practical* certainty. Al-Juwaynī achieves this result by redefining the process of reasoning, the nature of proofs, and the overall categorization of knowledge, replacing the definitions dominant in his time.

AL-JUWAYNĪ'S EPISTEMOLOGY IN THE *IRSHĀD* AND THE *SHĀMIL*

Reconstructing al-Juwaynī's epistemological framework is complicated, because elements of it are scattered throughout his various legal and theological treatises. To make the task more cumbersome still, the dating of his works – with the exception of the *Burhān* and the *Niẓāmiyya*, known to be his last texts – is unknown.[1] This problem is somewhat alleviated by the fact that al-Juwaynī wrote the majority of his books after assuming his position at the Niẓāmiyya, and therefore the *Burhān*,[2] the *Shāmil*,[3] the *Irshād*,[4] and the *Niẓāmiyya*[5] can all be taken as emblematic of his later thought. As such, they will form the central texts for the present inquiry, with primacy given to the *Burhān*, since this was al-Juwaynī's final and longest extant statement on the topic.[6]

[1] According to Michel Allard, the chronological order of al-Juwaynī's theological texts runs from the *Shāmil* through the *Irshād* and the *Luma'* to the *Niẓāmiyya*. See Thiele, "Between Cordoba and Nīsābūr," 235, and Michel Allard, *Textes apologetiques de Guwayni (m. 478/1085)* (Beirut: Dar el-Mashreq, 1968).

[2] The definitive critical edition of al-Juwaynī's *Burhān* was produced by 'Abd al-'Aẓīm al-Dīb. I rely on the 1997 Doha reprint of the 1979 edition.

[3] Al-Juwaynī, *al-Shāmil fī uṣūl al-dīn*, translated as *Al-Shāmil fī Uṣūl al-Dīn: The Exposition of al-Bāqillānī's Commentary on the Kitāb al-Luma'*. The latter version will be cited in notes as *Shāmil* (Frank). The first publication of the *Shāmil* is not referenced as it was an incomplete preproduction of the manuscript that al-Nashshār subsequently published in full. For comparative purposes, one can consult *al-Shāmil fī uṣūl al-dīn*, ed. Helmut Klopfer (Cairo: Dār al-'Arab, 1959).

[4] Al-Juwaynī, *Kitāb al-Irshād ilā qawāṭi' al-adilla fī uṣūl al-i'tiqād*, translated as *A Guide to the Conclusive Proofs for the Principles of Belief.*

[5] I rely primarily on al-Kawtharī's edition of *al-'Aqīda al-Niẓāmiyya*. Another reliable edition is al-Juwaynī, *al-'Aqīda al-Niẓāmiyya*, ed. Muḥammad al-Zubaydī (Beirut: Dār al-Sabīl al-Rashād, 2003).

[6] In addition, I draw on numerous other texts by al-Juwaynī and commentaries on his works. These include al-Juwaynī, *al-Talkhīṣ fī uṣūl al-fiqh*, ed. 'Abd Allāh al-Nībālī and Shubbayr al-'Amrī (Mecca: Maktabat Dār al-Bāz, 1996); al-Juwaynī, *al-Kāfiya fi al-jadal*; 'Alī b. Ismā'īl al-Abyārī, *al-Taḥqīq wa-l-bayān fī sharḥ al-Burhān fī uṣūl al-fiqh* (Doha: Wizārat al-Awqāf wa-l-Shu'ūn al-Islāmiyya, 2013); al-Māzarī, *Īḍāḥ al-maḥsūl min Burhān al-uṣūl*; al-Anṣārī, *al-Ghunya fī al-kalām*; and Ibn al-Amīr, *al-Kāmil fī ikhtiṣār al-Shāmil*. Al-Juwaynī's most extensive theological work, the *Shāmil*, contains many crucial epistemological discussions, but because of corruptions in the manuscript, many of these are not fully elaborated or cogent. Despite this obstacle, a foray into the *Shāmil* does provide certain insights into al-Juwaynī's epistemology, and it, together with sections of the *Irshād*, the abridgment of the *Shāmil*, and the *Burhān*, yields a full picture. Also useful is the *Kāmil* of Ibn al-Amīr, which is a commentary on and abridgment of the *Shāmil*. However, it is important to recognize that many of al-Juwaynī's ideas evolved from the *Shāmil* and the *Irshād* to the *Burhān*, and therefore I will evaluate the *Shāmil* and the

The cornerstone of all disquisitions on epistemology that I have discussed is an investigation into the intellect, and al-Juwaynī follows suit. In the *Irshād*, al-Juwaynī commences his discussion by agreeing with al-Bāqillānī's definition that the intellect (*ʿaql*) is equivalent to some elements of necessary knowledge.[7] By this statement, al-Juwaynī means that basic knowledge is always present in the intellect and forms the foundation of the process of reasoning, whether one is reasoning about complicated matters or simple ones. Examples of such basic knowledge include knowledge of the impossibility of impossibilities, such as the union of black and white; knowledge of the possibility of possibilities, such as the affirmation or negation of all known things; and the understanding that existent entities can be either eternal or created.[8] Though this list is not exhaustive, implicit in al-Juwaynī's argument that the intellect contains a portion of necessary knowledge is the claim that the primary function of the intellect is to reason in order to arrive at knowledge. Speaking of knowledge (*ʿilm*), then, al-Juwaynī invokes the definition of knowledge proposed by al-Bāqillānī – namely, knowing something knowable as it truly is[9] – but criticizes this definition for its singular emphasis on the notion of "knowing" without any indication of the process.[10] To remedy this omission, he amends the definition in his *Irshād*, where he states that knowledge is produced by a process of speculative reasoning (*naẓar*) when a specific matter of investigation has been delineated.[11] This process of speculative reasoning, however, can be either sound (*ṣaḥīḥ*) or unsound (*fāsid*). Sound speculative reasoning leads the individual to what is indicated (*madlūl*), or the thing that the individual desires to know, whereas unsound reasoning does the opposite, leading to falsity, doubt, and confusion.[12] What connects speculative reasoning to the object sought is the proof (*dalīl*), which, al-Juwaynī argues, "indicates on the basis of its essential characteristic ... the knowledge of what is indicated."[13] Proofs are either rational or scriptural; in either case, they allow the reasoner to attain a specified knowledge item. Although al-Juwaynī establishes the primacy of speculative reasoning and proofs in the *Irshād*, he does not provide the reader with any clarity as to how the reasoner arrives at the proofs, nor how the proofs bring the reasoner to the correct conclusion.

Irshād together before moving on to his more comprehensive epistemological discussions in the *Burhān*.

7 Al-Juwaynī, *al-Irshād*, 15. 8 Ibid., 14–16.

9 Al-Bāqillānī, *al-Tamhīd*, 6, and *al-Taqrīb*, 174. For a longer discussion of al-Bāqillānī's definition, see Chapter 3.

10 Al-Juwaynī, *al-Irshād*, 10. 11 Ibid., 10–11. 12 Ibid., 3. 13 Ibid., 7.

Whereas the Muʿtazila hold that the reasoner reaches the correct conclusion thanks to the indications that God has placed in the world, the Ashʿarīs reject this notion on the basis that it limits God's power. They argue that indications do not necessarily lead to the correct conclusion and thus can give rise to incorrect as well as correct knowledge.

Al-Juwaynī addresses this issue in greater detail in his *Shāmil*, where he first qualifies his definition of speculative reasoning thus: "Know that speculative reasoning (*naẓar*) entails (*yataḍamman*) knowledge (*ʿilm*) according to the people of truth if it is correct and exhaustive and is not followed by opinions that oppose the knowledge [ascertained]. And the people of truth reject those who describe speculative reasoning as necessitating (*mūjib*) knowledge, and reject the notion of causality (*tawallud*) entirely."[14] In this definition, al-Juwaynī specifies that speculative reasoning is correct not simply because of the discovery of proofs, as stipulated in the *Irshād*, but also thanks to an exhaustive process of reasoning in which the reasoner adequately responds to any objections raised against the conclusion. Al-Juwaynī also argues that knowledge is not caused or necessitated by speculative reasoning, as the Muʿtazila claim, but rather is entailed (*yataḍamman*) by it.[15] By using the language of "entailing," al-Juwaynī is arguing *not* that either a proof (*dalīl*) or speculative reasoning (*naẓar*) will necessarily bring about knowledge, but instead that an element within the process of speculative reasoning, if the process is sound, entails the knowledge desired. He thus introduces the idea of the "aspect of the proof" (*wajh al-dalāla*)[16] as the element that entails knowledge. For al-Juwaynī, "correct speculative reasoning is thinking connected to the search for the aspect of the proof in a manner that arrives at [what is indicated]."[17] Two longer passages further clarify his position:

14 Al-Juwaynī, *Shāmil* (Frank), 10.

15 Al-Bāqillānī also uses this language of reasoning's "entailing" knowledge in the *Taqrīb*, but his discussion is fairly truncated. See al-Bāqillānī, *al-Taqrīb*, 210–14.

16 Ayman Shihadeh rightly notes that not enough attention has been paid to the notion of *wajh*, which appears both in discussions of moral values and in discussions of proofs. In the discussion of moral values, Shihadeh argues that *wajh* can be understood as circumstance; however, I do not think the concept of circumstance fits well in the context of the discussion of proofs. Therefore, I am translating *wajh* as "aspect," to indicate a certain element of the proof or a certain understanding of the proof that entails the conclusion, as opposed to the circumstance of its discovery. See Shihadeh, "Theories of Ethical Value," 392–95.

17 Al-Juwaynī, *Shāmil* (Frank), 19.

Speculative reasoning is useful (*mufīd*) if the one reasoning discovers the aspect (*wajh*) of the proof. If [the reasoner] attains knowledge from this aspect, from which the proof is indicated, then the research is complete and the quest is finished. And knowledge from the aspect of the proof is outside consideration as one of the pillars of speculative reasoning because it is clear that the knowledge of the proof, and knowledge of that which is indicated, exist simultaneously after the completion of speculative reasoning ...[18]

We say that knowledge of the aspect of the proof *is* knowledge of that which is indicated. And when the act of knowing takes place (*ḥādith*), it applies to two knowledge items in some cases, as in this one, where the two objects are knowledge of the aspect of the proof (*wajh al-dalāla*) and knowledge of that which is indicated (*madlūl*), since one cannot conceive of the aspect of the proof without attaching it to that which is indicated, and there is no meaning to the aspect of the proof without necessitating (*iqtiḍā'*) that which is indicated. So, it springs forth from this that the knowledge of the aspect of the proof *is* knowledge of that which is indicated.[19]

In these passages, al-Juwaynī argues that the most important element in the process of speculative reasoning is the aspect of the proof, which the reasoner may or may not discover during the process of reasoning. Furthermore, even if the reasoner arrives at the correct proof, he or she may nonetheless fail to arrive at the correct conclusion, because the latter requires the specific "aspect" of the proof. Though al-Juwaynī is not explicit in his various writings about what exactly the *wajh* is, a closer reading of his texts suggests that it refers to a specific element or understanding of the proof that allows the reasoner to reach knowledge. By emphasizing the "aspect" of the proof instead of the proof itself, al-Juwaynī is able to avoid asserting a causal relationship between the proof and knowledge, while still arguing for a relationship between sound speculative reasoning and knowledge. This is why he argues in both passages that the aspect of the proof is what is indicated (*madlūl*) by sound speculative reasoning and is, therefore, the knowledge desired. Consequently, merely discovering the proof does not necessarily lead to knowledge, but identifying the specific aspect of the correct proof through sound speculative reasoning means that the reasoner has arrived at knowledge. At this point, in al-Juwaynī's words, "knowledge of the proof, and knowledge of that which is indicated, exist simultaneously after the completion of speculative reasoning."

A sound process of speculative reasoning (*al-naẓar al-ṣaḥīḥ*) is, therefore, an exhaustive one in which the reasoner evaluates all possible proofs

[18] Ibid., 12. [19] Ibid.

and refutations until he or she arrives at a specific element of one specific proof; at this moment, the reasoner simultaneously arrives at the knowledge sought. For al-Juwaynī, the aspect of the proof is thus almost a eureka moment for the reasoner, who, having identified the correct proof, suddenly realizes a specific configuration of it that instantaneously grants him or her knowledge. By emphasizing the aspect of the proof and its simultaneity with knowledge, al-Juwaynī avoids the causal argument of the Muʿtazila, but he does not embrace the opposite argument of the Ashʿarīs; rather, he acknowledges that the process of sound reasoning can successfully bring about knowledge if the individual identifies the specific aspect of the proof that yields the desired knowledge. At the same time, by equating the aspect of the proof with knowledge of what is indicated as one and the same thing, al-Juwaynī avoids acknowledging a causal connection between two discrete moments in the process of speculative reasoning.

After broadly addressing the topic of speculative reasoning and knowledge, al-Juwaynī turns to a discussion of the various types of knowledge. Here, too, he departs from his Ashʿarī predecessors, who distinguished firmly between necessary knowledge (*ʿilm ḍarūrī*) and acquired/speculative knowledge (*ʿilm kasbī/naẓarī*). In the *Irshād*, al-Juwaynī begins by identifying three main categories of knowledge: necessary knowledge (*al-ʿilm al-ḍarūrī*), innate knowledge (*al-ʿilm al-badīhī*),[20] and acquired knowledge (*al-ʿilm al-kasbī*).[21] The first category refers to knowledge attained without speculative reasoning (*naẓar*) that is formed on the basis of what the individual identifies as harmful or beneficial. The second, innate knowledge, is similar to the first in that it is devoid of speculative reasoning, but it is not connected to individual harm or benefit. Two examples that demonstrate the difference between these two types are the need for food when afflicted by hunger and knowledge of one's own existence; the former is necessary knowledge, involving a need that also avoids harm, whereas the latter is simply innate knowledge. The subtle distinction that al-Juwaynī draws was not universally acknowledged by theologians in his time, and he notes that most scholars have in fact collapsed these two categories and refer to them interchangeably – a practice he does not consider a grave problem and in fact does himself in other texts. His willingness to accept the conflation of these two types

[20] Although innate knowledge and necessary knowledge are typically collapsed into one category, al-Juwaynī separates them in the *Irshād*, though he fails to retain this distinction in his other writings. Al-Juwaynī, *Irshād*, 10–15.

[21] Ibid., 13.

of knowledge is due to his identification of a common element in them, namely, the absence of speculative reasoning. Because of the absence of speculative reasoning, once knowledge of either of these two types is concretized within the intellect, it is not vulnerable to doubt or confusion.[22] Given the absence of doubt and speculative reasoning, al-Juwaynī makes the argument that such knowledge forms part of the intellect.

In conceptualizing necessary knowledge as part of the intellect, al-Juwaynī confronts a tension. Recall that the first type of necessary knowledge, *ḍarūrī*, is related to either the positive need for something or the negative need to avoid something. These desires, though necessary to the mind at a certain point, are born of experience, custom, or circumstances. For example, it is only after one experiences being burned by fire that one avoids touching it. The aggregation of repeated instances of witnessing fire burning then leads one to the necessary knowledge that fire burns. Although reaching this conclusion does not require extensive reasoning, it does rely on experiential knowledge and observation. The importance of experiential knowledge and repetition to necessary knowledge is absent in the *Irshād* but discussed in the *Shāmil*. There, al-Juwaynī argues that the parameters of necessary knowledge encompass knowledge devoid of reasoning as well as any knowledge that is the product of recurrent habit (*iṭṭirād al-ʿāda*).[23] In the case of fire, the knowledge that fire burns is not necessary to the human intellect ab initio, but it becomes so through its repeated experiential occurrence. With this addition, al-Juwaynī's definition of necessary knowledge now contains two elements – the absence of speculative reasoning and customary occurrence or repetition.[24]

The last category of knowledge, acquired knowledge (*al-ʿilm al-kasbī*), is defined by al-Juwaynī as knowledge of created and eternal things by way of sound speculative reasoning.[25] To ascertain such knowledge, the reasoner is dependent on proofs (*dalāʾil*) or indications that guide him or her toward the knowledge sought. The proofs may be manifold or singular, reason-based or scriptural[26] – al-Juwaynī is preoccupied not so much with their number or nature as with the end result, the creation of knowledge.[27] However, as noted earlier, the mere presence of proofs or indications does not necessitate correct knowledge for al-Juwaynī, as that

22 Ibid., 14.

23 Al-Juwaynī, *Shāmil* (Frank), 88–90; al-Juwaynī, *al-Shāmil*, 102–3, 111–14.

24 Ibn al-Amīr, in his commentary on this discussion in the *Shāmil*, does not dwell on the means of attaining necessary knowledge; rather, he simply explicates the various forms of knowledge to which al-Juwaynī subscribes. See Ibn al-Amīr, *al-Kāmil*, 296–302.

25 Al-Juwaynī, *al-Irshād*, 14. 26 Ibid., 8. 27 Al-Juwaynī, *al-Shāmil*, 110–11.

would imply a causality that al-Juwaynī is keen to avoid. But proofs do affect the process of speculative reasoning, and therefore, in the *Shāmil*, much as in the *Irshād*, al-Juwaynī differentiates between sound (*ṣaḥīḥ*) and unsound (*fāsid*) speculative reasoning.[28] The distinction between the two types of speculative reasoning does not translate into a categorization of some knowledge as more evident (*jalī*) to the intellect and other knowledge as hidden (*khafī*); for al-Juwaynī, all matters requiring reason are equal, and although some may require more effort to penetrate, this does not mean they are different in their reality.[29]

The idea of the uniformity of knowledge that al-Juwaynī puts forward in the *Shāmil* probably represents the most glaring difference from his discussion of knowledge, its classification, and the process of speculative reasoning in the *Irshād*. In the *Irshād*, as described earlier, al-Juwaynī divides knowledge into necessary/innate knowledge (*al-ʿilm al-ḍarūrī/al-badīhī*) and acquired/speculative knowledge (*al-ʿilm al-kasbī/al-naẓarī*). In the *Shāmil*, al-Juwaynī nonetheless argues that the two categories can be collapsed. He uses the example of action, juxtaposing voluntary and involuntary action and pointing out that in spite of their difference, both remain, at the most basic level, forms of action.[30] Similarly, irrespective of the differentiation between various types of knowledge based on the presence or absence of certain elements, once one can claim knowledge of something, this knowledge is equivalent to all other knowledge that one has.[31] Despite this equivalence, al-Juwaynī accepts that there are ways to distinguish forms of knowledge from one another on the basis of the process or degree of speculative reasoning required:

> Knowledge of what is reflected (*manẓūr*) upon is not arrived at except through speculative reasoning. One with intellect does not differentiate between the capacity of an individual to reason and the absence of capacity for knowledge, except when one finds that it is connected to two types of knowledge. And the impossibility of distinguishing between two types of knowledge is clarified if they are similar, and one of them is evaluated as necessary and the other as acquired. [In this scenario], nothing is left except to differentiate on the basis of capacity to arrive at subtle knowledge. And this is clear for one who thinks.[32]

[28] Al-Juwaynī, *al-Irshād*, 3; *Shāmil* (Frank), 18; *al-Shāmil*, 99–104.
[29] Al-Juwaynī, *al-Shāmil*, 101–4. [30] Ibid., 103.
[31] Ibn al-Amīr describes the notion that all knowledge is equal as odd, because in his view the presence of reasoning naturally sets some types of knowledge apart. Ibn al-Amīr, *al-Kāmil*, 297.
[32] Al-Juwaynī, *Shāmil* (Frank), 90.

In this passage, al-Juwaynī argues that there is no need to distinguish between different intellects and types of knowledge except when a classification already exists, at which point one is forced to adopt the dual classification and to characterize one form of knowledge as necessary and the other as speculative. If one is forced to engage in this form of differentiation, al-Juwaynī contends that the only possible way of differentiating between intellects is on the basis of the fact that certain intellects are more judicious and can grasp subtle knowledge, whereas others are less so and cannot comprehend more complex matters. For al-Juwaynī, therefore, all knowledge resulting from speculative reasoning is the same. One can distinguish between types of reasoners and their capacity to reason,[33] but once an individual classifies something as "knowledge," be it a complex matter requiring reasoning or an observation simply acquired through the senses, it occupies the same genus with all other knowledge, and there is no need for further classification on the basis of the process of acquisition.

This belief in the uniformity of all knowledge mirrors al-Juwaynī's discussion of the aspect of the proof, in which he argues that two individuals could arrive at the same proof but only one of them might identify the specific aspect of the proof and therefore attain knowledge. What differentiates the individual discovering the proof from the individual perceiving the aspect of the proof is the process of speculative reasoning. To the extent that one identifies the aspect of the proof through sound speculative reasoning, one has reached knowledge, and all knowledge ascertained through the aspect of the proof constitutes knowledge without further distinction. Therefore, although al-Juwaynī accepts the bifurcation of knowledge into necessary and acquired from the perspective of process, recognizing that some knowledge requires extensive speculative reasoning whereas other knowledge is obtained through abbreviated forms of reasoning, his theoretical acceptance of two forms of knowledge does not translate into an epistemological differentiation. He thus flatly rejects the assertion of his Ashʿarī predecessors of an epistemological difference between necessary knowledge, which is certain, and acquired knowledge, which is merely probable. Al-Juwaynī does not explicate the epistemological ramifications of his argument regarding the uniformity of knowledge in the *Irshād* or the *Shāmil*, but they are apparent in the *Burhān*.

33 Ibid.

AL-JUWAYNĪ'S EPISTEMOLOGY IN THE *BURHĀN*

The most striking element of al-Juwaynī's epistemological discussion in the *Burhān* is its sheer volume and range. In contrast to his other works, which survey discrete epistemological issues over a few pages, the *Burhān* contains an entire section dedicated to epistemological inquiries aimed at the formulation of a coherent theory to account for all forms of knowledge and any counterarguments that might be raised against the theory.[34] Al-Juwaynī begins his discussion with the common launching point of all epistemological inquiries – the reality of the intellect (*ʿaql*). Whereas in the *Irshād* he accepts al-Bāqillānī's position that elements of necessary knowledge are embedded within the intellect, in the *Burhān* he amends his opinion and asserts that the intellect is an instinct (*gharīza*) or a quality (*ṣifa*) that allows one to derive reason-based knowledge from foundational knowledge (*al-ḍarūriyyāt*), as opposed to containing knowledge itself.[35] Conceived of in this manner, the intellect is the central mechanism for capturing knowledge, not a vessel that always contains an element of it.

After offering this definition of the intellect, al-Juwaynī turns to the concept of knowledge. Here he rejects his earlier definition (and that of al-Bāqillānī) of knowledge as the understanding of what is knowable (*maʿlūm*) as it really is because, in his view, this definition excludes knowledge of eternal things and thus removes any possibility of "knowing" God. He argues that despite the inability of human beings to comprehend God in totality because of His eternality, some elements of His being can be apprehended by human beings. If knowledge of God is possible, then the definition of knowledge must accommodate the comprehension of eternal things.[36] The new definition of knowledge that al-Juwaynī proposes is "arriving at the reality (*ḥaqīqa*) of knowledge through research (*mubāḥatha*) in a way that enables one to differentiate what is sought from all else."[37] Knowledge, he continues, is comprehended internally and need not be expressed vocally. As an example, he uses the smell of incense: a person can know the smell of incense but be incapable of cogently relaying this knowledge to another individual. Such inability to articulate knowledge does not negate the presence of

[34] See al-Juwaynī, *al-Burhān*, 1:111–78.

[35] Al-Juwaynī, *al-Burhān*, 1:112. One of the commentators on the *Burhān*, al-Māzarī, also picks up on this shift regarding the definition of the intellect. See al-Māzarī, *Īḍāḥ al-maḥṣūl*, 38.

[36] Al-Juwaynī, *al-Burhān*, 1:119. [37] Ibid., 1:119–20.

knowledge in the individual. With this addendum, al-Juwaynī's definition can now be conceptualized as resting on three pillars: speculative reasoning, differentiation, and internal understanding.[38]

After offering new definitions of the intellect and of knowledge, al-Juwaynī outlines in much greater detail the argument for the interconnectivity and uniformity of all knowledge that he alludes to in the *Shāmil*. As I have noted, al-Juwaynī's main Ashʿarī influence was al-Bāqillānī, who differentiated between two types of knowledge – epistemically certain necessary knowledge and epistemically probable reason-based knowledge. This classification assumes an epistemological barrier between the two types that precludes fluidity: probable knowledge cannot become necessary, and vice versa. Following al-Bāqillānī's lead in the *Irshād*, al-Juwaynī accepts the distinction between these two forms of knowledge and even adds a third, innate knowledge. However, in the *Shāmil*, he rejects the notion of an impermeable barrier between the types, arguing that continual repetition or custom can bring about necessary knowledge.[39] His discussion in the *Burhān* shows further development of this idea to the point that a distinct departure from his predecessors can clearly be identified. To illustrate his new framework, he presents what he describes as ten grades (*marātib*) of knowledge:

The scholars have said – may God be pleased with them – that the comprehensive division of the classes of knowledge is ten.

The first: The human being's knowledge of himself. And a corollary to this [knowledge] is what he discovers necessarily from his states, such as pain and existence.

The second class [of knowledge] consists of necessary knowledge such as the impossibility of the impossible. This [class] is lower than the first grade because it is based on knowledge that requires reflection (*fikr*)[40] on opposites and their contradictions.

The third [class] consists of the knowledge [ascertained] by the senses. This class is lower than the second because sensory [perception] is vulnerable to imagination and temporary defects.

The fourth class consists of knowledge of the truthfulness of concurrent reports. This [class] is lower than the knowledge of the senses because concurrence is

[38] Ibid., 1:121. [39] Al-Juwaynī, *Shāmil* (Frank), 103–4, 109–11.

[40] In this passage, al-Juwaynī uses the term *fikr* instead of the more usual *naẓar*. Throughout the *Burhān*, al-Juwaynī uses a variety of terms, such as *tadabbur* (contemplation), thinking (*taʾammul*), and reflection (*fikr*), to indicate a process of speculative reasoning (*naẓar*). However, I have not seen him use *tadabbur*, *taʾammul*, or *fikr* in a technical sense, so although it seems likely that the terms refer to a process of speculative reasoning or types of speculative reasoning, he never defines them the way he does *naẓar*.

attained [only] if the number of transmitters is sufficient. There is no doubt that this requires reflection (*fikr*), and thus al-Kaʿbī[41] considered it a type of speculative knowledge.

The fifth class is that of skill and handicraft. This knowledge is contingent on previous [knowledge] because of the difficulty and possibility of error within it.

The sixth class is contingent on circumstantial states, such as the knowledge of the shyness of the bashful, the fear of the fearful, and the anger of the angry. This is placed below the previous classes because of the ambiguity of circumstantial evidence and the absence of decisive categorization.

The seventh class is attained through reasoned proofs (*adillat al-ʿuqūl*). There is no doubt that this is lower than the necessary knowledge mentioned in the previous classes.

The eighth class is the knowledge of the possibility of prophecy, the sending of prophets, and the sending of divine law.

The ninth class is the knowledge of miracles, if they occur.

The tenth class is revelatory knowledge based on the Quran, the Sunna, and consensus (*al-ijmāʿ*).[42]

To summarize, the ten grades of knowledge are (1) knowledge of the self, (2) knowledge of logical impossibilities, (3) sensory knowledge, (4) historical knowledge conveyed concurrently, (5) theoretical knowledge leading to practical knowledge, (6) knowledge of the bodily states and emotions of others, (7) reasoned knowledge, (8) knowledge of prophecy, (9) knowledge of miracles, and (10) knowledge contained in revelation. These grades of knowledge are arranged in a particular order, starting with knowledge that requires no reasoning, such as knowledge of the self, and proceeding through to knowledge that requires extensive reasoning, such as revelatory knowledge. The distinguishing factor between the grades is the amount of reasoning needed to arrive at the knowledge, not the epistemic value of the resulting knowledge as either certain or probable. This presentation is thus in line with al-Juwaynī's earlier argument in the *Shāmil* regarding the equivalence of all knowledge, with the sole distinction between types being the extent of reasoning required to attain each. In addition, in the middle categories of theoretical knowledge and knowledge of bodily states, al-Juwaynī emphasizes the function of continual repetition and custom that he originally proposed in the *Shāmil*. As one moves down from the first grade toward the later grades, a

41 Al-Juwaynī is referring to the famous Basran Muʿtazilī scholar Abū al-Qāsim al-Balkhī (also known as al-Kaʿbī), a common interlocutor for Ashʿarī scholars. For more on al-Balkhī, see El Omari, *Theology of Abū l-Qāsim al-Balkhī/al-Kaʿbī*.

42 Al-Juwaynī, *al-Burhān*, 1:131–33.

progressively higher degree of reason, repetition, and customary knowledge is required to claim each type of knowledge.

In this schema, reasoning is the main anchor of most knowledge types. After outlining the ten grades of knowledge, al-Juwaynī defines reasoning as follows:

> Speculative reasoning (*naẓar*) is an attempt to capture knowledge by roaming around its paths and corners. The resulting knowledge is necessary knowledge (*ḍarūrī*), as has previously been established. These paths result in exhaustive categories (*taqāsīm munḍabiṭa*) between negation and affirmation, or they are limited between the two. Thus the person of intellect engages in critical examination (*al-fikr al-ʿaqlī*) and determines through it either negation or establishment, for the establishment of either is certain (*qaṭʿī*). And the proof [for either] cannot be attained except through the divestment of thinking (*tajrīd al-fikr*) and the correct inclination toward the place to which the intellect leads.[43]

For al-Juwaynī, the process of speculative reasoning is a process of reflection[44] based on prior knowledge and aimed at obtaining new knowledge. This process has to be both precise and exhaustive, so that the reasoner, on arriving at the aspect of the proof, reaches the conclusion of the investigation and can be confident that the knowledge obtained is not adulterated by doubt. According to al-Juwaynī, if this process of extensive speculative reasoning is executed correctly, the resultant knowledge will be necessary – and it is this assertion that stands in stark contrast to the positions of his predecessors.

Recall that although al-Bāqillānī accepts the primacy of reason, he argues that knowledge ascertained through reason is acquired and epistemically probable as opposed to necessary and epistemically certain. For al-Bāqillānī, the latter kind of knowledge is only presumptive because even if it has been attained through sound speculative reasoning, its veracity is not certain given that there is no causal relationship between reasoning and knowledge or between proofs and knowledge.[45] As noted earlier, in the *Shāmil* al-Juwaynī rejects the existence of a causal relationship between proofs and knowledge, but he does assert that the goal of speculative reasoning is to discover the specific aspect of the proof that entails the conclusion, since the aspect of the proof and what is indicated (*madlūl*) are one and the same in his mind.[46] In this sense, even though he

[43] Ibid., 1:138. [44] See note 40.

[45] For more on this, see the section on al-Bāqillānī's epistemology in Chapter 3.

[46] See previous section on al-Juwaynī's epistemology as elaborated in the *Irshād* and the *Shāmil*.

maintains that there is no causal relationship between proofs and knowledge, there seems to be a strong relationship between sound speculative reasoning and knowledge, as sound reasoning facilitates the reasoner's arrival at the aspect of the proof. In the *Burhān*, al-Juwaynī does not invoke the same language of entailment (*taḍammun*), but he goes into more detail regarding the process of speculative reasoning and proofs, fully revealing the contours of his argument regarding the potential epistemic certainty of all knowledge and its relationship to reasoning and proofs.

Beginning with the process of speculative reasoning itself, al-Juwaynī argues that there are two types of speculative reasoning:

> These are [all] vacillations in the corners of necessary knowledge (*ḍarūriyyāt*). But when they are divided according to what needs categorization and reasoning, one of the types is called *acquired* and the other *necessary*.
>
> To describe the purpose of this section concisely, it is that everything that leads to an exhaustive categorization (*taqsīm munḍabita*) and then to the specification of either one of them [the possibilities] is what the intellect will incline toward. [Thus,] that which is not regulated [by categorization] and to which the intellect does not incline with prolonged reasoning is from the puzzles of the intellect.[47]

Later, at the end of the section on speculative reasoning, he summarizes his remarks and asserts:

> The objective [in saying this] is the following: rational matters are divided into the innate, which are those matters that the intellect penetrates without the need for contemplation (*tadabbur*), and those that necessarily require extensive thinking (*ta'ammul*). If [reasoning] happens to follow the right path, without any obstruction, then necessary knowledge will follow. In this regard, in reality there is no difference in reasoned matters between what is apparent and what is hidden, for all of the results are necessary knowledge. But one can make two types of distinction. The first is that a thing may be in need of extensive contemplation by a highly intelligent mind because of the distance that the normal intellect cannot bear reflecting on it. But there is no difference between prolonged reflection (*fikr*) and condensed reflection as long as the reflection proceeds in the correct manner. This is one of the distinctions between the two types of speculative reasoning (*naẓarayn*). The second is that the reasoner may seek something remote that may be obtained through the proposed ten steps of speculative reasoning, but the time [the reasoner spends on the quest] is so prolonged that the reasoner forgets the primary and middle [steps], and so the reasoning fails. Or suppose the conclusion requires only three stages of thinking; then the distance is short, and the path is not full of obstacles. Therefore, there may be a difference in the length of the speculative reasoning required or in the capacity for speculative reasoning;

[47] Al-Juwaynī, *al-Burhān*, 1:140.

otherwise, in reality, there is no difference in knowledge in the case of intellectually beneficial speculative reasoning.[48]

In these passages, al-Juwaynī maintains that once a person legitimately claims knowledge of something, the claimed knowledge is epistemologically equivalent to all other knowledge the person possesses. But he also makes two sets of distinctions.

The first distinction, encountered previously, is the difference between matters requiring no speculative reasoning and matters requiring at least some speculative reasoning. In the *Irshād*, this idea is encapsulated in the distinction between necessary/innate knowledge (*ʿilm ḍarūrī/badīhī*) and speculative/aquired knowledge (*ʿilm naẓarī/kasbī*). The second distinction falls within the realm of matters requiring reason, and it distinguishes between matters requiring simple reasoning by simple intellects and those requiring complex reasoning by complex intellects. If a reasoner investigating a matter requiring complex reasoning can analyze the matter systematically and proceed exhaustively step by step, addressing all doubts and queries, then the reasoner attains knowledge, and for al-Juwaynī this knowledge possesses the same epistemic value as necessary knowledge, though the paths of acquisition are markedly different. The equation applies only once the process of reasoning is complete; as long as no firm conclusion has been reached and avenues of inquiry remain unexplored, the specific knowledge item cannot be considered necessary. Once the process is complete, the resulting knowledge can be conceptualized as *acquired necessary knowledge*. It forms one end of a spectrum of necessary knowledge from innate necessary knowledge to acquired necessary knowledge, with the first free of reason and the last fully dependent on it.

Al-Juwaynī's distinctions in the *Burhān* are rooted in a focus not on the epistemic value of knowledge but rather on the process of knowledge acquisition and the role, if any, of speculative reasoning in it. The difference between al-Juwaynī's argument as presented in the *Irshād* and that found in the *Burhān* and the *Shāmil*, therefore, should not be read as evidence that he changed his mind, or even as a rejection of his Ashʿarī predecessors; rather, it reflects al-Juwaynī's analysis of the question of knowledge and its acquisition from different perspectives. At the end of al-Juwaynī's epistemological inquiries in the *Burhān*, he finally turns to the nature of proofs (*adilla*) and their relationship to speculative reasoning. In the *Shāmil*, al-Juwaynī argued that knowledge is attained

48 Ibid., 1:155–57.

in the moment in which the reasoner perceives the aspect of the proof (*wajh al-dalāla*). For al-Juwaynī, therefore, speculative reasoning entails knowledge to the extent that it leads the reasoner to the aspect of the proof. Here, once again, al-Juwaynī emphasizes the process of reasoning, as an individual could theoretically identify the correct proof but remain ignorant of the knowledge sought if he or she fails to recognize the specific aspect of the proof that entails the knowledge item. In the *Burhān*'s discussion of proofs, al-Juwaynī uses less technical language but conveys a similar idea:

> The jurisprudents have said: reasoned proofs (*al-adilla al-ʿaqliyya*) are those that bring complete speculative reasoning (*al-naẓar al-tāmm*) to the knowledge of what is indicated. They indicate from themselves, not from characteristics, and it is not permissible to classify them as "not indicating" (*ghayr dālla*), for an action indicates an actor, the specification performed by an intending actor indicates the existence of that actor, and mastery/precision (*iḥkām*) indicates one who is knowledgeable. So, if these proofs occur, they indicate intrinsically from themselves (*dallat li-aʿyānihā*), without need for intention (*qaṣd*) to arrive at the proofs.[49]

Although al-Juwaynī does not use the language of entailment (*taḍammun*) in this passage as he does in the *Shāmil*, he argues that proofs intrinsically indicate the knowledge item sought in the same way in which an action indicates the existence of a capable actor. Here, the line between al-Juwaynī's argument and the argument of causality that he explicitly rejects in the *Shāmil* and the *Irshād* becomes woefully thin. Al-Juwaynī is arguing that if an individual fails to reach correct knowledge of something, it is either because the process of reasoning is faulty and does not lead to the correct proof or because the reasoner is simply not capable of sufficiently complex reasoning. If the individual is capable of sound reasoning and does not face obstacles to such reasoning, then as long as the individual reaches the correct proof, the individual will attain knowledge. This argument is a slight, but important, departure from the *Shāmil*, where al-Juwaynī's focus was more on the specific aspect of the proof as the key to knowledge, as opposed to the *Burhān*'s focus on the proof itself. In more concrete terms, in the *Shāmil*, a failure to arrive at knowledge could be due to three factors: unsound reasoning, a lack of intellectual capacity on the part of the reasoner, or misapprehension of the specific aspect of the proof. In the *Burhān*, the possible reasons for not reaching knowledge seem to be limited to the first two factors, as

[49] Ibid., 1:155.

al-Juwaynī claims that the proof indicates knowledge intrinsically, without the intentionality of the reasoner. Although he maintains his rejection of the causal argument embraced by the Muʿtazila, in the *Burhān* he once again comes very close to accepting it when he argues that sound reasoning and proofs lead to knowledge. Combining al-Juwaynī's argument regarding the relationship between sound reasoning, proofs, and knowledge with his argument regarding the uniformity of all knowledge opens up an expansive realm of acquired necessary knowledge; for to the extent that one reasons soundly and identifies, according to the *Burhān*, the correct rational proof or, according to the *Shāmil*, the exact aspect of the proof, one attains knowledge that cannot be epistemologically differentiated from any other knowledge item possessed by the intellect.

So far, in my exposition of al-Juwaynī's epistemology in the *Burhān*, the focus has been on his argument for the uniformity of all knowledge and his belief that sound speculative reasoning leads to correct proofs and epistemically certain knowledge. However, al-Juwaynī's ten grades of knowledge hint at another mechanism of attaining epistemically certain knowledge in addition to exhaustive reasoning – namely, continuous repetition and custom. The notion that repetition and custom can change the epistemic value of knowledge was alluded to in the *Shāmil*, where the parameters of necessary knowledge include matters that an individual knows not through speculative reasoning but through recurrent habit.[50] In the *Burhān*, al-Juwaynī revisits this idea when he discusses his fifth and sixth categories of knowledge, theoretical knowledge and knowledge of bodily states, respectively.[51]

The fifth category, theoretical knowledge evolving into practical knowledge, is probably the most emblematic of al-Juwaynī's ideas regarding custom, as it entails the gradual aggregation of information over time until the individual can be said to have attained knowledge. As an example, al-Juwaynī discusses the craft of a blacksmith. According to him, the knowledge that blacksmiths have of their vocation is necessary because it does not require reasoning; however, their knowledge does not enjoy such an elevated epistemic status from the start. To an apprentice blacksmith approaching a piece of iron with a hammer without any previous knowledge, both the tools and the craft appear foreign; however, through repetition and practice the novice perfects the craft of forging to the point that it becomes almost innate and little reflection is required.

[50] Al-Juwaynī, *Shāmil* (Frank), 109–11. [51] Al-Juwaynī, *al-Burhān*, 1:133.

A more modern example might be learning to drive a car. At first, the novice driver is preoccupied with cumbersome rules and takes deliberate care with every rotation of the wheel; however, once the driver is acclimated to driving, the process comes to feel natural, and even after a prolonged hiatus, the skill returns almost instantaneously. These examples show that knowledge derived from repetition, despite being initially foreign to the intellect and of limited epistemic value, can gradually increase in epistemic strength in tandem with the aggregation of instances of occurrence. Referring to the example of the blacksmith, al-Juwaynī argues that once the blacksmith's knowledge is fully embedded in his or her intellect, there is no way to describe it except as necessary; however, like knowledge produced through reasoning, it constitutes acquired necessary knowledge.

The other type of knowledge achieved through repetition is knowledge of bodily states, which al-Juwaynī describes as "contingent on circumstantial states such as the knowledge of the shyness of the bashful, the fear of the fearful, and the anger of the angry." Like theoretical knowledge, knowledge of emotional or bodily states is not something individuals know intrinsically, but rather something they attain through continual observation. If a person recognizes observable signs, such as facial redness in the case of anger or laughter in the case of jubilation, and repeatedly sees these signs in a variety of circumstances, that person will begin to associate anger with facial redness and jubilation with laughter to the point that he or she will be confident that when a specific bodily sign appears, a specific emotional state is indicated. This type of knowledge, being contingent on "circumstantial states," requires a certain amount of deduction and reasoning, but once it is cemented by repeated observation and custom, it, too, is categorized as necessary.

Equipped with this understanding of al-Juwaynī's views on knowledge, reason, and customary repetition, we can now divide his ten grades of knowledge into three main categories. The first four grades of knowledge – knowledge of the self, knowledge of logical impossibilities, sensory knowledge, and historical knowledge – can be called innate necessary knowledge, as they are reached without the medium of speculative reasoning and are intrinsically certain. The next two – theoretical knowledge and knowledge of bodily states – are acquired necessary knowledge, because they are products of continual repetition and/or custom and provide the individual with practical certainty. This leaves the final four grades, which are primarily related to religious matters such as prophecy and revelation, miracles, and religious law. By ranking them the lowest on the scale of knowledge acquisition (though not attaching to them a lower epistemological value), al-Juwaynī is subtlely acknowledging that matters of religion require the most reasoning and effort to comprehend. Nonetheless, once such religious knowledge is attained, it, too, is classified as acquired necessary knowledge and affords believers practical certainty in their conclusions.

Beyond the first three grades of knowledge, which are the same for all human beings, all other forms of knowledge approach the realm of necessary knowledge and are ranked according to the subjective knowledge reservoir and capacity for sound reasoning of each individual. Therefore, the degree to which an individual's acquired knowledge can be considered to be necessary and to provide practical certainty is as contingent on continual practice and repetition as it is on the discovery of the correct proof through sound reasoning. This conclusion harks back to al-Juwaynī's basic premise that all knowledge is ultimately equal; differentiation is possible in terms of the path by which knowledge was acquired and the cognitive capabilities of the reasoner, but not in terms of any substantive differences within the body of knowledge. This typology of knowledge also reveals that for al-Juwaynī there are three main sources of knowledge: reason, revelation, and custom. Sometimes these sources of knowledge work collaboratively to produce knowledge, whereas at other times they function independently.

Although al-Juwaynī was clearly a strong proponent of human reason and a believer in its ability to reach knowledge, he recognizes that the human intellect cannot penetrate all matters. In fact, he explicitly states that there are matters the intellect cannot understand, and in those matters the best position for an individual to adopt is to accept the limits of the intellect (*tawaqquf*).[52] In matters that are susceptible to comprehension by human reason, al-Juwaynī sees the ability to understand as contingent on the complexity of the matter at hand and the capacity of the reasoner. Simple matters can be easily apprehended by any individual as long as he or she can undertake the inquiry, systematically analyze all its elements, and identify the correct proof, or aspect of the proof, that produces knowledge. More complex matters, by contrast, require a greater capacity for reasoning, but they, too, necessitate an exhaustive process of systematic analysis until the inquiry culminates in the correct proof that indicates knowledge. In the end, whether one attains

[52] Ibid., 1:137–38.

knowledge of a simple matter or a complex one, through speculative reasoning or without recourse to it, the resulting knowledge is, from al-Juwaynī's perspective, necessary. Therefore, the terminological distinction that best reflects al-Juwaynī's framework is that between acquired necessary knowledge and necessary knowledge, not that between necessary knowledge and speculative or acquired knowledge. Acquired necessary knowledge is especially important for al-Juwaynī because as long as it follows a successful process of reasoning, it affords the individual practical certainty. Beyond exhaustive reasoning, the other important mechanism for obtaining knowledge, which al-Juwaynī describes most clearly in the *Burhān*, is custom. His understanding of custom-derived knowledge includes knowledge of matters subject to personal repetition and habit as well as knowledge of circumstantial states that can be repeatedly observed by an onlooker. The combination of the various discussions on knowledge and the intellect in the *Irshād*, the *Shāmil*, and the *Burhān* shows clearly that al-Juwaynī is preoccupied not simply with knowledge but also with the question of certainty and the path to correct knowledge. Consequently, instead of limiting epistemologically certain knowledge to a narrowly defined realm, as his Ashʿarī predecessors did, al-Juwaynī argues for a relationship between sound reasoning and proofs, allowing reason, custom, and repetition to exist as parallel valid paths to knowledge. By expanding the realm of necessary knowledge, al-Juwaynī enables individuals to attain practical certainty on the basis of either sound reasoning or custom. This theory, of course, has profound implications for jurisprudential discussions, something al-Juwaynī himself recognized when he placed his most extensive epistemological engagement at the beginning of his magnum opus on *uṣūl al-fiqh*, the *Burhān*.

IMPLICATIONS OF AL-JUWAYNĪ'S EPISTEMOLOGY FOR LAW

The previous chapter demonstrated that basic epistemological discussions have significant ramifications for the conceptualization and articulation of law and moral values. In the case of the Muʿtazila, their valorization of human reason and their belief in causality led them to argue that the moral value of all actions could be ascertained rationally, without recourse to revelation, and that the purpose of revelation was simply to support the conclusions reached by the intellect or to provide clarity and details on more opaque matters. The Ashʿarīs responded to this epistemological system by emphasizing the importance of revelation as opposed to reason. They argued that although people are endowed with reason and are responsible for using it, especially to arrive at knowledge of God, human reason is fallible and there is no causal link between proofs and what they indicate that could guarantee the acquisition of sound knowledge. Therefore, while people can, and should, reason, the conclusions reached through reason are usually epistemically probable. In the realm of law, as described in the preceding chapter, Ashʿarī epistemology led to an emphasis on the centrality of revelation and a rejection of legal responsibility (*taklīf*) in its absence; a belief in scriptural universalism, which roots the legal and moral value of every action in scripture; an acceptance of legal indeterminacy; and the marginalization of the lay individual and the elevation of the jurist to a privileged position as the sole qualified deriver of legal rulings.

Al-Juwaynī's departures from the classical Ashʿarī paradigm in his epistemological framework, especially in his understanding of reasoning and proofs, led him to abandon some of the above positions. More specifically, whereas al-Juwaynī accepted and championed the centrality of revelation and scriptural universalism, his desire for certainty forced him to push against legal indeterminacy and the marginalization of the individual. These divergences from previous Ashʿarī doctrine give the impression that he conceded considerable ground to the Muʿtazila; however, he vigorously attacks the Muʿtazila at the beginning of the *Burhān*,[53] and nowhere in his epistemological discussion does he explicitly endorse any of their arguments. In fact, he is especially concerned about the ramifications of the Muʿtazilī doctrine of *taḥsīn wa-taqbīḥ*, which he believes undermines the centrality of revelation.[54] And although al-Juwaynī does acknowledge in the *Irshād* that part of necessary knowledge is what the individual judges to produce harm or good, this evaluation takes place on the basis of the individual's subjective understanding of what is good or bad in a given situation; in al-Juwaynī's view, these subjective assessments have no otherworldly consequences in terms of reward or punishment from God.[55]

Al-Juwaynī's resistance to legal indeterminacy is rooted in his belief that a proof (*dalīl*), in the case of the *Burhān*, or an aspect of a proof (*wajh al-dalāla*), in the case of the *Shāmil*, leads to knowledge, and that an individual can, on the basis of sound reasoning, arrive at correct

[53] Ibid., 1:87–99. [54] Ibid., 1:87–92.
[55] See Shihadeh, "Theories of Ethical Value," 384 and 407.

knowledge. The implication of this position is that reasoning individuals can reach practical certainty in the subject of their reasoning, since for al-Juwaynī all knowledge is necessary – though some necessary knowledge is innate, whereas other necessary knowledge is acquired. In addition, since people can also acquire necessary knowledge through repetition or the observation of customary occurrences, even individuals without refined cognitive abilities to reason about complex matters can attain practical certainty. The possibility of practical certainty applies also to the four final grades of knowledge in al-Juwaynī's ten-grade schema, namely, knowledge of prophecy and revelation, miracles, and religious law: their placement at the end of the scale simply reflects the fact that they require the greatest amount of reasoning. Individuals can obtain practical certainty also in religious matters to the extent that they reason soundly, and this religious knowledge constitutes part of their reservoir of acquired necessary knowledge. In the case of the jurist, knowledge of the law, and therefore practical certainty, is achieved through extensive juridical reasoning and proofs based on scriptural sources, whereas an individual is more likely to reach practical certainty on the basis of repetition. This possibility of practical certainty on the part of both the jurist and the lay individual leaves al-Juwaynī's epistemology at odds with the legal indeterminacy of the Ashʿarī epistemological framework. Furthermore, by allowing not only jurists but also laypeople to access sound knowledge and practical certainty, al-Juwaynī rejects the Ashʿarīs' marginalization of the individual.

Despite al-Juwaynī's novel epistemological framework, which grants individuals certainty in both mundane and religious affairs, he remains squarely an Ashʿarī who concedes all legislative power to God alone. Thus, his resolution of the question of certainty and his creation of an expansive realm for knowledge acquisition are tempered by a commitment to scriptural universalism and to the centrality of revelation; he affirms that human reason can never supersede revelation nor arrive at moral truths without it. Reason, in this paradigm, is a tool at the disposal of the individual to improve his or her understanding of revelation, not to render it irrelevant.

EPISTEMOLOGY BEYOND THE SELF

Al-Juwaynī's recognition that custom can be a source of knowledge beyond speculative reasoning is part of a broader debate in the field of epistemology between internalism and externalism. Epistemology is broadly seen as an inquiry within philosophy that seeks to explain the grounds of human knowledge. Traditionally, epistemologists have defined knowledge as justified belief on the basis of perception, memory, consciousness, or reason.[56] In this paradigm, knowledge is understood to be justified on the basis of the individual alone. This "internalist" model of knowledge has increasingly been challenged by "externalist" models, which recognize that human knowledge is not merely self-referential but also grounded in the individual's context, and a myriad of external factors can influence the four traditional sources of knowledge.[57] The recognition that human knowledge has an outward element led to the birth of social epistemology, which attempts to evaluate the external epistemic factors that relate to human cognition. In the case of al-Juwaynī, although he does not construct a theory of social epistemology, he recognizes that beyond an individual's ability to reason, the individual's ability to act, to reenact an action, and to observe social habits all contribute to his or her knowledge reservoir. This outward element of knowledge acquisition, important on its own for a full understanding of al-Juwaynī's epistemology, becomes especially important when we turn to al-Juwaynī's political thought. Because al-Juwaynī views custom as a source of knowledge and people as capable of achieving practical certainty in their daily affairs, stability and order are, in his political framework, guaranteed not only by institutions but by society itself. In this way, al-Juwaynī's arguments regarding knowledge relate directly to his concern with certainty as well as to his concern with continuity. The full scope of the relationship between al-Juwaynī's epistemology and his political thought is discussed in Chapters 9 and 10.

CONCLUSION

Despite some discrepancies in al-Juwaynī's treatment of knowledge and speculative reasoning in the various texts discussed in this chapter, the overall contours of his epistemology are relatively consistent. Above all, al-Juwaynī appears preoccupied with the question of knowledge and, more specifically, with certainty, and he sets out to articulate an epistemological system that can provide individuals with certainty in their reasoned conclusions while still safeguarding the ultimate legislative authority of God. He accomplishes this goal by focusing on speculative

56 Audi, "Sources of Knowledge."

57 BonJour, "Internalism-Externalism Controversy"; Vahid, "Externalism/Internalism."

reasoning as a process of exhaustive and systematic analysis culminating in a sound proof that yields correct knowledge. By virtue of the exhaustive process of reasoning and the relationship between the correct proof or "aspect of the proof" and knowledge, once knowledge is attained, it is epistemologically equivalent to all other knowledge. Al-Juwaynī does not uphold a distinction between necessary knowledge (*ʿilm ḍarūrī*) and speculative knowledge (*ʿilm naẓarī*). For him, all knowledge, to the extent that it is reached through correct reasoning and without doubt, is necessary, even though some knowledge is acquired without the medium of reason whereas other knowledge is contingent on it. His argument for the uniformity of knowledge affords individuals practical certainty in all soundly reasoned matters. Al-Juwaynī's theory is predicated on the belief that discovery of the correct proof necessarily leads to knowledge of what is sought; in other words, the entire process of speculative reasoning consists of arriving at the correct proof, which in turn entails the object of knowledge itself. This understanding of the relationship between reason, proofs, and knowledge departs from al-Juwaynī's Ashʿarī predecessors and forms the theoretical basis for the rest of his arguments regarding reason, certainty, and human knowledge.

While it may at first glance seem as if al-Juwaynī is laying the entire world bare for the human mind to comprehend, in fact he repeatedly stresses that not everything can be known through reason, nor can everyone reason about complex matters. Furthermore, human reasoning on matters of law and morality has ultimately no otherworldly significance, as it is God alone who legislates both morality and law. Despite the restriction on human legislation, al-Juwaynī sees the basic function of the intellect to consist of apprehending matters rationally and systematically so as to yield knowledge that is certain rather than indeterminate or presumptive. Simply put, the basic desire of a human being is to know things with certainty, and the intellect, utilized as a judicious tool, can fulfill this desire.

PART III

LEGAL THEORY

5

Certainty in Legal Sources

Ḥadīth

The previous two chapters argued that epistemological discussions have a direct bearing on the law, as jurists are concerned with both the epistemic value of rulings and the certainty by which the sources of the law are established as authoritative. With regard to the former, the self-conscious epistemology of the Ashʿarīs recognized the limits of human reason and the breadth of God's legislative authority, resulting in a legal theory that gave preference to the plain meaning of the text and to explicit legal injunctions, which required the least amount of reasoning on the part of the jurists.[1] However, Ashʿarī jurists could not simply turn to the scriptural sources – the Quran and *ḥadīth* – and interpret them directly to derive a ruling on an issue; instead, the first step was to confirm that the

[1] Standard books of *uṣūl al-fiqh* begin with extensive linguistic and hermeneutical inquiries, signaling that law rests on a robust theory of language and interpretation that serves as the foundation to legal derivation. One of the basic tenets is that the epistemic strength of a legal ruling is connected to its linguistic clarity as well as its linguistic form. This means that explicit scriptural prescriptions or proscriptions hold a higher epistemic value than do vague or ambiguous ones. Given the importance of the scriptural sources, their correct interpretation and epistemic weight were subjects of extensive debate. For more on the development of and disagreements in early legal hermeneutics, see Vishanoff, *Formation of Islamic Hermeneutics*; El Shamsy, *Canonization of Islamic Law*, part 1; Zysow, *Economy of Certainty*, chapter 2; Bernard Weiss, *The Search for God's Law: Islamic Jurisprudence in the Writings of Sayf al-Dīn al-Āmidī* (Salt Lake City: University of Utah Press, 2010), chapters 1 and 3; Joseph Lowry, *Early Islamic Legal Theory* (Leiden: Brill, 2007), chapter 2; and Joseph Lowry, "Some Preliminary Observations on al-Šāfiʿī and Later *Uṣūl al-Fiqh*: The Case of the Term *Bayān*," *Arabica* 55, nos. 5–6 (2008): 505–27. For a brief overview of various linguistic and hermeneutical classifications, see Sukri Ramic, *Language and the Interpretation of Islamic Law* (Cambridge: Islamic Texts Society, 2005).

scriptural sources themselves were indeed authentic.[2] For the Quran, which was transmitted in countless concurrent reports (*mutawātir*) and had been memorized by numerous individuals,[3] establishing the material validity of the text was relatively easy, but for *ḥadīth* the task was considerably more complex. By al-Juwaynī's time the issue had already been hotly debated with the canonization of the *ḥadīth* collections of al-Bukhārī and Muslim,[4] but al-Juwaynī undertakes his own evaluation of the validity of *ḥadīth* in his *Burhān*, once again preoccupied with the question of certainty. In contrast to his intellectual predecessors, who held overwhelmingly that concurrent reports (*aḥādīth mutawātira*) that met certain conditions constitute necessary (*ḍarūrī*) knowledge, al-Juwaynī rejects the proposed list of conditions and instead argues that from a procedural perspective, the knowledge gleaned from concurrent reports is *naẓarī*, or speculative, in nature. On the surface this position seems to contradict al-Juwaynī's concern with certainty, but a closer reading reveals that al-Juwaynī is actually arguing that this knowledge is *acquired* necessary knowledge. Furthermore, the conditions that he sets out for *mutawātir ḥadīth* show that his primary focus lies beyond the concern with formal criteria that characterizes his predecessors and on the *external* manifestation of *ḥadīth* within society. As a consequence, his analysis resembles less the formalized epistemological system of the jurists and more the early epistemological understanding of the *ahl al-ḥadīth* (partisans of *ḥadīth*).[5] This feature of al-Juwaynī's approach to *ḥadīth* is

[2] On the debates regarding the authenticity of *ḥadīth*, see Wael Hallaq, "The Authenticity of Prophetic Ḥadîth: A Pseudo-Problem," *Studia Islamica*, no. 89 (1999): 75–90; Zysow, *Economy of Certainty*, chapter 1; Lowry, *Early Islamic Legal Theory*, chapter 3; and Brown, *Canonization of al-Bukhārī and Muslim.*

[3] For some of the debates regarding the early compilation of the Quran, see the works of Andrew Rippin, such as "Revelation and Canon," in *Quranic Studies: Sources and Methods of Scriptural Interpretation*, ed. John Wansbrough (Amherst, NY: Prometheus Books, 2002); Shady Hekmat Nasser, *The Transmission of the Variant Readings of the Qur'ān: The Problem of* Tawātur *and the Emergence of* Shawādhdh (Leiden: Brill, 2013); Fred Donner, "The Qur'ān in Recent Scholarship – Challenges and Desiderata," in *The Qur'ān in Its Historical Context*, ed. Gabriel S. Reynolds (Abingdon: Routledge, 2008), 29–50; Fred Donner, "The Historian, the Believers, and the Qur'ān," in *New Perspectives on the Qur'ān*, ed. Gabriel S. Reynolds (London: Routledge, 2011), 25–37; and Fred Donner, "The Historical Context of the Qur'an," in *The Cambridge Companion to the Qur'an*, ed. Jane D. McAuliffe (Cambridge: Cambridge University Press, 2006), 21–39. See also the works of Angelika Neuwirth.

[4] See Brown, *Canonization of al-Bukhārī and Muslim.*

[5] According to Jonathan Brown, scholars in this period were divided on how to understand and employ *ḥadīth*. Some focused on the epistemic value of *ḥadīth*, seeing them as representing the *actual* actions of the Prophet, whereas others were more concerned with

important because his emphasis on external conditions illuminates the importance he places on both practice and society in the construction, preservation, and transmission of knowledge.

LEGAL THOUGHT AT THE TIME OF AL-JUWAYNĪ

Amid the intellectual animosity between the Ḥanafīs and the Shāfiʿīs and between the Ashʿarīs and the Muʿtazila in Nishapur, major intellectual developments continued to sweep the Islamic world. For present purposes, the two most important were the canonization of Islamic law and the canonization of *Ṣaḥīḥ al-Bukhārī* and *Ṣaḥīḥ Muslim*. These developments set the intellectual stage for al-Juwaynī by establishing the parameters within which he reasoned as an adherent of the Shāfiʿī school and an intellectual heir of the scholars who were most instrumental in the canonization of the two *ḥadīth* compilations.

The canonization of Islamic law, as Ahmed El Shamsy has termed this development, was a process that began with al-Shāfiʿī (d. 204/820), who sought to replace an emphasis on the community's normative tradition as encapsulated in the practice of Medina and the Mālikī school[6] with an emphasis on textual sources and hermeneutical techniques of legal derivation. The ultimate goal of al-Shāfiʿī's focus on textual authority,

the use of *ḥadīth* for a wide array of legal and social purposes. One might expect that the partisans of *ḥadīth* (*ahl al-ḥadīth*), defined by Brown as "those scholars who prioritized the derivation of norms from texts (*nuṣūṣ*) above consistency in legal analogy, selecting these proof texts through the emerging science of *ḥadīth* criticism," would be interested primarily in the epistemic value of *ḥadīth*; however, Brown argues that they were more concerned with their historical certainty. Therefore, despite their rigor in *isnād* criticism, they were willing to utilize *ḥadīth* that were not rigorously authenticated if circumstances necessitated it. See Brown, "Did the Prophet Say It or Not? The Literal, Historical and Effective Truth of Hadith," *Journal of the American Oriental Society* 129, no. 2 (2009): 259–85. For more on the distinction between partisans of *ḥadīth* and partisans of reason (*ahl al-ra'y*), see Christopher Melchert, "The Traditionist-Jurisprudents and the Framing of Islamic Law," *Islamic Law and Society* 8, no. 3 (2001): 383–406; Scott Lucas, "Where Are All the Legal *Ḥadīth*?," *Islamic Law and Society* 8, no. 3 (2001): 408–31; and Lucas, "Principles of Traditionist Jurisprudence Reconsidered," *Muslim World* 100, no. 1 (2010): 145–56.

6 See Umar Abd-Allah Wymann-Landgraf, *Mālik and Medina* (Leiden: Brill, 2013); Yasin Dutton, *The Origins of Islamic Law: The Quran, the Muwaṭṭa' and Madinan 'Amal* (London: Routledge, 2002); and Yasin Dutton, *Original Islam: Mālik and the Madhhab of Madina* (London: Routledge, 2012).

however, was to eclipse or displace tradition and, indeed, the community.[7] As El Shamsy argues,

> al-Shāfiʿī's canon-centered individualism was tempered by the reintegration of community into Islamic law through a new institution, the school of law (*madhhab*). Whereas the pre-canonization normative discourse had been embodied in a community of *tradition*, the novel institution of the legal school was first and foremost a community of *interpretation* that defined itself in terms of a shared hermeneutic stance vis-à-vis the canon of sacred sources.[8]

The community created in each *madhhab* was a community of interpretation with a common hermeneutical stance toward the sacred sources, which gave the *madhhab*'s members a distinct group identity and discourse. For El Shamsy, this distinct identity and discourse is evident not just in the existence of a school doctrine, but also in secondary literature that actively engages with both the eponym of the school and the dominant doctrine.[9] An evaluation of a school's secondary literature reveals the shared commitment to an interpretative methodology emblematic of a community of interpretation that crosses temporal constraints. In the Shāfiʿī school, the interpretative methodology characterizing the *madhhab* as a community was one that emphasized a "semantic approach" to the sacred sources alongside an interpretative one, recognizing that a deep understanding of the sources and a robust legal theory were both necessary. What differentiated the Shāfiʿī methodology from the Mālikī one at the time was what El Shamsy describes as the former's "radical individualism,"[10] which emphasized the individual interpretation of the jurist over the preservation of tradition in the communal practice of the people of Medina. These differences between the *madhhab*s meant that each

[7] Scholars have characterized the development of Islamic law in various ways, their focal points ranging from the rise of concretized jurisprudential methods to the emergence of regional schools out of local schools, the widespread practice of *taqlīd* (following of previous authorities), and the rise of a robust intra-school dialogue. It is likely that each of these explanations describes a particular phase in the maturation of the Sunnī legal schools, without which the schools could not have attained their dominance. For the various arguments, see Hallaq, *Origins and Evolution*; Wael Hallaq, "From Regional to Personal Schools of Law? A Reevaluation," *Islamic Law and Society* 8, no. 1 (2001): 1–26; Melchert, *Formation of the Sunni Schools*; Nimrod Hurvitz, "Schools of Law and Historical Context: Re-Examining the Formation of the Ḥanbalī Madhhab," *Islamic Law and Society* 7, no. 1 (2000): 37–64; Nimrod Hurvitz, "From Scholarly Circles to Mass Movements: The Formation of Legal Communities in Islamic Societies," *American Historical Review* 108, no. 4 (2003): 985–1008; Mohammad Fadel, "The Social Logic of *Taqlīd* and the Rise of the *Mukhtaṣar*," *Islamic Law and Society* 3, no. 2 (1996): 193–233; and El Shamsy, *Canonization of Islamic Law*.

[8] El Shamsy, *Canonization of Islamic Law*, 6.

[9] Ibid., chapter 3.

[10] Ibid., 84.

madhhab was an interpretive community unto itself, despite the fact that each was ultimately engaged in the same project of legal interpretation.

Beyond these methodological differences, these independently functioning communities of interpretation were united in two key ways – one legal and the other epistemological. From a legal perspective, as Wael Hallaq notes, the four primary Sunnī *madhhabs*[11] all recognized the validity and centrality of four legal sources, a recognition that is described as "the Great Synthesis."[12] These four sources – namely, the Quran, *ḥadīth*, consensus (*ijmāʿ*), and independent reasoning (*ijtihād*) – formed the cornerstone of all legal reasoning; sources beyond these four were subject to disagreement among the *madhhabs*. Epistemologically speaking, what united the four communities of interpretation is what Aron Zysow calls a formalist epistemology, which stood in contrast to the materialist epistemology embraced by nondominant legal schools such as the Ẓāhirī school.[13] For formalists, according to Zysow, "the practice (*ijtihād*) of the jurist is of paramount concern. Ordinarily the results of his practice are only probable, but their validity is ensured by the fact that the framework within which he practices is known with certainty. This framework is provided by the main legal institutions and by *uṣūl al-fiqh*."[14] Therefore, formalists are primarily concerned with ensuring that the process of legal reasoning, and thus legal theory, is established with certainty. The certainty of the legal framework allows jurists to overlook the lack of certainty in the resulting rulings. For materialists, on the other hand, "probability has no place in the formulation of the rules of law.

11 On the historical trajectory of the four *madhhabs*, see note 7.

12 Hallaq, *Origins and Evolution*, 109, 119, 123, and Wael Hallaq, "Was al-Shafiʿi the Master Architect of Islamic Jurisprudence?," *International Journal of Middle East Studies* 25, no. 4 (1993): 587–605.

13 The Ẓāhirī school was the most famous nondominant school characterized by a materialist epistemology. For full-length studies on the Ẓāhirī school, see Amr Osman, *The Ẓāhirī Madhhab: A Textualist Theory of Islamic Law* (Leiden: Brill, 2014), and Ignaz Goldziher, *The Ẓāhirīs: Their Doctrine and Their History* (Leiden: Brill, 2007). Research on Ibn Ḥazm's legal thought has played a crucial role in mapping the development of the Ẓāhirī school. See Adam Sabra's two-part article, "Ibn Ḥazm's Literalism: A Critique of Islamic legal Theory – Part 1," *Al-Qanṭara* 28, no. 1 (2007): 7–40, and "Ibn Ḥazm's Literalism: A Critique of Islamic legal Theory – Part 2," *Al-Qanṭara* 28, no. 2 (2007): 307–48. See also Camilla Adang, "Ibn Ḥazm on Homosexuality: A Case-Study of Ẓāhirī Legal Methodology," *Al-Qanṭara* 24, no. 1 (2003): 5–31; Devin Stewart, "Muḥammad Dāwūd al-Ẓāhirī's Manual of Jurisprudence," in *Studies in Islamic Legal Theory*, ed. Bernard Weiss (Leiden: Brill, 2002), 99–158; and Melchert, *Formation of the Sunni Schools*, 178–97.

14 Zysow, *Economy of Certainty*, 3.

Every rule must be certain in order to be valid. There is no balancing of certainty and probability in materialist systems, and the line between legal theory and law is erased."[15] Materialists thus focus on the scriptural sources themselves, limiting the derivation of legal rulings to epistemically certain sources. This means that any source lacking in epistemic certainty cannot be used to generate norms.[16]

Formalists, too, devote some attention to epistemological inquiries, as their four-source theory of the law requires them to verify the epistemological strength of the scriptural sources as well as to establish with certainty that their other two primary sources of law are indeed definitive. As Zysow notes, formalists are willing to accept legal probability in specific rulings only because they possess certainty in the process of legal reasoning, meaning that the sources that they use to derive the rulings must be definitively valid. However, al-Juwaynī's epistemology, driven foremost by his desire for certainty, shows that he was not a prototypical formalist fixated on the epistemological strength of the sources of the law; he was also concerned with the epistemological strength of derived rulings. This concern, however, does not make him a materialist, as materialists were unwilling to accept probability, which al-Juwaynī openly does. But his preoccupation with epistemological certainty for both the sources of the law and the rulings derived from them complicates his classification as a formalist and problematizes the simple categorization of jurists into one camp or the other.

The validity of the scriptural sources was directly connected to their transmission: if a jurist could be certain that a text was preserved in its revealed form or, in the case of a *ḥadīth*, in the exact form in which the Prophet articulated it, the text would be considered epistemically certain in terms of its transmission (*qaṭʿī al-wurūd/thubūt*).[17] If, on the other

[15] Ibid.

[16] It is important to note that while materialists were concerned with the epistemic certainty of sources, when it came to interpretation on the basis of these sources, they did not endorse simple literalism. See Robert Gleave, *Islam and Literalism: Literal Meaning and Interpretation in Islamic Legal Theory* (Edinburgh: Edinburgh University Press, 2013). See also the beginning of Sherman Jackson's article "Literalism, Empiricism and Induction: Apprehending and Concretizing Islamic Law's *Maqāsid al-Sharīʿa* in the Modern World," *Michigan State Law Review* (2006): 1469–86.

[17] Certainty in the transmission of a report was achieved if it was narrated concurrently, making it a *mutawātir* report. The theory of concurrency (*tawātur*) articulated by the jurists applied to both the Quran and *ḥadīth*. Although the textual legitimacy of the Quran is not usually discussed in texts of *uṣūl al-fiqh*, the *tawātur* doctrine obtains its gravity from its applicability to the Quran, for if one were to cast doubt on the doctrine of *tawātur*, one would be implicitly questioning the authenticity of the transmitted text of the Quran. Such doubt would disrupt the entire edifice of Islamic scholarship. From this

hand, the jurist was uncertain about the accuracy of the text's preservation and transmission, it would be deemed only probable in terms of its transmission (*ẓannī al-wurūd/thubūt*). In texts of *uṣūl al-fiqh*, this issue arises in the section on reports (*akhbār*), where jurists typically distinguish between two types of reports, concurrent reports (*al-akhbār al-mutawātira*) and unitary reports (*al-akhbār al-āḥād*),[18] the latter referring to *ḥadīth* related by a single person or only a few people. Concurrent reports are defined as reports that are mass-transmitted across successive generations; the jurist can be certain of their veracity because of the extreme improbability of undetected fabrication or error. Although most jurists accepted that concurrent reports are epistemically certain in terms of their transmission, they differed on whether the knowledge gleaned from such reports is necessary (*ḍarūrī*) or speculative (*naẓarī*).[19] By contrast, unitary

vantage point, the importance of the doctrine of *tawātur* can be seen as an outgrowth of the centrality of the textual sources themselves. While believing Muslims naturally acknowledge the primacy of these sources, jurists, through the doctrine, could justify it rationally. Secondary literature on abrogation (*naskh*) in English is limited and features only one full-length monograph, John Burton's *The Sources of Islamic Law: Islamic Theories of Abrogation* (Edinburgh: Edinburgh University Press, 1990). However, many elements of Burton's work are now outdated in light of newly discovered classical manuscripts. Shorter studies on abrogation in English include Daniel Brown, "The Triumph of Scripturalism: The Doctrine of *Naskh* and Its Modern Critics," in *The Shaping of an American Islamic Discourse: A Memorial to Fazlur Rahman*, ed. Earle Waugh and Frederick Denny (Atlanta: Scholars Press, 1997), 49–66; John Burton, "Abrogation," in *Encyclopaedia of the Qurʾān*, 11–19; Christopher Melchert, "Quranic Abrogation across the Ninth Century: Shāfiʿī, Abū ʿUbaid, Muḥāsibī, and Ibn Qutaibah," in Weiss, *Studies in Islamic Legal Theory*, 75–98; David Powers, "The Exegetical Genre *Nāsikh al-Qurʾān wa Mansūkhuhu*," in *Approaches to the History of the Interpretation of the Qurʾān*, ed. Andrew Rippin (New York: Oxford University Press, 1988), 117–38; Andrew Rippin, "Al-Zuhrī, *Naskh al-Qurʾān* and the Problem of Early *Tafsīr* Texts," *Bulletin of the School of Oriental and African Studies* 47, no. 1 (1984): 22–43; and Andrew Rippin, "The Exegetical Literature of Abrogation: Form and Content," in *Studies in Islamic and Middle Eastern Texts and Traditions in Memory of Norman Calder*, ed. G. R. Hawting, J. A. Mojaddedi, and Alexander Samely (Oxford: Oxford University Press, 2000), 213–31.

18 For a later comprehensive categorization of the types of *ḥadīth*, see Abū ʿAmr ʿUthmān b. ʿAbd al-Rahmān al-Shahrazūrī, *Muqaddimat Ibn al-Ṣalāḥ fī ʿulūm al-ḥadīth* (Cairo: Dār al-Maʿārif, 1990). A translation by Eerik Dickinson is also available, entitled *An Introduction to the Science of the Ḥadīth* (Reading: Garnet, 2006). For an overview of the development and role of *ḥadīth*, see Jonathan Brown, *Hadith: Muhammad's Legacy in the Medieval and Modern World* (London: Oneworld, 2009), and Muhammad Zubayr Siddiqi, *Hadith Literature: Its Origin, Development and Special Features* (Cambridge: Islamic Texts Society, 1993).

19 Al-Zarkashī identifies three opinions regarding the epistemic value of knowledge derived from *mutawātir ḥadīth*: (1) it is necessary (*ḍarūrī*); (2) it is speculative (*naẓarī*); and (3) it falls somewhere between acquired (*muktasab*) and necessary. Among those holding that

reports are only probable in terms of their transmission. The distinction between the two types of reports is primarily an epistemological one, with concurrent reports being certain and, according to the dominant view, producing necessary knowledge (*ʿilm ḍarūrī*), whereas unitary reports are considered probable and produce speculative knowledge (*ʿilm naẓarī*). Given the epistemological and legal ramifications of a *ḥadīth*'s classification as *mutawātir*, scholars paid great attention to the specific requirements that, if met, would endow a *ḥadīth* with the seal of epistemic certainty. The debates arose from the fact that jurists could not agree on these requirements.

Two important *uṣūl al-fiqh* texts that provide insight into the discussions surrounding *mutawātir ḥadīth* before al-Juwaynī are al-Bāqillānī's magnum opus *al-Taqrīb wa-l-irshād al-ṣaghīr* and Abū al-Ḥusayn al-Baṣrī's (d. 436/1044) *al-Muʿtamad fī uṣūl al-fiqh*, an abridgment of Qāḍī ʿAbd al-Jabbār's *ʿUmd*. As we have seen, al-Baqillānī had an undeniable impact on al-Juwaynī's thought, and in the *Burhān*, al-Juwaynī continually invokes al-Bāqillānī as one of his primary interlocutors. Unfortunately, the section on *akhbār* in al-Bāqillānī's *Taqrīb* is not extant; however, the basic discussion is captured in al-Juwaynī's abridgment of the text, *al-Talkhīṣ fī uṣūl al-fiqh*. Al-Baṣrī also appears as an interlocutor of al-Juwaynī in the *Burhān*, but while his *uṣūl* is considered either Ḥanāfī or Shāfiʿī,[20] he adheres to the epistemological framework of the Muʿtazila.

In his *Talkhīṣ*, al-Juwaynī presents what is probably a highly truncated version of al-Bāqillānī's discussion, focusing primarily on the three conditions required for a report to be considered *mutawātir*: (1) the report must be transmitted by a minimum of four narrators; (2) the narrators

it is necessary, al-Zarkashī lists al-Juwaynī, al-Ghazālī, and al-Bāqillānī. Those who hold that it is *naẓarī* include, according to al-Zarkashī, al-Kaʿbī, Imām al-Rāzī, Ibn al-Ḥājib, Abū al-Ḥusayn al-Basrī, and Ibn al-Qaṭṭān. Al-Zarkashī does not name any adherents of the middle view, but he says that they are similar to those who abstain from the discussion entirely, such as al-Āmidī. See Badr al-Dīn Muḥammad b. Bahādur al-Zarkashī, *al-Baḥr al-muḥīṭ fī uṣūl al-fiqh*, ed. ʿAbd al-Qādir ʿAbd Allāh al-ʿĀnī (Kuwait: Dār al-Ṣafwa li-Wizārat al-Awqāf, 1992), 5:240, and Sayf al-Dīn al-Āmidī, *al-Iḥkām fī uṣūl al-aḥkām* (Cairo: Maṭbaʿat Muḥammad ʿAlī Ṣubayḥ, 1917), 2:22. For a treatment in English of the epistemological differences surrounding *ḥadīth*, see Zysow, *Economy of Certainty*, 9–11. See also Murteza Bedir, "An Early Response to al-Shāfiʿī: ʿĪsā ibn Abān on the Prophetic Report," *Islamic Law and Society* 9, no. 3 (2002): 285–311, and Hallaq, "Authenticity of Prophetic Ḥadîth."

20 Given that al-Baṣrī's funeral was led by the famous Ḥanafī *qāḍī* Abū ʿAbd Allāh al-Ṣaymarī, it is most likely that he was a Ḥanafī. See Wilferd Madelung, "Abū l-Ḥusayn al-Baṣrī," in *Encyclopaedia of Islam*, 2nd edn.

must understand the content of the report that they convey; and (3) the report must be conveyed directly through sensory means.[21] The first condition is intended to exclude the possibility of collusion or error in transmission. The second condition is likewise aimed at safeguarding against error by requiring that the narrators understand the information contained in the report. Otherwise, they may inadvertently change the intended meaning of the report in their retelling of it.[22] Finally, al-Bāqillānī's last condition is tied to his belief that knowledge obtained through *mutawātir* reports is necessary (*ḍarūrī*) and, as such, must be established through one of the avenues of necessary knowledge, which he limits to sensory knowledge or axiomatic knowledge.[23] In al-Bāqillānī's view, hearing or receiving a *mutawātir* report is akin to coming into direct contact with the Prophet, in a sense "seeing" his actions. However, the fulfillment of the third condition alone does not establish the necessary nature of the knowledge contained in the report – all three criteria must be met. Al-Bāqillānī nonetheless insists that knowledge derived from a *ḥadīth* is not *naẓarī*, since considering such would imply not only that the transmission of the *ḥadīth* is only probable but also that the mass-transmitted text of the Quran is similarly probable. The primary objective of the three criteria, according to al-Bāqillānī, is to establish conclusively the veracity of *ḥadīth* reports, and it is therefore important that the criteria be both rigorous and practical. Al-Bāqillānī also discusses and criticizes alternative *tawātur* criteria proposed by others, arguing that any conditions beyond these three are unnecessary and make the process of verification unnecessarily complicated.[24] Because al-Bāqillānī's discussion reaches us only through al-Juwaynī's abridgment, it is not clear what other issues in addition to his criteria and the necessary nature of *mutawātir* reports al-Bāqillānī may have been interested in. In the *Talkhīṣ* al-Juwaynī does not explicitly disagree with al-Bāqillānī, but later in his *Burhān* he does criticize both al-Bāqillānī's criteria and his conclusion that the knowledge from such reports is necessary.

Abū al-Ḥusayn al-Baṣrī also holds that *mutawātir* reports yield epistemically certain and necessary knowledge, but he affirms only two of al-Bāqillānī's conditions: (1) the report must be transmitted by at least four

21 Al-Juwaynī, *al-Talkhīṣ*, 2:286–87.
22 For verbatim and non-verbatim transmission, see Brown, "Did the Prophet Say It?," 265–75.
23 For a review of al-Bāqillānī's epistemology, see Chapter 3.
24 Al-Juwaynī, *al-Talkhīṣ*, 2:296–300.

narrators in order to prevent collusion and (2) the report must be transmitted through sensory means.[25] When these conditions are met, al-Baṣrī argues, the resulting knowledge is necessary. Despite the abbreviated nature of al-Baṣrī's and al-Bāqillānī's discussions, it is clear that both scholars were primarily concerned with establishing the authenticity of *mutawātir* reports, leading them to focus on the reports' mode of transmission in terms of number and form. However, by detailing varying scholarly opinions regarding *tawātur*, they reveal that despite the foundational importance of concurrent reports, the conditions governing them remained fraught with disagreement.

This lack of agreement remained unresolved through al-Juwaynī's time and, indeed, well after. In the seventh/thirteenth century, the controversy is recorded in the *Iḥkām* of Sayf al-Dīn al-Āmidī (d. 631/1233). According to al-Āmidī, there are two types of conditions: those that scholars agree on and those that are contested. The first category contains five generally accepted requirements: (1) The number of narrations must be sufficiently high to preclude the possibility of collusion. (2) The narrators must be able to attest to the genuine nature of the report; in other words, the report must be based on *actual* knowledge of what transpired. (3) The knowledge conveyed must be based on sense perception and not on reason. (4) The recipient of the report must be capable of receiving it; individuals with cognitive impairments are thus excluded. (5) When a report is conveyed over successive generations, all of the above conditions must be met for each generation.

The first three conditions mirror those of al-Bāqillānī and al-Baṣrī, and though they did not explicitly articulate the fourth and fifth, their discussions indicate that they would probably have endorsed them, too. Like al-Bāqillānī and al-Baṣrī, al-Āmidī argues that once the minimum criteria have been fulfilled, the resulting knowledge is necessary.[26] As for the contested conditions, these likewise number five and concern the narrators of the report, who (1) should be numerous beyond counting, (2) should all be trustworthy Muslims, (3) may not be coerced, (4) should be immune to error, and (5) may not represent the lower social classes. Al-Āmidī argues that these conditions are unnecessary, since they do not help to establish the veracity or authenticity of the narration.

[25] Abū al-Ḥusayn al-Baṣrī, *al-Muʿtamad fī uṣūl al-fiqh* (Damascus: al-Maʿhad al-ʿIlmī al-Faransī li-l-Dirāsāt al-ʿArabiyya, 1964), 2:565 and 561.

[26] Al-Āmidī, *al-Iḥkām*, 2:34–42.

The first five conditions enumerated by al-Āmidī were adopted by the majority of jurists, and thus the slightly later al-Zarkashī (d. 794/1269) presents almost identical conditions for *tawātur*.[27] The jurists' ongoing preoccupation with *mutawātir* reports and their prominence in legal treatises is testament to their centrality in the Islamic tradition. And though disagreement regarding the conditions was never completely eliminated, it was greatly curtailed by the universal agreement on two key conditions – a large number of transmitters and the sensory conveyance of the report. As long as these two conditions were met, the majority of jurists accepted reports as epistemically certain in terms of transmission and the resulting knowledge as necessary. This meant that legal scholars had a source of scriptural knowledge in addition to the Quran on which they could confidently rely.

Given al-Juwaynī's formalist concern with establishing the validity of the process of legal reasoning, it is not surprising that he, too, is preoccupied with the legitimacy of *ḥadīth* as a source of law. Al-Juwaynī's justification of *ḥadīth* entails demonstrating that concurrent reports are epistemically certain because of their unassailable transmission and that unitary reports, although not similarly certain in terms of their transmission, can nonetheless constitute a valid source of law on the basis of a broader, epistemically certain principle. Al-Juwaynī is adamant that both types of *ḥadīth* must be justified rationally for their legitimacy to be established. He thus returns to the epistemological foundations laid out in the *Burhān* and ends up rejecting the two conditions for *tawātur* accepted by the majority of jurists.

AL-JUWAYNĪ AND REPORTS (*AKHBĀR*)

As noted earlier, the discussion regarding the epistemic value of *ḥadīth* was subsumed within a larger conversation in *uṣūl al-fiqh* texts regarding reports (*akhbār*). Al-Juwaynī starts this discussion in the *Burhān* by differentiating between three types of reports: (1) those whose veracity (*ṣidq*) can be conclusively established, (2) those whose falsity can be conclusively established, and (3) those whose veracity or falsity cannot

[27] Al-Zarkashī does list some conditions that would not meet with al-Āmidī's approval, such as the requirement that the report be conveyed by a trustworthy individual. He enumerates a total of seven agreed-on conditions and five that are subject to disagreement. See al-Zarkashī, *al-Baḥr al-muḥīṭ*, 6:231–34.

be determined conclusively.[28] The first category is further subdivided into reports whose veracity can be determined immediately and which thus produce necessary knowledge and those that require extensive speculative reasoning and thus yield the type of acquired necessary knowledge encountered earlier. Applying this typology to *ḥadīth*, al-Juwaynī argues that *mutawātir ḥadīth* constitute reports whose veracity can be established conclusively but whose use as an independent source of legal derivation must be justified through reasoning,[29] whereas unitary *ḥadīth* (*aḥādīth āḥād*) are reports whose veracity or falsity cannot be determined conclusively and whose legitimate use in legal derivation requires something external, a subject to which we will return.[30]

In his discussion of concurrent reports, al-Juwaynī veers away from a strictly textual and transmission-based analysis, which was the norm among scholars both before and after him, and instead relies on external indicators (*qarāʾin al-aḥwāl*) to establish the veracity of particular reports. In contrast to his predecessors, who focused on the number of narrators and the sensory transmission of reports, al-Juwaynī focuses on indicators that support the trustworthiness and uprightness of a *ḥadīth*'s transmitter and on the content of the *ḥadīth* itself. As he later details, verification of a report's content through external indicators draws in part on individual customary practice of the knowledge conveyed in the *ḥadīth*, which indicates not just the veracity of the text but also its acceptance in society more broadly. In this way, whereas earlier scholars fixated on conditions internal to the *ḥadīth*, al-Juwaynī moves outward to argue that if a concurrent report is sound, then external indicators will work in tandem to produce an aggregation of knowledge, resulting in conviction regarding the report. By appealing to conditions outside the report itself, al-Juwaynī acknowledges that texts stand in a dialectical relationship with the individuals who receive and convey them, such that both are contingent on one another. In other words, texts cannot exist or be substantiated without the individuals who enact their contents, and the practice of individuals cannot exist without the explicit knowledge conveyed in texts.

28 Al-Juwaynī, *al-Burhān*, 1:583. The section on reports starts earlier, on p. 540, with a discussion on the conditions for *mutawātir ḥadīth* put forward by his predecessors. Later scholars complicate the distinction of true versus false speech and delve into questions such as whether the speech is singular or compound and the reality of true and false speech. For a detailed discussion, see al-Zarkashī, *al-Baḥr al-muḥīṭ*, 6:215–30.

29 Recall that concurrent reports made an appearance in the fourth grade of al-Juwaynī's ten grades of knowledge; see Chapter 4 and al-Juwaynī, *al-Burhān*, 1:132 and 1:574–79.

30 Al-Juwaynī, *al-Burhān*, 1:564–66 and 582–84.

RESPONDING TO HIS PREDECESSORS AND ESTABLISHING HIS OWN CRITERIA

Al-Juwaynī starts his discussion by rejecting the conditions for *tawātur* proposed by his predecessors, arguing that they are meritless and ineffective in establishing the veracity of reports. The most problematic condition for al-Juwaynī is the stipulation that the information be conveyed through sensory means (*maḥsūs*). The rationale for this criterion is the view, mentioned earlier, that hearing or receiving a *mutawātir* report is analogous to direct contact with the Prophet.[31] Since the report is conceptualized as "seeing" the Prophet's actions, it is included in the realm of sensory knowledge and thus counts as necessary knowledge. In response to this logic, al-Juwaynī argues that the sensory perceptions of individuals are not uniform, and in contrast to sensory knowledge, which is innate, knowledge of a concurrent report's veracity requires some mental effort to attain. This additional effort means that knowledge of the report's veracity is not immediate in the way that sensory knowledge of light and darkness is, and therefore it cannot be classified alongside sensory knowledge. By equating sensory knowledge with innate knowledge (*ʿilm badīhī*), which requires no reasoning, al-Juwaynī precludes any form of equivalence between naturally occurring sensory knowledge and knowledge derived from concurrent reports, which does require reasoning.

For al-Juwaynī, reasoning on the basis of external indicators is a very specific form of reasoning, which occupies the sixth grade in his discussion on the ten grades of knowledge in the *Burhān*. In that discussion, al-Juwaynī uses the example of knowledge of bodily states obtained through external indicators (*qarāʾin al-aḥwāl*), such as the redness that accompanies anger and the blushing that indicates shyness. This type of knowledge is not equivalent to innate sensory knowledge, but it, too, can be deemed necessary.[32] The necessary nature of this knowledge is based on al-Juwaynī's assertion that knowledge derived from continual observation of patterns in the world of phenomena can reach practical certainty and be necessary to the intellect.[33] Since this kind of knowledge is necessary but nonetheless independent of the senses, al-Juwaynī argues that

31 Zysow, *Economy of Certainty*, 15.

32 Al-Juwaynī, *al-Burhān*, 1:568. Al-Juwaynī uses the same example in his description of the ten grades of knowledge. For his argument regarding practical certainty and necessary knowledge, see Chapter 4.

33 Al-Juwaynī, *al-Burhān*, 1:568.

mutawātir knowledge can also be established without the aid of the senses. In illuminating what he sees as the falsity of the sensory condition and explicating his rationale, al-Juwaynī relies on customary behavior and/or the customary appearance of the world of phenomena – a concept I will discuss more fully later.

The second condition for *tawātur* that al-Juwaynī likewise rejects is the stipulation of a minimum number of narrators. He cites various numbers proposed by scholars as the threshold figure; these range from five to forty, or even the total number of inhabitants in a country.[34] Though he does not identify the scholars advocating each opinion,[35] he finds equal fault in all of them, criticizing them for a lack of adequate reasoning. According to al-Juwaynī, the importance of *tawātur* stems from its acceptance as a fundamental source of religious knowledge, and to function as such, it must be justified on purely rational grounds, otherwise the foundation of religion will be susceptible to critique. Applying this requirement to the conditions suggested for concurrent reports, he is unable to identify a rational justification for any of the numbers proposed as a minimum requirement. He speculates that the various figures are either taken from Quranic stories or borrowed from other legal situations such as witnessing that have no direct bearing on the doctrine of *tawātur*.[36] Instead of specifying a fixed minimum number of narrators, al-Juwaynī makes the argument that as a growing number of people convey a single report, the accumulation of evidence and knowledge will prevent a rational individual from dismissing the report. As this aggregation of knowledge cannot be rigidly defined and varies from case to case, al-Juwaynī refrains from specifying a minimum number of narrators.

The final condition repudiated by al-Juwaynī is the requirement that the other conditions for the *mutawātir* report, including the minimum number of narrators, be present in every generation of transmitters up to the present moment. Al-Juwaynī dismisses this condition as unreasonable, arguing that as a concurrently transmitted report takes root in customary practice, its narration by a large number of individual narrators is not exigent. As a result, after a few generations the report will be relayed by fewer narrators than at the beginning, but it is now attested to by customary practice or general knowledge. Deeming such a report unitary because of the absence of continuous concurrency would amount to ignoring the multifaceted ways in which knowledge is manifested and

[34] Ibid., 1:570–73 and 578–80. [35] Ibid., 1:573. [36] Ibid., 1:572 and 580.

preserved within a community. For al-Juwaynī, a report that is transmitted concurrently early on and subsequently incorporated into manifest social practice should be considered *mutawātir* even if its actual transmission tapers off.[37]

After rejecting the three widely agreed-on conditions for the concurrence of reports, al-Juwaynī offers his own mechanism for evaluating reports. Returning to his basic distinction between true and false speech, he states that concurrent reports are those that are true; therefore, the veracity of each report needs to be determined individually on the basis of metrics that produce an aggregation of evidence regarding the report's veracity. These metrics are dynamic, so what establishes the veracity of a report in one situation may not do so in another. The two main factors that al-Juwaynī identifies are the nature of the information conveyed in the report and the indicators of truth (*qarāʾin al-ṣidq*) based on patterns in the world of the phenomena that facilitate an analysis of both the narrator and the content of the report.

Before delving into al-Juwaynī's method of establishing the veracity of *mutawātir ḥadīth*, we should recall his understanding of proofs as described earlier.[38] In his discussion of decisive proofs (*burhān*), al-Juwaynī diverges from the early understanding of them as divine legislative pronouncements and instead adopts what Joseph Lowry has described as the "linguistic turn in mature *uṣūl al-fiqh*."[39] Instead of defining *bayān* in relation to scriptural sources, as al-Shāfiʿī did,[40] al-Juwaynī argues that a *bayān* is the same as a *dalīl* (proof) and can be either rational (*ʿaqlī*) or scriptural (*samʿī*). Since he is here interested in establishing the validity of the scriptural sources of the law rationally, he does not use scriptural proofs, as that would result in a circular argument. In speaking of rational proofs, he states:

37 Ibid., 1:580–82 and 586–88.

38 For a full review of al-Juwaynī's notion of proofs, see Chapter 4.

39 By the phrase "linguistic turn," Lowry is highlighting the way in which *bayān* as a term evolved from al-Shāfiʿī to later *uṣūl al-fiqh* scholars. Lowry argues that the former was more concerned with instances of apparent contradiction between scriptural sources, whereas later scholars focused on communication and the linguistic nature of that communication. Lowry, "Preliminary Observations," 526.

40 According to Lowry, "[A]l-Shāfiʿī's concept of *bayān* can therefore be summarized as follows: God always communicates norms in ways that are structured exclusively by the Qurʾān and the Sunna: by the Qurʾān alone, by the Qurʾān and Sunna together, by the Sunna alone, or by inference based on the Qurʾān and/or the Sunna." Lowry, "Preliminary Observations," 507–8. See also the more detailed exposition in his monograph, *Early Islamic Legal Theory*, chapter 1.

The jurisprudents have said: reasoned proofs are those that bring complete speculative reasoning to the knowledge of what is indicated (*madlūl*). They indicate from themselves, not from characteristics, and it is not permissible to classify them as "not indicating," for an action indicates an actor, the specification performed by an intending actor indicates the existence of that actor, and mastery/precision (*iḥkām*) indicates one who is knowledgeable. So, if these proofs occur, they indicate intrinsically from themselves, without need for intention to arrive at the proofs.[41]

In this passage, al-Juwaynī argues that rational proofs, unlike scriptural proofs, are dependent on the inference of the reasoner with respect to what is signified. So, for example, the presence of an action implies capability to perform the action, and mastery of something implies knowledge of it. In the realm of *akhbār* and *ḥadīth*, this argument raises a question: How do proofs allow a reasoner to infer the veracity of a report? If, as al-Juwaynī asserts, rational proofs "indicate *intrinsically* from themselves, without need for intention to arrive at the proofs," little reasoning is required for the reasoner to apprehend the report's veracity. However, in some scenarios, reasoning, even extensive reasoning, is necessary, as he himself acknowledges. Consequently, rational proofs can be subdivided into those open to direct apprehension and thus requiring little reasoning or inference, and those necessitating more substantial reasoning and inference. This division maps nicely onto al-Juwaynī's distinction between simple and complex reasoning.[42] An example of an innate rational matter is the impossibility of combining opposites, such as black and white, whereas noninnate rational matters include the veracity of reports, the establishment of which requires reflection. In his discussion of reports and more specifically of *mutawātir ḥadīth*, al-Juwaynī asserts that the conditions for *tawātur* accepted by the majority of jurists do not suffice to establish knowledge, and they must thus be replaced by sound rational proofs.

Before presenting these rational proofs, al-Juwaynī points out that since the subject of a report can range from sensory knowledge to reasoned, religious, or secular knowledge, the rational proof that establishes the report's veracity must match the type of knowledge conveyed in the report.[43] He gives the example of a report concerning a king's conquest of a city. The report of such an event will be transmitted by multiple

[41] Al-Juwaynī, *al-Burhān*, 1:155. [42] Ibid., 1:155–56.

[43] This is a notion with which scholars after al-Juwaynī agreed as well. See al-Āmidī, *al-Iḥkām*, 2:21–26.

people for a few generations. But as the event recedes further into the past, instances of the report's transmission will decrease in frequency.[44] Historical knowledge is, therefore, most likely to be mass-transmitted only by generations in close temporal proximity to the events described. Al-Juwaynī argues that the drop in transmissions in such cases should not lead to the report's downgrading to the status of unitary (*wāḥid*) and thus merely probable – it remains *mutawātir*. Religious knowledge, by contrast, is more likely to be transmitted continuously thanks to internal religious motivations. However, the transmission of religious knowledge may also decline if there is a decrease in religiosity or if the knowledge becomes widespread and customary for people.[45] In this case, even in the absence of sustained mass transmission, the report is not immediately removed from the category of *tawātur*. The possibility of religious knowledge becoming customary and embedded in individual practice brings al-Juwaynī to his discussion of the rational proofs required to establish the veracity of *mutawātir* reports. The two rational proofs he proposes are ongoing custom (*al-ʿāda al-mustaqirra*) and customary indicators (*al-qarāʾin al-ʿurfiyya*),[46] both subsumed under the broader rubric of external indicators (*qarāʾin al-aḥwāl*).

According to al-Juwaynī, an individual's confidence in a transmitted report is not based on the report itself or on the number of individuals attesting to it; rather, it is based on external indicators or, more specifically, on indicators of truth (*qarāʾin al-ṣidq*), which the individual ascertains rationally alongside the report. To illustrate this point, al-Juwaynī offers two example scenarios. In the first, a wet nurse is observed to be suckling a baby not by direct witnessing of the act of suckling itself but on the basis of the noises associated with suckling and of the baby's movements. In this situation, according to al-Juwaynī, one does not need to see the milk reach the mouth of the baby to conclude that the baby is suckling, because the external indicators are sufficient to establish that fact.[47] These rational external indicators are known customarily: as an individual experiences repeated instances of suckling, he or she becomes familiar with the indicators signifying its occurrence. In this case, then, knowledge of customary patterns in the world of phenomena and in human action leads to an understanding of external conditions that allow the individual to infer the occurrence of a certain action, in this case a

[44] Al-Juwaynī, *al-Burhān*, 1:586. [45] Ibid., 1:577.
[46] On al-Juwaynī's concept of custom, see further Chapter 6.
[47] Al-Juwaynī, *al-Burhān*, 1:575.

baby's suckling. As in al-Juwaynī's example of action indicating the existence of an actor, the sounds of suckling and the movement and placement of the baby indicate the action of suckling. Since it is likely that the observer is aware of these external signs before coming into contact with them, extensive reasoning is not required, and the individual almost instantaneously infers that the baby is suckling.

In the second example scenario, an individual is informed of the death of someone else. The indirect nature of this knowledge raises the possibility of misinformation on the part of the transmitter, and it thus requires more reasoning compared with the directly observable case of suckling. To confirm the veracity of the report, al-Juwaynī argues that the individual must consider two things: the trustworthiness of the narrator and the soundness of the report. There is a natural overlap between the two, but the truthfulness of the narrator does not necessarily mean that the report is true. Ascertaining the narrator's truthfulness requires basic information about him or her, including the reliability of his or her memory, intelligence, and scrupulousness in such matters. Then, to verify the report, one must again consider rational external indicators. In this example scenario, indicators that point to the veracity of the report include the presence of a grieving family, the sight of a grave being dug, and evidence of the body being prepared for burial. As in the case of suckling, this supporting knowledge, or circumstantial knowledge, is based on practice and customary experience (*ḥukm al-ʿādāt*).[48] In both examples, the observer infers the veracity of the report through external indicators, the difference being that the first situation involves direct observation whereas the second rests on circumstantial evidence. Since the judgment regarding a report's veracity relies on rational external indicators, knowledge is sometimes produced instantaneously and at other times delayed, depending on the complexity of the information conveyed and the number of external indicators present.

Through his presentation of these two scenarios, al-Juwaynī provides a broad methodology for evaluating reports, which he subsequently applies to the realm of *ḥadīth*. According to his method, an individual receiving a *ḥadīth* must establish first the truthfulness of the narrator and then the veracity of the report. The former criterion is satisfied by gathering information supporting the honesty and uprightness of the narrator,[49] whereas the latter calls for evidence regarding the number of narrators and the

[48] Ibid., 1:576. [49] Ibid., 1:577.

extent to which the knowledge conveyed in the *ḥadīth* has become customary and is thus reflected in rational external indicators supporting its signification. Widespread practice of the knowledge embodied in a *ḥadīth* attests to its prior transmission and thus constitutes an external indicator of its veracity. Al-Juwaynī is not here arguing that widespread practice can retroactively indicate the presence of a *mutawātir ḥadīth*;[50] rather, he is claiming that when a *ḥadīth* already exists, customary practice can attest to its authenticity. This view relies on some form of continuous transmission and a communal religious imperative to incorporate knowledge conveyed in *ḥadīth* into the daily practice of believers.[51]

If both the reliability of the narrator and the veracity of the report are established and the *ḥadīth* is narrated by an adequate number of individuals (al-Juwaynī does not specify a minimum number), there is sufficient evidence to declare the *ḥadīth* to be *mutawātir*. Though al-Juwaynī focuses primarily on rational external indicators in this process of verification, the central force behind his argument is customary practice. This becomes apparent at the end of the chapter on *mutawātir ḥadīth*, where he states, "Any report that is contradicted by customary practice is false" (*kull khabar yukhālifuhu ḥukm al-ʿurf, fa-huwa kadhib*).[52] Al-Juwaynī's dominant reliance on custom reflects his epistemology, which has at its heart the notion that custom and repetition can give rise to knowledge and also move it from the realm of the probable to the realm of the certain.

The emphasis on custom and practice is part of al-Juwaynī's pervasive tendency to seek epistemically certain knowledge through the rational mechanisms available to individuals. In his discussion of *tawātur*, this preoccupation is evident in his denunciation of what he deems to be the erroneous conditions set by his predecessors and the promulgation of his own conditions on the basis of rational external indicators. The emphasis on external indicators is rooted in al-Juwaynī's ten grades of knowledge,

50 Al-Juwaynī does not make the argument here that widespread practice can indicate a lost *ḥadīth*, but he does make it as part of his defense of *ijmāʿ*, discussed in Chapter 6.

51 Al-Juwaynī was not the only one to appeal to practice for the verification of *ḥadīth*. According to Brown, early jurists among the *ahl al-ḥadīth* were willing to accept a weak *ḥadīth* if it "was buttressed substantially by the practice of Muslim scholars." Brown notes that in such cases, it was not clear whether the "driving evidence" was the *ḥadīth* or the practice. See Brown, "Did the Prophet Say It?," 277–78. For al-Juwaynī, practice plays an essential role in verifying that a *ḥadīth* is indeed *mutawātir*. In the case of weak or unitary *ḥadīth*, al-Juwaynī does not focus on external indicators.

52 Al-Juwaynī, *al-Burhān*, 1:596.

where they occupy the sixth grade and facilitate the creation of acquired necessary knowledge.[53] In his earlier discussion, al-Juwaynī argues that external indicators reflect the customary appearance of phenomena in the world and can form the basis of an individual's inference of certain conclusions. His primary examples are shyness and anger, both of which are manifested in the external indicator of facial redness. Since the two states involve the same indicator, differentiation between them is possible only once one has become accustomed to the ways in which human beings typically display particular emotions. Al-Juwaynī invokes the same examples in his discussion of *mutawātir ḥadīth* to argue that external indicators can provide true knowledge (*ʿilm*), but it is impossible to specify as a general rule exactly what the indicators are or how many are needed.[54] By enshrining external indicators and custom as the key criteria of *tawātur*, al-Juwaynī provides a completely rational mechanism for establishing the concurrency of reports that also accords with his overarching epistemology and his desire to defend his legal methodology in a rational manner.

On the surface, it may seem that al-Juwaynī departs from his usual formalist approach to the sources of the law in his assertion that *mutawātir ḥadīth* produce *naẓarī* knowledge; however, his rejection of the dominant opinion that *mutawātir ḥadīth* yield necessary knowledge is not a substantive move, but a procedural one. For al-Juwaynī, knowledge conveyed in *mutawātir ḥadīth* is epistemically certain and true, but that knowledge is not immediate to the intellect since it relies on rational external indicators that are not always easily discernible. In his discussion of epistemology, al-Juwaynī makes it clear that for him, all true knowledge is of the same epistemic standing, but it can be classified on the basis of the presence or absence of reasoning, which constitutes the only true distinction between *ḍarūrī* knowledge and *naẓarī* knowledge. The fact that an individual evaluating a *ḥadīth* must rely on reasoning prevents the resulting knowledge from being considered innate or instantaneous and thus *ḍarūrī*.[55] Therefore, although *mutawātir ḥadīth* produce knowledge and conviction in the veracity of the knowledge conveyed, because obtaining this knowledge requires reason, it is not innate and cannot be classified as necessary ab initio. In using the typically Ashʿarī distinction between *ḍarūrī* knowledge as knowledge that does not involve reasoning and *naẓarī* knowledge as knowledge that does involve reasoning, al-

[53] Ibid., 1:132–33. [54] Ibid., 1:576. [55] Ibid., 1:574–79.

Juwaynī is not contradicting his own earlier assertion in the *Burhān* that once an individual acquires knowledge, this knowledge is equivalent to all other elements of knowledge possessed and is therefore necessary. He is simply classifying knowledge from *mutawātir ḥadīth* as *acquired* necessary knowledge, distinguishing it from other forms of knowledge methodologically but not epistemically.

Though al-Juwaynī's emphasis on external indicators is directly linked to his ten grades of knowledge, he was not the first to grant external indicators an important role in the verification of reports. Suheil Laher traces this view to al-Naẓẓām (d. between 220/835 and 230/845), a prominent early Basran Muʿtazilī.[56] Though al-Naẓẓām was frequently attacked for his skepticism regarding *ḥadīth* and his rejection of *ijmāʿ*, al-Juwaynī adopted his argument for external indicators.[57] Another element in al-Juwaynī's discussion of reports that is likely influenced by the Muʿtazila is his procedural defense of the necessary nature of knowledge conveyed in reports. This position, Laher notes, was associated with Abū al-Ḥusayn al-Baṣrī as well as the Baghdadi Muʿtazila, who held that the necessary nature of knowledge conveyed in reports "requires contemplation of the premises of the sufficient number of narrators and the infeasibility of their collusion."[58] Though al-Juwaynī does not stress the need for a minimum number of narrators to prevent collusion, he agrees with the Muʿtazila that contemplation is required in order to verify a *mutawātir ḥadīth*. These two borrowings from Muʿtazilī ideas may seem unremarkable, but they indicate that al-Juwaynī's interactions with the Muʿtazila on occasion resulted in direct appropriation.

The preceding chapter argued that al-Juwaynī's concern with epistemological certainty was a direct result of his intellectual exchanges with the Muʿtazila, who were able to tout certainty for the individual in both reasoned and revealed matters. Al-Juwaynī does not follow the

[56] Suheil Laher, "Twisted Threads: Genesis, Development and Application of the Term and Concept of *Tawātur* in Islamic Thought" (PhD diss., Harvard University, 2014), 27 and 112–16. Racha El Omari describes three main early Muʿtazilī stances toward *ḥadīth*: they were simply transmitted, accepted as long as they were *mutawātir*, or considered unreliable because of their use as a "polemical ideological tool." This last, skeptical position was adopted by al-Naẓẓām, who rejected both *mutawātir* and *wāḥid ḥadīth*. See Racha El Omari, "Accommodation and Resistance: Classical Muʿtazilites on Ḥadīth," *Journal of Near Eastern Studies* 71, no. 2 (2012): 234–35. On al-Naẓẓām's view of *ḥadīth*, see also Josef van Ess, "Ein unbekanntes Fragment des Naẓẓām," in *Der Orient in der Forschung: Festschrift fur Otto Spies zum 65. Geburtstag*, ed. Wilhelm Hoenerbach (Wiesbaden: Harrassowitz, 1967), 171–201.

[57] Al-Juwaynī, *al-Burhān*, 1:574, 584.

[58] Laher, "Twisted Threads," 113.

Muʿtazila in his epistemology, but he does on the issue of *ḥadīth*. The Shāfiʿī appropriation of Muʿtazilī ideas did not begin with al-Juwaynī: as Kevin Reinhart and Ahmed El Shamsy have demonstrated, there was a "speculative" strand within Shāfiʿism beginning with Ibn Surayj (d. 306/918) that drew on Muʿtazilism.[59] Reinhart and El Shamsy observe that the two discussions most heavily influenced by the Muʿtazila concerned the status of human actions before revelation and the idea of a connection between human benefit (*maṣlaḥa*) and the rationality of the law. Although al-Juwaynī is not as skeptical of *ḥadīth* as al-Naẓẓām is, his framework must be able to withstand the Muʿtazilī critique given his aim of establishing the foundational sources of the law with certainty. His new, rational criteria for reports not only supersede the usual requirements for reports stipulated by his Shāfiʿī predecessors but also directly placate some of the staunchest critics of *ḥadīth*.

THE RECEPTION OF AL-JUWAYNĪ'S ARGUMENTS ON REPORTS

Al-Juwaynī's attempt to provide a novel justification for *mutawātir ḥadīth* based on external indicators was not well received by his commentators. One of the most famous commentators on the *Burhān*, ʿUmar b. Muḥammad al-Tamīmī al-Māzarī (d. 546/1141), vehemently disagrees with al-Juwaynī's rejection of the conventional Ashʿarī conditions for *mutawātir ḥadīth* as well as with his new proposed conditions. Al-Māzarī argues that external indicators are a poor way to judge the veracity of a report because even unitary narrations could be supported by external indicators, so how could one adequately distinguish between the two? Using the specific example of the suckling baby, he argues against al-Juwaynī's view that external indicators of suckling are sufficient. In al-Māzarī's opinion, an individual can be *certain* that the baby is suckling only if he or she actually witnesses the act, rendering it sensory knowledge; otherwise the possibility that the baby is simply moving without suckling remains open.[60] Al-Māzarī also argues that al-Juwaynī overlooks the natural variance in cognitive abilities that could result in one individual identifying a plurality of indicators while another struggles to find a single one.[61] In this sense, al-Māzarī sees al-Juwaynī's conditions as

[59] El Shamsy, "Bridging the Gap" and "Wisdom of God's Law"; Reinhart, *Before Revelation*, 15–18.

[60] Al-Māzarī, *Īḍāḥ al-Maḥṣūl*, 424. [61] Ibid., 532.

too subjective and open to misunderstanding. Better, he maintains, are the three conditions previous scholars had agreed on, since they provide an objective set of criteria and a methodological apparatus by which to judge the veracity of reports and thus produce *ḍarūrī* knowledge.[62] Another commentator on the *Burhān*, Shams al-Dīn ʿAlī b. Ismāʿīl al-Abyārī (d. 616/1219), similarly attacks al-Juwaynī's claims, most vehemently the notion that *mutawātir ḥadīth* yield *naẓarī* knowledge. Al-Abyārī criticizes al-Juwaynī's notion of customary knowledge more broadly, asserting that it is not custom that allows one to deduce the emotional states of others, as al-Juwaynī claims, but rather one's sensory perception, and al-Juwaynī's reliance on custom is thus misplaced.[63] Taking his critique a step further, al-Abyārī declares that if al-Juwaynī is looking for external indicators, then the sheer number of individuals relating a *ḥadīth* counts as an external indicator. In this way, al-Abyarī takes al-Juwaynī's notions of customary knowledge and external indicators and relates these to sensory knowledge and the number of narrators, respectively, to argue that in fact al-Juwaynī's conditions mirror those of the scholars before him. Even as al-Abyārī attempts to salvage al-Juwaynī's conditions in this manner, he disagrees with their articulation in the *Burhān* and, like al-Māzarī, rejects al-Juwaynī's classification of knowledge from *mutawātir ḥadīth* as *naẓarī*.[64]

Though commentators on the *Burhān* criticized al-Juwaynī's reliance on external indicators, these were eventually accepted as a valid mechanism of establishing the veracity of reports. According to Laher, al-Ghazālī, al-Rāzī, al-Āmidī, Ibn al-Ḥājib, and most importantly Ibn Ṣalāḥ (d. 643/1245) all endorsed al-Juwaynī's argument that external indicators can indicate the veracity of the report and thus that the knowledge conveyed in such a report is considered true.[65] However, it is important to note that for al-Juwaynī external indicators were the only measure of the veracity of a report, whereas later scholars continued to maintain the importance of other conditions. For example, al-Zarkashī, in his *al-Baḥr al-muḥīṭ*, states that external indicators can be useful in ascertaining the veracity of reports, but they are not as important as the other conditions put forward by scholars. Al-Zarkashī then outlines seven necessary conditions for the

[62] Ibid., 426. [63] Al-Abyārī, *al-Taḥqīq wa-l-bayān*, 2:577.

[64] For the complete discussion, see ibid., 2:580–603.

[65] Laher, "Twisted Threads," 114–16.

narrator of the *ḥadīth* and three for the receiver of the *ḥadīth*[66] that, he believes, collectively yield certainty in the information relayed. Al-Zarkashī's ten conditions make it clear that he, like others before him, is primarily interested in establishing objective criteria for the evaluation of *ḥadīth* based on the *ḥadīth* itself, as opposed to investigating indicators that are external to, and separate from, the *ḥadīth*.

Given that external indicators were eventually accepted as an effective means of *ḥadīth* verification, some scholars sought to qualify exactly what these external indicators are. In the *Burhān*, al-Juwaynī is adamant that they cannot be easily described or quantified.[67] But Laher notes that Ibn al-Najjār al-Futūḥī (d. 973/1564) divided external indicators into *ʿādī* (customary), *ʿaqlī* (rational), and *ḥissī* (sensory) and also evaluated the circumstances of the report, the individuals conveying it and their comprehension, and the nature of the events being conveyed.[68] This further classification is likely a later development, as the earlier scholars who accepted al-Juwaynī's position did not further qualify it.

Another element of al-Juwaynī's discussion on *mutawātir ḥadīth* that subsequently became commonplace was his rejection of a specific minimum number for narrators. Although there were scholars before al-Juwaynī who also held this position, such as al-Bāqillānī, and it would be difficult to assert that al-Juwaynī single-handedly popularized it, scholars eventually accepted that stipulating a specific number of narrators was unnecessary.[69] While al-Juwaynī's positions on external indicators and narrators eventually became dominant, other elements of his argument, such as the claim that the information need not be conveyed through sensory means, were rejected.[70] Critics of al-Juwaynī, both immediately after his time and later, saw his criteria as arbitrary and subjective and disagreed with his rejection of the more conservative static and objective conditions of his predecessors. However, placing his criteria

[66] The seven conditions that al-Zarkashī outlines with regard to the narrator of the *ḥadīth* are the following: (1) the narrator must have knowledge of what he or she relates; (2) this knowledge must be known through the senses or witnessing; (3) at least two people must convey the report; (4) the narrator must be a trustworthy and upright individual; (5) in each generation the number of narrators must be sufficient to preclude collusion on a falsity; (6) the narrators must agree regarding the meaning of the report; and (7) all conditions must be met at every stage of narration. Conditions applying to the receiver of the *ḥadīth* include the receiver's capability to acquire knowledge and his or her not believing in anything that opposes the narration. See al-Zarkashī, *al-Baḥr al-muḥīṭ*, 4:241 (for his response to al-Juwaynī) and 4:243 (for his conditions).

[67] Al-Juwaynī, *al-Burhān*, 1:580.

[68] Laher, "Twisted Threads," 117–18.

[69] Ibid., 107–8.

[70] Ibid., 108–9.

within his overall intellectual project shows that his proposed conditions are part and parcel of his belief that the customary appearance of the phenomenal world as apprehended through rational external indicators can provide a path to knowledge. And although from a methodological perspective the use of reasoning in the process of verifying *ḥadīth* renders the resulting knowledge *naẓarī* in nature, al-Juwaynī's conviction in the equivalence of all knowledge means that *mutawātir ḥadīth* nonetheless remain a source of verifiable and sound knowledge.

AL-JUWAYNĪ ON UNITARY REPORTS (*AKHBĀR ĀḤĀD*)

Though al-Juwaynī is able to develop an argument for the authenticity and validity of *mutawātir ḥadīth* and their ability to give rise to knowledge, the task is much more complicated for unitary reports and *ḥadīth* (*akhbār/aḥādīth āḥād*), which are not transmitted with the same rational external indicators that are so critical to establishing the veracity of *mutawātir ḥadīth*.[71] For jurists before al-Juwaynī, the most glaring difference between *mutawātir* and *wāḥid ḥadīth* lay in their transmission; for al-Juwaynī, who emphasized external indicators more than chains of transmission, the main dividing line between the two types of *ḥadīth* was that the former are transmitted alongside external indicators attesting to their veracity whereas the latter are not. In al-Juwaynī's tripartite classification of reports–reports whose veracity can be conclusively determined, reports whose falsity can be conclusively determined, or reports whose veracity or falsity cannot conclusively be determined,[72] –unitary reports thus occupy the last category.[73]

Nonetheless, given that the majority of *ḥadīth* are classified as *āḥād*, the opinion of the formalists was that such *ḥadīth* are valid sources of legal derivation even though their validity cannot be established with certainty. In other words, jurists can use unitary *ḥadīth* to derive legal rulings, but the *ḥadīth* remain epistemically only speculative (*naẓarī*).[74] Therefore, the formalists argued that it was obligatory to act in accordance with *āḥād ḥadīth*, even though from an epistemological perspective

71 For the use of unitary reports in law, see Zysow, *Economy of Certainty*, 22–46, and Brown, "Did the Prophet Say It?," 279–84.

72 Al-Juwaynī, *al-Burhān*, 1:583. 73 Ibid., 1:598.

74 The materialists, by contrast, argued that there are some unitary reports whose authenticity is beyond doubt and which may thus be used for the derivation of law. Zysow, *Economy of Certainty*, 22.

such *ḥadīth* do not yield true knowledge.[75] Typically, formalists justified the obligation to act on unitary narrations by appealing to the practice of the Prophet's companions, asserting that the companions, through their consensus, conclusively established not merely the permissibility but also the necessity of adhering to the precedent of unitary narrations.[76] As Zysow has shown, the Muʿtazila originally developed this argument as a "master rule" that establishes "the obligation to conform to the norm contained in the tradition" such that "the unit consisting of the master rule along with the relevant tradition now bears the load of certainty."[77] This master rule was most often rational: the Muʿtazila argued that acting in accordance with what is probable is normal in ordinary life and must be so in religious life as well. Another version of the argument appealed to *maṣlaḥa* (public welfare), maintaining that if individuals could not act on the basis of overwhelming probability, they would be paralyzed in both their sacred and their mundane affairs. Zysow observes that later Ashʿarī scholars such as al-Ghazālī adopted this line of argumentation; but before al-Ghazālī, al-Juwaynī had already done so.

As noted earlier, al-Juwaynī believed it important to establish rationally the validity of each source of law. Therefore, after rationally arguing for the validity and veracity of concurrent *ḥadīth*, al-Juwaynī turns to unitary *ḥadīth*. In this relatively succinct section, he argues that unitary *ḥadīth* are valid sources of legal derivation for two reasons: (1) they support the purpose of prophecy and (2) their use is supported by the companions' precedent and consensus.[78] With regard to the first reason, he argues that the entire purpose of prophecy is to guide human beings with regard to what is permissible and impermissible so that they can lead their lives in accordance with God's desire for humanity. The Prophet fulfilled this obligation by guiding his followers, but sometimes his instructions were relayed by only a single companion. Therefore, if jurists limit their acceptance to *mutawātir ḥadīth*, they undermine the purpose of prophecy as guidance. Al-Juwaynī adds that the role of the Prophet as a legislative guide has been established through concurrent reports, so unitary reports are connected to an epistemically certain "meta-principle." From this perspective, "it is because our own state of being

[75] When speaking about the epistemic value of *ḥadīth*, one must distinguish between authenticity and validity. An authentic *ḥadīth* can be used to generate legal norms; a valid one provides sound knowledge. This means that a *ḥadīth* could, in theory, be valid in terms of the knowledge conveyed, but not authentic for juristic purposes.

[76] Zysow, *Economy of Certainty*, 24. [77] Ibid., 27.

[78] Al-Juwaynī, *al-Burhān*, 1:600–601 and 606–11.

is a condition for the obligation of action that the uncertain authenticity of the tradition is of no importance. All that matters is our knowledge of the master rule, and that is certain."[79] The second reason al-Juwaynī provides for the validity of unitary *ḥadīth* is that the companions of the Prophet agreed to act on unitary narrations, and the consensus of the companions is conclusively binding.[80] Because both of these proofs are epistemically certain and binding, and because human beings are in need of guidance, acting in accordance with unitary *ḥadīth* is obligatory. Although al-Juwaynī adopts the Muʿtazilī argument in favor of unitary *ḥadīth*, he does not stray from the basic Shāfiʿī-Ashʿarī position that following such *ḥadīth* is obligatory; accordingly, later commentators on the *Burhān* do not censure his opinion on this issue as they did his opinion on *mutawātir ḥadīth*.[81] It may seem surprising that al-Juwaynī spends significantly less time defending the validity of *wāḥid ḥadīth*, compared with his treatment of *tawātur*, but having linked his arguments for the former to his already established principles on the latter, he evidently does not see a need to prolong the discussion further.

One brief digression al-Juwaynī does make is to affirm the opinion of his Shāfiʿī-Ashʿarī predecessors that unitary *ḥadīth* can provide only *naẓarī* knowledge.[82] Other scholars address this point more exhaustively, but al-Juwaynī's argument is simple. Since a unitary *ḥadīth* is not accompanied by any external indicators that could confirm either its veracity or its falsity, it is intrinsically only probable (*maẓnūn fī nafsihī*) and cannot give rise to true knowledge. If a *ḥadīth* is conveyed with external indicators that enable determination of its falsity or veracity, given that al-Juwaynī does not require a minimum number of narrators for *tawātur*, that *ḥadīth* would be classified not as *wāḥid* but as *mutawātir* in his typology. From a methodological perspective, since the process of evaluating a *ḥadīth* and searching for external indicators inevitably requires reason, the knowledge provided by both *wāḥid* and *mutawātir ḥadīth* is *naẓarī* in nature, but from an epistemological vantage point, *wāḥid ḥadīth* are limited to producing *naẓarī* knowledge, whereas *mutawātir ḥadīth* result in acquired necessary knowledge. Regardless of their epistemological value, both types of *ḥadīth* require action on the part of the

79 Zysow, *Economy of Certainty*, 28.

80 While al-Juwaynī has not yet proven the legitimacy of *ijmāʿ* at this point in the *Burhān*, he views the *ijmāʿ* of the companions as especially sound and as beyond the critique of even those who do not accept the overall legitimacy of the doctrine. Al-Juwaynī, *al-Burhān*, 1:601–11.

81 Al-Abyārī, *al-Taḥqīq wa-l-bayān*, 2:640–50.

82 Al-Juwaynī, *al-Burhān*, 1:599.

individual. In the case of *mutawātir ḥadīth*, the action is compelled by the person's knowledge of the *ḥadīth*, whereas in the case of *wāḥid ḥadīth*, it is the precedent of the Prophet's companions that dictates action in accordance with the *ḥadīth*.

CONCLUSION

The process of canonizing Islamic law resulted in communities of interpretation that relied on hermeneutical methods of interpretation and verification over and above tradition. This development led to the rise of what Zysow has termed a "formalist" methodology, whose adherents focused on the validity of the formal apparatus of legal derivation. The starting point for formalists was the verification of the scriptural sources, as these were the foundation of legal derivation. Their investigation into the Quran and *ḥadīth* took place in books of *uṣūl al-fiqh* in the section on reports (*akhbār*). Reports were broadly divided into concurrent (*mutawātir*) and unitary (*wāḥid*). The former included the Quran as well as concurrently transmitted *ḥadīth*. Ashʿarī jurists before al-Juwaynī largely agreed on a set of conditions required for a report to be considered *mutawātir*; when these conditions were satisfactorily met, the report was deemed certain in terms of its transmission (*qaṭʿī al-wurūd*) and considered to yield necessary knowledge (*ʿilm ḍarūrī*). In his discussion of reports in the *Burhān*, al-Juwaynī does not adopt the typical formalist argument for *mutawātir ḥadīth* but instead constructs his own, rational argument, often borrowing from the Muʿtazila, in accordance with his own epistemological framework. He does the same for *wāḥid ḥadīth*, further demonstrating his concern for epistemically certain proofs for the sources of the law. Although al-Juwaynī's general desire for proofs aligns in some ways with the formalism dominant among the Shāfiʿīs, he diverges from their focus on epistemically certain proofs and their acceptance of probability in the realm of legal derivation. Al-Juwaynī's challenge to the typical formalist arguments for the sources of the law resurfaces in his discussion of *ijmāʿ*, where he again seeks to establish definitively the validity of the source within his own epistemological framework.

6

Certainty in Legal Sources

Ijmāʿ

Beyond the Quran and *mutawātir ḥadīth*, the only other legal source that the majority of scholars accepted as producing certain knowledge was *ijmāʿ* (consensus). On the surface, this privilege granted to *ijmāʿ* may seem counterintuitive, as the justification for the heightened epistemic status of the Quran and *ḥadīth* derives from their conceptualization as the true articulation of God's desires, whether in the formal form of the Quran or through the Prophet as a vessel of interpretation,[1] whereas no direct connection to God can be claimed for the consensus of the community. Consequently, the Quran and *ḥadīth* represent the core textual sources of the law, but *ijmāʿ* is a derivative or secondary source. Nonetheless, *ijmāʿ* attained an elevated status in the jurisprudential tradition thanks to extensive arguments for its validity based on proofs from *ḥadīth* and the Quran, as well as its ability to curb juristic agreement (*ikhtilāf*) and provide epistemic certainty for agreed-on rulings.

In his discussion of *ijmāʿ* in the *Burhān*, al-Juwaynī finds that the scriptural sources used in defense of *ijmāʿ* leave it highly susceptible to criticism, because the relevant Quranic verses are ambiguous and the *ḥadīth* on the topic are not *mutawātir*. Given that *ijmāʿ* elevates the epistemic value of rulings and thus constitutes a central source of law, al-Juwaynī sets out to establish its authority on firmer rational and scriptural grounds. He proceeds in a manner that mirrors his discussion

[1] On the authority of the Prophet, see Lowry, *Islamic Legal Theory*, chapter 3. See also Lowry, "The Prophet as Lawgiver and Legal Authority," in *The Cambridge Companion to Muḥammad*, ed. Jonathan Brockopp (Cambridge: Cambridge University Press, 2010), 83–102.

of *mutawātir ḥadīth*, beginning by attacking the faulty reasoning of his predecessors and then moving on to advance his own argument based on reasoning, custom, and revelation.

THE ROOTS OF *IJMĀʿ*

With the death of the Prophet and the cessation of revelation, the Muslim community was left with the orally preserved Quran and *ḥadīth* and the task of maintaining the religion in accordance with the Prophetic message. The Prophet was understood to be infallible (*maʿṣūm*), protected from error in matters of religion,[2] but in the Sunni view this station was unattainable by anyone else in the Muslim community.[3] This being the case, the pronouncement of an individual companion of the Prophet on any issue was not considered definitive, although the specific practices and rulings of prominent companions were granted special status as they were seen to reflect Prophetic practice. The absence of a single definitive authority made the institution of *shūrā* (consultation) the modus operandi of the early Muslim community.[4] Both the idea of *shūrā* and the value attributed to the practice of the companions reveal the early community's desire to ground normative knowledge in proximity to the Prophet.[5]

2 The infallibility of the Prophet was established in religious matters, but not in mundane affairs. For example, Rāfiʿ b. Khudayj relates a *ḥadīth* according to which the Prophet came across some Medinans cross-pollinating their date palms. The Prophet did not recognize the practice and so inquired about it; he then said that he does not think it brings any benefits. The Medinans promptly abandoned the practice, but then saw that the season's crop was not as plentiful as usual. Finding out about this, the Prophet declared, "I am only a human being. When I command you regarding your religion, accept it. When I command you based on my own opinions, then I am only a human being." *Ṣaḥīḥ Muslim*, no. 2362. In another narration of the *ḥadīth* provided by Muslim, the Prophet said, "You know best the affairs of your worldly life" (*Ṣaḥīḥ Muslim*, no. 2364).

3 The Sunnī belief in the exclusive infallibility of the Prophet contrasts with the Shīʿī belief in the infallibility of also the divinely guided imams. For more on the Shīʿī doctrine, see Heinz Halm, *Shiʿism* (Edinburgh: Edinburgh University Press, 2004).

4 For the development of the concept of *shūra*, see Muhammad Nazeer Ka Ka Khel, "The Conceptual and Institutional Development of Shura in Early Islam," *Islamic Studies* 19, no. 4 (1980): 271–82; Muhammad Shafiq, "The Role and Place of Shura in the Islamic Polity," *Islamic Studies* 23, no 4 (1984): 419–41; and Patricia Crone, "*Shūrā* as an Elective Institution," *Quaderni di Studi Arabi* 19 (2001): 3–39.

5 The concept of the "community of tradition" is taken from El Shamsy, who defines it in contrast to a community of interpretation, which came to dominate the ethos of the legal schools. See El Shamsy, *Canonization of Islamic Law*, chapters 1 and 3. See also the brief discussion of El Shamsy's ideas in Chapter 5 of the present work.

In some ways, *shūrā* and companion practice were the roots for the nascent doctrine of *ijmāʿ*, whose full articulation emerged alongside the formalized discipline of *uṣūl al-fiqh*. Even though *uṣūl al-fiqh* did not take concrete shape until the fourth/tenth century, starting in the late second/eighth century Muslim jurists living in Iraq, Syria, and Medina partook in systematic discussions on both Islamic law and its methods of derivation in order to deduce legal rulings believed to be sanctioned by God. These discussions gave rise to what Joseph Schacht has termed the "ancient schools,"[6] which represented the collective efforts of the early Muslim community to reason with respect to God's law. These ancient schools developed their own distinctive doctrines, which incorporated consensus. The consensus conceptualized by the schools was not a universal consensus of all Muslim jurists but rather a more narrowly defined agreement in specific locations of certain individual jurists who were considered erudite enough to engage in advanced legal reasoning. The most important individuals in this context were the companions themselves. As Ahmed El Shamsy explains, "the companions settled and lived in towns throughout the Islamic empire, and their unique characteristics and experiences combined with local cultures and practices to form distinctive regional traditions."[7] According to Bernard Weiss, the consensus that coalesced in these nascent legal schools around companion practice was taken as emblematic of the "Sunna of the Prophet," constituting, in effect, a communal recollection of his practice.[8] In part, this conceptualization was due to the scarcity of *ḥadīth* in circulation at this time, which made the retrieval of the *actual* Sunna arduous.

As *ḥadīth* became increasingly available and the Sunna of the Prophet could be reconstructed more directly, the emphasis on the Prophetic precedent as encapsulated in local consensus and practice was trumped by the Prophet's actual practice in both textually preserved and orally conveyed forms. This new emphasis on *ḥadīth* was exemplified in the *Risāla* of al-Shāfiʿī, which was dedicated to explicating the role and authority of *ḥadīth* and included scholarly consensus only as a subsidiary issue at the behest of an insistent interlocutor.[9] Despite the rising status of

6 Joseph Schacht's complete articulation of his view of Islamic law can be found in his *Introduction to Islamic Law* (Oxford: Clarendon Press, 1964), 23–76.

7 El Shamsy, *Canonization of Islamic Law*, 48.

8 Weiss, *Search for God's Law*, 180.

9 Lowry, *Early Islamic Legal Theory*, 320. For Lowry's full discussion of *ijmāʿ*, see ibid., chapter 7.

ḥadīth, however, *ijmāʿ* did not fall completely by the wayside. In fact, an early defense of *ijmāʿ* was based on *ḥadīth* itself.

EARLY DEFENSES OF *IJMĀʿ*

One of the earliest attempts to justify the doctrine of consensus was made by Muḥammad b. al-Ḥasan al-Shaybānī (d. 189/805), the lauded student of Abū Ḥanīfa. In his commentary on Imam Mālik's *Muwaṭṭaʾ*, he relates a decision of Mālik regarding supererogatory *tarāwīḥ* prayers and states that "Muslims agreed on this and approve of it." He then substantiates his statement with the following Prophetic pronouncement: "Whatever the Muslims see as good is good with God, and whatever the Muslims see as bad is bad with God."[10] Although this *ḥadīth* appears to endow the Muslim community with the ability to delineate what is good and bad, on a theological level it is potentially problematic as it contravenes the basic theological postulate that God is the ultimate legislative authority in all matters.[11]

In addition, the *ḥadīth* does not address the community's collective infallibility in sufficient detail to allow the theory of *ijmāʿ* to be extrapolated from it. Regardless of these shortcomings, the *ḥadīth* nonetheless sanctions the community's collective authority on the basis of Prophetic legislative power.

Al-Shāfiʿī's articulation of the doctrine of and proofs for *ijmāʿ* followed that of al-Shaybānī. Joseph Lowry argues that for al-Shāfiʿī, *ijmāʿ* was a juristic tool intended to support the interpretation of the Quran and

[10] The exact wording of the *ḥadīth* is "*mā raʾāhu al-muʾminūn ḥasanan fa-huwa ʿinda Allāh ḥasanun, wa-mā raʾāhu al-muslimūna qabīḥan fa-huwa ʿinda Allāh qabīḥun.*" See Ahmad Hasan, "The Argument for the Authority of Ijmāʿ," *Islamic Studies* 10, no. 1 (1971): 40. Hasan notes that the attribution of this statement to the Prophet is contested; al-Shaybānī endorses it, but Aḥmad b. Ḥanbal, in his *Musnad*, argues that it comes from ʿAbd Allāh b. Masʿūd, not the Prophet.

[11] The notion that human beings can decree what is good and bad relates to the debate between the Muʿtazila and the Ashʿarīs regarding whether things are intrinsically good or bad or whether they are so because God deems them so. The Muʿtazila adhered to the former view, espousing the doctrine of *taḥsīn wa-taqbīḥ*, whereas the Ashʿarīs adhered to the latter. For a more detailed account of the distinction and its relationship to the larger questions of theodicy and free will, see Heemskerk, *Suffering in Muʿtazilite Theology*; George F. Hourani, *Islamic Rationalism: The Ethics of ʿAbd al-Jabbār* (Oxford: Clarendon Press, 1971); Reinhart, *Before Revelation*; Vasalou, *Moral Agents and Their Deserts*; W. Montgomery Watt, "Suffering in Sunnite Islam," *Studia Islamica*, no. 50 (1979): 5–19; and Shihadeh, "Theories of Ethical Value."

Sunna, not a tool of independent legal derivation.[12] It could not authorize the community to formulate a ruling not rooted in the Quran or *ḥadīth* and to treat the ruling as certain. Rather, the function of *ijmāʿ* was to establish the meaning of Quranic verses or *ḥadīth* that were ambiguous or open to multiple interpretations: the interpretation that scholars agreed on was the correct one. In this manner, *ijmāʿ* was restricted to the source texts and was of secondary importance to the scriptural sources. Since *ijmāʿ* was limited to the realm of textual interpretation, it became the exclusive province of legal scholars versed in the textual sources as opposed to encompassing the entirety of the Muslim community.[13]

In the *Risāla*, al-Shāfiʿī first argues in favor of the utilization of *ijmāʿ* and then defends its legitimacy on the basis of *ḥadīth*. In the principal *ḥadīth* that al-Shāfiʿī proposes as proof, the Prophet warns the believers that after the companions and their successors pass away, untruthfulness about the religion will be rampant, so those who desire proximity to the truth should follow the community.[14] Al-Shāfiʿī does not substantiate the *ḥadīth* with any Quranic verses supporting the authority of *ijmāʿ*, maintaining that this tradition provides sufficient justification. However, like the *ḥadīth* used by al-Shaybānī, it is neither unequivocal in meaning nor clear in its prescription, making it a weak basis for the doctrine of *ijmāʿ*.

In recognition of this shortcoming, defenses of *ijmāʿ* after al-Shāfiʿī move from *ḥadīth*-based arguments to appeals to an array of Quranic verses and Prophetic *ḥadīth*. Abū Bakr al-Jaṣṣāṣ (d. 370/981), one of the first scholars marking this shift, cites a total of seven *ḥadīth*, including two

12 Lowry, *Early Islamic Legal Theory*, 327–31.

13 Scholars prior to Lowry held that al-Shāfiʿī's articulation of *ijmāʿ* includes the majority opinion, but Lowry argues convincingly that this is not the case. See Lowry, *Early Islamic Legal Theory*, 319–22.

14 The complete text of the *ḥadīth* is as follows: "Sufyān told us from ʿAbd Allāh b. Abī Labīd from ʿAbd Allāh b. Sulaymān b. Yasār from his father, who said: ʿUmar b. al-Khaṭṭāb made a speech at al-Jābiya in which he said: The Apostle of God stood among us by an order from God, as I am now standing among you, and said, 'Believe my companions, then those who succeed them, and after that those who succeed the successors; but after them untruthfulness will prevail when people will swear [in support of their statements] without having been asked to swear, and will testify without being asked to testify. Only those who seek the pleasure of Paradise will follow the community, for the devil can pursue one person but stands far away from two. Let no man be alone with a woman, for the devil will be the third among them. He who is happy with his right [behavior], or unhappy with his wrong behavior, is a [true] believer.'" Translation from Majid Khadduri, *Al-Shāfiʿī's Risāla* (Cambridge: Islamic Texts Society, 1987), 186. See also Joseph Lowry, trans., *The Epistle on Legal Theory: A Translation of al-Shāfiʿī's Risālah* (New York: New York University Press, 2013), 337.

mentioned by al-Shāfiʿī, and five Quranic verses. Of the *ḥadīth* he presents, the most important to later scholars are "My community will not agree on an error"[15] and "The hand of God is over the community."[16] The five Quranic verses are the following:[17]

1. We have made you [believers] into a just community, so that you may bear witness [to truth] before others and so that the Messenger may bear witness [to it] before you. (2:143)
2. [Believers], you are the best community singled out for people: you order what is right, forbid what is wrong, and believe in God. (3:110)
3. If anyone opposes the Messenger, after guidance has been made clear to him, and follows a path other than that of the believers, We shall leave him on his chosen path – We shall burn him in Hell, an evil destination. (4:115)
4. Do you think that you will be left untested without God identifying which of you will strive for His cause and take no supporters apart from God, His Messenger, and other believers? God is fully aware of all your actions. (9:16)
5. Yet keep their company in this life according to what is right, and follow the path of those who turn to Me. (31:15)

Al-Jaṣṣāṣ interprets these five verses as a Quranic argument to the effect that the way of the Muslim community is binding on its members and overseen by the Prophet, who serves as its witness and guardian.[18] Additionally, he argues that the description of the Muslim community as virtuous and encouraging of the good implies that its agreement on anything evil or wrong is unlikely, as such agreement would negate the quality of encouraging the good that these verses describe and thus cast doubt on the words of God. Though these arguments are individually weak, since none of the verses provides explicit evidence to support the authority of *ijmāʿ*, al-Jaṣṣāṣ asserts that taken collectively they uphold the elevated normative position of the Muslim community and the doctrine of *ijmāʿ*.

15 Al-Tirmidhī, no. 2167, and Ibn Māja, no. 1303.

16 Al-Nasāʾī, no. 4020; al-Ṭabarānī, nos. 362 and 368.

17 The verses are listed in Hasan, "Argument for the Authority of Ijmāʿ," 46–47. All translations are from M. A. S. Abdel Haleem, *The Quran* (Oxford: Oxford University Press, 2004).

18 Hasan, "Argument for the Authority of Ijmāʿ," 43. The notion that the Prophet is a witness to the Muslim community appears explicitly in Quran 2:143 and is substantiated in the other verses.

The early defenses of *ijmāʿ* put forward by al-Shaybānī, al-Shāfiʿī, and al-Jaṣṣāṣ had evolved greatly by the time of al-Juwaynī, as proponents of *ijmāʿ* were confronted by others who rejected its validity as a legal source. This meant that the relatively modest space allotted to *ijmāʿ* in early legal works was replaced by elaborate discussions that strove to answer the growing number of internal and external critiques. Emblematic of this change is Abū al-Ḥusayn al-Baṣrī's (d. 436/1044) defense of *ijmāʿ* in his *Muʿtamad.* He begins his discussion by acknowledging the critics of *ijmāʿ*, the most prominent and important for him being Abū Isḥāq al-Naẓẓām (d. between 220/835 and 230/845).[19] In response to their arguments, al-Baṣrī cites the same Quranic verses used by al-Jaṣṣāṣ and focuses particularly on the idea of the "path of the believers" (*sabīl al-muʾminīn*).[20] Al-Baṣrī accepts that each verse alone fails to establish the validity of *ijmāʿ*, but he maintains that collectively they point to the importance and unified strength of the community. He then bolsters these verses with *ḥadīth*, which, despite being weak, support the basic premise of the community's infallibility. After responding to critics of the scriptural proofs for *ijmāʿ*, al-Baṣrī turns to two other criticisms: the claim that a real-world *ijmāʿ* is actually impossible and the impossibility of defining a process by which *ijmāʿ* can be recognized.[21] To rebut the first argument, al-Baṣrī points to the precedent of the companions and the successors as evidence that *ijmāʿ* can indeed take place. Although he acknowledges the difficulties presented by the subsequent increase in the Muslim population, he argues that there are mechanisms that can facilitate *ijmāʿ*. The notion of an "assistive mechanism" provides a segue to his response to the second criticism, namely, that there is no clear way of determining the presence of *ijmāʿ*. Al-Baṣrī retorts that one of the advantages of *ijmāʿ* is that there is no single way to identify it. It may be expressed in the explicit vocal agreement of jurists or may be implicitly assumed from the jurists' silence on a given issue.[22] Although this rebuttal is not entirely convincing, al-Baṣrī moves on to discuss details of the doctrine of *ijmāʿ*, such as the qualifications of those whose agreement counts toward it, the handling of disagreement, and the ramifications of *ijmāʿ* for later generations.

Comparing the discussion of *ijmāʿ* in the respective writings of al-Shaybānī, al-Shāfiʿī, al-Jaṣṣāṣ, and al-Baṣrī we can see that although the treatment of the subject increases in complexity over time, all four scholars attempt to justify the infallibility of the community and the validity of *ijmāʿ* as sanctioned by revelation itself. The weakness of the

[19] Al-Baṣrī, *al-Muʿtamad*, 2:458.
[20] Quran 4:115.
[21] Al-Baṣrī, *al-Muʿtamad*, 2:478.
[22] Ibid., 2:478–93.

revelatory texts that tout the preeminence and virtues of the community, as noted earlier, is their lack of explicit detail regarding the phenomenon of *ijmāʿ* and the procedure for ascertaining its presence. This basic criticism of the scriptural validity of *ijmāʿ* finds a sympathetic ear with al-Juwaynī, who argues that the ambiguous nature of the proofs renders the entire doctrine only probable. He concludes that if jurists maintain that *ijmāʿ* as a source can provide epistemic certainty, the speculative foundation of its validity must be replaced with a more robust rational one.

A NOTE ON CUSTOM

Al-Juwaynī's defense of *ijmāʿ*, like his defense of *ḥadīth*, draws on his two central sources of knowledge: speculative reasoning and custom. By now, the way in which al-Juwaynī employs reason should be clear; however, a clarifying note regarding his invocation of custom is in order. In large part, the need for clarification is due to al-Juwaynī's inconsistent use of terminology – he most frequently refers to custom as *ʿāda*, but sometimes he also uses the terms *ʿurf* and *ʿamal*.[23] His preference for *ʿāda* over *ʿurf* is surprising, since the latter became the standard term used in juridical treatises to refer to custom. According to Ayman Shabana, al-Juwaynī's use of both *ʿurf* and *ʿāda* in the *Burhān* "facilitated the transformation of both the perception and the use of the concept of *ʿādah* from purely theological debates into mainstream Sunni juristic discourse."[24] Though Shabana differentiates linguistically between *ʿurf* and *ʿāda*,[25] he notes that some jurists use the two terms interchangeably.

23 *ʿAmal* eventually came to be associated primarily with the practice of the people of Medina. For the most comprehensive study on the idea of the "practice of Medina" as well as the jurisprudential understanding of the early Mālikī school, see Abd-Allah, *Mālik and Medina*. Another important monograph that takes a broader view of these issues and their importance for the development of the law is Dutton, *Origins of Islamic Law*. Before its development as a separate concept in law, Dutton argues that *ʿamal* was used early on to refer to the specific normative practice of the Prophet. See Dutton, "*ʿAmal v. Ḥadīth* in Islamic Law: The Case of *Sadl al-Yadayn* (Holding One's Hands by One's Sides) When Doing the Prayer," *Islamic Law and Society* 3, no. 1 (1996): 13–40.

24 Ayman Shabana, *Custom in Islamic Law and Legal Theory: The Development of the Concepts of* ʿUrf *and* ʿĀdah *in the Islamic Legal Tradition* (New York: Palgrave Macmillan, 2010), 70.

25 Shabana notes that "linguistically, *ʿurf* refers to any common practice, whether good or bad. Juristically, it refers exclusively to the common practice that has been established as good by the testimony of reason and has become acceptable to people's dispositions ... The word *ʿādah* ... refers to a habit or a continuous practice. Juristically, it refers to a continuous practice whose repetition cannot be explained rationally." Ibid., 50.

Al-Juwaynī's more frequent use of the term *ʿāda* can perhaps be explained by his role in inaugurating the move toward the juridical employment of the term *ʿāda*. Another possible reason for his use of *ʿāda* is the fact that it emphasizes the idea of repetition without ethical signification, a connotation that is absent from the alternative terms *ʿurf* and *ʿamal*. Taken in its widest sense, *ʿāda* can refer to any habitual practice or natural phenomenon, be it mundane or sacred. In al-Juwaynī's epistemology, this expansive definition of custom allows him to subsume both the practice of the blacksmith, as described in Chapter 4, and the practice of individuals enacting *ḥadīth*, discussed in Chapter 5, under the banner of *ʿāda*. When speaking of *ijmāʿ*, he invokes *ʿāda* once again, but this time he adds a layer of subtlety, distinguishing between common custom and juristic custom.

AL-JUWAYNĪ ON *IJMĀʿ*

Despite the number of textual proofs that scholars prior to al-Juwaynī offered in support of the doctrine of *ijmāʿ*, al-Juwaynī rejects them wholesale, citing their ambiguous nature, in the case of the Quranic verses, and their disputable transmission, in the case of *ḥadīth*.[26] He instead grounds the authority of *ijmāʿ* in its continual juristic practice and in the jurists' censure of those individuals who reject it: for him, these phenomena constitute a definitive proof that has not been adequately preserved in verbal form but is manifest in the customary practice of individuals. This defense of the doctrine of *ijmāʿ* on the basis of an untransmitted text recalls al-Juwaynī's argument that even if the transmission of a concurrent report lapses, the report's content may survive in customary practice. In the case of *ijmāʿ*, according to al-Juwaynī, although its authority cannot be traced to a reliable transmitted report, continuing juristic practice attests to the past existence of such a legitimating report and thus acts as an intermediary indicator of that source text. As the proof for *ijmāʿ* rests first on customary practice and only then on a

26 Al-Juwaynī, *al-Burhān*, 1:676–79. In addition to his discussion of *ijmāʿ* in the *Burhān*, al-Juwaynī also addresses the topic in his *Ghiyāthī* when discussing the obligatory nature of the imamate. There are no glaring dissimilarities between the two discussions, so here I am relying primarily on that in the *Burhān*. See al-Juwaynī, *Ghiyāth al-umam fī iltiyāth al-ẓulam* (i.e., *al-Ghiyāthī*), ed. ʿAbd al-ʿAẓīm al-Dīb (Qatar: Kulliyyat al-Sharīʿa, Jāmiʿat Qatar, 1980), 43ff. Wael Hallaq has also discussed al-Juwaynī's treatment of *ijmāʿ*; see Hallaq, "On the Authoritativeness of Sunni Consensus," *International Journal of Middle Eastern Studies* 18 (1986): 427–54.

source text, the dialectical nature between the text and the community is once again highlighted – and though the text is the ultimate basis for communal adherence, in the text's absence, communal practice attests to its having once existed.

Broadly speaking, the conversation over *ijmāʿ* unfolded between two groups, one that accepted *ijmāʿ* as a source of law and another that rejected it.[27] The former group can be further subdivided into those, such as al-Shaybānī, al-Shāfiʿī, al-Jaṣṣāṣ, and al-Baṣrī, who accepted it on textual foundations alone, and those who accepted it on the basis of rational arguments. Al-Juwaynī straddles the two camps, positioning himself against both those who reject *ijmāʿ* altogether and those who ground it solely in texts.

In the *Burhān*, the section on *ijmāʿ* follows al-Juwaynī's discussion of reports and addresses three topics: the concept of *ijmāʿ* and its occurrence, the proof of *ijmāʿ*, and the conditions for *ijmāʿ*. On the first topic, al-Juwaynī responds to the following four criticisms of the possibility of *ijmāʿ*: (1) it is impossible to gather the scholars of a single generation in one location, given the vastness of the Islamic world; (2) even if it were somehow possible to accomplish this, it is inconceivable that the gathered scholars, given their naturally varying dispositions, would unanimously agree on an issue; (3) even in the event of such agreement, it is unlikely that it would be consistently conveyed so that people could be sure the information they receive regarding *ijmāʿ* was accurate; and (4) most fundamentally, the scriptural proofs for *ijmāʿ* are too weak to establish it as a definitive source.[28]

To the first objection, al-Juwaynī responds that just as the caliph or king can summon his forces from distant lands, so, too, can he order that scholars gather in a specific location to reach an agreement on a particular issue.[29] And although he acknowledges that scholars are naturally susceptible to varying opinions (the second objection), he believes that because *ijmāʿ* is invoked in matters fundamental to religion and relies on proof texts, the extent of disagreement will be minimal. To the third objection – that the transmission of the agreed-on ruling will not meet the standards of *tawātur* – al-Juwaynī provides no rebuttal. His lack of

[27] Al-Āmidī, in his *Iḥkām*, provides a list of deniers of *ijmāʿ* that includes the Shīʿa, the Khawārij, al-Naẓẓām, and Aḥmad b. Ḥanbal. This is not entirely accurate, since Aḥmad b. Ḥanbal did not deny *ijmāʿ* in toto, as Ibn Taymiyya explains, though he did reject all noncompanion *ijmāʿ*. See al-Āmidī, *al-Iḥkām*, 1:262.

[28] Al-Juwaynī, *al-Burhān*, 1:670–75. [29] Ibid., 1:673–74.

engagement with this point may be attributed to his belief, discussed in the preceding chapter, that continuous transmission is not a condition of *tawātur*; from this perspective, the objection is beside the point. The succinctness of al-Juwaynī's response to the first three criticisms of *ijmāʿ* indicates his perception of their relative weakness. For him, it is not the occurrence of *ijmāʿ* and its transmission that represents the Achilles' heel of the doctrine, but rather the proof offered for it, which is what he turns to next.[30]

Instead of providing additional Quranic verses or *ḥadīth* to prove the authority of *ijmāʿ* textually, as al-Shāfiʿī and al-Baṣrī did, al-Juwaynī concedes to his interlocutor that the available textual proofs for *ijmāʿ* do not adequately justify its usage in law. According to him, the problem with all of the relevant Quranic verses is their lack of clarity. As an example, he uses the commonly cited verse 4:115, which says: "If anyone opposes the Messenger, after guidance has been made clear to him, and follows a path other than that of the believers, We shall leave him on his chosen path – We shall burn him in Hell, an evil destination." This verse was interpreted by many as God exhorting the believers to follow the way of the Prophet and the community and their consensus on matters, but al-Juwaynī argues it could also be interpreted in another way: that God is addressing the disbelievers' rejection of the Prophet and warning them of what will happen if they continue to shun the Prophet and the Muslim community.[31] Since the ambiguity in the verse is impossible to resolve, al-Juwaynī insists that it be precluded from use as a proof for *ijmāʿ*. He claims that all the other potential proof verses are similarly laced with ambiguity, and none of them can thus establish the authority of *ijmāʿ* as a fundamental source of law.[32] As for the main *ḥadīth* used in the justification of *ijmāʿ*, "My community will not agree on an error," al-Juwaynī argues that it, too, fails to explicitly establish the doctrine of *ijmāʿ*, nor is it a concurrent report. Because *ijmāʿ* is a considered a cardinal source of law and imbues rulings with epistemic certainty, it has to be grounded in sources that are likewise epistemically certain.[33] If these sources are not certain, it is impossible to hold that *ijmāʿ* can elevate or support the epistemic value of rulings. Having rejected all the textual proofs put forward by al-Shaybānī, al-Jaṣṣāṣ, al-Shāfiʿī, and al-Baṣrī for the authority of *ijmāʿ*, al-Juwaynī is left with the task of proving it by other means.

[30] Ibid., 1:677–80. [31] Ibid., 1:677. [32] Ibid. [33] Ibid., 1:678–80.

Instead of proposing a direct proof for *ijmāʿ*, al-Juwaynī sketches two scenarios in which *ijmāʿ* occurs and lays out a rational justification for the presence of *ijmāʿ* in each. In the first scenario, scholars from across the Muslim lands are asked to judge an issue deemed probable (*ḥukm maẓnūn*). When the scholars gather, their naturally different dispositions and tendencies should in all likelihood preclude agreement, yet somehow consensus is reached.[34] Because the agreement of so many individuals on a probable matter is unlikely, al-Juwaynī argues that there must be a source external to the issue in question that is definitive (*qaṭʿī*) and serves as the touchstone for the scholars' agreement.[35] Even if this definitive text is not explicitly mentioned by the scholars agreeing on the ruling, the fact that they converge in *ijmāʿ* indicates the existence of a unifying text.[36] This argument is similar to that made by al-Shāfiʿī, who claims that when *ijmāʿ* is reached, it is reached because it reflects a text that supports the agreed-on interpretation. In this scenario, al-Juwaynī provides an explanation for scholarly consensus but does not address the legitimacy of *ijmāʿ* directly or provide a proof for it.

In the second scenario, *ijmāʿ* is established on an issue, and subsequently anyone breaking with the consensus is censured and rebuked for contravening the *ijmāʿ*. In this case, al-Juwaynī argues, the jurists' collective censure of those who reject *ijmāʿ* demonstrates its validity as a binding doctrine, since divergence from it is universally disapproved. The jurists' unanimity on this point also indicates, in al-Juwaynī's eyes, that a text existed that clearly communicated the Prophet's intent for the doctrine of *ijmāʿ*; the text itself had been lost, but continuing juristic practice was evidence of the once extant source. *Ijmāʿ* is thus legitimized by a definitive text that al-Juwaynī is confident existed, despite his inability to cite it directly.[37] This rationalization for *ijmāʿ*, though it seems relatively weak,

[34] Ibid., 1:680. Al-Juwaynī also discusses this in the *Ghiyāthī*, 50–52.

[35] Al-Juwaynī, *al-Burhān*, 1:680 and 694–96.

[36] Al-Juwaynī is not explicit about whether the unifying text comes from the Quran, but since he clearly states that it is a definitive text, it has to be either be an explicit Quranic verse or a *mutawātir ḥadīth*.

[37] Al-Juwaynī, *al-Burhān*, 1:682. This argument from an "absent" source seems feeble, but al-Juwaynī was not the only one to make it. Ahmad Ahmad has argued that the emphasis on the four-source theory of the law has led to the neglect of numerous other rational sources invoked by jurists in the derivation of the law, and this argument is one such case. A "lost text" was also invoked later by al-Sharīf al-Tilmisānī (d. 771/1369), who, like al-Juwaynī, argues that the consensus of the companions or of the community as a whole is an indicator of a lost Sunnaic text. See Ahmad Atif Ahmad, *Structural Interrelations of Theory and Practice in Islamic Law* (Leiden: Brill, 2006), 132–34, 137–38.

is consistent with al-Juwaynī's view of the logic behind concurrent reports. On the issue of *tawātur*, as described in the preceding chapter, al-Juwaynī believed that some concurrent reports will cease to be transmitted continuously once knowledge of their content becomes ubiquitous. He noted that this occurs typically with historical reports but insisted that it can also apply to religious matters if the knowledge transmitted in the report is manifested through widespread enactment of it within the community. In the case of *ijmāʿ*, then, al-Juwaynī's argument is that the report legitimizing it was originally transmitted concurrently, but at some point its transmission lapsed and the practice survived only in the form of communal juristic practice. In this practice, *ijmāʿ* has become so entrenched that its rejection elicits unanimous juristic disapproval. In short, censure is indicative of juristic acceptance of consensus, which is in turn indicative of a concurrent and definitive proof that once existed in textual form but has not been continuously transmitted to the present.

Through these two scenarios, al-Juwaynī contends that the practice of *ijmāʿ* by the juridical community and the disdain for those who abandon it constitute the central proofs for its legitimacy. This argument poses the following question: If al-Juwaynī dismisses the putative textual proofs as too ambiguous and/or weak of transmission and thus not capable of justifying the doctrine of *ijmāʿ*, how do his proposed proofs acquire such an elevated status, especially since they seem susceptible to the charge of circularity? The answer lies in al-Juwaynī's conception of knowledge as rooted in two primary sources – reason and custom/repetition. Applying these to the case of *ijmāʿ*, al-Juwaynī asserts,

> there is no hope of relating it [*ijmāʿ*] to the intellect (*al-ʿaql*), and likewise there is no hope of relating it to a definitive textual proof (*dalīl qaṭʿī samʿī*) without consideration of an intermediary. The intermediary that is the pillar of reflection in rulings is the continuity of customs (*iṭṭirād al-ʿādāt*), as demonstrated previously in the two scenarios. Then, if the researcher (*bāḥith*) looks attentively, he will connect it to a definitive textual proof, which brings about consensus in the matter.[38]

According to this passage, the customary practice of *ijmāʿ* serves as an intermediary indicator of a definitive textual proof, and as discrete instances of *ijmāʿ* accrue, they collectively prove its legitimacy. This means that the initial occurrence of *ijmāʿ* is founded on a definitive source text, but the subsequent accumulation of instances serves to impress the

[38] Al-Juwaynī, *al-Burhān*, 1:683.

authority of the doctrine on people and eventually makes continuing transmission unnecessary.[39] Important to note here is al-Juwaynī's focus on juristic custom: he limits the scope of participants in *ijmāʿ* to the juristic class, since the jurists are the only ones qualified to engage in legal derivation.[40] By limiting the scope of *ijmāʿ* to jurists, al-Juwaynī is also emphasizing that it is the *juristic* practice of consensus that indicates the presence of a source text, not merely any customary practice.

Al-Juwaynī's reliance on juristic custom did not go uncriticized. In the *Burhān* itself, a hypothetical interlocutor rebuts his argument, asserting that for a proof to be valid it must be found directly in a source text without reliance on an intermediary indicator. In response, al-Juwaynī concedes the preference for a direct proof but defends the sufficiency of a definitive proof accessed through an intermediary indicator. To support his claim, he notes that the Prophet's speech itself was not a proof but was construed as one because it served as an intermediary to the truthful speech of God.[41] Extending this claim analogically, al-Juwaynī argues that once the validity of the intermediary proof is firmly established, the existence of the source follows. In the case of the Prophet, the veracity of his Prophetic message was established through the intermediary of miracles, which also indicate the truthfulness of God's speech. Similarly, the authority of *ijmāʿ* is based on the intermediary indicators of widespread juristic practice of *ijmāʿ* and the censure directed at those who diverge from it, both of which indicate a definitive text that establishes its legitimacy.

Given that al-Juwaynī champions the notion of intermediary proofs, an interlocutor could argue that the scriptural sources commonly cited in defense of *ijmāʿ* could also be construed as intermediary proofs. Although al-Juwaynī does not address this potential criticism, it is likely that he would have rejected it because of the scriptural ambiguity of the sources. For him, intermediary indicators must be unequivocal, and customary juristic practice and the censure of those who disregard *ijmāʿ* are undeniable proofs, unlike the vague scriptural proofs that he criticizes. However, the intermediary indicators of juristic practice and censure may not be as definitive as al-Juwaynī imagines. What if incidents of juristic practice are not widespread? And if the main intermediary indicator is juristic

[39] Al-Juwaynī's notion that the habitual practice of an action over time can lead to the creation of knowledge is addressed in Chapter 4. See also al-Juwaynī, *al-Burhān*, 1:132–36.

[40] Al-Juwaynī, *al-Burhān*, 1:687.

[41] Ibid., 1:683.

practice, does the proof not become circular, as the juristic practice of *ijmāʿ* itself constitutes the proof for it? Also, what if those who contravene *ijmāʿ* do not make their disagreement public? Even as al-Juwaynī is keen to avoid the shaky probable grounds of typical defenses of *ijmāʿ*, his own defense does not appear to be as strong as he believes.

Despite his failure to provide a satisfying custom-based or reason-based proof for *ijmāʿ* that could convincingly replace the usual scriptural proofs, al-Juwaynī's discussion of *ijmāʿ* is one of the most important sections of the *Burhān* for a number of reasons. For one thing, it once again highlights his concern with epistemic certainty. In the case of *ijmāʿ*, because rulings resulting from juristic agreement are considered certain, a status afforded to only a small subset of legal norms, al-Juwaynī is keen to ensure that the source itself is valid. Although, counterintuitively, this goal leads him to reject the suggested scriptural proofs, his alternative approach highlights the emphasis he places on custom and communal action more broadly. This emphasis, which is perhaps the most important element of al-Juwaynī's discussion of *ijmāʿ*, brings to the fore the dialectical relationship between texts and community, something we encountered already in his discussion on *mutawātir ḥadīth*. In the case of *ijmāʿ*, although the authority of the community is ultimately bound up with the authority of an untransmitted text, without the juristic community's embodiment of the text and knowledge of its practice, the doctrine of *ijmāʿ* would remain unsubstantiated. This means that although religious knowledge regulates human behavior, individual acceptance and embodiment of this knowledge safeguards it and ensures its continuity; in essence, religious knowledge cannot continue to exist without the religious practice of individuals. Acknowledging the multifaceted nature of texts and their manifestation in society allows al-Juwaynī to conceptualize religious knowledge as not merely the direct product of texts but also the product of communal knowledge and practice.

Having laid out his proof for *ijmāʿ*, al-Juwaynī turns to subsidiary issues that establish the parameters for the effective functioning of *ijmāʿ*, such as the eligibility and minimum number of the participants and the process through which *ijmāʿ* comes into existence. Al-Juwaynī excludes the laity from those eligible to partake in *ijmāʿ*, restricting participation only to *mujtahid*s,[42] who possess intimate knowledge of the law and its jurisprudential process. He acknowledges that some scholars, such as al-

[42] The definition of a *mujtahid* was much debated between the fourth/tenth and fifth/eleventh centuries. I will discuss al-Juwaynī's unique definition later; before him, Abū al-Ḥusayn al-Baṣrī formulated an early comprehensive definition of a *mujtahid* that was

Bāqillānī, include *muftī*s and other jurists with in-depth legal knowledge among the eligible participants of *ijmāʿ*, but he argues that the opinion of anyone classified as a follower (*muqallid*)[43] should not be considered for *ijmāʿ*, and such followers include both *muftī*s and laypersons.[44] Al-Juwaynī's persistence in limiting the participants of *ijmāʿ* to *mujtahid*s is due to his desire to avoid delays in reaching consensus on a matter, a goal that he believes would be compromised by allowing the participation of individuals with lower levels of knowledge.

With regard to the number of *mujtahid*s required to conclude *ijmāʿ*, al-Juwaynī rejects any fixed minimum, recognizing that the number of *mujtahid*s is in constant flux, as are social circumstances; thus, specifying a number without taking into account the specific historical moment in which *ijmāʿ* is sought would render the number arbitrary and could unnecessarily constrain future generations.[45] To provide some guidance on the matter, however, he does say that the required number relates to the repetition of custom (*ṭard al-ʿāda*), by which he likely means that the number of *mujtahid*s declared necessary for *ijmāʿ* in a given situation should take into consideration the precedent of earlier generations while remaining cognizant of the constraints present at the moment of inquiry.[46] This approach allows for a sense of continuity with the past while remaining accommodating of historical shifts and limitations.

The discussion on the qualifications of the participants and the minimum number of *mujtahid*s required leads naturally to al-Juwaynī's last inquiry, concerning the means by which *ijmāʿ* occurs. Al-Juwaynī divides instances of *ijmāʿ* into two categories, the first involving a probable (*ẓannī*) determination relating to a definitive (*qaṭʿī*) source text[47] and the second involving a probable determination with no recourse to a

accepted by later scholars such as al-Shīrāzī, al-Ghazālī, and al-Āmidī, with minor variations. See al-Baṣrī, *al-Muʿtamad*, 2:929–31. The most important requirement for al-Baṣrī is a sound understanding of the Quran and Sunna as well as of the principles of inference (*istidlāl*) through which *qiyās* can be conducted. He also emphasizes command of the Arabic language so as to prevent misinterpretation of the sources. Among secondary requirements, al-Baṣrī argues that the *mujtahid*s must fully understand the objectives of the Sharīʿa and be able to distinguish between strong and weak reasoning in matters of logical deduction. Finally, a *mujtahid* must be a sincere person and free from corruption.

[43] Al-Juwaynī, *al-Burhān*, 1:677. [44] Ibid., 1:686–87. [45] Ibid., 1:691. [46] Ibid.

[47] This means that the text is definitive with regard to its mode of transmission (*wurūd*), that is, it is concurrently transmitted (*mutawātir*), but the meaning conveyed in the text is unclear and thus subject to probability. The juristic classification of this type of text is "definitive in transmission and probable in signification" (*qaṭʿī al-wurūd wa-ẓannī al-dalāla*).

definitive text. In the first scenario, *mujtahid*s will assemble and, after brief deliberation and reflection, reach unanimous agreement by locating the issue in the definitive text.[48] The unanimity of the agreement and short deliberative process are due to the existence of an explicit source text that expedites agreement and minimizes dissent.

The second situation is more complicated because of the absence of a definitive source text. In this scenario, it is less likely that the assembled jurists will naturally come to an agreement, and al-Juwaynī predicts that the process of deliberation will continue until the *mujtahid*s naturally begin to apply the most probable ruling on the matter, even if they have not explicitly reached *ijmāʿ*. The absence of an explicit consensus does not preclude action; the tacitly accepted ruling is acted on, and if anyone objects to it, the dissenter is seen as unnecessarily prolonging reasoning on an agreed-on matter. In this case, then, *ijmāʿ* is not achieved explicitly on the basis of a definitive source text but rather emerges implicitly over time through juristic practice, as scholarly disagreement wanes and the ruling is implemented in spite of the absence of formal *ijmāʿ*. Al-Juwaynī finds the occurrence of this form of *ijmāʿ* unlikely in reality, as probabilistic issues will not enjoy silent agreement for long; however, if they do, the tacit *ijmāʿ* is valid. *Ijmāʿ* in such a case is a product of the accumulation of action.[49] These two cases of *ijmāʿ* thus mirror al-Juwaynī's defense of *ijmāʿ*, which similarly relies on the presumed existence of an untransmitted definitive text and on juristic practice.

THE RECEPTION OF AL-JUWAYNĪ'S NOTION OF *IJMĀʿ*

Al-Juwaynī's defense of *ijmāʿ* and his departure from his predecessors signal a lack of agreement regarding the doctrine of *ijmāʿ* in his time that goes beyond the disagreements during the formative period. Despite jurists' best efforts to identify scriptural evidence for *ijmāʿ*, dissent on the proofs and on the doctrine itself persisted. Al-Juwaynī's contribution to the debate was his attempt to replace scriptural proofs with rational proofs; however, his proposal was not wholeheartedly embraced. Al-Abyārī, in his commentary on the *Burhān*, is sympathetic to al-Juwaynī's criticism that the Quranic proofs for *ijmāʿ* are weak,[50] but he argues that the *ḥadīth* provide strong enough scriptural grounds for its validity. In response to al-Juwaynī's charge that all of the proffered reports are unitary transmissions, al-

[48] Al-Juwaynī, *al-Burhān*, 1:694. [49] Ibid., 1:694–96.
[50] Al-Abyārī, *al-Taḥqīq wa-l-bayān*, 2:806.

Abyārī evaluates their collective strength and concludes that together they guarantee the infallibility of the community and can serve as the basis of the doctrine of *ijmāʿ*.[51] He argues that the proofs provided by *ḥadīth* are further bolstered by the practice of the companions; together, the two sources decisively prove the validity of *ijmāʿ*.[52] Despite disagreeing with al-Juwaynī's overall attempt to provide rational proofs for *ijmāʿ*, al-Abyārī does concede that a *mutawātir ḥadīth* could have existed that was not transmitted in textual form because of its alternative perpetuation through communal practice. He mentions the examples of fasting and praying as matters that are epistemically certain even though no extant *ḥadīth* attest to their exact form.[53] However, al-Abyārī limits the applicability of the missing text argument to universal matters (*kulliyyāt*) of ritual practice, seemingly rejecting its usage for establishing the validity of a legal source.

Despite al-Juwaynī's intervention, the preference for scriptural arguments for the validity of *ijmāʿ* continued in later legal treatises. Al-Āmidī, in his *Iḥkām*, compares the rational and scriptural proofs for *ijmāʿ* and concludes that the scriptural proofs are far stronger.[54] His own discussion is then dominated by exegesis of the five Quranic verses he presents to support the authority of *ijmāʿ* and the infallibility of the community more broadly.[55] In addition to Quranic proofs, al-Āmidī endorses *ḥadīth* as an efficacious proof for *ijmāʿ* since relevant reports are related by some of the most prominent companions, such as ʿAbdallah b. Masʿūd, Abū Hurayra, and Ibn ʿUmar. Although these source texts cannot justify the doctrine of *ijmāʿ* individually, he follows the early defenders of *ijmāʿ* and al-Abyārī in asserting that their collective strength is sufficient to legitimize *ijmāʿ*.[56] Despite his emphasis on the scriptural sources, al-Āmidī also cites al-Juwaynī's rational proof of an untransmitted source text.[57] However, he overlooks the connection to custom, the linchpin of al-Juwaynī's argument, and custom's ability to substantiate scriptural proofs. This oversight is probably due to al-Āmidī's belief that the textual proofs are more forceful and that delving into rational proofs once the authority of *ijmāʿ* has been established scripturally is a needless endeavor.

After al-Āmidī, al-Zarkashī takes on the justifications of *ijmāʿ* proposed by various scholars in *al-Baḥr al-muḥīṭ*, paying particular attention to al-Juwaynī. In al-Zarkashī's view, al-Juwaynī fails to provide a convincing proof for the doctrine of *ijmāʿ*, as his proof, which al-Zarkashī describes as

51 Ibid., 2:811–12. 52 Ibid., 2:826. 53 Ibid., 2:816–17.
54 Al-Āmidī, *al-Iḥkām*, 1:262–66. 55 Ibid., 1:266–90. 56 Ibid., 1:290–95.
57 Ibid., 1:296.

a "definitive customary proof" (*dalāla qaṭʿiyya ʿādiyya*), circles the issue without actually addressing it directly.[58] Although al-Zarkashī is not altogether opposed to advancing rational proofs for the defense of legal sources, he disagrees with al-Juwaynī's claim that the scriptural proofs are inadequate and argues that the rational argument constructed by al-Juwaynī is in fact weaker because of its overreliance on custom.

Both al-Āmidī and al-Zarkashī reject al-Juwaynī's defense of *ijmāʿ*, implicitly in the former case and explicitly in the latter. Their dismissal of al-Juwaynī's argument seems to hinge on his rejection of the scriptural sources that the majority of scholars accepted as sufficient proof for the doctrine of *ijmāʿ* and his embrace instead of a rational proof that remained unconvincing to most. The natural mode of defense for the validity of *ijmāʿ*, whether in the formative period, in the works of early scholars such as al-Shaybānī and al-Jaṣṣāṣ, or in the postclassical period, in the works of al-Āmidī and al-Zarkashī, was textual. Although the text retains its importance for al-Juwaynī, as demonstrated by his ultimate reliance on the hypothesis of a definitive missing source, he insists that custom cannot be neglected, because the knowledge conveyed in the text is preserved through it. This reliance on custom reveals the relationship al-Juwaynī envisions between reason, custom, and knowledge, with the former two working in tandem to provide individuals with knowledge and certainty. Al-Juwaynī's primary motive for abandoning scriptural proofs for *ijmāʿ* is that in his opinion they simply cannot provide the epistemic certainty he believes is necessary for a foundational source of law. Such certainty is especially important in the case of *ijmāʿ*, since the majority of jurists held that once the jurists of a generation agree on a ruling, the ruling is elevated from the status of being probable (*ẓannī*) to that of being certain (*qaṭʿī*). For al-Juwaynī, preoccupied with the epistemic value of knowledge and legal rulings, this elevation makes a rationally adequate defense of *ijmāʿ* imperative. Though scriptural proofs provide some indication of the validity of *ijmāʿ*, their vague nature precludes complete confidence, forcing him to look elsewhere, toward reason and custom.

TWO CASES OF CUSTOM: *MUTAWĀTIR ḤADĪTH* AND *IJMĀʿ*

As noted earlier, al-Juwaynī's departure from the conventional scriptural defense of *ijmāʿ* and his turn to a reason-based and custom-based

[58] Al-Zarkashī, *al-Baḥr al-muḥīṭ*, 5:442.

approach mirror the rational defense that he sought to construct for *mutawātir ḥadīth*, which likewise accorded a significant role to custom. Al-Juwaynī's quest to provide novel, rational proofs for *ijmāʿ* and *mutawātir ḥadīth* is a direct outgrowth of his larger concern with epistemic certainty. This concern is most salient in the discussion of these two issues, as both sources of law produce necessary knowledge (*ʿilm ḍarūrī*) and, as such, require epistemically certain foundations. To his dismay, he finds the available juridical defenses of these sources to be weak, which undermines their validity within the jurisprudential framework. In the case of *mutawātir ḥadīth*, he argues that the conditions used to ensure the veracity of such *ḥadīth* are arbitrary and inconclusive; in the case of *ijmāʿ*, he concludes that the scriptural proofs are vague and susceptible to many plausible interpretations. The new proofs that al-Juwaynī proposes for both sources of law rely on custom. For *mutawātir ḥadīth*, custom takes the form of external indicators derived from the customary appearance of the world of phenomena and of the customary order in the communal practice of individuals; for *ijmāʿ*, it consists of the continuous practice of *mujtahid*s, which goes back to a definitive text. In both situations, the aggregation of customary evidence over time abates any initial doubt and gives rise to knowledge.

Within the realm of custom, al-Juwaynī confines authoritative practice to the agreement of jurists alone in the determination of *ijmāʿ* but broadens it to encompass the customary practice of individual believers in the area of *tawātur*. In the latter case, the practice of individuals serves as an external indicator of the authority of a *ḥadīth* under scrutiny. Therefore, juristic custom can be used to establish the past existence of a now absent source text, whereas the customary practice of laypeople can support the veracity of an extant source text but cannot independently indicate the existence of an absent one. In al-Juwaynī's schema, both juristic custom and ordinary custom have a direct relationship with texts, but the latter is limited in its formal application to the authentication of knowledge within the realm of law.

The variant conceptualizations of custom offered by al-Juwaynī operate outside the text and demonstrate the relationship that he conceives between custom and knowledge. Al-Juwaynī articulates the relationship in its most basic form in his categorization of knowledge, when he argues that the continuous customary existence of a phenomenon creates knowledge of it. The aggregation of knowledge through continuous customary practice, like reasoned reflection and the abatement of doubt, serves to elevate knowledge from epistemically probable to epistemically certain.

Applying this basic principle to *ijmāʿ*, al-Juwaynī asserts that overwhelming juristic practice of and adherence to a doctrine over a lengthy period of time not only indicates the existence of a lost source text but also serves as a replacement for its continued transmission. In this way, texts and their embodiment in actions stand in a dialectical relationship: the text informs action, and action, in turn, serves to authenticate the text and to communicate and preserve the knowledge contained within it, despite the material absence of the text. This idea of textual extension into action turns collective actions into a reservoir of knowledge that secures the knowledge conveyed in texts. Granting such an elevated status to custom has profound implications, especially since customs change; however, al-Juwaynī declares that, once established, customs rarely change,[59] and this is especially true of religious customs. For al-Juwaynī, therefore, custom does not merely bolster independent human knowledge of the mundane affairs of the world; rather, it can function meaningfully in the realm of law to legitimate sources and safeguard the transmission of knowledge.

CONCLUSION

Al-Juwaynī's discussion of *ijmāʿ* is rooted in his desire for absolute certainty in the authority of this source of the law and in his realization of the inadequacy of scriptural proofs for it. *Ijmāʿ* was particularly important for the same reason that *mutawātir ḥadīth* were: both could generate epistemically certain legal norms. Al-Juwaynī's replacement of the hitherto dominant scriptural proofs for *ijmāʿ* with rational proofs grounded in juristic custom was motivated by his conviction that the latter afforded a more secure basis for this important source of the law. By conceptualizing custom as a manifestation of a conclusive *ḥadīth* whose text has been lost but whose meaning endures in juristic practice, al-Juwaynī was able to link the authority of *ijmāʿ* to that of *mutawātir ḥadīth* without having to actually cite one.

Juxtaposing al-Juwaynī's use of custom in his defense of *ijmāʿ* with that in his discussion of *mutawātir ḥadīth* reveals that his understanding of custom is not uniform. In the context of *tawātur* al-Juwaynī focuses on customary patterns in the phenomenal world, whereas in the context of *ijmāʿ* he limits custom to the practice of qualified jurists. In both instances, custom yields knowledge, but juristic custom has the additional ability to

59 Al-Juwaynī, *al-Burhān*, 1:694.

indicate the past existence of a now-lost scriptural source. Custom thus stands in a dialectical relationship with the scriptural sources. Al-Juwaynī is particularly interested in custom that has been imbued with scriptural and religious mores. Such religiously informed custom is, for him, the element that binds society together, a notion discussed in detail in the context of al-Juwaynī's political thought in Chapters 9 and 10.

But before delving into al-Juwaynī's politics, the most complex element of his *uṣūl al-fiqh* remains to be explored. His use of custom alongside scriptural sources to justify the certainty afforded by *ijmāʿ* was facilitated by the general juristic agreement that this source can produce epistemically certain rulings. But such agreement did not apply to the last of the four primary legal sources, *qiyās* – for in contrast to *ijmāʿ*, jurists overwhelmingly considered *qiyās* to be incapable of providing epistemic certainty. Given that it is the most expansive source of law and enables legislative continuity, its epistemic weakness presented al-Juwaynī with a quandary.

7

The Rise of Legal Uncertainty

Qiyās al-Maʿnā

My presentation of al-Juwaynī's thought so far has demonstrated his relentless desire for certainty and his efforts to achieve it through an epistemological framework relying on reason and repetition/custom. Applying this epistemological method to religious matters and more specifically to legal knowledge, al-Juwaynī seeks to prove rationally the necessity and authority of the cardinal sources of the law. In the case of both *ijmāʿ* and *mutawātir ḥadīth*, he rejects as inadequate attempts to ground the sources in revelation and instead constructs rational arguments for their validity. Success in this endeavor, he believes, can establish the certainty of these two central sources of law beyond reproach. However, these sources are finite, and the Ashʿarīs, including al-Juwaynī, adhere to the position of legal universality, which assumes that all human actions are subject to legal rulings. Therefore, when confronting a legal query that does not admit direct recourse to a definitive text or consensus, jurists turn to a nonscriptural legal source, *qiyās*, which allows a *mujtahid* to derive a legal ruling for the case at hand using a variety of rational methods. This derived ruling is only tangentially related to a source text and therefore cannot reach beyond epistemic probability. For al-Juwaynī, the inability of rulings based on *qiyās* to rise to the level of epistemic certainty poses an intellectual dilemma.

Given al-Juwaynī's preoccupation with certainty, one might expect him to shun *qiyās* as a method of legal derivation; in fact, however, he argues for its necessity, allowing his desire for continuity to trump his desire for certainty. But he does not entirely forgo the prospect of legal certainty, and he seeks grounds for such certainty in the epistemic status of the *ʿilla*, the rationale for legal rulings and the basis of *qiyās*. The *ʿilla* poses its own challenges, as it is not easily ascertainable, nor is there any mechanism to ensure that a jurist has identified the correct *ʿilla*. Faced with a choice between legal continuity and legal uncertainty, al-Juwaynī accepts the indeterminacy associated with *qiyās*, but not without erecting a hierarchy of probability within the realm of *qiyās* to assist the jurist in differentiating between degrees of probability.

QIYĀS AND THE *ʿILLA*: PRELIMINARY INVESTIGATIONS

Perhaps no discussion has received as much attention in *uṣūl al-fiqh* as *qiyās*.[1] Even a cursory glance at works of *uṣūl al-fiqh* attests to its dominance, with the chapter on *qiyās* invariably being the longest and most exhaustive. The increasing space granted to *qiyās* in later works marks a move away from the revelatory texts of the Quran and *ḥadīth* and the infallibility of the community toward independent legal derivation. Though the activity retains connections to the text and consensus, in *qiyās* each *mujtahid* derives rulings independently based on textual indicators isolated from the scriptural sources. The distance from the text required jurists to establish parameters for this source of law to prevent it from degenerating into arbitrary lawmaking and legal relativism[2] under the guise of *uṣūl*

[1] My decision to leave the term *qiyās* untranslated throughout this chapter is a conscious one, based on Wael Hallaq's argument that rendering it into English as, for example, "analogy," as is frequently done, does not adequately express the multifaceted nature of the doctrine. According to Hallaq, analogy is merely one mode of argumentation and legal derivation within *qiyās*, others being the a fortiori argument and the reductio ad absurdum argument. In the *Burhān*, al-Juwaynī uses the term *qiyās* to denote the jurist's derivation of law based on rational and logical tools. See Wael Hallaq, *A History of Islamic Legal Theories: An Introduction to Sunnī Uṣūl al-Fiqh* (Cambridge: Cambridge University Press, 1997), and, for a more detailed exposition, Wael Hallaq, "Non-Analogical Arguments in Sunnī Juridical *Qiyās*," *Arabica* 36 (1989): 286–306, and Hallaq, "Logic, Formal Arguments and Formalization of Arguments in Sunnī Legal Thought," in *Islamic Law and Jurisprudence*, ed. Nicholas Heer (Seattle: University of Washington Press, 1990), 3–31. Other scholars insist on *qiyās* as analogy; see Noel J. Coulson, *A History of Islamic Law* (Edinburgh: Edinburgh University Press, 1964), 59–60, 72–73; Schacht, *Introduction to Islamic Law*, 37; and Weiss, *Search for God's Law*, 546. Aron Zysow, in his seminal text *Economy of Certainty*, accepts that there are various modes of *qiyās* but argues that analogy is the most prominent of them and thus focuses solely on it. See Zysow, *Economy of Certainty*, chapter 4.

[2] Here I am employing the term "legal relativism" in a specific way, as a charge brought by critics of *qiyās* who argue that the open-ended use of *qiyās* results in the formulation of laws that reflect merely jurists' intuitions and cannot be deemed legally binding as dictates of the Lawgiver since they have no explicit textual mandate attached to them. Permitting

al-fiqh. Rising to the occasion, legal scholars strictly defined the process of *qiyās* (including all of its substantive elements) and restricted its usage to only the most qualified of legal scholars, the *mujtahid*s.

Al-Juwaynī's preoccupation with *qiyās* differs from his regular juristic inquiries because it brings into acute tension his dual desires for certainty and continuity. Recall al-Juwaynī's belief that individuals, on the basis of sound and exhaustive reasoning, can attain knowledge and practical certainty in their conclusions whether or not that knowledge is epistemically certain. This belief in human reason is tempered by al-Juwaynī's belief in, and adherence to, scriptural universalism,[3] which delegates all legislative power to God, meaning that although human beings have the capacity to reason and to achieve certainty in their conclusions, God is the ultimate lawgiver. This tension between human cognitive abilities and divine legislative authority comes to the fore in *qiyās*, which is, most fundamentally, a rational tool that jurists call on in situations in which the scriptural sources do not provide sufficient divine legislative guidance and scriptural universalism is thus threatened. Instead of accepting the absence of a divine ruling in such situations, the jurists who endorse *qiyās* argue that the scriptural sources can be extended on the basis of indicators to provide legal rulings in situations not obviously addressed by the text. In this manner, scriptural universalism and legal universalism are two sides of the same coin for al-Juwaynī: in his framework, every human action is covered by a specific legal ruling. In other words, there is no action that a human being can undertake that has no legal ruling attached to it; and every such legal ruling must find its roots in divine legislation,

the proliferation of juristic interpretation, according to the critics, will open the door not only to contradictions in the law but also to the displacement of the truth. This criticism was made by the Ẓāhirīs, who vehemently rejected the authority of *qiyās*. For an overview of the anti-*qiyās* position, see Zysow, *Economy of Certainty*, 167–96. For the Ẓāhirīs and their conception of legal theory, see Camilla Adang, "'This Day I Have Perfected Your Religion for You': A Ẓāhirī Conception of Religious Authority," in *Speaking for Islam: Religious Authority in Muslim Societies*, ed. Gudrun Krämer and Sabine Schmidtke (Leiden: Brill, 2006); Melchert, *Formation of the Sunni Schools*, 178–90; Stewart, "Muhammad b. Dawūd al-Ẓāhirī's Manual"; Goldziher, *Ẓāhirīs*; and Sabra, "Ibn Ḥazm's Literalism."

[3] I am using the term "scriptural universalism" as employed by Sherman Jackson, who argues that as Ashʿarīs rejected ethical objectivism and strove to place moral and ethical values beyond the reach of the intellect, they elevated the status of scripture as the sole repository of legal guidance. In doing so, they overlooked the subjectivities of the jurist, leading to both scriptural universalism and the potential problem of juristic authoritarianism. See Jackson, "The Alchemy of Domination: Some Ashʿarite Responses to Muʿtazilite Ethics," *International Journal of Middle East Studies* 21, no. 2 (1999): 185–201.

even if it is simply the extension of scriptural sources through *qiyās*.[4] Framed in this way, al-Juwaynī's section on *qiyās* in the *Burhān* challenges both his rationalism and his scripturalism, forcing him to account for the epistemic uncertainty of legal rulings as well as for the limited nature of direct scriptural guidance.

Since the section on *qiyās* is the longest and the most complicated in the *Burhān*, a couple of methodological notes are in order. First, my exposition of al-Juwaynī's views on *qiyās* will follow the order of al-Juwaynī's own arguments as presented in the *Burhān*. Adopting this order will allow the reader to experience more fully the development of al-Juwaynī's thought while also providing a road map for those who want to refer to the text itself. Second, later opinions that diverge from al-Juwaynī's will be noted, but they should not be taken as fundamental disagreements, since linguistic and semantic differences do not necessarily translate into substantive theoretical divergences. An accurate understanding of the reception of al-Juwaynī's ideas by later scholars would require a detailed comparative study, which is beyond the scope of the current book. Third, and following from the previous point, the reception of al-Juwaynī's ideas on *qiyās* will be evaluated through the commentary of al-Abyārī, as it is the only complete extant commentary.[5] In sum, my presentation of al-Juwaynī's discussion of *qiyās* consists predominantly of a close textual reading of his *Burhān*, with occasional references to later opinions.

QIYĀS: DEFINITION AND DEFENSE

Al-Juwaynī opens his discussion on *qiyās* by examining the definition of *qiyās* and the justification of its use. He borrows al-Bāqillānī's definition of *qiyās* as the process of "the linking of a known (*maʿlūm*) [situation] with a known [situation], as regards the confirmation or negation of a *ḥukm* (ruling) for both of them, by way of something which unites them, whether [such is] the confirmation or negation of a [shared] *ḥukm* or *ṣifa* (property)."[6] The

4 Al-Juwaynī lays out both of these ideas in the opening paragraphs of his discussion on *qiyās* (*al-Burhān*, 2:743) and also makes continual references to them throughout his exposition.

5 The commentary of al-Māzarī, *Īḍāḥ al-maḥsūl*, referenced for the reception of al-Juwaynī's epistemology, is only partly extant, and the section on *qiyās* is missing. For that reason, I will be relying primarily on the commentary of al-Abyārī, *al-Taḥqīq wa-l-bayān*.

6 Ibid., 2:745. For al-Bāqillānī's definition of *qiyās*, see al-Juwaynī, *al-Talkhīṣ*, 3:145. Al-Juwaynī concedes that al-Bāqillānī's definition is not ideal but asserts that it is the "closest" in that it captures – for him – the foundational idea of discovering the ruling on a matter

definition has three constituent parts, which form the foundational elements of *qiyās*: drawing an equivalence between two cases, establishing or rejecting a ruling for them, and isolating a connecting matter (*jāmiʿ*). These three elements of *qiyās* were also emphasized by scholars before al-Juwaynī and al-Bāqillānī, though the exact wordings of the definitions varied.

In al-Baṣrī's *Muʿtamad*, for example, *qiyās* is defined as the "attainment (*taḥṣīl*) of the ruling (*ḥukm*) of a thing (*al-shayʾ*) by considering the causation (*taʿlīl*) of another."[7] This definition refers explicitly to two of the three elements above, the presence of two cases and the transfer of the ruling, and hints at the "connecting matter" by using the word *taʿlīl*. The ambiguity is cleared later in al-Baṣrī's text, when he redefines *qiyās* as "the establishment of a ruling for a thing by relating it (*al-radd*) to another due to [the presence] of a *ʿilla*."[8] In this definition, al-Baṣrī makes explicit reference to what al-Bāqillānī and al-Juwaynī call a "connecting matter" and labels it the *ʿilla*. These two definitions just pages apart are verbally different but conceptually identical in their identification of the three constituent elements outlined above. We find the same central elements identified even earlier in the writings of al-Shāfiʿī.

In al-Shāfiʿī's *Risāla*, *qiyās* is introduced in the course of a discussion of *ijtihād* (independent juridical investigation) and remains closely connected to it. Al-Shāfiʿī writes:

> There is, for everything that befalls a Muslim, a binding ruling (*ḥukm lāzim*) or, by means of pursuing the correct answer in regard thereto, some extant indication (*dalāla mawjūda*). He must, if there is a rule concerning that specific thing, follow

on the basis of a previously known matter. Al-Juwaynī, *al-Burhān*, 2:745, 748. Al-Āmidī reports that the definition provided by al-Juwaynī and al-Bāqillānī was accepted by the majority of later Shāfiʿī jurists, though al-Āmidī himself rejects it. Al-Āmidī lists nine definitions that he disagrees with before proposing his own definition. For the listing, see al-Āmidī, *al-Iḥkām*, 3:262–65. His discussion continues until p. 276, where he finally provides his definition: "The linking of one thing to another in respect to one of the rulings governing it, the grounds for this linking being some sort of likeness between the two things" (translated by Bernard Weiss in *The Search for God's Law*, 757). One of the most comprehensive discussions regarding the definition of *qiyās* is provided by Ibn Taymiyya, who outlines more than twenty definitions and his objections to each of them. See Taqī al-Dīn Aḥmad b. ʿAbd al-Ḥalīm Ibn Taymiyya, *Kitāb al-Radd ʿalā al-manṭiqiyyīn*, ed. ʿAbd al-Ṣamad Sharaf al-Dīn al-Kutubī (Bombay: Qayyimah Press, 1949), 6.

7 Al-Baṣrī, *al-Muʿtamad*, 2:699. Earlier he provides definitions given by others but disagrees with most of them, with the exception of the definition of Abū Hāshim; however, at the end, he ultimately prefers his own definition. For Abū Hāshim's definition and others, see ibid., 2:697.

8 Ibid., 2:1031. Al-Āmidī disagrees with this definition; see al-Āmidī, *al-Iḥkām*, 3:262–65.

it. If there is no such rule, then one seeks the indication by pursuing the correct answer in regard thereto by means of *ijtihād*. *Ijtihād* is, in turn, *qiyās*.[9]

In this definition, al-Shāfiʿī equates *ijtihād* with *qiyās*, arguing that there will always be a textual indicant (*dalāla*) guiding the jurist in his search for God's law.[10] However, as we progress through the *Risāla* it becomes apparent that al-Shāfiʿī conceptualizes *qiyās* in a very particular manner, and this passage merely signals that *qiyās* always involves independent inquiry, though its forms are multiple. Al-Shāfiʿī eventually elaborates several distinct types of *qiyās*,[11] all of which contain the same three constituent elements:

Qiyās is that which is sought by indications of conformity with a previously identified revealed text, whether from the Book or the Sunna. This is because they are the signs of the correct result (*ʿalam al-ḥaqq*), the pursuit of which is an obligation ...

It [that which is sought] might agree with it [the revealed text] in two ways: One is when God or his Messenger forbids a thing by means of an explicit text, or makes it licit for a particular policy reason (*maʿnā*). If we find something that is covered by that reason in a matter for which neither a passage from the Book nor a Sunna has provided an explicit rule for precisely that thing, then we could make it licit or forbid it, because it is covered by the reason for making [the earlier thing] licit or forbidden. Two is when we find something to resemble (*shabah*) one thing [that has been forbidden or made licit, as in the previous paragraph] or another thing, and we find nothing that resembles it more than one of those two things. Then we would bring it into a certain relation with the one of the [two] things that best resembles it.[12]

The two forms of *qiyās* that al-Shāfiʿī outlines in this passage comprise one in which a potentially efficient rationale (*maʿnā*) for the ruling has been extracted and another that is based on similarity (*shabah*). In both types, the ruling for a known case is transferred to an undetermined case by virtue of something connecting the two cases, either a specific rationale or an identifiable similarity.

Comparing the definitions of al-Juwaynī, al-Bāqillānī, al-Baṣrī, and al-Shāfiʿī reveals a consistent assertion of the three constituent elements beyond their minor differences in wording. One of the elements, the connecting

[9] Translated in Lowry, *Early Islamic Legal Theory*, 145. Lowry argues that a similar idea is articulated elsewhere in the *Risāla*.

[10] The argument that the indicator is textual is made elsewhere in the *Risāla* and expounded in Lowry, *Early Islamic Legal Theory*, 149.

[11] In addition to the two described here, he recognizes a third type, for which see Lowry, *Early Islamic Legal Theory*, 153–56.

[12] Ibid., 150.

matter, is present in all definitions but under different labels: al-Juwaynī and al-Bāqillānī refer to it as the *amr jāmiʿ*, al-Baṣrī as the *ʿilla*, and al-Shāfiʿī as the *maʿnā*. But does the terminological variation denote substantive conceptual differences? Western scholars long thought that the emerging field of *uṣūl al-fiqh* initially produced a variety of terms for a single phenomenon, but Walter Young has recently demonstrated that *ʿilla* and *maʿnā* refer to two distinct concepts. Young argues that *maʿnā* indicates a property that can *potentially* occasion a ruling, whereas the *ʿilla* is the specific rationale that brings about the ruling. Thus every *ʿilla* is a *maʿnā*, but not every *maʿnā* can be considered an *ʿilla.*[13] Al-Juwaynī's concern with ascertaining the correct *ʿilla* within *qiyās al-maʿnā* supports this assertion, as does his discussion on terminology in the *Kāfiya* where he distinguishes between the two.[14] Al-Juwaynī eventually goes into great detail regarding how to ascertain the correct *ʿilla*, but before that we must return to his defense of *qiyās*.

Al-Juwaynī's defense of *qiyās* has two parts: a rational defense and a scriptural one. The rational defense is based on necessity and reflects his adherence to legal universalism, described earlier. He notes that potential legal queries are unlimited, whereas the sources of the law are limited (*maḥṣūr*).[15] Since, according to the universalist position, every situation is governed by a ruling, a jurist seeking to deduce a ruling for a case that lacks an explicit textual indication is compelled to reach beyond the text to reason independently on the basis of indirect textual indicators. Al-

[13] Wael Hallaq argues that when al-Shāfiʿī uses the term *maʿnā*, he is in fact speaking of the *ʿilla*, which Hallaq translates as the *ratio legis*, or the rationale. Hallaq concludes that *maʿnā* was a precursor to the term *ʿilla*, which gained popularity later as the sole technical term referring to the rationale of the ruling. See Hallaq, "The Development of Logical Structure in Sunni Legal Theory," *Der Islam* 64 (1987): 42–67; Hallaq, *History of Islamic Legal Theories*, 23. The reason I have chosen not to use his term *ratio legis* is twofold. First, according to Lowry, *maʿnā*, strictly speaking, means "the purpose of a statute," a concept intended to resolve ambiguities in the law by appeal to the identifiable rational purpose of any law. However, in Islamic law, the purpose of the *maʿnā* or the *ʿilla* is not to resolve ambiguities; it is to extend one case to another case, and the removal of ambiguity occurs first and foremost through jurisprudential methodology. See Lowry, *Early Islamic Legal Theory*, 150–51. Second, Young argues that al-Shāfiʿī uses *maʿnā* to refer to "a potentially-shared and potentially-efficient 'property' or 'quality' or 'intension,'" supporting his assertion that *maʿnā* and *ʿilla* are indeed distinct. He translates *maʿnā* as a potentially efficient property and *ʿilla* as the occasioning factor for a ruling. See Walter Young, *The Dialectical Forge: Juridical Disputation and the Evolution of Islamic Law* (Cham: Springer, 2016), 161 n. 247 and 175–76.

[14] Al-Juwaynī, *al-Kāfiya*, 1–6, 59–61.

[15] Al-Juwaynī, *al-Burhān*, 2:743, 764–65, 805. Other rational arguments were also proposed for the authority of *qiyās*, but they were made by only a few scholars and did not become the principal mode of defending *qiyās*. See Zysow, *Economy of Certainty*, 166.

Juwaynī's rational argument was not accepted by al-Abyārī, who states that the position of legal universalism does not give any support to the necessity of *qiyās*. In fact, he goes even further to assert that there is no proof that every issue actually has a specific ruling applicable to it and that many scholars have argued the contrary;[16] thus, al-Juwaynī's larger point about legal universalism should not be taken as a broadly accepted rational proof for the necessity and validity of *qiyās*.

Although al-Juwaynī presents the rational proof repeatedly in his discussion on *qiyās*, he primarily grounds the validity of *qiyās* in companion precedent and consensus, arguing that these establish the obligatory nature of *qiyās* with complete certainty.[17] According to al-Juwaynī, the companions of the Prophet, on his passing, were required to legislate in circumstances for which no explicit ruling could be found in the Quran or the practice of the Prophet. The ability of the companions to do so was sanctioned by the Prophet himself during his lifetime. The evidence that al-Juwaynī provides for this view consists of the famous exchange that took place when the Prophet sent Muʿādh b. Jabal to Yemen to take up the position of *qāḍī*. The Prophet asked,

> "How will you decide when a question arises?" He [Muʿādh] replied, "According to the Book of God." – "And if you do not find the answer in the Book of God?" – "Then according to the Sunna of the Messenger of God." – "And if you do not find the answer either in the Sunna or in the Book?" – "Then I shall come to a decision according to my own opinion without hesitation." Then the Messenger of God slapped Muʿādh on his chest with his hand, saying, "Praise be to God who has led the Messenger of God to an answer that pleases him."[18]

According to al-Juwaynī and other jurists, this *ḥadīth*, beyond permitting companions to legislate on the basis of the textual sources, approves independent reasoning in the Prophet's absence.

16 Al-Abyārī, *al-Taḥqīq wa-l-bayān*, 3:7–8.

17 Al-Juwaynī, *al-Burhān*, 2:763, 767–83. For a more detailed examination of consensus in the justification of *qiyās*, see Zysow, *Economy of Certainty*, 163–66. In his discussion, Zysow problematizes the use of consensus, since many jurists are not clear as to what sort of consensus was reached by the companions. Zysow notes that al-Juwaynī, who normally does not accept tacit consensus, makes an exception in the case of *qiyās* based on exigency.

18 Related by Abū Dawūd and al-Nasāʾī. Fakhr al-Dīn al-Rāzī goes into greater detail on the use of this *ḥadīth* to justify *qiyās* in his *al-Maḥṣūl fī ʿilm uṣūl al-fiqh*, ed. Ṭāhā Jābir al-ʿAlwānī (Riyadh: Imam Ibn Saʿūd Islamic University, 1979), vol. 5, pp. 38ff. As al-Juwaynī notes, al-Shāfiʿī also used this report as a proof for *qiyās*. Joseph Schacht briefly evaluates al-Shāfiʿī's use of this tradition in *The Origins of Muhammadan Jurisprudence* (n.p.: American Council of Learned Societies, 2008), 106.

Al-Juwaynī then goes on to recount other instances in which the companions freely used their independent reasoning to legislate when they had no recourse to textual sources. These additional instances indicate to al-Juwaynī a pervading consensus on the permissibility of *qiyās* and the use of independent reasoning more generally, which can be extended to later generations. Surprisingly, al-Juwaynī relies on *ḥadīth* for his justification and does not attempt to fashion proofs from Quranic verses. This is unexpected because for many other scholars the Quran provided the most convincing defense of the doctrine of *qiyās*. For example, al-Jaṣṣāṣ's defense of *qiyās* cites at least eighteen Quranic verses and numerous *ḥadīth*.[19] Similarly, al-Shāfiʿī and Abū al-Ḥusayn al-Baṣrī also invoke Quranic verses and *ḥadīth* as their primary defense before calling on companion precedent or consensus.[20] The absence of a Quranic defense in the *Burhān*, while peculiar, signals the authority that al-Juwaynī affords to companion consensus, even against his adversaries who reject *qiyās*.[21] One possible reason for the absence of scriptural proofs lies in al-Juwaynī's general unwillingness to rely on vague scriptural proofs that do not provide unequivocal evidence, as evinced in his discussion of *ijmāʿ* in the preceding chapter. Al-Juwaynī's preference for nonscriptural sources in both discussions arises from a desire to secure the authority of the foundational sources of jurisprudence through definitive proofs. A definitive proof in the case of *qiyās* is especially important because, as Aron Zysow notes, in the realm of *qiyās* the only rule that can be known with certainty is the obligation to undertake *qiyās* itself. Certainty is thus not desired in individual instances, "but the rule of the

19 Ahmad Hasan, "The Justification of Qiyās," *Islamic Studies* 20, no. 3 (1981): 204–6. The most prominent verse used to justify *qiyās* is "Reflect, you who have understanding" (59:2). However, the strength of this verse is contested. For the arguments against it and other Quranic verses used in the defense of *qiyās*, see Abū Bakr Muḥammad b. Aḥmad al-Sarakhsī, *Uṣūl al-Sarakhsī*, ed. Abū al-Wafāʾ al-Afghānī (Hyderabad: Lajnat Iḥyāʾ al-Maʿārif al-Nuʿmāniyya, 1953), 2:138.

20 Al-Basri, *al-Muʿtamad*, 2:726–36.

21 The main opponent al-Juwaynī identifies for his own position on *qiyās* is Ibrāhīm al-Naẓẓām (d. between 220/935 and 230/845); however, there were also others, including the Ẓāhirīs, many of the Muʿtazila, the Khārijīs, and the Shīʿīs. Zysow notes that these disparate groups were connected by their epistemological discomfort with *qiyās*, rooted in their respective standards for valid expressions of Islamic law. See Zysow, *Economy of Certainty*, 167–95. Zysow also supplies an important quotation from Ibn ʿAbd al-Barr (d. 463/1071) summarizing the various scholars and groups who opposed the doctrine of *qiyās* in his time. Ibn ʿAbd al-Barr's words are particularly salient because he was a contemporary of al-Juwaynī and provides a description of the latter's interlocutors who remain unnamed in the *Burhān*. Translation in Zysow, *Economy of Certainty*, 168.

case derives its validity from the certainty of the master rule."[22] This "displacement of certainty," as Zysow terms it, allows the certainty regarding the necessity of *qiyās* to be transferred to the rulings obtained through it, even though technically the rulings remain only probable. Al-Juwaynī himself makes this argument at the end of his defense of *qiyās*, stating that the obligation to act in accordance with a ruling derived through *qiyās* relates not to the ruling itself, which is probable, but to the certainty of the proof on which *qiyās* is based. Though al-Juwaynī primarily considers the consensus of the companions and the *ḥadīth* of Muʿādh to constitute this certain proof, the rational proof derived from scriptural and legal universality serves to further bolster his argument.

Considering al-Juwaynī's defense of *qiyās* within the framework of his broader epistemological concerns, we can characterize his approach to *qiyās* as an exploration of how knowledge is acquired through reason and revelation, in contradistinction to his discussions on *mutawātir ḥadīth* and *ijmāʿ*, which focused on how knowledge can be acquired through reason and custom. Therefore, it is no surprise that al-Juwaynī subsumes his discussion of *qiyās* under the larger topic of *al-naẓar al-sharʿī* (reasoning in scriptural matters), indicating that *qiyās* in its most basic form is a process of arriving at rulings through reasoning. Within this broad category of scriptural reasoning, the first grade of reasoning is "the application (*ilḥāq*) of a thing not covered by the text (*al-maskūt*) to a [thing] enunciated explicitly in the text (*manṭūq*)."[23] As an example, he gives a *ḥadīth* in which the Prophet states that if a man urinates in stagnant water, the water becomes impure. This *ḥadīth* conveys an explicit ruling without need for reasoning or extensive consideration and, as such, can easily be extended to similar cases. So, pouring urine from a pitcher into standing water will similarly make the water impure.[24] Al-Juwaynī argues that because little mental exertion is needed in this case because of the obviousness of the impurity, the ruling from the *ḥadīth* is easily transferable to an analogous case. The ruling in the second case then takes on the epistemic value of the original case and is likewise considered epistemically certain (*maqṭūʿ*).[25] In other situations, when the matter is not as clear (*khafī*) and reasoning is required, the epistemic value of the ruling will be dependent on the semantic clarity of the original injunction. Al-Juwaynī does not consider this first grade of *al-naẓar al-sharʿī* to constitute *qiyās*; instead, he labels it *istinbāṭ* (deduction),

[22] Zysow, *Economy of Certainty*, 266. [23] Al-Juwaynī, *al-Burhān*, 2:782–84.
[24] Ibid., 2:783. [25] Ibid., 2:787.

defining it as the easy transference of a ruling to an analogous situation.[26] It is anything beyond such simple legal deduction and extension that falls within the formal realm of *qiyās*.

TYPES OF *QIYĀS* AND EXTRACTING THE *ʿILLA* AND *MAʿNĀ*

Although deduction, the most basic form of scriptural reasoning, is an ideal interpretative scenario for the jurist, al-Juwaynī recognizes that the majority of cases cannot be resolved through this simple type of legal extension, and this acknowledgment brings him to the realm of *qiyās* proper. He argues that there are two main types of *qiyās*: *qiyās al-maʿnā* and *qiyās al-shabah*. Some scholars identify a third type of *qiyās*, known as *qiyās al-dalāla*, that shares in the characteristics of both of the first two types and oscillates between them,[27] but al-Juwaynī does not formally endorse this third category. The difference between the two forms of *qiyās*

[26] Ibid., 2:786. He acknowledges disagreement among scholars on this point, with some including *istinbāṭ* under the banner of *qiyās*; however, he argues that this is merely a matter of semantic preference. He also states that some jurists call this type of reasoning *faḥwā al-khiṭāb*, *mafhūm al-khiṭāb*, or *laḥn al-khiṭāb*. Al-Shāfiʿī gives as an example of this type of reasoning the conclusion that if God or His messenger forbids a small quantity of something, a larger quantity is also prohibited. As a specific example, he argues that since God promises in the Quran that an atom's weight of good as well as an atom's weight of evil will be seen on the Day of Judgment, this means that more than an atom's weight of either will also be seen (al-Shāfiʿī, *al-Risāla*, paras. 1482–85). Although al-Shāfiʿī calls this form of reasoning *qiyās*, most later jurists, like al-Juwaynī, deem it a natural inference from the text itself. Al-Āmidī agrees with al-Juwaynī in this regard and calls this type of reasoning *mafhūm al-muwāfaqa*, asserting that it is more of a linguistic argument as opposed to a *qiyās*-based one. See al-Āmidī, *al-Iḥkām*, 2:18–20, 210, 281–82. Hallaq refers to this type of argument as an a fortiori argument and discusses the various views surrounding it in his article "Non-Analogical Arguments," 289–96.

[27] Al-Juwaynī did treat *qiyās al-dalāla* as an independent form of *qiyās* in his much shorter work on *uṣūl al-fiqh*, *al-Waraqāt*, but he explicitly ignores it in the *Burhān*. It is most likely that his opinion evolved between the earlier *Waraqāt* and the later and more comprehensive *Burhān*. In brief, in the *Waraqāt* al-Juwaynī describes *qiyās al-dalāla* as a separate grade between *qiyās al-maʿnā* and *qiyās al-shabah*, defining it as "analogy on the basis of signification (*dalāla*) which leads to the occasioning factor (*ʿilla*) and not the injunction directly"; see Jalāl al-Dīn al-Maḥallī, *Sharḥ al-Waraqāt fī ʿilm uṣūl al-fiqh ʿalā Waraqāt Abī al-Maʿālī Imām al-Ḥaramayn* (Mecca: Maktabat Nazār Muṣṭafā al-Bāz, 1996), 45. In contrast to the other two forms of *qiyās*, which are based on the occasioning factor or on resemblance between the two cases, respectively, *qiyās al-dalāla* is founded on the notion of signification: an established case is connected to a new case on the basis of a quality signifying the presence of the *ʿilla*, which can be used to extend the case in a novel situation. For al-Juwaynī's discussion of *qiyās al-dalāla* in the *Burhān*, see al-Juwaynī, *al-Burhān*, 2:863–67.

is related to the semantic clarity of the original ruling, which in turn is tied to the confidence the jurist has in the potential occasioning factors (*ma'ānī*) extracted from the original case. The stronger form of *qiyās*, *qiyās al-ma'nā*, is possible only if the jurist has a relatively clear scriptural ruling from which he or she can, with overwhelming probability, isolate the actual rationale (*'illa*). Conversely, in *qiyās al-shabah*, the jurist is unable to ascertain the exact *'illa* and instead bases the connection between the source (original) case and the branch (new) case on resemblance between the two. Because the two types of *qiyās* are distinguished most fundamentally on the basis of the *'illa* identified by the jurist, al-Juwaynī dedicates the bulk of the section on *qiyās al-ma'nā* to a discussion of the mechanism for ascertaining the *'illa* with overwhelming probability.

Al-Juwaynī formally defines *qiyās al-ma'nā* (or *qiyās al-'illa*, as he also calls it)[28] as "the extraction of suitable (*munāsib*) and indicative (*mukhīl*) *ma'nā* qualities (*istinbāṭ al-mā'ānī*) from an established ruling, which is based on [divinely sanctioned] univocal texts (*al-manṣūṣ*) or [cases of] *ijmā'*."[29] Based on this definition, the extracted *ma'nā* qualities must satisfy two conditions in order to be sound – it must be both *munāsib* and *mukhīl*.[30] Consequently, al-Juwaynī's investigation centers on defining the terms *munāsib* and *mukhīl* and the mechanisms used to extract possible rationales.[31]

28 Though he uses these two terms interchangeably, *qiyās al-ma'nā* eventually comes to dominate in the *Burhān*.

29 Al-Juwaynī, *al-Burhān*, 2:787.

30 Felicitas Opwis rightly notes that al-Juwaynī's usage of these two terms is vague and made more so by the lack of examples. She argues that both terms denote "suggestiveness" in the sense that particular elements within the source case "suggest to the jurist the specific rationale." See Opwis, *Maṣlaḥa and the Purpose of the Law* (Leiden: Brill, 2010), 46–47. Zysow observes that many Shāfi'ī jurists used the term *mukhīl* as a synonym for *munāsib*, but al-Juwaynī differentiates between the two. It will become clear in the course of this chapter that he is primarily concerned with the notion of *munāsaba*. Zysow, *Economy of Certainty*, 196–204.

31 Although al-Juwaynī provides a general definition of *qiyās al-'illa*, he does not give details regarding its constituent parts, with the exception of the *'illa*. Scholars both before and after him did the opposite, spending a considerable amount of time defining both the source case (*aṣl*) and the branch case (*far'*) and delineating conditions governing their utility. Al-Baṣrī, for example, lists three main definitions for *aṣl*, arguing that they are all valid because they arrive at the same end; see al-Baṣrī, *al-Mu'tamad*, 2:700–703. However, scholars differed on the conditions of the *aṣl*, a discussion on which al-Juwaynī is silent. For a more extensive treatment of *aṣl*, see al-Āmidī, *al-Iḥkām*, 2:278–91; Abū Ḥāmid al-Ghazālī, *Shifā' al-ghalīl* (Baghdad: Maṭbā'a al-Irshād, 1971), 635–37; and al-

Al-Juwaynī uses the term *munāsaba* broadly to refer to the congruence of the ruling either with the original case presented in the source text or with the overarching principles of the law. In the first of these cases, *qiyās* connects the source case and a seemingly identical case on the basis of textual evidence. The extracted "rationale" is *munāsib* if it can be deemed identical to that behind the original ruling. In its second usage, *munāsaba* applies to a rationale that corresponds to general human welfare (*maṣāliḥ kulliyya*) in situations in which the source text is unclear and no clear *ʿilla* can be identified.[32] Therefore, in the case of a clear source text, the suitability of the putative rationale is based on the original ruling, whereas with an unclear source text, it depends on the factor's congruence with public welfare and human good.[33]

Among the scholars who support al-Juwaynī's notion of *munāsaba* is al-Ghazālī, who provides two detailed definitions for the term. In his *Mustaṣfā*, he defines it as "that which proceeds by way of the manner of human good (*minhāj al-maṣāliḥ*), in such a way that when the rule is attributed to it, it becomes uniform (*intazama*)."[34] He gives the example of wine, stating that intoxication leading to rational impairment is an appropriate rationale for its prohibition; by contrast, the liquid form, smell, or other external qualities of wine cannot be deemed fitting reasons for the ban.[35] In another text, *Shifāʾ al-ghalīl*, al-Ghazālī defines *munāsaba* as "the *maʿnā* easily intelligible to the intellect (*maʿqūl ẓāhiran fī al-ʿaql*) that can be established against the opponent by simple reasoning

Shawkānī, *Irshād al-fuḥūl*, 179–85. The branch case was subject to less disagreement overall. Al-Baṣrī mentions two main definitions, one proposed by the jurists and the other by the theologians: the former define the *farʿ* as an object or case for which a rule is sought by means of *qiyās*, whereas the latter define it as the rule that must be established through causation (*taʿlīl*). See al-Baṣrī, *al-Muʿtamad*, 703. The difference in the definitions reflects the respective ideologies of their proponents – the jurists being focused on the determination of a ruling and the theologians on its causality. As for the conditions of the *farʿ*, the jurists generally agreed that there were five, but they differed on their details; see the sources listed above for the *aṣl*. Al-Shawkānī notes that later scholars proposed a new definition in order to transcend the early disagreements regarding the definition and conditions of the *aṣl* and the *farʿ*, calling the *aṣl* "the object of agreement" (*maḥall al-wifāq*) and the *farʿ* "the object of disagreement" (*maḥall al-khilāf*). See al-Shawkānī, *Irshād al-fuḥūl*, 179. Al-Juwaynī provides brief definitions of the *aṣl* and the *farʿ* in *al-Kāfiya*, 59–60.

32 Al-Juwaynī, *al-Burhān*, 2:876.

33 According to al-Abyārī, the idea of *maṣlaḥa* provides the primary way of understanding *munāsaba* in the *Burhān*; al-Abyārī, *al-Taḥqīq wa-l-bayān*, 3:117–19. Al-Juwaynī also says as much. See al-Juwaynī, *al-Burhān*, 2:876.

34 Abū Ḥāmid Al-Ghazālī, *al-Mustaṣfā* (Mecca: al-Jāmīʿa al-Islāmiyya, 2008) 3:620.

35 Ibid.

(*naẓar ʿaqlī*)."[36] He explains that if the rationale is established on the basis of an apparent textual indication, an opponent's denial of the factor's suitability would indicate sheer obstinacy. Though this definition focuses on the easily ascertainable nature of the rationale, he subsequently argues that suitable potential occasioning factors (*al-maʿānī al-munāsiba*) indicate and preserve the general good (*maṣāliḥ*) of the people. This notion of "general good" evolves into an articulation of the five basic principles (*al-kulliyyāt al-khams*) of the law, namely, the preservation of life, reason, lineage, property, and religion.[37]

In both definitions, al-Ghazālī equates *munāsaba* with *maṣlaḥa*, deeming the latter an efficacious criterion for evaluating the suitability of a ruling. In addition, he is emphatic that agreement on a rationale reduces the possibility of future disagreement. These two elements are interrelated, because if a ruling promotes human welfare, it is less likely to provoke future disagreement. Al-Ghazālī's conceptualization of *munāsaba* was adopted by later scholars such as al-Āmidī. In his *Iḥkām*, al-Āmidī states that a *munāsib* rationale "is apparent (*ẓāhir*) and bound (*munḍabiṭ*), and if the law is applied in accordance with it, it necessitates the achievement of what is fitted to being the purpose of the rule, whether the rule is negative or positive, and whether the purpose is to seek utility or to avert harm."[38] By defining a *munāsib* rationale as apparent and bound, he implicitly relates it to either a source text or an irrefutable argument – much like al-Ghazālī did in his definition. The addendum at the end, which links the rationale to the two poles of seeking utility or averting harm, also echoes al-Ghazālī's assertion that considerations of *maṣlaḥa* play a role in the identification of a *munāsib* rationale.[39]

[36] Al-Ghazālī, *Shifāʾ al-ghalīl*, 143.

[37] Tying the notion of *munāsaba* to the welfare of the Muslim community is something al-Ghazālī most likely borrows from al-Juwaynī, as will be seen in the next chapter in the section on al-Juwaynī's use of *maṣlaḥa*. Al-Ghazālī divides *munāsaba* into four main categories. The first type applies to a *ʿilla* that fits the relevant rule and is supported by a source of law, making it the strongest type of *munāsaba* and the one utilized in *qiyās*. The second type involves a *ʿilla* that is neither appropriate to the rule nor supported by a source of law, and thus cannot be used for *qiyās*. Al-Ghazālī calls the latter *istiḥsān* (preferential reasoning). The third type of *munāsaba* describes a *ʿilla* that is supported by a legal rule but is not congruent with the rule; this type falls in the realm of *ijtihād*. And the final type relates to a *ʿilla* that fits the rule but is not supported by the law; it, too, belongs to the realm of *ijtihād*, and al-Ghazālī equates it with *al-maṣlaḥa al-mursala* (public benefit). Al-Ghazālī, *Shifāʾ al-ghalīl*, 188–89 and 209ff.

[38] Al-Āmidī, *al-Iḥkām*, 3:338–39.

[39] For a detailed discussion of the relationship between *munāsaba* and *maṣlaḥa*, as well as the various degrees of *maṣlaḥa*, see al-Āmidi, *al-Iḥkām* , 3:390–404.

Given later scholarly support for the relationship between *munāsaba* and *maṣlaḥa*, jurists had to be aware of the suitability of a ruling for fostering the general welfare of individuals. Al-Juwaynī's justification for this departure from the text rests on the companions' use of general welfare as a guide when deriving legal rulings in matters lacking a direct textual basis.[40] Drawing on their precedent, al-Juwaynī defends the generation of rulings without obvious textual indicators, though he is careful to define the parameters of this allowance and later dedicates an entire section to *maṣlaḥa*, discussed later in this chapter.

After the first requirement that the *ʿilla* be *munāsib* comes al-Juwaynī's second condition that it be indicative or suggestive (*mukhīl*).[41] This requirement, too, al-Juwaynī relates to the precedent of the companions, who would reflect on an issue in an effort to derive a ruling, and if nothing opposed their interpretation and it was in accordance with the principles of the Sharīʿa (*uṣūl al-sharīʿa*) and public interest (*maṣāliḥ*), they would decide on the ruling with overwhelming probability.[42] The key element in al-Juwaynī's description of the companions' legal reasoning is the attainment of overwhelming probability, as al-Juwaynī goes on to remark that *ikhāla* can be understood as the overwhelming probability in the mind of the *mujtahid* regarding the suitability and indicativeness of the *ʿilla* deduced for the rule. This conceptualization of *ikhāla* is supported by al-Juwaynī's distinction between *qiyās al-maʿnā*, in which the *ʿilla* is relatively clear and the jurist can thus have confidence in it, and the other types of *qiyās*, which all pose a degree of interpretational difficulty due to the absence of indicativeness.[43] However, the requirement that the *ʿilla* be *mukhīl*, while useful in supporting juristic interpretation, is susceptible to subjectivity, as determining what is indicative is at the discretion of the jurist. This subjectivity, if pushed further, could give rise to a form of juristic relativity. Thus, some jurists, such as the Ḥanafīs, challenge both the effectiveness and the validity of *ikhāla* on the grounds that it

[40] Throughout the text, al-Juwaynī is concerned with the companions' usage of *qiyās*, since the practice of the Companions is what makes *qiyās* both legitimate and authoritative. See al-Juwaynī, *al-Burhān*, 2:757, 767, 789, 803.

[41] Al-Juwaynī occasionally uses *uṣūl al-sharīʿa* interchangeably with *munāsaba*, but it becomes clear that the two are actually distinct for him.

[42] Al-Juwaynī, *al-Burhān*, 2:803.

[43] The distinction between *qiyās al-maʿnā* and *qiyās al-shabah* on the basis of *ikhāla* will be discussed in greater detail later.

constitutes pure conjecture.[44] Al-Juwaynī and other proponents of *ikhāla* disagree: they see the requirements of *ikhāla* and *munāsaba* as creating a defined methodology without which robust juristic interpretations could not easily be fashioned.

If we return to al-Juwaynī's original definition of *qiyās al-maʿnā* as "the extraction of suitable (*munāsib*) and indicative (*mukhīl*) *maʿnā* qualities (*istinbāṭ al-māʿānī*) from an established ruling, which is based on [divinely sanctioned] univocal texts (*al-manṣūṣ*) or [cases of] *ijmāʿ*"[45] and insert the definitions for *ikhāla* and *munāsaba*, a more complete definition emerges. The validity of *qiyās*, then, is dependent on the extraction of potential occasioning factors (*maʿānī*) from an explicit text that is in overall accordance with the public good and the objectives of the Sharīʿa (broadly, the notion of *munāsaba*) with the goal of convincing the *mujtahid* with overwhelming probability that he or she has ascertained the correct ruling (broadly, the definition of *ikhāla*). Put more simply, the formal condition for the validity of the *ʿilla* is the presence of the two qualities of *munāsaba* and *ikhāla*. This definition is corroborated by a later statement of al-Juwaynī's, which lists three elements of a sound *ʿilla*: (1) that it is *munāsib* and *mukhīl*, (2) that it is free of objections, and (3) that it is in accordance with the *uṣūl*.[46] Once these three conditions are satisfied, the proposed *ʿilla* is accepted as the rationale for the source ruling and can be extended to branch cases. Given that the *mujtahid* must consider the correctness of the extracted *ʿilla* overwhelmingly probable, al-Juwaynī outlines three specific methods to help the jurist in the discovery and validation of the correct *ʿilla*: textual extraction, *al-sabr wa-l-taqsīm* (examination and division), and *al-ṭard wa-l-ʿaks* (coextensiveness and coexclusiveness).

Of the three methods, the first is scripturally based and functions independently, whereas the other two are rational, nontextual, and act in tandem to reveal the *ʿilla*. The first method, textual extraction, is contingent on the presence of a lucid Quranic verse or *ḥadīth* (*naṣṣ ẓāhir*)[47] that enables the jurist to detect linguistic indications in the

[44] For a summary of the Ḥanafī rejection of *ikhāla*, see al-Sarakhsī, *Uṣūl al-Sarakhsī*, 2:183–87. See also Zysow, *Economy of Certainty*, 215–36.

[45] Al-Juwaynī, *al-Burhān*, 2:787.

[46] Al-Juwaynī does not explain what he means here by *uṣūl*, so he could be referring to the jurisprudential procedure itself, *uṣūl al-fiqh*, or the general objectives of the law as encapsulated in the doctrine of *maṣlaḥa*. Ibid., 2:802.

[47] Here al-Juwaynī is implying that a *ẓāhir* text indicates the justification of the *ʿilla*, but this was a matter of disagreement. Generally, jurists distinguished between two types of

structure of the words themselves.[48] For example, derived nouns (*ism mushtāq*) and/or proper nouns (*ism al-ʿalam*) are both apparent (*ẓāhir*) in their meanings and can easily direct the jurist toward the rationale. To illustrate this method, al-Juwaynī uses the example of the punishment for theft, namely, amputation, which is specified in the Quran. The verse dictating this punishment uses a derived noun in the form of the doer of the verb (*fāʿil*) to indicate the thief – *al-sāriq*.[49] Al-Juwaynī argues that using a derived noun indicates a justification of the rationale, which then signifies indicativeness (*ikhāla*).[50] However, the presence of a clear text (*naṣṣ ẓāhir*) indicating suitability satisfies only one of the conditions; the jurist still has to ensure that all objections are answered and the ruling is in accordance with public welfare.[51]

Using direct textual indicators is the optimal way to deduce the *ʿilla* with overwhelming probability, but given the relative scarcity of such clear indicators, the jurist is compelled to make use of the other two rational methods suggested by al-Juwaynī. The first, *al-sabr wa-l-taqsīm* (examination and division),[52] is defined as a process in which "the reasoner investigates various potential occasioning factors (*maʿānī*) for the source ruling one by one and isolates one of them as being correct with respect to the justification (*taʿlīl*) for the ruling."[53] In this method, the

scriptural texts, *qaṭʿī* or *sarīḥ*, and *ẓāhir*. Texts of the former type indicate justification (*taʿlīl*), whereas texts that are *ẓāhir* (obvious) or *muḥtamal* (equivocal) may not convey justification directly, and the *mujtahid* will have to exert more effort to isolate the rationale. In both cases a direct link is possible, the difference being the amount of effort needed to demonstrate the exact relationship.

48 This definition is taken from a summary that al-Juwaynī provides after discussing various examples of textual extraction. As noted earlier, he does not give this mode of extraction a name, nor does he provide a definition for it. See al-Juwaynī, *al-Burhān*, 2:809–11.

49 See Quran 5:38. He also cites 24:2, which dictates the punishment due for an adulterer and likewise uses a derived noun, *al-zānī*.

50 Al-Juwaynī, *al-Burhān*, 2:710–11.

51 Al-Juwaynī's articulation of this method of deducing the *ʿilla* is similar to the method of *al-tanbīh wa-l-īmāʾ* found in the work of later scholars. However, the two are not exactly the same, as most scholars agree that in *īmāʾ* the cause of the ruling is established not directly from the text but rather from the literal meaning of the word and its typical use. See al-Āmidī, *al-Iḥkām*, 3:336; al-Subkī, *Jamʿ al-jawāmiʿ*, 3:32; and al-Shawkānī, *Irshād al-fuḥūl*, 185.

52 In logic, this method is called the separational-conditional proposition (*al-sharṭī al-munfaṣil*) and constitutes a type of syllogism used in finding rational occasioning factors (*ʿilal ʿaqliyya*) in rational matters. According to Zysow, the majority of Ḥanafīs rejected this method of discovery unless the various possible rationales were excluded on the basis of consensus. See Zysow, *Economy of Certainty*, 217.

53 Al-Juwaynī, *al-Burhān*, 3:815.

jurist examines all possible *maʿānī* for a specific ruling individually to discern which is the *ʿilla* for that ruling.[54] Because it may not be possible to extract all *maʿānī*, al-Juwaynī divides this method into two categories: *ḥāṣir* (exhaustive) and *ghayr ḥāṣir* (nonexhaustive). In the first, the *maʿānī* for the ruling are limited to the binary of negation (*nafī*) and establishment (*ithbāt*), making the process of evaluating these properties relatively manageable and straightforward for the jurist.[55] For al-Juwaynī, exhaustive categorization is superior to the other form of *sabr wa-taqsīm*, because it expedites arrival at overwhelming probability. In this process, some *maʿānī* may be eliminated, either because they are excluded by companion consensus[56] or because of the independent realization of the *mujtahid* that one is more suitable and indicative than another. Companion precedent, once again, plays an important function, as the *ʿilla* is discovered through the interplay of the companions' rulings in specific instances and the insight of the *mujtahid*.

In the nonexhaustive type of *sabr wa-taqsīm*, the *maʿānī* are not limited to the dichotomy between establishment and negation, and the evidence for eliminating some is merely probable. Al-Juwaynī is not keen on this method, fearing that it will breed continuous disagreement because of the lack of overwhelming probability. He also faults it for being more prone to juristic subjectivity, since the evidence for negation is not substantiated by companion consensus.[57] For these reasons, al-Juwaynī argues that this mode of *sabr wa-taqsīm* should not be used to deduce the *ʿilla*, as any *ʿilla* identified through it is not likely to yield overwhelming probability.

Al-Juwaynī's preference for the exhaustive mode of *sabr wa-taqsīm* is due to its comprehensiveness and its corroboration of the selected *ʿilla* through the precedent of the companions. However, the companions were not exhaustive in their legal pronouncements, so jurists must necessarily fall back on their own opinions in the process of excluding certain *maʿānī*. Therefore, al-Juwaynī's critique of the subjectivity inherent to the nonexhaustive mode of *sabr wa-taqsīm* is also to some extent applicable

54 Ibid. 55 Ibid.

56 Abū al-Ḥusayn al-Baṣrī expands on this point, arguing that once the justification for a case has been established either through *ijmāʿ* or by the *mujtahid*s, disagreement regarding the exact occasioning factor is impossible and various potentially efficient properties can be rejected on the basis of juristic understanding or precedent. See al-Baṣrī, *al-Muʿtamad*, 2:784–85.

57 Al-Juwaynī, *al-Burhān*, 2:818.

to his preferred mode of this method.[58] The juristic prerogative to exclude certain *maʿānī* on the basis of *ikhāla*, or indicativeness, relies heavily on the legal acumen of *mujtahid*s and their ability to conceptualize the actual *ʿilla*. Some legal schools disapproved of granting such power and interpretive freedom to jurists.[59] The majority of Ḥanafī and Ḥanbalī jurists held this view, rejecting *al-sabr wa-l-taqsīm* as a method for extracting the *ʿilla*. In addition to their suspicion of juristic subjectivity, they also argued that if companion precedent is invoked, the rationale is not technically derived using *al-sabr wa-l-taqsīm*. The Ḥanafīs and the Ḥanbalīs insisted that the derivation of the *ʿilla* remain authentic to the text or *ijmāʿ* to the maximum possible extent. In their view, reliance on rational methods was a poor path to the overwhelming probability needed in religious matters.[60]

Despite these critiques, Shāfiʿī scholars after al-Juwaynī, such as al-Ghazālī, continued to assert that in rational matters (*ʿaqliyyāt*), *al-sabr wa-l-taqsīm* can result in certain knowledge.[61] At the same time, however, al-Ghazālī acknowledges that in religious and legal matters *al-sabr wa-l-taqsīm* can yield only probability and that it is therefore not necessary to reject all *maʿānī* except for the selected one; one has only to establish that the latter predominates over the rest, with the selected one becoming the *ʿilla*.[62] This opinion is shared by al-Āmidī, who adds the caveat that the overwhelming probability of *al-sabr wa-l-taqsīm* applies only to the one undertaking the investigation (*nāẓir*), not to the opponent (*munāẓir*), who has not independently undertaken the process. This implies that two *mujtahid*s can carry out *al-sabr wa-l-taqsīm* on the same original and branch cases and arrive at two contradictory conclusions, even though each is characterized by overwhelming probability.[63] In adding this

58 Al-Juwaynī acknowledges that in the end there could be two occasioning factors for a single ruling. In such cases, it is the jurist's responsibility to choose one over the other. If one *ʿilla* is clearly more suitable than the other, then the jurist uses the process of *al-sabr wa-l-taqsīm* to select the best one. If the two factors are very similar, precluding simple elimination, al-Juwaynī advocates evaluating the two cases through the principle of preponderance, a process he details in his *kitāb al-tarjīḥ*. See al-Juwaynī, *al-Burhān*, 2:1142–293.

59 This same criticism was directed at the condition of *ikhāla*, as noted earlier.

60 Zysow, *Economy of Certainty*, 217–18.

61 This resembles al-Juwaynī's view, presented in Chapter 4. Al-Juwaynī's belief that certain knowledge is accessible through exhaustive reflection is in many ways another expression of his doctrine of *al-sabr wa-l-taqsīm* in *qiyās*.

62 Al-Ghazālī, *al-Mustaṣfā*, 3:618–19; Al-Ghazālī, *Shifāʾ al-ghalīl*, 450–51.

63 Al-Āmidī, *al-Iḥkām*, 3:384–85. This scenario foreshadows a later discussion on the assessment of two contradictory rulings issued by qualified *mujtahid*s. This issue will be

caveat, al-Āmidī implicitly accepts the Ḥanafī critique that the method entails juristic subjectivity, but for al-Āmidī and other Shāfiʿī jurists complete eradication of the jurist's subjectivity is impossible since *qiyās* is at its most fundamental level a juristic act.

The second rational method for deducing the *ʿilla* is *al-ṭard wa-l-ʿaks* (coextensiveness and coexclusiveness). This method rests on the proposition that if the jurist has identified the correct rationale, then whenever the factor is present in a case, the same ruling applies to it, and whenever the factor is absent, that ruling is not applicable. If these conditions hold, the jurist can be relatively confident that the rationale selected is indeed the correct one.

Al-Juwaynī commences his discussion of this method by engaging with jurists who reject *al-ṭard wa-l-ʿaks* as an appropriate or valid way of deducing the *ʿilla*.[64] He names al-Bāqillānī as an opponent of the method, citing the latter's position that the companions relied first on textual indicators and then, if no textual indicators were available, on public welfare (*maṣlaḥa*) in deriving their rulings. Remaining true to the companions' example would, from al-Bāqillānī's perspective, invalidate *al-ṭard wa-l-ʿaks* because there is no evidence that the companions made use of it. Al-Juwaynī retorts that the general use of reason by the companions reveals that they did not confine themselves solely to the text; moreover, the sphere of reason encompasses various methods, of which *al-ṭard wa-l-ʿaks* is one.[65] Al-Juwaynī's own argument for the permissibility of this method relates to his assertion that the main objective of *qiyās* is the creation of overwhelming probability through textual indicators and/or reason. Therefore, to the extent that *al-ṭard wa-l-ʿaks* can assist in ascertaining the *ʿilla*, it is valid. However, although he defends the method, he recognizes that it is not as methodologically sound as *al-sabr wa-l-taqsīm* is and cannot serve as the sole mechanism for identifying the *ʿilla*.

In part, the weakness al-Juwaynī associates with *al-ṭard wa-l-ʿaks* is rooted in the fact that to extract a *maʿnā*, the ruling, and therefore *ṭard*, is logically necessary. As for *ʿaks*, the inapplicability of the ruling in the absence of the *ʿilla* reinforces the *ʿilla* selected by the jurist, but it cannot by itself establish the *ʿilla*, nor does it definitively point toward justification (*taʿlīl*) because it is possible that there is a correlation between a

taken up in Chapter 8 in the context of diversity and disagreement within the realm of *qiyās*.

64 For the critiques of this method, see Zysow, *Economy of Certainty*, 217.

65 Al-Juwaynī, *al-Burhān*, 2:837–39.

maʿnā and the ruling without causal connection.[66] Therefore, al-Juwaynī concludes, *al-ṭard wa-l-ʿaks* can aid in the discovery of the *ʿilla* of a ruling but cannot function independently without support from the other two methods. By adding this qualification, al-Juwaynī accepts that *al-ṭard wa-l-ʿaks*, unlike *al-sabr wa-l-taqsīm* and textual indicators, cannot by itself establish overwhelming probability.[67]

Al-Juwaynī's reservations regarding *al-ṭard wa-l-ʿaks* were echoed by al-Ghazālī, but the latter takes them a step further, invoking the Ḥanafī charge that if one needs to reinforce the conclusions obtained through *al-ṭard wa-l-ʿaks* by recourse to other methods such as *al-sabr wa-l-taqsīm*, then it is more accurate to say that it was the latter method that enabled identification of the *ʿilla*. For al-Ghazālī, the dependency of *al-ṭard wa-l-ʿaks* on other methods of deduction means that it is not an appropriate method for discovering the *ʿilla* and can at best be used as a secondary tool after the *ʿilla* has already been established with overwhelming probability by a stronger method.[68]

Al-Juwaynī and al-Ghazālī agree that the deficiencies inherent in the method of *al-ṭard wa-l-ʿaks* prevent it from functioning independently without qualification to guide the jurist to the most probable *ʿilla*. To be effective, it must either be coupled with other methods of discovery or fulfill certain stringent conditions. Rational methods of identifying the *ʿilla* were a point of general contention among the various legal schools and especially between the Ḥanafīs and the Shāfiʿīs, but the method of *al-ṭard wa-l-ʿaks* was particularly contested. According to Zysow, this is because the argument of coextensiveness and coexclusiveness – or as he calls it, consistency and convertibility – brings the ontology of the *ʿilla* into sharp relief. What is at stake in this discussion is the issue of causality: if coextensiveness and coexclusiveness were accepted as a condition for the *ʿilla*, this would mean that for any given ruling there is only one correct *ʿilla*, and the *ʿilla* has a causal relationship with the ruling such that if the *ʿilla* were incorrect, the jurist would not reach the same ruling.

The issue of causality was part of a larger epistemological debate that we encountered in Chapter 3 regarding rational proofs (*dalāʾil ʿaqliyya*) and knowledge.[69] The standard Ashʿarī position was to deny a causal

[66] Ibid., 2:849–52, 854.

[67] Al-Basrī, much like al-Juwaynī, argues that *al-ṭard wa-l-ʿaks* can be used but cannot establish anything with certainty.

[68] Al-Ghazālī, *al-Mustaṣfā*, 3:636–39.

[69] For the full contours of the debate, see Zysow, *Economy of Certainty*, 222–36.

relationship between rational indicators and knowledge. In legal discussions, their stance entailed the absence of causal relationships between revelatory indicators and the rationales, on the one hand, and the rulings connected to them, on the other. The absence of causal relationships meant that although *al-ṭard wa-l-ʿaks* was a useful tool, it ultimately could not serve as an independent definitive proof. However, al-Juwaynī rejected the classical Ashʿarī view of rational proofs and argued that proofs, or aspects (*wajh*) of proofs, lead to or – in his terminology – entail (*taḍammun*) knowledge of the conclusion, meaning that to the extent that human beings reason correctly, they will arrive at sound knowledge. But does the argument for rational proofs apply also to revelatory proofs and indicators? In other words, does knowledge of the *ʿilla* similarly entail knowledge of a specific ruling, as al-Juwaynī maintained for rational proofs?

Consistency would require that al-Juwaynī evaluate rational and scriptural proofs and indicators in the same way, but in fact he does not do so. Instead, he says that revelatory proofs (*dalāʾil sharʿiyya* or *ʿilal samʿiyya*) "are indicators (*amārāt*) on the path to probability (*ẓann*)."[70] Al-Juwaynī thus emphasizes that there is no causal relationship between the *ʿilla* as a revelatory rationale and the ruling associated with it. Beyond this difference, revelatory proofs, according to him, are also unique because they take into consideration the welfare (*maṣāliḥ*) of individuals.[71] Al-Abyārī, while disagreeing with al-Juwaynī's broad argument regarding rational indicators,[72] agrees with the assertion that the difference between revelatory and rational proofs lies in the role of welfare in the former.[73] It is clear why al-Juwaynī does not see *al-ṭard wa-l-ʿaks* as an independent verifier of the *ʿilla*: doing so would mean accepting legal and revelatory causality, which would not only limit the scope for extending the ruling but also undermine the notion of legal plurality.[74]

70 Al-Juwaynī, *al-Burhān*, 2:843, 849–51. 71 Ibid., 2:849.

72 See the discussion of al-Juwaynī's argument regarding rational proofs in Chapter 3.

73 Al-Abyārī, *al-Taḥqīq wa-l-bayān*, 3:229–31.

74 In Chapter 4, I argued that the Ashʿarī emphasis on divine legislative authority entailed an acceptance of legal indeterminacy, as jurists could not be absolutely certain that they had correctly ascertained the legal rule in any given situation. A natural corollary to legal indeterminacy is legal plurality, since jurists can come to different conclusions and all are considered legitimate as long as they were derived using an acceptable methodology. Despite the general acceptance of legal plurality, the existence or otherwise of a single correct answer in any situation was subject to heated debate. This debate, encapsulated in the question *Hal kull al-mujtahid muṣīb* (Is every jurist correct?), was carried on primarily between the *mukhaṭṭiʾa*, who argued that there is always a single correct answer, and the

In addition to al-Juwaynī's ontological concerns invoked by the question of causality, he concludes his section on *qiyās al-maʿnā* by noting his suspicion of the possibility of truly parallel cases. In his view, no two situations can ever be fully parallel, and any attempt to draw a definitive connection between two cases will inevitably highlight some lack of congruence. Therefore, the objective in using various methods of extracting the rationale is not the identification of completely equivalent cases but the extraction of a multitude of *maʿānī* from a specific case in order to facilitate the jurist's attempt to deduce the most plausible rationale for the source ruling and the one *most* appropriate for the branch case, not one that is necessarily identical.[75] Moreover, even if a jurist is able to identify a suitable (*munāsib*) and indicative (*mukhīl*) *ʿilla* with overwhelming probability, given inevitable variance among jurists, coupled with the impossibility of true parallels, rulings derived through *qiyās al-maʿnā* – the strongest type of *qiyās* – remain probable, not certain.

CONCLUSION

The discussion of *qiyās* in the *Burhān* is based on al-Juwaynī's belief in legal universality: every human action has a corresponding legal ruling rooted in the revealed law. Since the scriptural sources are limited in the legal guidance they can provide, *qiyās* becomes an important legal mechanism for extending these limited scriptural sources and indicators to a wide array of novel legal scenarios. The mode of extending legal rulings is contingent on the legal acumen of the jurist; therefore, the entire section on *qiyās* can broadly be read as an exploration of how knowledge, and more specifically legal knowledge, is produced through a combination of reason and revelation. In contrast to his assertion in the *Burhān*'s section on epistemology that rational indicators entail their conclusions, here al-Juwaynī argues that scriptural indicators, in the form of legal rationales

musawwiba, who held that there is not. I will not delve into the details of the debate, but it should be kept in mind that both groups accepted juristic plurality as theoretically valid. By endorsing *qiyās* as a valid source of law and by accepting the possibility of more than one *ʿilla*, al-Juwaynī, too, had to accommodate legal plurality despite his concern with legal certainty. For more on the relationship between legal indeterminacy and legal plurality, see Zysow, *Economy of Certainty*, chapter 5; Khaled Abou El Fadl, *Speaking in God's Name: Islamic Law, Authority and Women* (Oxford: Oneworld, 2001), 147–50; Weiss, *Spirit of Islamic Law*, chapter 5; and Anver Emon, "The Most Likely to Know the Law: Objectivity, Authority and Interpretation in Islamic Law," *Hebraic Political Studies* 4, no. 4 (2009): 431–38.

[75] Al-Juwaynī, *al-Burhān*, 2:841–43.

(*ʿilal*), do not entail their conclusions, and it is thus the job of the jurist to extract all possible *maʿānī* from a scriptural source. The extraction of possible *maʿānī* is connected to the clarity of the scriptural source itself, necessitating a distinction between two types of *qiyās*: *qiyās al-maʿnā* and *qiyās al-shabah*. In the former – the focus of this chapter – the ruling in the original case is relatively clear, allowing the jurist to identify possible *maʿānī* with relative ease. In evaluating the *maʿānī*, the jurist must satisfy the dual conditions of suitability (*munāsaba*) and indicativeness (*ikhāla*) and eliminate unsuitable rationales using various rational tools. Once a single conceivable rationale remains, the jurist can reach a conclusion with overwhelming probability.

The challenge of *qiyās* for al-Juwaynī lies in its juxtaposition of his overall desire for epistemic certainty with his desire for legal universality and continuity. In the discussion on *qiyās al-maʿnā*, he is able to mitigate uncertainty to some extent thanks to the presence of a scriptural text; however, in the discussion of *qiyās al-shabah*, the second and weaker form of *qiyās*, an added degree of probability emerges, forcing al-Juwaynī to develop strategies to manage the increasing probability in the realm of law.

8

Coping with Legal Uncertainty

Qiyās al-Shabah

In the case of *qiyās al-maʿnā*, the jurist's recourse to textual indicators in either the Quran or *ḥadīth* elevates the probability that the rationale (*ʿilla*) extracted by the jurist is the correct one. However, not all legal queries relate to textual sources, and on some queries the jurist is thus forced to venture beyond textual reliance to derive rulings by other means. The departure from the textual reliance of *qiyās al-maʿnā* brings al-Juwaynī to his other principal type of *qiyās*, *qiyās al-shabah*. The main distinction between *qiyās al-maʿnā* and *qiyās al-shabah* is that the latter is based on a resemblance (*shabah*) whereas the former is based on a clearly definable, suitable, and indicative rationale identified through textual evidence. The absence of textual recourse means that *qiyās al-shabah* involves even more juristic subjectivity than does *qiyās al-maʿnā*. Though al-Juwaynī accepts legal uncertainty in his discussion on *qiyās al-maʿnā*, in order to mitigate the proliferation of competing juristic interpretations brought on by *qiyās al-shabah* he constructs a hierarchy within the realm of *qiyās*, urging jurists not merely to accept probability but also to isolate the most probable ruling when presented with multiple options. To further control the spread of legal uncertainty and the multiplicity of competing rulings, at the end of his discussion on *qiyās* he also seeks to limit the domain of jurists who can practice *ijtihād* to *muftī-mujtahid*s alone.

QIYĀS AL-SHABAH: A DEBATED SOURCE

Qiyās al-shabah is the most controversial element within the doctrine of *qiyās*. Rejected by a great many legal scholars as an illegitimate source of law,[1] it enjoyed a mixed reception among Shāfiʿī scholars, some of whom opposed it despite al-Shāfiʿī's own approval of the doctrine in his *Risāla*. Critics of this form of *qiyās* saw it as an untethered, unwieldy source of law – unbound by textual indicators or scripturally derived rationales and too open to juristic subjectivity and interpretation. Defenders of the doctrine, al-Juwaynī and al-Shāfiʿī among them, viewed it as a nonideal but legitimate source of legal derivation and, in fact, as necessary for extending the law to cover new circumstances. Unlike *qiyās al-maʿnā*, which connects two cases on the basis of a textual indicator and a derived occasioning factor, *qiyās al-shabah* is constructed on the basis of a resemblance, meaning that there could be multiple possible source cases and multiple resemblances connecting the cases. Al-Juwaynī illustrates this point with the example of a slave's putative right to own property.[2] If one argues that the slave resembles a free person in that both have intellects and are capable of managing property, then the slave should be permitted to own property. If, on the other hand, one argues that the slave, like an animal, is owned by a master, then one would conclude that just as an animal does not possess the independence or means to own property, neither does the slave. This example is often put forward by opponents of *qiyās al-shabah* to demonstrate that the method can result in completely opposed rulings and that the possibilities of resemblance are practically endless. Why should the slave be compared only to a free person or an animal? Is it not possible to draw a comparison between the slave and an orphan, a woman, or a child, potentially leading to a different ruling in each case?[3] Those skeptical of *qiyās al-shabah* argue that if nothing guides the resemblances proposed methodologically or textually, the proliferation of conflicting rulings resulting from the use of *qiyās al-shabah* could threaten the very stability of the law. Al-Juwaynī, instead of defending the resemblance between a slave and an animal or between a slave and a free person, argues that this is simply a bad case of *qiyās al-shabah* because even though *qiyās* on the basis of resemblance is allowed, the resemblance must still be indicative (*mukhīl*)

[1] Zysow, *Economy of Certainty*, 159–88.

[2] Al-Juwaynī notes that the example was originally provided by al-Bāqillānī. See al-Juwaynī, *al-Burhān*, 2:864.

[3] I am making no judgments as to the suitability of these analogies, merely highlighting the fact that classical jurists often constructed analogies between these categories of individuals, so it is worth asking why in the case of property ownership jurists chose the two potential analogies that they did.

and suitable (*munāsib*) based on the original case.[4] This means that the specific resemblance chosen must be justified and other possible resemblances rationally eliminated. Before delving into the specifics of al-Juwaynī's argument, I will revisit that of al-Shāfiʿī, which is the font for later Shāfiʿī debates surrounding *qiyās al-shabah*.[5]

Al-Shāfiʿī's succinct discussion of *qiyās* is rooted in the assertion that there is an "all-encompassing structural coherence to the source texts and their legislative components."[6] Given this coherence between the law and the scriptural sources, extending textual rulings through analogy or resemblance is a legitimate legal method. As Joseph Lowry describes it, al-Shāfiʿī's idea of *qiyās al-shabah* involves three cases, two with rulings and one without, in contrast to *qiyās al-maʿnā*, which features only two cases, the source and the branch. All three cases are connected by resemblances, and the job of the jurist is to ascertain the strongest resemblance between two cases and extend the ruling accordingly.[7] But al-Shāfiʿī stops short of explaining how resemblances are to be identified and eliminated. Lowry notes that despite endorsing *qiyās*, al-Shāfiʿī harbors reservations about it because of the epistemological problem it poses: *qiyās* necessarily involves a greater degree of legal uncertainty, and this is particularly apparent in *qiyās al-shabah*, where juristic subjectivities are front and center. Moreover, given al-Shāfiʿī's primary desire in the *Risāla* to demonstrate the "structural coherence" of scriptural sources in relation to law, dwelling too much on cases that showcase an absence of that coherence or the difficulty of realizing it would undermine the very objective of the *Risāla*.[8]

[4] Al-Juwaynī, *al-Burhān*, 2:864.

[5] For a full exposition on al-Shāfiʿī's understanding of *qiyās* in relation to his broader argument in the *Risāla*, see Lowry, *Early Islamic Legal Theory*, chapter 2. Lowry is part of a long line of scholars who have attempted to excavate al-Shāfiʿī's legal thought in the *Risāla*, in particular. He departs from the others in important ways that are, however, beyond the scope of this work. Those interested may consult a number of secondary sources: Joseph Lowry, "Does Shāfiʿī Have a Theory of 'Four Sources' of Law?," in Weiss, *Studies in Islamic Legal Theory*, 23–40; Schacht, *Origins of Muhammad Jurisprudence*; Coulson, *History of Islamic Law*; and Melchert, *The Formation of the Sunni Schools*, chapters 4 and 5.

[6] Lowry, *Early Islamic Legal Theory*, 151. Al-Shāfiʿī does not endorse *qiyās* without reservation, as he is worried about overextending the text, betraying the intent of the legislator, and creating scripturally unsupported rulings. Like al-Juwaynī, he notes the epistemological limitations of *qiyās* due to its inability to provide the jurist with anything beyond overwhelming probability. For more, see ibid., 156–63.

[7] Ibid., 151.

[8] According to Lowry, the only case al-Shāfiʿī discusses is the classification of a gazelle as more like a sheep or a camel when it comes to the rules of reparation (*jazāʾ*). The basic rule is that if a person kills an animal while in the state of *iḥrām* (consecration for pilgrimage),

In contrast to al-Shāfiʿī, who provides only a brief elaboration on *qiyās al-shabah*, al-Juwaynī seeks to defend the legitimacy of the doctrine by proving its utility and validity. Shāfiʿī scholars after al-Shāfiʿī were divided on *qiyās al-shabah*. Most importantly for al-Juwaynī, his preeminent intellectual predecessor al-Bāqillānī rejects it, arguing that since no precedent in companion practice can be found for it, this form of *qiyās* is not a legitimate tool of legal derivation.[9] However, al-Juwaynī finds al-Bāqillānī's persistent objection feeble at best. In his defense of the practice, al-Juwaynī argues that the companions used reason in legal derivation, and this usage of reason on their part legitimates all rational methods of legal derivation, including *qiyās al-shabah*. Al-Bāqillānī's claim to the contrary is based on the idea that each mode of *qiyās* must be founded on explicit precedent, instead of a general precedent sufficing to permit the application of reason.

In addition to casting doubt on the legitimacy of *qiyās al-shabah*, al-Bāqillānī asserts that it does not produce overwhelming probability, a condition for any ruling to be considered valid. This is because any "resemblance" between two cases can be considered broadly suitable (*munāsib*), which renders the condition ineffective. Since suitability and indicativeness are what engender overwhelming probability, the absence of clearly identifiable appropriateness means the absence of overwhelming probability. And if one moves away from these two conditions and buttresses the argument with other evidence, such as companion precedent, then, al-Bāqillānī argues, the *qiyās* is no longer based on resemblance, but rather on companion opinion.[10] To this last criticism al-Juwaynī does not offer a direct response, but he does reiterate that the driving purpose of *qiyās* is to extend the scope of the law to novel situations, thereby securing the continuity of the law. For al-Juwaynī, the jurist will always yield to textual indicators and companion precedent when available, but the law cannot be circumscribed by these sources alone – rational methods, too, must be employed. This position reveals al-Juwaynī's sense of a pressing need both to justify the doctrine of *qiyās* and to safeguard the continuity of the law. Though al-Juwaynī appears more

he or she must make reparations by sacrificing an animal similar to the one killed. Al-Shāfiʿī uses *qiyās al-shabah* to determine whether a sheep or a camel should be killed as reparation for a gazelle. Ibid., 157–58.

9 Al-Bāqillānī used the same argument against the method of *al-ṭard wa-l-ʿaks*, discussed in the previous chapter. On that issue, too, al-Juwaynī rejected his critique, asserting that the companions broadly sanctioned the use of reason in the realm of legal derivation.

10 Al-Juwaynī, *al-Burhān*, 2:871–72.

willing than al-Bāqillānī to depart from obvious textual indicators in this regard, he does uphold a single criterion for all forms of *qiyās*, both textual and nontextual, namely, overwhelming probability (*ghalabat al-ẓann*).[11]

Although al-Bāqillānī's early criticisms of *qiyās al-shabah* found some sympathetic ears in the Shāfiʿī school,[12] defenses of *qiyās al-shabah* continued to accumulate. Al-Ghazālī takes particular interest in this discussion and provides an extensive defense of *qiyās al-shabah*. In his *Shifāʾ al-ghalīl*, he not only defends the doctrine but also amends it, asserting that the condition of suitability (*munāsaba*) is unnecessary; it is sufficient, in his view, that the jurist reaches overwhelming probability based on resemblance in terms of the ruling and the form.[13] On this point, al-Juwaynī and al-Ghazālī diverge slightly, as al-Juwaynī maintains *munāsaba* as a condition for *qiyās al-shabah* and as integral to the achievement of overwhelming probability. Al-Ghazālī elaborates his argument in greater detail in his *Mustaṣfā*, arguing that whereas *qiyās al-maʿnā* is based on a *munāsib ʿilla* directly suited to the ruling, *qiyās al-shabah* is based on a resembling quality that is not directly appropriate to the ruling, which renders the condition of *munāsaba* superfluous. Though al-Juwaynī and al-Ghazālī disagree on some of the more nuanced elements of *qiyās al-shabah*, both recognize its value in ensuring the continuous derivation of legal rulings. It is precisely with this recognition of the centrality of *qiyās al-shabah* to legal continuity that al-Juwaynī opens his discussion of this form of *qiyās*.

QIYĀS AL-SHABAH ACCORDING TO AL-JUWAYNĪ

In the beginning of his discussion on *qiyās al-shabah* in the *Burhān*, al-Juwaynī struggles to provide a clear definition and instead explores problematic definitions or problematic cases, such as the abovementioned question of slave property rights. When he finally proposes a definition, he does so by relating *qiyās al-shabah* to *qiyās al-maʿnā*, the main distinction being that the suitability and indicativeness of the occasioning factor (*ʿilla*) in the former will not rise to the same level as it does in the latter.[14] Further, he explains that *qiyās al-shabah* "is divided into that which informs by way of an indicative and suitable *maʿnā* quality (*al-maʿnā al-mukhīl al-munāsib*) with clear notification (*ishāran bayyinan*),

[11] Ibid., 2:871–75. [12] Zysow, *Economy of Certainty*, 192–96.
[13] Al-Ghazālī, *Shifāʾ al-ghalīl*, 306–11. [14] Al-Juwaynī, *al-Burhān*, 2:865, 873.

and that which utilizes pure resemblance."[15] This first type of *qiyās al-shabah* thus resembles *qiyās al-maʿnā*, whereas the second type gives the jurist neither knowledge nor overwhelming probability (*ẓann*).[16] In a case of *qiyās al-maʿnā* in which the rationale is unclear and the jurist's confidence is wavering, the eventual decision to choose one potentially efficient rationale over another is due not to explicit textual indications but to a subjective assessment of which potentially efficient rationale is more indicative and suitable than the others. On this basic level, the subjective assessment of the jurist in such a case of *qiyās al-maʿnā* is the same as that in the first grade of *qiyās al-shabah* regarding resemblance.[17] The true distinguishing factor between the various grades of *qiyās*, according to al-Juwaynī, is indicativeness (*ikhāla*). He notes that indicativeness is not a unitary concept but rather comprises degrees, the strongest being *jalī* (evident) and the weakest *khafī* (latent).[18] In *qiyās al-maʿnā* the indicativeness of the rationale is apparent, whereas in *qiyās al-shabah* it is not. Therefore, "what preponderates (*yaghlib*) in [the *mujtahid's*] mind, in his judgement without indicativeness, is the matter of resemblance (*shubh*)."[19]

Al-Juwaynī divides resemblance, on which *qiyās al-shabah* rests, into two types: resemblance on the basis of legal rulings (*rabṭ al-aḥkām bi-l-aḥkām*) and pure resemblance (*shubh maḥḍ*).[20] As an example of the first and stronger form of *qiyās al-shabah*, he cites the cases of *ẓihār* (divorce through likening one's wife to one's mother) and *ṭalāq* (divorce), which have the same legal consequence, namely, the prohibition of intercourse (*taḥrīm al-buḍʿ*), and which also share the same occasioning factor, the suspension of a formal spousal relationship. A strong resemblance is most evident in legal consequences and appears obvious at first glance: *ẓihār* and *ṭalāq* are joined not only by the same legal consequence but also by an obvious relationship to one another.[21] In other cases of *qiyās al-shabah*, however, the resemblance between the cases is not easily ascertainable by the jurist. In this category, al-Juwaynī places the resemblance between ablution (*wuḍūʾ*) and dry ablution (*tayammum*), and the resemblance between a ritual bath (*ghusl*) prompted by impurity (*janāba*) and

[15] Ibid., 2:866–67. [16] Ibid., 2:862. [17] Ibid., 2:872–76, 885.
[18] Ibid., 2:864–65. [19] Ibid., 2:870. [20] Ibid., 2:866–67.
[21] Al-Juwaynī acknowledges that some jurists call this stronger form of *qiyās al-shabah* *qiyās al-dalāla*, but because the occasioning factor is not completely clear, al-Juwaynī subsumes it under *qiyās al-shabah* while acknowledging that it represents a higher grade since its rationale is somewhat *munāsib* and *mukhīl*. Ibid., 2:867–77.

the ritual bath given to the dead.[22] In the latter case, even though there is a legal resemblance between a ritually impure individual and a deceased one as indicated by the requirement of a ritual bath for both, the obvious difference between a living and a deceased individual means that equivalence between the two cases is not based on an easily ascertainable rationale, and it thus constitutes a weaker form of *qiyās al-shabah*.

Whether *qiyās al-shabah* is based on a ruling or on pure resemblance, the similarities between the cases allow the jurist to transfer the ruling of one case to another even if a clearly indicative rationale cannot be identified. The condition for the employment of this form of *qiyās* is that the indicativeness ensures overwhelming probability in the mind of the jurist. This idea of overwhelming probability is most important for al-Juwaynī, and thus he says at the end of his defense of *qiyās al-shabah* that "speculative reasoning (*naẓar*) in [matters of] resemblance, when continuous in terms of habit, arrives at overwhelming probability, just as speculative reasoning in [*qiyās*] *al-maʿnā* necessitates it."[23] The methods for generating overwhelming probability are identical to the ones in *qiyās al-maʿnā – al-sabr wa-l-taqsīm* and *al-ṭard wa-l-ʿaks*.

Al-Juwaynī's conditions for *qiyās al-shabah* and *qiyās al-maʿnā* and the methods by which the rationales are determined in each case are the same, even though al-Juwaynī classifies them in distinct categories. The main differentiating factor between these two forms of *qiyās* is thus not the epistemic strength of the resulting ruling, which is probable in either case, or the presence versus the absence of a text, but the clarity with which the jurist discerns the rationale on the basis of indicativeness and suitability. Although this distinction grants a higher status to *qiyās al-maʿnā*, the importance of *qiyās al-shabah* is not diminished, and in view of al-Juwaynī's concern for legal continuity and universality, it may even be more exigent in certain circumstances.

The centrality of *qiyās al-shabah* for al-Juwaynī is most evident at the end of his discussion, where he again returns to the issue of overwhelming probability in cases of *qiyās al-shabah*:

> In my view, overwhelming resemblances in the mind, even if they do not fit the ruling, can nonetheless create a connection between the branch and the original [cases] for the purposes of a ruling. This is the greatest secret in this chapter. It is as if a suitable *maʿnā* for the ruling [can be given] without mention of the original [case], [by] reflecting on the general benefit (*al-maṣāliḥ al-kulliyya*). [As] the

[22] Ibid., 2:868–69. [23] Ibid., 2:874.

original [case] is for safeguarding the benefit (*maṣlaḥa*) [of people] in the foundations of the Sharīʿa.[24]

Though al-Juwaynī so far in his discussion on *qiyās al-shabah* has been keen to emphasize the connection between cases on the basis of rulings or the resemblance that brings about indicativeness, in this quotation he broadens the scope of *qiyās al-shabah* to include reasoning on the basis of *maṣlaḥa*. While on the surface this seems like a departure from his more textual approach to *qiyās*, for al-Juwaynī, it is in fact a necessary result of his subscription to the notion of legal universality.

MAṢLAḤA IN *QIYĀS*

The cornerstone of al-Juwaynī's defense of *qiyās* is the notion of legal universality – the two-pronged argument that every human action has a corresponding legal judgment and that whereas potential legal cases are innumerable, the scriptural sources are limited. The finite number of sources and the infinite number of legal queries necessitates that jurists, when possible, create relationships between nonidentical cases in order to extend the rulings of established cases to new ones. The main challenge in this system is posed by the limited number of original cases or textual indicators in the face of countless and variable legal scenarios. When the jurist cannot extend the rationale from one case to another or identify a resembling feature between two cases, to what can the jurist have recourse?

Legal rulings are not created in a vacuum. They are the result of novel social, political, or economic situations that demand, in the case of Islamic law, religiously conscious legal rulings. Rulings are thus requested by laypersons and provided by scholars in a specific context that shapes the form of both the question and the answer. This dialectical nature of legal queries means that legal scholars must be aware of the needs of the questioner and of society more broadly. Al-Juwaynī traces this cognizance required of the jurist to the companions, who often justified their juristic interpretations on the basis of communal public interest.[25] Since the companions were seen as the emblematic representation of the juristic class, al-Juwaynī asserts that *maṣlaḥa* constitutes a measure of the soundness of jurists' legal interpretations.[26]

[24] Ibid., 2:876. For the most comprehensive analysis of the development of the doctrine of *maṣlaḥa*, see Opwis, *Maṣlaḥa and the Purpose of the Law*.

[25] Al-Juwaynī, *al-Burhān*, 2:804–11, 876. [26] Ibid., 2:876, 923–26.

By grounding the usage of *maṣlaḥa* in the practice and consensus of the companions, al-Juwaynī fixes it with an authoritative status, as he does in his broader defense of *qiyās*. But despite identifying a broad desire on the part of the companions to take public interest into consideration, al-Juwaynī is unable to point to a single historical instance in which the companions explicitly referred to *maṣlaḥa* in the course of legal derivation.[27] This inability makes his defense of *maṣlaḥa* tenuous, reliant more on his own conceptualization and imagination of what the companions did and thought than on actual historical proof. It is especially surprising that al-Juwaynī advances such a weak defense of *maṣlaḥa* given that most of his discussions on *uṣūl al-fiqh*, especially his revisionary ones,[28] hinge on the definitive establishment of the validity of a source. The discussion on *maṣlaḥa*, therefore, appears to be an occasion on which al-Juwaynī prioritizes continuity over certainty: recognizing that the textual sources are limited whereas possible legal queries are not, he reasons that it is better to use *maṣlaḥa* if it enables the creation of laws since the alternative is forfeiting the possibility of a legal ruling altogether. Though this rational defense of the need for *maṣlaḥa* satisfies al-Juwaynī, it fails to meet the standards of epistemic certainty that he generally upholds for the validity of legal sources.[29]

Al-Juwaynī's approach becomes more precise when he turns to the operational role of *maṣlaḥa* within the domain of *qiyās*. As described earlier, one of al-Juwaynī's conditions for the validity of a putative rationale is its suitability (*munāsaba*) in relation to the ruling. Al-Juwaynī did not explicitly equate the notion of *munāsaba* with *maṣlaḥa*, but later jurists saw them as naturally synonymous.[30] Al-Juwaynī employs the term *munāsaba* in two ways. In the first usage, the suitability of the rationale depends on its connection to the original ruling in a source text and the extent to which the rationale in both cases can be deemed identical. The second usage appears in situations in which the rationale

[27] Recall that al-Juwaynī likewise justifies *qiyās* by appeal to companion practice, but he also provides a scriptural proof in the form of the exchange between the Prophet and Muʿādh b. Jabal in which the former sanctions the use of independent reasoning; see Chapter 7.

[28] By "revisionary," I mean discussions in which al-Juwaynī departs from the standard proofs proffered by his Shāfiʿī predecessors, as he did in the cases of *ijmāʿ* and *ḥadīth*; see Chapters 5 and 6.

[29] Al-Juwaynī, *al-Burhān*, 2:804–11. He also provides another defense on pp. 1113–14, where he argues that this practice was generally accepted in the Shāfiʿī school as long as the guiding *maṣlaḥa* was in accordance with the textual sources.

[30] See Opwis, *Maṣlaḥa and the Purpose of the Law*, 59–131.

is unclear and the suitability of the ruling, instead of being connected to an explicit textual source, is linked to principles of general benefit (*maṣāliḥ kulliyya*) governing all legal rulings.[31] In this context, al-Juwaynī conceptualizes general benefit as the rationale underpinning all legal rulings and facilitating the overall welfare of believing Muslims. He illustrates this notion of *maṣlaḥa* through the example of the marriage contract. Its formal contractual elements resemble those of all other financial or commercial contracts; however, it is unique because it is an open contract that can be terminated and is intended to promote the birth of progeny by way of a legally sanctioned sexual relationship. Underlying the formal rules and regulations of the marriage contract is, according to al-Juwaynī, the welfare (*istiṣlāḥ*) of human beings, and in the event of an unprecedented situation involving marital contracts, the jurist should not derive a ruling from contractual law[32] but rather find a suitable ruling that is commensurate with the *maṣlaḥa* guiding marriage contracts.[33]

Having defended the permissibility and validity of determining rulings on the basis of *maṣlaḥa*, al-Juwaynī addresses legal rulings in broad terms along with the general principles that they uphold. For him, each ruling, besides being associated with a rationale, is governed by and upholds the general good.[34] However, it is not enough simply to assert that all rulings foster the *maṣlaḥa* of the community, as some things are necessary for general welfare whereas others, while beneficial, are superfluous. Therefore, he creates a graduated scale from indispensable to nonessential to reflect how integral any given legal matter is to promoting the general good of the Muslim community. In this section, al-Juwaynī refers to

31 Al-Juwaynī, *al-Burhān*, 2:876.

32 Kecia Ali argues that the dominant conceptualization of the marital contract in classical books of *fiqh* is as a commercial contract, involving an exchange of goods and ownership rights. Though there were differences among the legal schools regarding the exact mode of exchange, all agreed that the husband acquired ownership of the wife's body, entailing complete sexual access to her. Other scholars, such as Judith Tucker, have demonstrated that despite the restrictive language in the *fiqh* texts, women acted as independent agents in divorce and often in cases involving abuse. See Kecia Ali, *Sexual Ethics and Islam: Feminist Reflections on Quran, Hadith and Jurisprudence* (London: Oneworld, 2016), chapters 1 and 2; Judith Tucker, *In the House of the Law: Gender and Islamic Law* (Berkeley: University of California Press, 2000).

33 Al-Juwaynī, *al-Burhān*, 2:903–5, 908.

34 The idea of legal rulings upholding the general good was not introduced by al-Juwaynī. One of the most prominent proponents of this argument is al-Qaffāl al-Shashī, an early Shāfiʿī scholar, who argues in his *Maḥāsin al-sharīʿa* that all rulings have a specific purpose and are aimed at the benefit of human beings. For more on his argument, see El Shamsy, "Wisdom of God's Law."

rationales (*ʿillas*) and *uṣūl al-sharīʿa* (foundations of the Sharīʿa) interchangeably, effectively arguing that groups of legal rulings share a common reasoning. He enumerates five categories of *uṣūl al-sharīʿa*: rulings intended to preserve something necessary (*amr ḍarūrī*), rulings involving a general need (*ḥāja ʿāmma*), rulings promoting noble deeds (*makārim*), rulings encouraging actions that are recommended (*mandūb*), and, finally, rulings whose reason is unintelligible.[35]

In rulings falling into the first category, the reasoning behind the legal ruling is intelligible and relates to a matter necessary for the overall order and maintenance of people's affairs (*īyāla*) and for the political welfare (*siyāsiyya*) of the Muslim community.[36] Though the scope of necessary (*ḍarūrī*) matters is vast, al-Juwaynī limits his discussion to things that are essential for the physical and spiritual integrity of the Muslim polity. The primary example he provides is rulings mandating equal retribution (*qiṣāṣ*),[37] which, he argues, are intended to protect life by deterring people from physically injuring others.[38] A difficulty arises in situations in which a group of people kill an individual, and the imposition of equal retaliation – that is, the death penalty on all perpetrators – appears to lead to disproportionate bloodshed. On the other hand, however, the rule of commensurate requital supports *maṣlaḥa* by recognizing the sanctity of the victim's life and avenging its violation. Al-Juwaynī rules, therefore, that in such a situation the *maṣlaḥa* supported by retaliation must be upheld and retaliation applied to all members of the guilty group. He points out that if the multiplicity of perpetrators were permitted to avert the penalty of death, a potential criminal might deliberately recruit an accomplice in order to avoid retaliation. Beyond demonstrating the application of *maṣlaḥa* in legal reasoning, al-Juwaynī's presentation of this case is particularly interesting since it preserves the universal *maṣlaḥa* of the sanctity of life and the laws regarding retaliation even as it contravenes the particular rule of commensurate retribution.[39]

35 Al-Juwaynī, *al-Burhān*, 2:923–26. After providing this basic outline, he then delves into further detail on each category. See ibid., 2:937–51.

36 Ibid., 2:923.

37 The rules of retribution apply to any intentional unlawful or unjust killing. According to Rudolph Peters, these rules are governed by three ideas: "(a) the principle of private prosecution; (b) the principle that redress consists in retaliation or financial compensation; (c) the principle of equivalence, which means that retaliation is only allowed if the monetary value of the victim is the same as or higher than that of the perpetrator." For more on these rules, see Rudolph Peters, *Crime and Punishment in Islamic Law* (Cambridge: Cambridge University Press, 2005), 38–53.

38 Al-Juwaynī, *al-Burhān*, 2:927.

39 Ibid., 2:927–28.

Once rulings based on necessity (*ḍarūra*) have been established, they can be extended to similar situations. Al-Juwaynī analogizes the above example of loss of life caused by a group of people to the question of retaliation against a group of people who have inflicted bodily harm on another individual. He thus extends the ruling based on the *maṣlaḥa* of protecting life and providing the right of retaliation from one particular case to another.[40] However, a *particular* ruling based on necessity cannot be extended to an entire category of rulings. Thus, the permissibility of eating carrion in a situation of necessity (for example, when facing imminent starvation) is a particular ruling that cannot form the basis for a general ruling allowing the eating of carrion.[41] When the notion of necessity functions in a particular case, it applies to a discrete juristic inquiry; the rulings issued on its basis can be extended only to similar particular cases and cannot be generalized. In al-Juwaynī's example, a particular case based on *maṣlaḥa* (retaliation against the lives of all members of a group of perpetrators for intentional killing) is extended to another particular case (retaliation against the limbs of all members of the group for bodily injury), but the law of commensurate retaliation remains intact.

Another mode of applying this form of *maṣlaḥa* involves the opposite process: a general or universal ruling is applied to a particular case on the basis of necessity. As an example, al-Juwaynī cites the permissibility of sale (*bayʿ*), which is necessary for the development of society. The permission to sell covers both the general category (*jumla*) of sale and specific instances (*nawʿ*) of selling.[42] Because the specific instances of sale are included under the general rule, there is a general sanction for all contracts, though their constituent elements remain subject to juristic criticism or approval. In sum, then, in matters involving societal necessity, a general rule can subsume within it all particular instances, as in the case of sale, or a particular rule can be extended to an analogous situation, as with the principle of requital.

In the second category of *maṣlaḥa*-based rulings, the reasoning relates to a general need (*ḥāja ʿāmma*) but not one that constitutes a necessity whose absence would result in direct social harm.[43] Although a general need may become an individual necessity in specific cases, the jurist using *maṣlaḥa* to derive rulings must be guided by the general good of the Muslim community and not the circumstances of any individual

[40] Ibid., 2:929–30. [41] Ibid., 2:942–43. [42] Ibid., 2:923. [43] Ibid., 2:924.

Muslim.[44] At the same time, if individual needs are exacerbated to the extent that they affect society as a whole, the ensuing general need can serve as the basis of a ruling aimed at averting a specific harm from the community. As an example, al-Juwaynī offers the case of rent (*al-ijāra*).[45] Rental contracts are not a necessity for individuals seeking housing, but they may alleviate the financial difficulty associated with ownership. The *maṣlaḥa* that underpins their permissibility is people's general need for shelter regardless of their financial status. However, the unique features of a rental contract pose a challenge to the rules governing commercial contracts, which generally require the physical transfer of ownership in exchange for material payment. In the case of rent, no property changes hands, nor is payment made in full at the time of the contract. The *maṣlaḥa* behind the general rule is the protection of both parties from being wronged in the exchange. However, in the case of *ijāra*, the general need for shelter overrides the *maṣlaḥa* of requiring such safeguards for commercial contracts.[46] Therefore, rental contracts are permitted on the basis of need (*ḥāja*), even though they violate one aspect of the soundness of a contract.

The third category of rulings comprises rulings that are not connected to any necessity or need but rather are aimed at encouraging noble deeds. Rulings in this category are also informed by an underlying *maṣlaḥa*, but the *maṣlaḥa* is not immediately apparent to people, because it is established by God as an imposition (*waẓīfa*) on believers. Since the *maṣlaḥa* behind these rulings is inaccessible to the jurist, they cannot be extended to novel situations. Al-Juwaynī gives as an example the obligation of ablution after ritual impurity (*ḥadath*), which reflects human beings' natural inclinations and promotes a noble goal, cleanliness; however, the precise reasoning behind the legal obligation cannot be ascertained.[47]

The fourth category is similar to the third one in that its rulings promote people's benefit, but the actions these rulings encourage have the added benefit of being explicitly recommended (*mandūb*). Al-Juwaynī cites the example of the contractual manumission (*al-kitāba*) of a slave, an agreement by which a slave can buy his or her freedom through service or money.[48] The permissibility of *kitāba* is peculiar because the slave technically has no ownership over his or her labor and thus no right to use it

[44] Ibid., 2:923–24. [45] Ibid., 2:924. [46] Ibid., 2:930–31. [47] Ibid., 2:925, 936.

[48] On the laws of manumission, see Ulrike Mitter, "Unconditional Manumission of Slaves in Early Islamic Law: A Ḥadīth Analysis," *Der Islam* 78, no. 1 (2001): 35–72. For the application and development of these laws in the Ottoman period, see Nur Sobers-Khan, *Slaves without Shackles: Forced Labor and Manumission in the Galata Court Registers, 1560–1572* (Berlin: Klaus Schwarz, 2014).

as the currency of exchange. This makes the case of *kitāba* akin to that of *ijāra*, in which one element of the exchange is absent at the time of the contract. However, because manumission is a meritorious act in its own right, *kitāba* is permitted. Rulings in this category do not have intelligible rationales and as such cannot be the basis of further *qiyās*, since their permissibility comes directly from the Lawgiver.

Rulings in the fifth and final category do not fall into any of the other categories, and their logic or reasoning is difficult to discern. In this category, al-Juwaynī includes rulings relating to worship, which can be understood only as a sign of submission to God and a way of warding off character deficiencies such as evilness and laziness. Rulings in this category, such as the obligation to pray or the prescription of a specific number of prostrations for each prayer, are generated with a certain rationale in the mind of the Lawgiver that is not ascertainable by textual or rational means. Therefore, like those in the previous two categories, rulings in this category cannot be used as the basis for *qiyās*.[49] This category is distinguished from the third one by its focus on matters of worship (*ʿibādāt*), whereas the third category covers any action considered beneficial for the cultivation of noble character.

Al-Juwaynī's typology of the five *uṣūl al-sharīʿa* is based on a hierarchy of needs and of the potential ascertainability of the legal reasoning behind the rulings.[50] Only the first two categories of rulings, aimed at safeguarding necessities and basic human needs and characterized by intelligible rationales, can serve as the basis of *qiyās*. In these limited cases, the jurist is permitted to abandon text-based *qiyās* for *qiyās* based on *maṣlaḥa*, even though the former is methodologically and textually more valid.[51] However, al-Juwaynī does not restrict the use of *maṣlaḥa* to this form of *qiyās*. Felicitas Opwis observes that

[49] Al-Juwaynī, *al-Burhān*, 2:926, 958–60.

[50] Aron Zysow points out an interesting tension present between the doctrine of *maṣlaḥa* and what he labels Ashʿarī ethics. He notes that the doctrine of *maṣlaḥa* presupposes that jurists are able to ascertain the purpose of the law in general as well as in specific rules so as to be able to identify them as the legal cause. Zysow argues that this creates a theological problem, since the jurists are implicitly arguing that they can indeed deduce what the purpose of the law really is – in other words, they are claiming, through their use of *maṣlaḥa* in *qiyās*, that they have understood the Lawgiver's intent. According to Zysow, this demonstrates that "the Ashʿarī ethical doctrine was false, and their own practice of analogy pointed to its falsity." He also notes that this apparent contradiction became one of the many Achilles' heels of the Ashʿarī *uṣūlī*s and that it demonstrates how detached the disciplines of theology and legal theory were. See Zysow, *Economy of Certainty*, 199–200.

[51] Al-Juwaynī, *al-Burhān*, 2:909–10.

al-Juwaynī's interpretation of *maṣlaḥa* reflects two different ways of reasoning with which to approach the authoritative texts. When using the considerations of *maṣlaḥa* in the form of suitability in the method of analogy, a jurist moves in a deductive fashion from one particular statement/ruling in the texts to another particular. The basis (*aṣl*) as well as the derivation (*far'*) refers to a particular case, and in each legal instance the jurist has to establish that the same *ratio legis* exists in the new and original case. A different approach is used when postulating *maṣlaḥa* as a universal precept. A jurist extracts inductively from several particular statements in the texts a general ruling that is then applied in law-finding without direct reference to the particular pieces of textual evidence from which it was extracted.[52]

In the first instance, *maṣlaḥa* is used to evaluate a specific case in order to determine the suitability (*munāsaba*) of the rationale tentatively identified for the ruling; in the second instance, a general *maṣlaḥa* is derived from multiple rulings and then serves as the basis for the formulation of future rulings. In the example of retaliation, the jurist is already familiar with the broad *maṣlaḥa* of the preservation of life, conveyed in the cumulative message of the scriptural sources. In the specific case of a group killing, the jurist looks to this universal *maṣlaḥa* to determine a suitable ruling instead of engaging in direct *qiyās*. Whether using *maṣlaḥa* to isolate the most suitable rationale or to create a legal ruling, jurists invoke *maṣlaḥa* when no clear textual indicator is available and a legal ruling is desired. By endorsing the second function of *maṣlaḥa*, which does not necessitate a direct textual indicator, al-Juwaynī presents *maṣlaḥa* as the antidote, along with *qiyās*, to the dilemma posed by the principle of legal universality and the limited nature of the scriptural texts. Although *maṣlaḥa*-based rulings related to necessities and needs are textually derived and extended, in other instances, where there is no direct ruling or parallel case, the jurist is not limited to scriptural legal derivation. Therefore, al-Juwaynī's theory of *qiyās*, and the role of *maṣlaḥa* in it, can be read as a means of justifying his claim of legal universality while at the same time providing a tangible mechanism for its realization.

THE HIERARCHY WITHIN *QIYĀS*

Both Al-Juwaynī's detailed analysis of *qiyās* and his introduction of *maṣlaḥa* serve his belief in legal universality, which necessitates a framework open to continued legal derivation free of textual constraints.

[52] Opwis, *Maṣlaḥa and the Purpose of the Law*, 59.

However, this belief in legal universality is tempered by the competing ideal of certainty, which preoccupies him in the early pages of the *Burhān*. Al-Juwaynī's two seemingly irreconcilable needs thus create a quandary. On the one hand, legal universality entails the continuing ability to fashion legal rulings despite textual insufficiency and epistemic uncertainty. On the other, the standard of epistemic certainty requires the individual and the jurist to have complete confidence in the rulings produced. The tension between these two competing desires is in many ways unresolvable, as satisfying one undermines the other. Al-Juwaynī is thus compelled to prioritize one over the other, recognizing that a true balance is often unachievable in the interplay between continuity and certainty. His acceptance and promotion of the doctrine of *qiyās*, alongside his willingness to champion *maṣlaḥa* as a tool of legal derivation, suggests that at least in this area he is more concerned with continuity and legal universality than he is with legal certainty. However, his desire for certainty reenters the picture in the form of a gradation for *qiyās*, which seeks to enable the jurist to identify the most epistemically sound ruling in each case. The relative strength of each mode of *qiyās* occupies an independent section in the *Burhān* entitled "Grades of *qiyās*" (*marātib al-aqyisa*).[53]

After a review and refutation of gradations proposed by other scholars, al-Juwaynī introduces his own gradation with a basic epistemological distinction between what is known (*al-ma'lūm*) and epistemically certain, and what is merely probable (*al-maẓnūn*). As for what is known, al-Juwaynī reiterates his earlier contention[54] that there is no distinction between types of knowledge (*'ilm*) in terms of their epistemic strength because any knowledge, once acquired fully, cannot be substantively differentiated from other knowledge: "One cannot conceive of knowledge more apparent (*abyan*) than knowledge."[55] Therefore, the sole criterion for distinguishing between acquired knowledge items is the amount of reflection (*naẓar*) each requires. So whereas sensory knowledge and knowledge of advanced algebra may occupy the same epistemological level by virtue of both being objects of knowledge, the latter requires more

53 Al-Juwaynī, *al-Burhān*, 2:877–89.

54 See Chapter 4 for a discussion of al-Juwaynī's epistemology. In a slight revision to his earlier position, here he asserts that the distinction between *'ilm naẓarī* and *'ilm ḍarūrī* is merely a semantic one and that if an individual reasons exhaustively to reach a conclusion and is confident in it, that new knowledge item is "necessary" (*ḍarūrī*) to the intellect and no epistemological distinction can be drawn between it and other knowledge items.

55 Al-Juwaynī, *al-Burhān*, 2:881.

reflection than does the former. This lack of differentiation within knowledge does not apply to the results of *qiyās*, because rulings derived through it are epistemically only probable and thus are not considered knowledge proper. Therefore, they do admit epistemological gradation.

The basic epistemic classification of *qiyās*-based rulings as probable reflects the absence of a transparent and direct textual indicator. This weakness cannot be circumvented, since *qiyās* is a valid mode of legal derivation only in the absence of a source text addressing the legal situation at hand. The lack of textual evidence leaves the jurist epistemically restricted, unable to conclude with certainty that he or she has identified the correct rationale or a valid resemblance between two cases. Consequently, the jurist's objective, as al-Juwaynī repeatedly states, is not certainty but overwhelming probability. Despite this inherent limitation, the existence of multiple forms of *qiyās* enables al-Juwaynī to categorize them according to how much confidence they grant to the jurist. On this basis, he identifies four grades of *qiyās*: evident (*jalī*) *qiyās al-maʿnā*, latent (*khafī*) *qiyās al-maʿnā*, *qiyās al-shabah* on the basis of rulings, and *qiyās al-shabah* on the basis of resemblance.[56]

The two first grades, featuring *qiyās al-maʿnā*, are distinguished by the indicativeness of the rationale. If the rationale is indicative (*mukhīl*), then it, and the *qiyās* procedure relying on it, is classified as evident, yielding the strongest type of *qiyās*. If, on the other hand, the jurist encounters difficulty in ascertaining the rationale, it falls under the rubric latent.[57] Even though al-Juwaynī earlier outlines two conditions for the validity of the rationale, indicativeness and suitability, differentiation of *qiyās al-maʿnā* in terms of strength is contingent only on indicativeness. This means that *maṣlaḥa*, which is most closely tied to suitability, does not affect the strength of *qiyās al-maʿnā*. *Qiyās al-shabah*, constituting the second two grades, is divided according to the basis of the relationship postulated between the two cases – a shared ruling or resemblance.[58] In the former type of *qiyās al-shabah*, al-Juwaynī still stipulates the

[56] Al-Juwaynī first describes the grades of *qiyās al-maʿnā*, then explains the various grades, and finally details the grades of *qiyās al-shabah*; ibid., 2:882–85. The *Burhān* contains two discussions on the grades of *qiyās*. The first is presented at the end of the section on *qiyās* and forms the basis for this exposition. The second comes much later in the *Burhān*, in the chapter on preponderance (*tarjīḥ*); for that discussion, see ibid., 2:1142–84. In the latter section, he first claims that it is not possible to describe fully the various grades of *qiyās al-maʿnā* since its subject matter is probable (*maẓnūn*), but he nonetheless goes on to outline two principal grades.

[57] Al-Juwaynī, *al-Burhān*, 2:882–85. [58] Ibid., 2:886.

condition of indicativeness, though he recognizes that it will not be met to the same degree as in *qiyās al-maʿnā*. In the latter form of *qiyās al-shabah*, the rationale's indicativeness is even weaker; this is the realm in which rulings can be constructed on the basis of *maṣlaḥa*.

The gradation of *qiyās* proposed by al-Juwaynī advocates juristic reliance on the mode of *qiyās* that affords the highest degree of probability for the resulting ruling – with the degree of probability being in relation to the clarity and indicativeness of the rationale in the first two grades and to the nature of the resemblance between the two cases in the second two. However, whether the ruling is based on an explicit textual indicator or a tenuous resemblance, for al-Juwaynī all instances of *qiyās* fall under the broad banner of epistemic probability. Within the realm of legal knowledge, epistemically certain rulings can be achieved only through *mutawātir ḥadīth* and Quranic verses explicit in their signification, along with rulings from *ijmāʿ*. As rulings from these unassailable sources constitute only a small subset of all rulings, the majority of rulings must be accepted as probable, ushering in plurality and mutual juristic critique. This situation raises two important questions. First, given al-Juwaynī's preoccupation with certainty and its overall importance for individuals, how does he justify the enactment of probable rulings? Second, how is the inevitable diversity produced by varying juristic subjectivities and acumen regulated? The first question appeared already in al-Juwaynī's discussion of unitary *ḥadīth*, where he argued for their use in law despite their epistemic deficiencies on the basis of necessity, with the justification that people need legal guidance in all of their affairs. He bolstered his argument further by asserting that the companions accepted the use of unitary narrations. The principle of legal universality and the use of epistemically probable sources are established unequivocally, and these metarules justify each subsequent ruling.[59] Al-Juwaynī applies the same argument to the case of *qiyās*, pointing out, first, that the companions certainly utilized *qiyās*, and second, that human beings' need for continuous legal guidance is likewise certain. These two foundational principles justify the acceptance of probable rulings, as rejecting them would not only contravene companion precedent but also leave people without legal guidance. As for the second question regarding juristic and legal variability, al-Juwaynī recognizes the complexity of the issue and devotes an entire section to addressing it.

[59] See al-Juwaynī's defense of *qiyās* in Chapter 7 and of *wāḥid ḥadīth* in Chapter 5 for detailed discussion of this idea.

REGULATING VARIANCE: THE ROLE OF THE *MUJTAHID*

According to al-Juwaynī, legal variance is mitigated by two main mechanisms. On the one hand, a restrictive mechanism is built into the legal methodology, which permits only jurists at the rank of *muftī-mujtahid* to perform *qiyās*.[60] On the other hand, a theoretical restriction operates through the doctrine of *taswīb*, which imputes correctness to each individual *muftī-mujtahid*'s legal opinion while maintaining the existence of a singular ontologically correct ruling.

The permission given to jurists to derive rulings meant that they were charged with interpreting the scriptural sources and regulating basic human affairs. The gravity of this vocation translated into stringent requirements that had to be met before an aspiring jurist was granted license to issue legal verdicts.[61] The requirements focus on the mastery of various disciplines that demonstrate breadth of knowledge and legal acumen. Within the parameters of professional engagement, the range of each jurist depended on his or her knowledge: some were limited to sermonizing and issuing legal verdicts based on precedent, whereas others enjoyed the freedom to create new rulings through *qiyās*.[62] This

[60] I have chosen to use the term *muftī-mujtahid* because early legal discussions on juristic qualifications focused on the requirements for the *muftī*, and one of the main such requirements was that the *muftī* be capable of *ijtihād*. Consequently, texts written before the time of al-Juwaynī did not have a separate section on the qualifications of the *mujtahid*. It was only later that the status of a *mujtahid* was disassociated from that of a *muftī*. My choice of *muftī-mujtahid* is thus based on a desire to reflect the early doctrine accurately. See Wael Hallaq, "Ifta' and Ijtihad in Sunni Legal Theory: A Developmental Account," in *Islamic Legal Interpretation: Muftis and Their Fatwas*, ed. Muhammad Khalid Masud, Brinkley Messick, and David S. Powers (Cambridge, MA: Harvard University Press, 1996), 33–44.

[61] I am using "license" here in a loose sense. Although the notion of licenses (*ijāzāt*) did exist, referring to authorization to teach particular texts, ascent to the level of a *muftī-mujtahid* was not based on *ijāza*s but rather was a matter of acceptance into a scholarly class by others already in that class.

[62] The continuing derivation of new rulings by jurists within the *madhhab* framework is one of the principal ideas scholars have used to rebut the notion that the "doors of *ijtihād*" had closed. Sherman Jackson points to the emergence of a *madhhab*-internal phenomenon of "legal scaffolding" in which jurists build on existing legal foundations to create new rulings. For him, *taqlīd* signals the existence of legal scaffolding and a more mature form of law as opposed to one constantly in flux. Other scholars have also demonstrated the existence of legal innovation within the *madhhab*, either through *qiyās* or through engagement with existing doctrines. They argue that legal derivation within the *madhhab* was an advanced form of jurisprudence and enabled continuity alongside change. See Sherman Jackson, "Taqlīd, Legal Scaffolding and the Scope of Legal Injunctions in Post-Formative Theory," *Islamic Law and Society* 3, no. 2 (1996): 165–92; Mohammad

categorization was based on the model of the companions, who identified select individuals among themselves as capable of issuing legal verdicts.[63] As the discipline of Islamic law matured, the practice of the companions informed later doctrines, resulting in the tenet that only the foremost legal scholars, early on referred to as *muftīs*, were qualified to issue independent legal verdicts known as fatwas.[64] This restriction confined *qiyās* to the realm of the *muftī-mujtahids* and served as the catalyst for defining the qualities that distinguished the *muftī-mujtahid* from other legal scholars. Al-Shāfiʿī provides an early articulation of the qualifications of the *muftī-mujtahid*,[65] among which he includes knowledge of the Quran, *ḥadīth*, *ijmāʿ*, and the Arabic language; an understanding of what is equitable and just; and sociological insights into varying societies.[66] After al-Shāfiʿī, the most exhaustive exposition of the qualities of a *muftī-mujtahid* was provided by al-Baṣrī in his *Muʿtamad*. He acknowledges the importance of all the qualities al-Shāfiʿī enumerates but fixates on legal knowledge, which for him encompasses other forms of religious and rational knowledge.[67] Al-Baṣrī also adds that once a legal scholar achieves the requisite qualifications and is considered a *muftī-mujtahid*, he is required to issue opinions on the

Fadel, "The Social Logic of *Taqlīd* and the Rise of the *Mukhtaṣar*," *Islamic Law and Society* 3, no. 2 (1996): 193–233; and Wael Hallaq, "Was the Gate of Ijtihad Closed?," *International Journal of Middle East Studies* 16, no. 1 (1984): 3–41.

63 According to al-Juwaynī, the first four caliphs, as well as Ṭalḥa b. ʿUbayd Allāh and Saʿd b. Abī Waqqās, were all *mujtahids*. His full discussion of *mujtahids* among the companions and the successors can be found in the *Burhān*, 2:1333–37.

64 For a complete historical overview of the development of the *muftī*'s vocation and the institutional apparatus supporting it, see Muhammad Khalid Masud, Brinkley Messick, and David Powers, "Muftīs, Fatwas and Islamic Legal Interpretation," in Masud, Messick, and Powers, *Islamic Legal Interpretation*; and Hallaq, "Iftaʾ and Ijtihad." Hallaq's article is especially useful for mapping how the discussion regarding the qualifications of the *mujtahid/muftī* evolved over time. Broadly speaking, Hallaq argues that scholars from al-Shāfiʿī to al-Baṣrī, al-Juwaynī, and al-Ghazālī all upheld similar requirements and approached the discussion in a similar manner; however, after al-Āmidī the qualifications of the *mujtahid* began to be considered from the specific standpoint of the *madhhab*. Al-Āmidī also introduced the question whether a non-*mujtahid muftī* was permitted to issue fatwas. Until this point, the assumption had been that a *muftī* was always a *mujtahid*; al-Āmidī's discussion thus called that basic assumption into doubt.

65 Al-Shāfiʿī does not explicitly state that the *muftī* must be capable of *ijtihād*, but the qualifications he enumerates are similar to those listed by later scholars such as al-Baṣrī and al-Juwaynī for the *muftī-mujtahid*.

66 For a full discussion of the qualifications and the various positions taken, see al-Khaṭīb al-Baghdādī, *al-Faqīh wa-l-mutafaqqih*, ed. ʿĀdil b. Yusūf al-ʿAzāzī (Mecca: Dār Ibn al-Jawzī, 1996). For al-Shāfiʿī's discussion, see Muḥammad b. Idrīs al-Shāfiʿī, *Kitāb al-Umm* (Bulaq: al-Maṭbaʿa al-Kubrā al-Amīriyya, 1907–8), 7:274.

67 Al-Baṣrī, *al-Muʿtamad*, 2:929–31.

basis of his *ijtihād* without recourse to other juristic opinions, as such recourse would undermine his position as a *muftī-mujtahid*.

The early conditions outlined by al-Shāfiʿī and al-Baṣrī remained relatively constant, and there is little historical evidence of disagreement regarding the qualifications.[68] This stability continues with al-Juwaynī; however, he adds a psychological dimension. The required qualifications he lists comprise maturity and knowledge of Arabic, the Quran, *ḥadīth*, grammar, morphology, rhetoric, exegesis, abrogation, history, jurisprudence, and *fiqh*, as well as *fiqh al-nafs*. This last item, *fiqh al-nafs*, is not mentioned in earlier works, and al-Juwaynī does not elaborate on it. Its linguistic meaning suggests a knowledge of the self (*nafs*), referring to either the *muftī-mujtahid*'s internal awareness of his or her own subjectivity or an external understanding of the psyche of the questioner. The introduction of this apparently psychological element indicates that al-Juwaynī is aware that the proclivities and subjectivity of both the jurist and the questioner are implicated in legal derivation, and these have to be recognized even if they cannot be fully overcome.

The prerequisites for legal derivation determine which jurists are capable and qualified to issue rulings on the basis of *qiyās* and which jurists are bound to scriptural sources and the precedent of their more erudite peers. The requirements serve to limit the actual number of *muftī-mujtahids*, thereby controlling the amount of legal diversity produced by *qiyās*. Narrowing the scope of diversity, however, does not eliminate the possibility of contradictory rulings on individual issues. Since each *muftī-mujtahid* is granted free range to discover the law within the parameters of the sanctioned jurisprudential methods, it is plausible that two jurists may evaluate a single issue in contrasting ways. This poses the questions of how the two contradictory opinions can be reconciled and whether diversity can be tempered further by declaring only one of them correct.

To address these questions, al-Juwaynī begins with the claim that each legal query has only one ontologically true ruling in the mind of the Lawgiver, whether or not it is actualized by the jurist. This axiom upholds ontological unity and coherence within the law even in situations of actual juridical diversity.[69] With this argument, al-Juwaynī partakes in a larger debate between the position of *takhaṭṭu*ʾ (admission of error or

[68] There were, of course, countless other scholars who enumerated the qualities of the *muftī-mujtahid*. For an overview of these various opinions, see Hallaq, "Iftaʾ and Ijtihad," 31–35.

[69] Al-Juwaynī, *al-Burhān*, 2:1325.

fallibility) and that of *taswīb* (admission of soundness or infallibility). Proponents of the former argue that there is always one correct answer in the mind of God, the Lawgiver, and a *muftī-mujtahid* unable to identify it has erred. This thesis emphasizes the necessary soundness of the final legal opinion, as it is the locus of God's judgment. By contrast, advocates of *taswīb* contend that as long as the *muftī-mujtahid* endeavors sincerely to ascertain the correct ruling, the effort is rewarded even if the selected ruling is not, in fact, the one chosen by the Lawgiver. Defenders of this position emphasize the methodology of derivation rather than the resulting judgment, arguing that if the correct methodology is applied, the jurist is considered to have discharged his or her duty successfully.[70]

Al-Juwaynī himself adopts the doctrine of *taswīb* on the basis that *ijtihād* is a process of legal reasoning aimed at overwhelming probability.[71] Thus, the duty of the *muftī-mujtahid* is to reach overwhelming probability, not the ontologically correct ruling according to God. That said, al-Juwaynī acknowledges the existence of a correct answer and claims an additional reward from the Lawgiver to be due to the jurist who successfully identifies it. To illustrate his argument, he provides two examples. In the first, a *muftī-mujtahid* rules that a specific act is prohibited, whereas another *muftī-mujtahid* rules that the same act is virtuous and acts accordingly. Al-Juwaynī argues that the second jurist is correct from the procedural perspective because he or she followed their judgment but wrong from the formalistic perspective, since he or she did not arrive at the correct conclusion of prohibition.[72] In this case, the jurist is rewarded for their effort, but not for their action. In the second, more explicit example, two *muftī-mujtahid*s reach conflicting conclusions regarding the correct direction of prayer (*qibla*), with each subsequently praying according to their own opinion. In this case, as in the first one, the *muftī-mujtahid* who acts incorrectly on the basis of a faulty but sincere opinion is correct from the perspective of procedure but wrong in terms of the decision itself.[73] In both examples, al-Juwaynī emphasizes the utmost importance of the jurisprudential process in the derivation of new rulings.

[70] For a more detailed look at the various arguments and their proponents, see Zysow, *Economy of Certainty*, chapter 5. Zysow shows that there was a great deal of diversity even within the Shāfiʿī school with regard to the doctrine, so it cannot be said that al-Juwaynī represents the only view within the school, although al-Bāqillānī and others relate that al-Shāfiʿī himself held the same opinion. See also Ahmed Fekry Ibrahim, *Pragmatism in Islamic Law: A Social and Intellectual History* (Syracuse, NY: Syracuse University Press, 2015), 49–60.

[71] Al-Juwaynī, *al-Burhān*, 2:1323. [72] Ibid., 2:1325. [73] Ibid., 2:1325–26.

For each new legal query, the *muftī-mujtahid* should first investigate the textual sources, then *ijmāʿ*, and then the opinions of previous scholars and the companions, turning only after these sources have been exhausted to his or her own independent reasoning and pursuing this until a conclusion is reached of overwhelming probability. By focusing on the method, al-Juwaynī demonstrates that divergent opinions arising from *ijtihād* are not necessarily due to individual juristic subjectivities but rather may reflect conceivable differences in the practice of a single mode of reasoning. Thanks to the emphasis on the methodology of derivation as opposed to the judgment, the incorrect *muftī-mujtahid* escapes censure for the failure to reach the ontologically correct answer. Finally, by maintaining that there is an ontologically correct answer, al-Juwaynī is issuing an indirect rejoinder to those that consider the doctrine of *taswīb* of legal relativism.[74]

CONCLUSION

Al-Juwaynī's extensive engagement with the doctrine of *qiyās* is best conceptualized as a negotiation between his preoccupation with epistemic certainty and his commitment to legal universality and continuity. The exigency al-Juwaynī associates with the latter leads him to elevate it over the competing need for certainty by authorizing the *muftī-mujtahid* to extend the law to novel cases through *qiyās*. Central to his doctrine of *qiyās* is *maṣlaḥa*, the welfare of the Muslim community, which the jurist seeks to promote by taking the community's needs into consideration in the process of *qiyās*. The coupling of *qiyās* and *maṣlaḥa* creates a mechanism through which the law can be extended to cases with no explicit textual grounding. All laws generated through *qiyās* are limited to epistemic probability, but the unassailable independent authority of *qiyās* and *maṣlaḥa* legitimizes acting on such probable rulings. Al-Juwaynī defends the legitimacy of these two sources through the practice of the companions and the rational need of individuals for legal guidance. By establishing the legitimacy and epistemic certainty of *qiyās* and *maṣlaḥa*, al-Juwaynī is able to mitigate unease with the probabilistic nature of the resulting rulings and to bolster both jurists' and the laity's confidence in the jurisprudential method.

[74] See Zysow, *Economy of Certainty*, 272–77.

On the surface, *qiyās* and *maṣlaḥa* appear unrestricted. However, al-Juwaynī laboriously constructs an overarching jurisprudential procedure in the *Burhān* that constrains and regulates them. It is also important to note that he sees both as "last resort" sources. Scriptural rulings always take precedence, and al-Juwaynī erects a hierarchy within *qiyās* to ensure that the jurist issues the most probable ruling possible. Nonetheless, in spite of these mechanisms, the application of *qiyās* and *maṣlaḥa* engenders a great deal of legal diversity that seems to contravene al-Juwaynī's overall objective of certainty. In order to prevent legal pluralism from slipping into legal chaos, al-Juwaynī limits the use of *qiyās* to *muftī-mujtahids*, thus severely narrowing the population of individuals permitted to engage in it. He also upholds the view that there is a single ontologically correct ruling for every scenario, whether or not the jurist successfully identifies it. This means that material plurality within the law is sanctioned but restricted, and ontological plurality is barred entirely. Al-Juwaynī's belief in a single correct answer, coupled with his authoritative defense of *qiyās* and *maṣlaḥa*, demonstrates the internal congruity between his epistemological pursuit of certainty and his legal discussions. Although he ultimately accepts uncertainty in legal rulings, he insists on establishing rationally the certainty of each source of law utilized by the jurist in an attempt to move the legal framework itself beyond critique.

In this chapter, my focus has been on demonstrating the inevitable tension between al-Juwaynī's two desires for certainty and continuity given the limited nature of the scriptural sources. In response, he upholds *qiyās* instead of rejecting it in favor of certainty, and it is thus his desire for continuity that prevails. This choice between certainty and continuity in the case of *qiyās*, as discussed in this chapter, is negotiated within the realm of law. But does the same analysis apply to al-Juwaynī's views on politics and the Muslim community? The idea of the Muslim community appears in al-Juwaynī's discussion of *maṣlaḥa*, but the full contours of the interplay between certainty, continuity, and the community emerge only in his political treatise, the *Ghiyāthī*.

PART IV

POLITICAL THOUGHT

9

The Search for Continuity

Al-Juwaynī's Political Thought

My investigation of al-Juwaynī's thought thus far has demonstrated the connection between his epistemological framework, with its emphasis on certainty, and his defense of the foundational sources of law. His treatment of *qiyās*, analyzed in Chapters 7 and 8, provided the first glimpse of the tension between al-Juwaynī's dual desiderata of certainty and continuity; in that case, his belief in legal universality and in the importance of continuity won the day in spite of the inherent inability of *qiyās* to provide legal certainty. This friction between continuity and certainty comes to the fore again in this chapter, which investigates al-Juwaynī's political thought and the future of the Islamic polity and the Muslim community.

The *Ghiyāthī*,[1] al-Juwaynī's main political text, begins like many political treatises written before his time: with a discussion of the

[1] The full title of the work is *Ghiyāth al-umam fī iltiyāth al-ẓulam*, but it is commonly (and throughout this book) referred to as the *Ghiyāthī*. This is the title al-Juwaynī himself uses, analogizing it to the title of his work *al-ʿAqīda al-Niẓāmiyya*, which is commonly known as the *Niẓāmiyya*. See al-Juwaynī, *al-Ghiyāthī*, 15. The text is divided into three parts, each analyzing a different situation. In the first section, al-Juwaynī addresses a situation in which an ideal imam exists and adequately discharges the duties associated with the office. In the second part, he discusses a nonideal situation featuring an imam who does not meet all of the stipulated requirements for the office. In this section, al-Juwaynī envisions the possibility both of the office's usurpation and of its abolishment altogether. In the third and final section, he discusses a situation in which the *ʿulamāʾ*, and more specifically the *mujtahid*s, assume guardianship over the people. This section also considers the possible absence of the *mujtahid*s and attempts to formulate a solution that guarantees the continuity of society even without formal government of the *mujtahid*s' guidance. This chapter will provide an overview of the first two sections; Chapter 10 then focuses on the third section, in which al-Juwaynī's notion of continuity and its connection to his epistemology is most apparent.

qualifications of the imam, or the political leader of the community, and the responsibilities related to the imamate. After laying out an ideal scenario in which a fully qualified imam discharges all of the duties of the office, he considers a scenario in which there is no qualified imam, and the responsibilities of the imamate go unfulfilled. In envisioning this scenario as a possibility, al-Juwaynī adopts a pragmatic approach to politics, responding and adapting to the political exigencies of the time. In contrast to scholars before him, who accepted a separation between symbolic power (the caliph) and formal power (the sultan) but maintained the sacrosanct nature of the caliphate, al-Juwaynī willingly compromises on the need for the continuous presence of the ideal imam and the formal institution of the imamate itself. His willingness to allow both a nonideal imam and the wholesale absence of the imamate again demonstrates his preoccupation with continuity. This time, however, the preoccupation extends beyond the realm of law to the realm of politics and society.

ISLAMIC POLITICAL THOUGHT: AN OVERVIEW

As Islamic intellectual history unfolded, the Muslim community had, so to speak, one eye directed ahead to newly emergent issues, while the other eye was trained backward, seeking guidance from the Prophetic ideal and from the most tangible manifestation of that ideal in the life of the early companions. From its vantage point in the present, authority and justification were sought retrospectively, whereas innovation and ingenuity were sought prospectively. Accordingly, the fundamentals for the construction of an image of the ideal Islamic polity were absorbed from the early Islamic political model as formulated by the Prophet and his four successors.[2] Scholars of later generations, grappling with the political contingencies of their times, needed to develop a political theory responsive to conditions both in the present and beyond it in the future. But the challenge that confronted this Islamic political theory was that the earliest example of an Islamic polity was unattainable – it centered on the charismatic character of the Prophet, whose connection to God allowed his decisions to transcend the temporal realm and rendered them automatically legitimate, the locus of divine support. Later generations of Sunnīs had no recourse to a central figure possessing unchallenged and divinely

[2] These four successors were the four caliphs, Abū Bakr, ʿUmar, ʿUthmān, and ʿAlī.

ordained legitimacy, so they had to find other ways of justifying their political frameworks as legitimate and authoritative.

Gerhard Böwering argues that the birth of Islamic political thought as a discipline was shaped by certain historical events that threatened the very existence of the Muslim polity. He outlines five distinct phases of Islamic political thought. The first is the early medieval phase, from 132/750 to 446/1055, during which legal scholars, theologians, philosophers, and clerical administrators attempted to respond to the death of the Prophet and the early model of the caliphate as forged by the four caliphs by formulating theories of what makes an imam legitimate and what duties were incumbent on one. In the middle phase, from 446/1055 to 656/1258, Muslim thinkers were primarily concerned with the delegation of power and the legitimacy of an imam who obtains power through usurpation. These preoccupations were a direct result of the upheaval caused by the Seljuk invasion and the weakening of the ʿAbbasid Empire. The next phase extended from 656/1258 to 905/1500 and was prompted by the defeat of the ʿAbbasid Empire at the hands of Mongol invaders, which forced scholars to grapple with urgent questions regarding the preservation of the community and governance under non-Muslim rule. During the subsequent phase, from 906/1500 to 1215/1800, political thought was influenced by the dominance of the three monarchic empires of the Ottomans, the Safavids, and the Mughals, each with its distinct cultural and religious practices and leaders. In the final phase, stretching from the 1800s to the present, Islamic political thought becomes, according to Böwering, geared toward addressing the ascendancy of the West, the loss of the caliphate, and the rise of nation-states.[3] Böwering's overall assessment points to the important fact that Islamic political thought has not been uniform over time and indeed could not have been so, since it was always responding to shifting political arrangements and recurring political crises. This is not to say that nothing connects the five phases: certain inquiries persisted across time and space despite political and local variations. Specifically, Ann Lambton argues that the various strands of Islamic political thought cohere around four main issues: (1) the sovereignty of God, (2) the preservation of Islam, (3) the application of the Sharīʿa, and (4) the defense of religious orthodoxy.[4]

[3] Gerhard Böwering, *Islamic Political Thought: An Introduction* (Princeton: Princeton University Press, 2015), 4–23.

[4] Lambton, *State and Government*, 1–20.

In the second phase of development outlined by Böwering, the formalized articulation of Sunnī political thought between the fourth/tenth and fifth/eleventh centuries, which took place predominantly in Baghdad,[5] was in many ways spurred by Shīʿī ideological and political encroachment. The ʿAbbasids, though still asserting formal control over the Islamic empire, were increasingly facing Shīʿī intrusion from all sides: the Fatimids were steadily expanding in North Africa and Egypt; the Zaydīs established a stronghold in Yemen; the Hamdanids settled in Syria; and, in closest proximity to the ʿAbbasid center of power in Baghdad, the Buyids (345/945 to 446/1055) had seized effective control and forced the ʿAbbasid caliph to assume a status of titular power only.[6] Though politically the impotency of the Sunnīs was becoming increasingly obvious, intellectual life in the Sunnī world was becoming ever richer with the emergence of a new wave of intellectuals who were willing and able to address the most pressing issues of the time. It was in this context that Islamic political thought began to flourish, but it did so within three distinct disciplines. The first of these was the discourse of the religious intelligentsia, the *ʿulamāʾ*, who posed questions regarding the legitimacy and authority of the caliphate in works of *kalām* and investigated subsidiary issues in books of positive law, *fiqh*.[7] The second discipline in which Islamic political thought unfolded was the literature of statecraft – the "mirrors for princes" genre – which focused

[5] Although formal discussions within *kalām* multiplied at this time, they were predated by earlier discussions regarding the form of the Islamic polity that began almost immediately on the death of the Prophet. Discussions concerning issues such as the legitimacy of succession, the authority of the caliph, the role of the Sharīʿa and Quran, and the institution of *shūrā* (consultation) likewise appeared almost immediately after the Prophet's death. For a detailed overview of these various discussions before they were concretized in *kalām* treatises, see Anjum, *Politics, Law, and Community*, chapter 1. For an earlier but valuable exposition, see Duncan B. Macdonald, *Development of Muslim Theology, Jurisprudence, and Constitutional Theory* (New York: Charles Scribner's Sons, 1903).

[6] For the rise of these various dynasties, see C. E. Bosworth, *Islamic Dynasties* (Edinburgh: Clark Constable, 1980).

[7] The overall issue of the caliphate, referred to in *kalām* treatises as a discussion on the imamate, was first and foremost a theological issue, and the *kalām* literature thus established the basic conceptualization and defense of the Sunnī doctrine of the imamate that juridical discussions then developed further. In *kalām* works, the imamate was usually addressed at the end, and the discussion covered the mode for understanding the necessity of the imamate (reason versus revelation), the fallibility of the imam (in response to the Shīʿī doctrine of infallibility), and the order of the imams or caliphs after the Prophet (in response to the Shīʿī belief that ʿAlī was the only true successor).

predominantly on the notion of a just ruler.[8] Finally, there was the translation movement, discussed earlier in Chapter 1, which exposed the Muslim intelligentsia to Platonic and broader Greek notions of politics and government and resulted in treatises drawing heavily on this tradition.[9] Al-Juwaynī's writings fall squarely in the first category.

[8] The mirrors for princes genre is broadly categorized as advice literature (*naṣīḥa*), primarily addressed to people in the higher echelons of leadership for the distinct purpose of elucidating the ideal conduct of leaders. Therefore, texts within this genre were principally concerned with notions of statecraft and were written in a homiletic fashion intended to provide exhortation to rulers. Because of their focus on statecraft, issues pertaining to the populace were of secondary concern and usually emerged only tangentially. Patricia Crone has argued that the development of this genre was rooted in its overwhelming presence in the literary tradition of the Sasanian Empire, from which it slowly seeped into the Islamic empire after Ibn al-Muqaffa''s (d. 139/756) translation of the fable collection *Kalīla wa-Dimna*. Ibn al-Muqaffa' also penned works of his own, of which those pertaining to government are *al-Adab al-kabīr*, *al-Adab al-ṣaghīr*, *al-Risāla fī al-ṣaḥāba*, and *al-Yatīma*. After Ibn al-Muqaffa', some of the most prominent contributions to this genre include al-Fārābī's (d. 339/950) *Fuṣūl al-madanī*, Abū 'Alī al-Ḥasan al-Ṭūsī Niẓām al-Mulk's (d. 485/1092) *Siyar al-mulūk*, and Abū Ḥāmid al-Ghazālī's (d. 505/1111) *Naṣīḥat al-mulūk*. See Patricia Crone, *God's Rule – Government and Islam: Six Centuries of Medieval Islamic Political Thought* (New York: Columbia University Press, 2004), as well as Lambton, *State and Government*, 44–68. Given Niẓām al-Mulk's political stature, his work has been studied carefully. See Ann Lambton, "The Dilemma of Government in Islamic Persia: The *Siyāsat-nāma* of Niẓām al-Mulk," *Iran* 22 (1984): 55–66, and Sayyid A. Rizvi, "Niẓām al-Mulk, His Contribution to Statecraft, Political Theory and the Art of Government" (PhD thesis, University of Karachi, 1977).

[9] However, as Muhsin Mahdi, in his study on al-Farabī, has pointed out, although the Greek translations provided a foundation for Islamic political philosophy, the latter evolved as a distinctive intellectual endeavor. Its development was fostered by Muslim philosophers' engagement with the philosophical inquiries of their Greek predecessors, coupled with the specific theological and philosophical concerns unique to Islamic political thought. Erwin Rosenthal calls this feature a "Platonic legacy" and names al-Fārābī, Ibn Sīnā (d. 418/1037), Ibn Bājja (d. 533/1038), and Ibn Rushd (d. 595/1198) as the central figures in this process. The list should also include one of the first Muslim philosophers to be influenced by the Greek and Hellenistic philosophers, al-Kindī (d. 252/866). Of these scholars, the two who wrote most prolifically on political thought under the influence of the eudaemonistic Greek political tradition are al-Fārābī and Ibn Rushd. Buttressed by the abundant interest in Islamic philosophy in general, much Western scholarly attention has been directed at the political writings of Islamic philosophers rooted in the Greek tradition. For an overview of the work of these thinkers, see Charles Butterworth, *The Political Aspects of Islamic Philosophy: Essays in Honor of Muhsin S. Mahdi* (Cambridge, MA: Harvard University Press, 1992), and Erwin Rosenthal, *Political Thought in Medieval Islam* (Cambridge: Cambridge University Press, 1958). The thought of al-Fārabī has been studied most extensively by Muhsin Mahdi, who is an invaluable resource for those wishing to explore the connections between Greek and Islamic articulations of political thought. See Muhsin Mahdi, *Al-Farābī and the Foundations of Islamic Political Thought* (Chicago: University of Chicago Press, 2001).

The *ʿulamāʾ* writing on Islamic political thought in the fourth/tenth to fifth/eleventh centuries occupied a somewhat precarious position in relation to the ruling elite in that although the elite bestowed patronage on the *ʿulamāʾ*, the latter remained detached from the political authorities because of their membership in particular *madhhab*s, which placed them in distinct legal circles as opposed to political ones. As a consequence, as Khaled Abou El Fadl observes, the relationship between the *ʿulamāʾ* and the ruling elite was a "reciprocal and dialectic process of accommodation and resistance."[10] Cognizant of their unique position and the socioreligious needs of the people,[11] the jurists sought to articulate a political theory that accommodated these competing needs while remaining authentic to the early model of the Prophet's polity. This balancing act was complicated by the political instability of the ʿAbbasid period, reflected in the continuous concessions made by the ʿAbbasids to powerful dynasties across the Islamic lands. It is important to place political writings against this sociopolitical backdrop. However, as Ovamir Anjum notes, although "the aforementioned political and intellectual conditions provided this discourse its context, limits, questions and direction, the theological, epistemological and political theories that emerged in response cannot be taken as 'logical' or predictable developments of these conditions and hence must be examined in their own right."[12] Therefore, even though al-Juwaynī's sociopolitical context most likely had a direct effect on his political thought, his own intellectual proclivities and interests formed the cornerstone of his discourse, as illustrated in this chapter.

At the time of the emergence of Sunnī political thought in the fourth/tenth through fifth/eleventh centuries, the two primary threats were the Shīʿa in the west and the Seljuk Turks in the east. The first threat, the growing Shīʿī presence, forced Sunnī theologians and jurists to provide an authoritative articulation of the caliphate that could challenge the Shīʿī notion of the caliphate as based on succession through the Prophetic line.[13] The second threat, the Seljuks' dynastic hold over the ʿAbbasid

[10] Abou El Fadl, *Speaking in God's Name*, 102.

[11] Baber Johansen, in his monograph *Contingency in a Sacred Law*, examines two types of rights as conceptualized by Ḥanafī jurists: those of fellow believers (*ḥuqūq al-ʿibād*) and those of God (*ḥuqūq Allāh*). The realm of the state was the domain for the preservation and negotiation of these rights, but these processes were arduous, as the rights of individuals were often in conflict with overall public interest.

[12] Anjum, *Politics, Law, and Community*, 109.

[13] For more on Shīʿī political thought, see Said Arjomand, "Crisis of the Imamate and the Institution of Occultation in Twelver Shiʿism: A Sociohistorical Perspective,"

caliphate, meant that the caliph was present only ceremonially and did not wield any actual power. Therefore, when scholars explicated a legitimate model of the caliphate, they had to take into consideration the emerging presence and de facto rule of the Seljuk sultans and address the legitimacy of these usurpers. They could have argued against the legitimacy of dynastic succession and promoted a model of the caliphate based on the Prophetic ideal, but in actual fact the *'ulamā'* made concessions to political realities at every turn. As a result, Anjum argues, the normative ideal of the Prophetic polity, centered on the community, was lost, and what remained was a political model that paid homage to the office of the caliph even though it had in reality become a powerless and defunct institution embroiled in dynastic disputes.[14]

One of the earliest texts discussing the caliphate at length from the period under study is al-Bāqillānī's (d. 403/1013) *Tamhīd*,[15] which approaches the issue of the imamate from an entirely theological perspective. Al-Bāqillānī's discussion is echoed in 'Abd al-Qāhir al-Baghdādī's (d. 429/1037) *Uṣūl al-dīn*,[16] a theological text that investigates the foundations of the imamate from the Sunnī-Ash'arī perspective. These works focus on a modest number of issues, including proof of the necessity of an imam, the imam's main duties, and the rightful order of the caliphs after the death of the Prophet.[17] These early writings, though important in the development of Sunnī political thought, were limited in the scope of their inquiry, because they were written as responses to the contrary and, in the Sunnī view, theologically problematic conceptions of the caliphate put forward by the Shī'īs, the Khārijīs, and the Zaydīs.

International Journal of Middle East Studies 28, no. 4 (1996): 491–515, and Arjomand, *The Shadow of God and the Hidden Imam* (Chicago: University of Chicago Press, 2010), chapters 1 and 2.

14 Anjum argues that emphasis on the legitimizing power of the community was absent from the discourse that emerged in the fourth/tenth and fifth/eleventh centuries but reappeared with Ibn Taymiyya in the eighth/fourteenth century. Anjum, *Politics, Law, and Community*, 26–31, 228–65.

15 One version of the title of al-Bāqillānī's work is *al-Tamhīd fī al-radd 'alā al-mulḥida al-mu'aṭṭila wa-l-rāfiḍa wa-l-khawārij wa-l-mu'tazila* (The Preliminary in the Refutation of the Deviant Deniers [of God's Attributes], the Rāfiḍīs, the Khārijīs, and the Mu'tazila), under which title it has been edited by Richard J. McCarthy (Baghdad: Publications of al-Ḥikma University of Baghdad, 1958). For a study of al-Bāqillānī's political thought, see Ibish, *Political Doctrine of al-Bāqillānī*.

16 Abū Manṣūr 'Abd al-Qāhir b. Ṭāhir al-Tamīmī al-Baghdādī, *Uṣūl al-dīn* (Istanbul: Maṭba'at al-Dawla, 1928).

17 For details on the differences between al-Bāqillānī and al-Baghdādī, see Lambton, *State and Government*, chapter 5.

The limitations of these early texts were transcended in a single watershed moment by Abū al-Ḥasan ʿAli b. Muḥammad b. Ḥabīb al-Māwardī's (d. 450/1058) treatise *al-Aḥkām al-sulṭāniyya* (The ordinances of government), which rejects the confines of theology to discuss the nature of the caliphate from a practical perspective.[18] According to Lambton, al-Māwardī's main "purpose was to give a legal exposition of the theory of government speculatively derived from the basis of theology and to set out the formal basis of government."[19] Although al-Bāqillānī and al-Baghdādī had already to some extent pushed back against the limits of a theological inquiry into political thought, al-Māwardī's exposition was more sophisticated, and he addressed issues of actual governance that his predecessors customarily left untouched. In addition, al-Māwardī found himself in the midst of the chaos brought about by the rise of the dynastic powers and had to take on the task of theorizing and legitimizing the concept of delegated power, an inquiry that al-Bāqillānī and al-Baghdādī could still ignore. Al-Māwardī thus opened the door for works of Islamic political thought to move beyond the basic inquiries and polemics of theology to issues of statecraft and governance. In general, these works addressed nine primary issues in relation to the imamate:[20] (1) the necessity of the imamate, (2) the circumstances of the imam's appointment, (3) the number of imams at any given time, (4) the race and tribe of the imam, (5) the qualifications of the imam, (6), the imam's impeccability, (7) the means through which the imam is established in office, (8) the appointment of the imam after the death of the Prophet, and (9) inheritance and testament with regard to the imamate (*naṣṣ*). Al-Juwaynī discusses all of these in his *Ghiyāthī* alongside two additional

[18] Hamilton A. R. Gibb notes that al-Māwardī's concessions to reality as well as his justification of the legitimacy of a usurper and the institution of the sultanate essentially undermined the legality of government and allowed for the acceptance of a continuous nonideal situation. See Gibb, *Studies on the Civilization of Islam* (Princeton: Princeton University Press, 1982), 140–43. For Gibb and others, al-Māwardī thus changed not only the content of political treatises but also what was considered legitimate in the realm of politics. Another work penned around the same time was Abū Yaʿlā al-Farrāʾ's (d. 458/1066) *al-Aḥkām al-sulṭāniyya*. It is similar to al-Māwardī's but maintains a more idealistic bent. For a discussion of the differences between the two, see Nimrod Hurvitz, *Competing Texts: The Relationship between al-Māwardī's and Abū Yaʿlā's "al-Aḥkām al-Sultāniyya"* (Cambridge, MA: Islamic Legal Studies Program, Harvard Law School, 2007). Also see Hanna Mikhail, *Politics and Revelation: Māwardī and After* (Edinburgh: Edinburgh University Press, 1995).

[19] Lambton, *State and Government*, 84.

[20] These nine topics reflect the headings of al-Baghdādī's work and are used by Lambton, *State and Government*, 77, and Anjum, *Politics, Law, and Community*, 111–15.

inquiries: (10) the possible absence of the imam and (11) the model of governance in the absence of the imam. Though al-Juwaynī differs from al-Māwardī as well as from al-Baghdādī and al-Bāqillānī in his explication of these topics, the full extent of his departure becomes apparent in the sections addressing the absence of government and the continuity of society. It is also in these sections that his epistemological framework reemerges.[21]

THE NECESSITY OF THE IMAMATE: ITS JUSTIFICATION AND PURPOSE

Al-Juwaynī begins the *Ghiyāthī* by asking whether the imamate is necessary and, if it is, whether this necessity is established by reason or revelation. In line with other Sunnī scholars, he confirms the necessity of an imam[22] based on revelation (*shar*ʿ). This position calls for justification, given the absence of explicit Quranic verses or *ḥadīth* supporting it. Accordingly, al-Juwaynī turns to the precedent of the companions, which serves as a recurrent mechanism for defending the legitimacy of various doctrines.[23] For al-Juwaynī, the fact that a caliph was installed immediately after the death of the Prophet, coupled with the agreement of the companions on the selection of Abū Bakr as the caliph, proves the authority and necessity of the imamate.[24] Momentarily placing this necessity aside, however, al-Juwaynī also notes that since there are times devoid of prophets and direct divine guidance, there can be times lacking an imam. In this sense, the necessity of appointing an imam does not

21 Although I will highlight basic disagreements between al-Māwardī, al-Baghdādī, al-Bāqillānī, and al-Juwaynī in this chapter, they are not my primary focus. Thus, any comparisons I make between the scholars must be understood as partial. For a more detailed analysis of the divergences between these scholars as well as general philosophical trends around them, see Anjum, *Politics, Law, and Community*, 115–25.

22 Some early scholars argued against the necessity of an imam. Generally, the Khārijīs held this position on the basis that individual Muslims could discharge the duties of the imam. Some early Baghdadi Muʿtazilī scholars, such as ʿAbd al-Raḥmān al-Kaysān, commonly known as al-Aṣamm (d. ca. 225/840), and Hishām al-Fuwaṭī (d. before 218/833) also took this position, but they qualified it as applying only to times of peace and order. For more, see Lambton, *State and Government*, 77–78. Al-Juwaynī, in his discussion, specifically refers to al-Aṣamm as someone who rejects the necessity of the imamate. Al-Juwaynī, *al-Ghiyāthī*, 24–25.

23 As described in Chapters 6 and 7, al-Juwaynī also relies on the consensus of the companions to establish the authority of *ijmā*ʿ and *qiyās*.

24 Al-Juwaynī, *al-Ghiyāthī*, 22–24.

preclude the possibility of a time without one, as circumstances can arise, as will be seen, in which legitimate rule by an imam is not possible.[25]

Though the precedent of the companions and consensus represent al-Juwaynī's primary means of establishing the necessity of an imam, he argues that the institution can also be defended rationally based on its formal utility. The basic function of the imamate, according to him, is twofold: to protect Muslim territories from external invasion and to maintain order and stability within the territories.[26] If Muslims were to be left to meet these two needs independently, natural disagreement and strife would preclude any long-term achievement of stability. Therefore, the unifying power of an imam is required to accomplish these tasks. In addition to overseeing the affairs of the populace, the imam also fosters agreement in areas of natural discord by instituting laws and general policies.[27] This rational defense of the imamate buttresses the authority of the institution and simultaneously emphasizes its two central functions of security and stability.

THE SELECTION OF THE IMAM

After establishing the necessity of the imamate, al-Juwaynī moves to the method of appointing the imam. In part, the predicament that he faces in this discussion arises from the plurality of models embodied in the precedent of the companions after the death of the Prophet. Abū Bakr was selected as the first caliph thanks to ʿUmar's pledge of allegiance (*bayʿa*) to him, which prompted others to follow suit. But Abū Bakr, on his deathbed, bequeathed the title of caliph to ʿUmar – bypassing any community involvement in the selection of the next caliph. ʿUmar reversed this trend before his own death, designating a committee of six companions[28] to choose the next caliph from among themselves. Thus, the precedent of the companions offers three contradictory models of selection: communal pledging, caliphal designation, and group consensus. Al-Juwaynī, instead of attempting to reconcile these various methods or focusing on a formal set of criteria, asserts that since the purpose of the imamate is the "attainment of obedience," the guiding objective in the selection of the imam must be the securing of obedience and allegiance from the masses.

[25] Ibid., 22. [26] Ibid., 132–33. [27] Ibid., 23–24.

[28] The six companions designated by ʿUmar were ʿAlī b. Abī Ṭālib, ʿAbd al-Raḥmān b. ʿAwf, Saʿd b. Abī Waqqās, ʿUthmān b. ʿAffān, Zubayn b. al-ʿAwwām, and Ṭalḥa b. ʿUbayd Allāh.

According to al-Juwaynī, scholars before him had proposed four mechanisms as valid methods for appointing the imam. These were appointment by textual designation (*naṣṣ*), appointment by the *ahl al-ḥall wa-l-ʿaqd* ("those who loosen and bind"), appointment by the previous imam (*tawliyat al-ʿahd*), and appointment through usurpation. He declares the first method, advocated by the Shīʿa, illegitimate, arguing that there is no definitive indication in the scriptural sources as to who should be the imam, nor is there any clear description of the method that should be followed to determine the rightful appointee. The other three methods he considers valid as long as they facilitate the obedience and allegiance of the masses and allow for a degree of flexibility in the actual method of selection. In al-Juwaynī's discussion, selection by *ahl al-ḥall wa-l-ʿaqd* is the most important, as the other two methods follow from the logic it establishes.

The task of the group of individuals denoted by *ahl al-ḥall wa-l-ʿaqd*[29] is to choose the imam through a process of selection and contraction (*al-ikhtiyār wa-l-ʿaqd*) after evaluating the qualities of each candidate. According to al-Juwaynī, the members of this select group must meet the following criteria: they must be male, free, Muslim, knowledgeable, pious, and powerful. Of these qualities, he places most emphasis on power, arguing that the electors must possess both punitive power (*shakwa*) and favor-based power (*munna qahriyya*), which endow them with legitimacy and distinguish them from ordinary individuals.[30] On this point, al-Juwaynī begins to deviate from al-Māwardī, who sets only three conditions for membership in the *ahl al-ḥall wa-l-ʿaqd*: probity (*ʿadāla*), sufficient knowledge to establish that the chosen candidate meets the qualifications, and sound judgment and wisdom.[31] Al-Juwaynī does not, however, consider al-Māwardī's conditions efficacious for securing the allegiance of the population, as they ignore the social and political strength needed to influence people and instead place undue emphasis on the specific qualifications of the electors. In al-Juwaynī's mind, whether the members of *ahl al-ḥall wa-l-ʿaqd* possess sound judgment is secondary to whether they are able to convince the masses of the legitimacy of the individual they select. His conditions, therefore, focus on the

[29] For a more extensive discussion of *ahl al-ḥall wa-l-ʿaqd* and how the concept developed from the classical to the modern period, see Muhammad Qasim Zaman, "Ahl al-ḥall wa-l-ʿaqd," in *Encyclopaedia of Islam*, 3rd edn.

[30] Al-Juwaynī, *al-Ghiyāthī*, 62–66.

[31] Abū al-Ḥasan ʿAli b. Muḥammad b. Ḥabīb Al-Māwardī, *al-Aḥkām al-sulṭāniyya* (Kuwait: Maktaba Dār Ibn Qutayba, 1989), 4. According to al-Juwaynī, al-Bāqillānī requires them also to be *mujtahid*s, but al-Juwaynī disagrees with this requirement.

social and political power of the electors, encapsulated in his requirements of *shakwa* and *munna qahriyya*.[32] Because of their power, he believes, these individuals hold unique sociopolitical influence over the community to the extent that their acceptance of a candidate for imam will naturally lead to the candidate's acceptance by the populace. That said, the electors must wield their power responsibly: their selection of an imam may not be arbitrary; rather, it must be contingent on the candidate's satisfactory fulfillment of the requisite qualifications and on the sociopolitical imperatives of the time. As for the number of electors required for legitimate selection of the imam, because al-Juwaynī's primary concern is with ensuring popular allegiance to the imam, he argues that the presence of even a single individual possessing the political and social strength of the *ahl al-ḥall wa-l-ʿaqd* is sufficient to appoint an imam.[33]

To defend this position of allowing a single elector, al-Juwaynī points to Abū Bakr's selection by ʿUmar, who was initially alone in pledging his allegiance to Abū Bakr as the caliph. It was ʿUmar's political and social power in both the Meccan and Medinan communities that elicited the subsequent allegiance of the others. On this point al-Juwaynī disagrees with his predecessors, who generally argue for a higher minimum number of electors,[34] and his disagreement is due to his belief that the formal conditions are not as important as the ultimate objective and role of the electors. Moreover, by arguing for the permissibility of a single persuasive elector, al-Juwaynī is implicitly legitimizing the mechanism of succession in which a living imam designates his successor (*tawliyat al-ʿahd*). Since a living imam naturally possesses *shakwa* and *munna qahriyya*, his designation of a successor should theoretically elicit the same allegiance as would the selection of a suitable candidate by a formal body of electors. The precedent of the companions once again legitimizes his position, as Abū Bakr designated ʿUmar as the caliph after himself, and given Abū Bakr's stature, the designation was unopposed by the community. Extending this argument even further, al-Juwaynī legitimizes the authority of an imam who has usurped power from a ruling imam. In al-Juwaynī's view, if the usurper is able to garner the allegiance and obedience of the people, the act of usurpation is overlooked and he is

32 Al-Juwaynī, *al-Ghiyāthī*, 70–71.

33 Before al-Juwaynī, al-Bāqillānī also permitted the appointment of the imam by a single individual. See Lambton, *State and Government*, 73–74.

34 According to al-Juwaynī, the various minimums proposed by earlier scholars range from two to forty. For the full discussion, see al-Juwaynī, *Ghiyāthī*, 69–70.

considered legitimate. In fact, he is deemed even more legitimate than his predecessor, since he has secured the support of the polity whereas the previous imam has presumably lost it.[35]

In these last two cases – direct designation and usurpation – the electors are redundant, demonstrating that the role of the electors is strategic, not necessary. If the strategic purpose of securing the widespread allegiance and obedience of the masses can be attained without the electors, as in the case of a usurper or a direct designee, then they are not necessary to the process. Al-Juwaynī's endorsement of the *ahl al-ḥall wa-l-ʿaqd* is motivated by the desire to secure the population's support in the most effective way possible. Often, this end can be best achieved through such a body of influential individuals, but they do not hold a monopoly on this ability.

THE QUALIFICATIONS OF THE IMAM

The previous section demonstrated that al-Juwaynī's ultimate aim is the attainment of allegiance and obedience to the imam. Similarly, his discussion of the qualifications required of the imam is shaped by a singular focus on a potential imam's competence to lead independently (*kifāya*). Al-Juwaynī begins by enumerating the ideal qualifications of the imam: he should be "a free man of Qurashī lineage, an independent jurist (*mujtahid*), possessing piety (*waraʿ*), power, and competence (*al-najda wa-l-kifāya*)."[36] The combined objective of these characteristics is to ensure

[35] The discussion of usurpation is one to which al-Juwaynī devotes considerable space. It is important to remember that al-Juwaynī was not the first to legitimize the rule of a usurper; al-Māwardī had already done so. In part, Gibb's assessment of al-Māwardī's willingness to compromise his ideals and make concessions to reality relates to this point. Al-Juwaynī analyzes three cases of usurpation, each more problematic than the last. The first involves a usurper who fulfills all the requirements of an imam, the second a usurper who is merely competent, and the third a usurper who does not meet any of the conditions. Demonstrating his pragmatism and the paramount importance he places on a functioning government, al-Juwaynī accepts the legitimacy of the first two types of usurpation, arguing that as long as the usurper is able to secure the allegiance of the population, the involvement of electors – whose primary function is to secure this allegiance for the selected imam – is superfluous. For the complete discussion of usurpation, see al-Juwaynī, *al-Ghiyāthī*, 316–43.

[36] Ibid., 90–91. He also repeats this point later: "He who reflects on what we have said understands from it that while we hope that they will all be met, the objective in stipulating the conditions for the imam, as we have described them, is ultimately competence (*kifāya*) and the ability to lead independently (*istiqlāl bi-l-amr*). This is the foundation of government, but it is not sufficient by itself if coupled with a poor character and

the independence of the imam entrusted with leadership over the Muslim polity. Though al-Juwaynī acknowledges that the imam will be supported by other individuals in the fulfillment of his duties, in theory he must be self-sufficient. This requirement reflects his trepidation at the idea of a weak imam. His fear is that if the imam is reliant on others, he cannot secure the allegiance of the people and properly discharge his duties. Consequently, al-Juwaynī focuses on the competence and independence of the imam – a preoccupation that is most apparent in his discussion of the appointment of an inferior candidate (*al-mafḍūl*).[37]

Since al-Juwaynī's discussion of the imamate began with the necessity of the office as a means of facilitating the unity of society and the security of the Islamic polity, the absence of the imam would seem to entail societal disintegration. To prevent the chaos associated with a lacuna in political leadership, al-Juwaynī prefers an imam who does not meet all the requirements over the complete abandonment of the office. He likewise accepts an inferior candidate in situations in which the appointment of a superior one threatens to lead to instability. In both scenarios, the desire for stability and authority trumps the benefits associated with the appointment of a more qualified candidate. Although al-Juwaynī compromises on the qualifications of the imam by accepting an inferior candidate, he does maintain certain restrictions by insisting that the appointee, whatever his weaknesses, be capable of independent leadership. This is why al-Juwaynī is willing to suspend all conditions except for the requirement of competence to lead independently, and he explicitly prioritizes this requirement over that of piety:

> It was mentioned at the beginning of the chapter that the most qualified is the most fit [for the imamate]. If we must identify the most prominent conditions, on one side is utmost piety and on the other competence (*kifāya*); but we put the second, competence, before it [piety], because it guides us to the path of politics and statesmanship, and piety cannot lead to this end. Therefore, competence is highest in priority ... Knowledge comes after competence and after good character, since knowledge is the best equipment and the strongest bond. With it, the leader can handle matters by applying the rules of Islam. Lineage, though considered when possible, does not fulfill an intelligible goal; previous consensus is the basis for considering it.[38]

deviation from the bonds of piety. And perchance it could be a source of corruption when coupled with the readiness to abuse power." Ibid., 313.

37 The status of an inferior candidate was first raised by al-Shāfiʿī, who noted that there may be situations in which the appointment of a superior candidate is not possible or would lead to chaos. See Böwering, *Islamic Political Thought*, 75.

38 Al-Juwaynī, *al-Ghiyāthī*, 170.

In this passage, al-Juwaynī lays out an explicit hierarchy of the qualities desired in an imam, making it clear that some qualities can be sacrificed in dire circumstances. The most important quality, as already seen, is *kifāya*, the competence to lead independently. Al-Juwaynī is adamant about the necessity of competence, arguing that an imam unable to display it will be seen as impotent and will naturally fail to obtain the support of the polity. Alongside competency, al-Juwaynī values knowledge and piety, as these characteristics give insight into religious affairs and prevent political corruption.[39] The importance of the remaining qualifications depends on on current sociopolitical needs. For example, in another passage al-Juwaynī compares two candidates, one more adept in legal affairs and the other an expert in warfare. If, at the time of selection, the country is safe from internal and external threats but is facing religious calamity through the spread of heretical opinions, the candidate who is learned in religious affairs is more suited to the office. If, on the other hand, the internal affairs of the country are in order but external threats are looming, the appointment of a candidate skilled in warfare is more appropriate.[40] This example shows that al-Juwaynī considers all conditions beyond competence and independence contingent on the community's needs at the time.[41]

In his discussion of the requirements for *ahl al-ḥall wa-l-ʿaqd* and the qualifications of the imam, al-Juwaynī posits ideal qualifications but is willing to accept fewer as long the overall objective is achieved. The purpose of the electors is to facilitate the community's allegiance to the new imam, so if this end can be attained by a single elector, or even a usurper, al-Juwaynī considers these alternatives legitimate. As for the characteristics of the imam, al-Juwaynī's extensive list of qualifications

[39] Ibid., 88–89, 311–15. [40] Ibid., 170–71.

[41] In connection with the discussion on the appointment of an inferior candidate to the imamate, al-Juwaynī also addresses the potential appointment of a transgressor (*fāsiq*). He argues that if the transgressing candidate is nonetheless able to garner the support of the masses, his appointment is legitimate, because deposing him given that support is a greater challenge than is accepting his rule. This position demonstrates the extent of al-Juwaynī's willingness to compromise for the sake of stability and continuity. However, it is important to note that al-Juwaynī's acceptance of the possibility of a transgressor as the imam is accompanied by a general belief that any person who possesses great authority is likely to possess some undesirable traits due to the corruptive force of money and power. His willingness to accommodate an inferior or transgressing imam is, therefore, predicated on his overall willingness to overlook the minor transgressions of those in power. But if the transgressions mount to the point of impeding the imam's judgment or making him pernicious, he ought to be deposed by either the electors or the people. For this discussion, see al-Juwaynī, *al-Ghiyāthī*, 164–69.

represents an ideal, but the bottom line consists of competence and independence. Therefore, he is willing to accept the imamate of an inferior candidate or a usurper, as long as the claimant meets the minimum requirements and secures the support of the people. This consistent willingness to compromise demonstrates al-Juwaynī's recognition of the need to make concessions when faced with nonideal circumstances and to focus pragmatically on the basic functionality of the imamate. Most emblematic of this stance is his legitimization of even an unqualified usurper if the alternative is the absence of any imam at all. Despite his willingness to grant extensive concessions in order to avoid this outcome, he is nonetheless forced to countenance it as a possibility.

THE PURPOSE OF THE IMAMATE

After presenting the necessary qualifications of the imam and defending the potential acceptability of an inferior candidate, al-Juwaynī elaborates on the actual duties of the imam. Interestingly, however, he begins with a lengthy exposition on how the nature of human beings justifies the necessity of the imam and what his central role is in society.[42] According to al-Juwaynī, although the ultimate goal of human beings should be to seek the pleasure of God, in reality humans are created with both praiseworthy and condemnable desires. To prevent the dominance of the latter, God has legislated laws for humans, which, if followed, will help them achieve the pleasure of God and keep their worldly affairs in order. However, there will inevitably be some individuals who do not conform to the legislated rules, creating discord in society and encouraging others to transgress as well.[43] To curb such behavior, society needs someone who can manage the community's affairs and prevent the proliferation of unlawful behavior. Al-Juwaynī analogizes the role of this individual to the role of prophets, who were similarly sent with laws in order to provide religious guidance for people's worldly affairs. Al-Juwaynī concludes that "the purpose [of the imamate] is religion, but the continuation of it is dependent on worldly affairs [*al-dunya*]."[44] The purpose of the imamate, for al-Juwaynī, is thus to ensure the continuity of religion by securing the community's worldly affairs through law and order. But despite the emphasis he places on the community's need for the imam, he also stresses the imam's need of the community, as it is the members of the community

[42] Ibid., 180–83. [43] Ibid., 182. [44] Ibid., 183.

who embody the law through their adherence to it. Because the function of the imam is a religious one contingent on certain worldly conditions, al-Juwaynī divides the duties of the imam between those related to worldly matters and those related to religious ones.

In the latter category, al-Juwaynī identifies two types of religious matters, foundational (*uṣūl al-dīn*) and subsidiary (*furūʿ al-dīn*). In his view, the imam's duty to safeguard foundational aspects of religion applies both within the boundaries of the Islamic empire and outside them. Beyond the empire, this duty translates into protecting the borders against potential invaders and sending missionaries to foreign lands to propagate and explain the faith. Internally, the imam is responsible for warding off negative innovations,[45] protecting religious scholars, maintaining a pure creed,[46] and following the opinions of the early companions (*al-salaf al-sābiqīn*). The imam's tasks in relation to foundational matters are targeted at two main objectives: "to preserve [the religion] and its people" and to spread the religion to those who are not yet believers.[47]

Subsidiary religious matters include public matters involving large numbers of people, public matters involving few people, and private matters. The first category consists of things for which the imam bears legal responsibility, meaning that he must ensure that the duty involved is properly discharged. Into this category falls, for example, the establishment and correct performance of the ʿĪd prayers and the *ḥajj*. By contrast, in private matters or matters that are public but involve only a few people, such as daily prayers or the call to prayer, the imam does not play the role of either legislator or enforcer. Al-Juwaynī emphasizes that the legal validity of an action is not contingent on the approval of the imam, as legal validity is established by revelation and through the investigation of legal scholars; rather, the imam's role, whether in foundational matters or subsidiary ones, is to facilitate the communal fulfillment of religious obligations.[48]

In the realm of worldly affairs, al-Juwaynī asserts that the imam should strive to "obtain what has not been acquired, and preserve what has been acquired" (*ṭalab mā lam yaḥṣul wa-ḥifẓ mā ḥaṣal*).[49] The former task,

[45] For a discussion on how, exactly, the imam is to prevent the spread of innovations, see ibid., 184–86.

[46] Al-Juwaynī states that the central elements of a pure creed are enumerated in his *Niẓāmiyya*. Ibid., 190.

[47] Ibid., 190. [48] Ibid., 198–200. [49] Ibid., 201.

which he mentions only briefly, likely refers to expanding the Muslim empire through territorial acquisition. The latter aim encompasses protecting Muslim lands from the external threat of disbelievers through military training and observation, and safeguarding the Muslims within the empire from internal sedition and rebellion. Internal protection is divided between matters of universal interest (*marātib al-kulliyya*), such as ensuring safety from highway robbers and preventing violence within the community, and matters pertaining to individuals (*al-juzʾiyyāt*). Individual or specific matters under the remit of the imam include criminal punishments (*ḥudūd*), discretionary punishments (*taʿzīr*), adjudication between conflicting parties, and assistance to people afflicted by disaster.[50] Overall, the primary duty of the imam in the area of worldly affairs is to ensure the survival and safety of the polity by protecting it from external and internal enemies. However, this duty, as al-Juwaynī notes in the section on religious affairs, is merely a means to ensure the preservation of religion – the primary function of the imam. Given the central role the imam plays in safeguarding Muslim lands and protecting the religion, it is fair to ask why al-Juwaynī is nonetheless willing to compromise on the ideal qualifications of an imam. Since the remit of the imam includes both internal and external affairs, secular as well as worldly ones, could a merely competent imam, even with assistance, discharge all of the required duties? By conceding the possibility of a minimally competent imam, al-Juwaynī appears to risk the fulfillment of the fundamental duties of the office. Since the imam, in al-Juwaynī's framework, acts as the worldly guarantor of the religion, what happens to religion if the appointed imam is weak or, worse yet, if there is no imam at all?

ENVISIONING THE ABSENCE OF THE IMAM

The leap from an ideal imam to a merely competent one and then to no imam at all seems a long one, but that is how al-Juwaynī proceeds through the *Ghiyāthī*. He makes the first transition from an ideal imam to a competent one to account for situations in which no candidate for the imamate meets all the requirements, forcing the acceptance of an inferior candidate. In such extreme situations al-Juwaynī, like al-Māwardī before him, legitimizes the rule of a usurper if the usurper successfully undertakes the duties of the imam and obtains the allegiance of the masses.

[50] Ibid., 202–31.

Additionally, al-Juwaynī is also willing to authorize usurpation by individuals who discharge the duties of the imam without formally assuming power. This addition most likely reflects al-Juwaynī's own political context, in which Seljuk sultans wielded actual power over the Islamic empire and undertook the duties that he associates with the imamate, even though the formal position of the ʿAbbasid caliph endured in name.[51] Al-Juwaynī's acceptance of this bifurcation between formal power (the ʿAbbasids) and actual power (the Seljuks) was aimed at preserving the strength and integrity of a united Islamic empire. From this vantage point, the legitimacy of usurpers is due not to the method of their selection or even the qualities they may possess but to the simple fact that they discharge the duties required of the imam and thereby ensure the imamate's continued functioning. Therefore, all of al-Juwaynī's conditions, whether pertaining to election, selection, or the requirements for the position, are ultimately expendable in nonideal situations, in which any ruler able to perform the essential functions of the office is considered legitimate, regardless of his characteristics or formal title. The legitimacy of such a ruler is still subject to his ability to secure the community's support, but it is not contingent on the formal mechanisms of selection or election, or on the possession of merit-worthy qualities; it is obtained simply by virtue of discharging the duties required of the imam.

Al-Juwaynī's focus on ensuring the continuity of the imamate, which preoccupies him in the first half of the *Ghiyāthī*, parallels his concern with legal continuity in the *Burhān*. Recall that in his discussion of *qiyās*, al-Juwaynī ultimately elevated continuity over certainty, the ultimate objective of his epistemology. Though the discussion in the *Ghiyāthī* is ostensibly about political continuity, given that the fundamental duty of the imam is the preservation of religion, religious continuity is just as much at stake. In this sense, whether in the *Burhān* or in the *Ghiyāthī*, al-Juwaynī is willing to make whatever concessions are necessary to guarantee the continuity of law, religion, and the community. In the realm of law, this means accepting *qiyās*; in the realm of politics, it entails legitimizing even inferior political leadership to stave off chaos.

Al-Juwaynī's belief that the strength and continuity of the religion are intimately tied to the strength and continuity of the imamate leads him to compromise the ideals he attaches to the office to the extent of accepting a

[51] That al-Juwaynī is referring to the Seljuk sultans here is underscored by the defense of Niẓām al-Mulk and the Seljuks that follows his discussion of other political authorities fulfilling the imam's role. Al-Juwaynī, *al-Ghiyāthī*, 340–54.

poorly qualified candidate and/or a bifurcation between symbolic power and actual power. In doing so, on the one hand, he maintains the unity of the empire and the continuity of the religion, but on the other, he diminishes the stature of the institution of the imamate by subjugating it to practical politics, even if that entails elevating a usurper over a living imam. If taken further, al-Juwaynī's concessions to political reality could depreciate the value of the institution to the point of rendering the imamate operationally defunct. Taken to an extreme, al-Juwaynī arrives at the end of the first section of the *Ghiyāthī* at a situation in which there is no competent and independent candidate to assume the position of imam, and no other individual can successfully undertake the duties associated with the office. In this scenario he accepts the dissolution of the imamate with little hope for the reestablishment of any form of centralized rule.

CONCLUSION

Al-Juwaynī's *Ghiyāthī* is a juridical-theological treatise falling within the broad genre of Islamic political thought, written in response to the progressive weakening of the ʿAbbasid Empire in the face of rising dynastic powers. In al-Juwaynī's lifetime, the most important of these dynasties was that of the Seljuk Turks, who effectively took over power from the ʿAbbasid caliph, leaving the latter a mere figurehead of the empire instead of its actual ruler. In addition to the Seljuk encroachment, al-Juwaynī was also responding to the rise of the Fatimid caliphate, which posed not just a political threat but also, as a Shīʿī caliphate, a theological one. Given this context, it is no surprise that the *Ghiyāthī* is centrally preoccupied with ensuring the continuity of the imamate, even at the cost of sacrificing some of the qualities desired in an imam. In fact, al-Juwaynī is willing to go as far as accepting the imamate of someone who is merely competent in political affairs or who usurps power from a sitting imam as long as this person is able to secure the allegiance of the masses. Al-Juwaynī's willingness to compromise on the ideal of the imam is due to his belief that the ultimate duty of the imam goes beyond the management of the community's worldly affairs to encompass the protection of its religion. Therefore, if there is no imam, religion itself is threatened. This threat can be either external, in the form of a potential invasion by a foreign power, or internal, in the form of heresy and devious innovations that are able to spread because of the imam's absence. At every turn, then, al-Juwaynī is willing to make concessions to the standard doctrine of the imamate in order to accommodate turbulent political realities for the sake of his ultimate goal – the continuity of religion. This stance echoes al-Juwaynī's arguments in the *Burhān*, where he similarly makes concessions in order to ensure legal continuity.

Despite his deep-seated fear of the complete absence of the imam and the associated threat to religion, al-Juwaynī concedes at the end of the first section of the *Ghiyāthī* that a situation in which not even a minimally qualified imam can be found is a possibility. However, instead of concluding that the loss of the imamate will necessarily result in the total loss of religion, in the final sections of the *Ghiyāthī* he finds hope for the continuity of both society and religion in the Muslim community and the individuals who compose it. This argument again reflects his epistemological framework, at the heart of which stands the individual's ability to reason and to attain religious knowledge with practical certainty.

10

Continuity, Custom, and Applied Epistemology in al-Juwaynī's Political Thought

> And of these curiosities, surely, the most curious is the endless discussion as to whether law consists in institutions or in rules, in procedures or in concepts, in decisions or in codes, in processes or in forms, and whether it is therefore a category like work, which exists just about anywhere one finds human society, or one like counterpoint, which does not.
>
> – Clifford Geertz[1]

The previous chapter demonstrated al-Juwaynī's pragmatism and concern with continuity within his political thought. His many compromises on the requirements surrounding the imamate illuminate the importance he places on continuity, but the relationship between this desire for continuity and his emphasis on epistemic certainty remains to an extent unclear in this discussion. This is a result of the structure of the *Ghiyāthī*, as the first section of the book is devoted to the ideal scenario in which authority and stability are connected to the imamate itself. Once al-Juwaynī concedes the possibility of the imam's absence in the latter portions of the *Ghiyāthī*, his focus on authority and stability gives way to a focus on the Muslim community and the epistemically certain knowledge that individuals possess.

In the absence of the imamate, al-Juwaynī envisions society ordered and governed by epistemically certain legal and social norms embodied in and internalized by individuals over time, with the result that the lacuna in formal structures of order, whether political or legal, does not lead to the immediate disintegration of society. This scenario indicates the

[1] Clifford Geertz, *Local Knowledge: Further Essays in Interpretive Anthropology* (New York: Basic Books Classics, 1985), 168.

interplay between continuity and certainty in al-Juwaynī's framework, as continuity is predicated on epistemically certain knowledge. But beyond this, the continuity of society also evinces a dialectical relationship between the Sharīʿa and the community in which the vitality of the Sharīʿa is fundamentally connected to the individuals practicing it.

LIVING WITHOUT RULERS: THE RISE OF THE *ʿULAMĀʾ*

The second part of the *Ghiyāthī* confronts a scenario in which there is no imam possessing even the minimum qualification of bare competence, and the institution of the imamate has thus lapsed. This hypothetical scenario signals al-Juwaynī's pessimistic, at times even apocalyptic, view of the future of the imamate. Though the first section of the *Ghiyāthī* can be read as a defense of Seljuk rule through the justification of the separation of formal and actual power, the second and third sections show al-Juwaynī coming to terms with the fact that excessive concessions to political circumstances can bring about an inferior imam, and that a time can exist in which no, even minimally suitable, imam can be found.[2] Be that as it may, al-Juwaynī's argument for the continuity of society in spite of political and institutional failure exemplifies his unyielding desire for continuity and his recognition of the multifaceted forces that govern society.

Considering the loss of the imamate as the new reality, al-Juwaynī shifts the focus of his inquiry from the functions of the imam to the community and societal continuity more broadly. The disappearance of the political authority embodied in the imamate does not extinguish al-Juwaynī's concern with societal ordering and stability. To the contrary, the obsolescence of formal political rule leads him to concentrate on the development of new mechanisms and institutions that can facilitate order in society. As the discussion of *ahl al-ḥall wa-l-ʿaqd* in the previous chapter shows, al-Juwaynī recognizes that certain individuals exert influence over others because of their elevated sociopolitical status. Under the imamate, the most valuable social currency is political and social power, as exemplified in the requirement that the electors possess both punitive power (*shakwa*) and favor-based power (*munna qahriyya*).[3] With the loss

[2] After the death of the Prophet, the arc of history was believed to tend toward decline, as suggested by the apocalyptic and millenarian messages within the Quran and *ḥadīth*. For the development of Islamic apocalyptic thought, see David Cook, *Studies in Muslim Apocalyptic* (Princeton: Darwin Press, 1966).

[3] Al-Juwaynī, *al-Ghiyāthī*, 62–66.

of the imamate, al-Juwaynī argues that the socially powerful individuals are no longer those with a proximal relationship to the imam but rather those close to God. The demise of the imamate, therefore, signals the transfer of religious authority from the imam to *muftī-mujtahid*s,[4] the highest rank of legal scholars, who are charged with the guardianship of the masses by virtue of their knowledge of the Sharīʿa and their piety. Al-Juwaynī's relegation of power to the religiously learned does not necessarily come as a surprise, as he argues throughout the first section of the *Ghiyāthī* that the imam must be surrounded by a council of learned men if he is lacking in religious qualifications himself. If the scholars surrounding the imam function in an advisory capacity, especially in religious affairs,[5] it is logical that they will assume a central role in the imam's absence. In addition, al-Juwaynī postulates that the end of the imamate will foster greater individual interest in religion, and this factor, too, supports the thesis that the *muftī-mujtahid*s are the best suited to assuming responsibility for the religious affairs of the community. This role of the scholars as the "overseers" of the community is reflected in al-Juwaynī's terminology, when he refers to the *muftī-mujtahids* as the "guardians of the believers" (*wulāt al-ʿibād*).[6]

[4] As explained in Chapter 8, al-Juwaynī uses the terms *muftī* and *mujtahid* interchangeably because one of the requirements of a *muftī* is that he be a *mujtahid*, so I have chosen to use the term *muftī-mujtahid* to reflect his usage. The qualifications required of the *muftī-mujtahid* in the *Ghiyāthī* mirror those specified in the *Burhān*: (1) knowledge of the Arabic language equivalent to that possessed by a native Arab; (2) knowledge of the law, including the opinions of past scholars; and (3) knowledge of jurisprudence. Al-Juwaynī disagrees with those who specifically stipulate knowledge of the Quran and *ḥadīth* as a requirement, because he understands this to be implied in the conditions requiring knowledge of jurisprudence and law. He also rejects conditions related to character, such as piety and God-consciousness, because he does not consider them to have a direct bearing on the skill of the *muftī-mujtahid* in determining the law. See al-Juwaynī, *al-Ghiyāthī*, 400–408.

[5] Al-Juwaynī accepts the possibility of an inferior imam (*imam mafḍūl*) because he assumes that the members of the imam's closest council will compensate for his deficiencies. If an imam is not knowledgeable in matters of war, he will have among his advisors someone skilled in warfare. Similarly, if he is not knowledgeable in matters of religion, he will have a *muftī-mujtahid* as a council member. See al-Juwaynī, *al-Ghiyāthī*, 164–71. He reiterates this point when addressing the guardianship of the *muftī-mujtahid*s, stating that if a minimally competent and independent candidate for the imamate is found, he should be appointed and his other deficiencies should be overlooked, but he should continuously turn to the *muftī-mujtahid*s for guidance. Ibid., 310.

[6] Ibid., 388–91. It is likely that al-Juwaynī uses the term "guardians" because he begins his discussion on the absence of the imam by mentioning the scenario of a woman's marriage without a guardian (*walī*). According to al-Shāfiʿī, if a previously unmarried woman seeks to marry but does not have a guardian to contract the marriage on her behalf, the ruler will

However, the unity promoted by the singularity of the imamate is difficult to achieve under the guardianship of the *muftī-mujtahid*s, since individual Muslims will naturally pledge themselves to the religious scholars who are closest to them. This means that the guardianship of the *muftī-mujtahid*s will lack uniformity in spite of widespread loyalty, leading to the rise of distinct communal affiliations. Though al-Juwaynī accepts the existence of multiple poles of authority in this scenario, he seeks to limit the potential for plurality and instability posed by the residence of multiple *muftī-mujtahid*s in a single location. Paralleling his unwillingness to countenance more than one legitimate imam at a given time,[7] al-Juwaynī's position here is that the population of a location with multiple *muftī-mujtahid*s should coalesce around the one who possesses the most knowledge and piety. If there are several *muftī-mujtahid*s of equal stature, one should be selected as the primary one by the community; otherwise, the conflicting opinions issued by the *muftī-mujtahid*s could sow discord and division.[8]

The selection of the most qualified *muftī-mujtahid* rests on the same religious criteria that al-Juwaynī proposed in the *Burhān*, with the exception of *fiqh al-nafs*, which is not required here.[9] Of the various intellectual requirements, the most important is juristic acumen and the ability to derive laws in response to new legal queries and quandaries. Once a locale's top *muftī-mujtahid* is selected, other *muftī-mujtahid*s should acquiesce to his decisions in order to preserve unity and order. In this way, each location will have a *muftī-mujtahid* overseeing the legal and

act as her guardian (*fa-l-sulṭān walī man lā walī lah*). If there is no ruler, instead of declaring such women unable to marry, al-Shāfiʿī assigns the duty of their guardianship to the *muftī-mujtahid*s. When al-Juwaynī later refers to *muftī-mujtahid*s as the guardians of the believers, he is likely drawing an analogy to this situation.

7 Since the overall objective of the imam is to preserve the unity of the Islamic empire, al-Juwaynī rejects the possibility of two imams under any circumstances. In addition to the negative implications for unity, he argues that the two imams would likely vie for power, spawning discord within the empire. If, for some reason, two imams are appointed in different areas, al-Juwaynī considers one of them the rightful imam and the other an *amīr* (commander) serving under the imam. In the *Irshād*, he does accept the possibility of two imams if they are geographically separated, as in the case of the Umayyad caliphate of Cordoba (317/929 to 422/1031), which existed alongside the ʿAbbasid caliphate, but in the *Ghiyāthī* he unequivocally rejects this arrangement, most likely because of his unease with the rise of the Shīʿī Fatimid caliphate in Cairo. In the *Ghiyāthī*, he also criticizes al-Ashʿarī and Abū Isḥāq al-Isfarāyīnī for their acceptance of the possibility of two imams. See al-Juwaynī, *al-Ghiyāthī*, 172–79, and *al-Irshād*, 425; and Lambton, *State and Government*, 80.

8 Al-Juwaynī, *al-Ghiyāthī*, 414–16.

9 See note 4.

religious affairs of the people in that location.[10] The masses who lack legal knowledge are obliged to refer all legal and religious queries to the *muftī-mujtahid*. Al-Juwaynī also addresses a scenario in which the questioner is himself a legal scholar and disagrees with the *muftī-mujtahid*'s judgment on the grounds that the founder of the *muftī-mujtahid*'s own legal school – in al-Juwaynī's example, al-Shāfiʿī – had reached a contrary ruling on the same matter. In situations of such interpretational conflict, al-Juwaynī favors the living *muftī-mujtahid*, recognizing that it is common for two jurists to reflect on the same matter and reach conflicting results. In such cases, both jurists are correct,[11] and there is no need to prefer the earlier one of the two. Perhaps more importantly still, the legal and religious authority of the *muftī-mujtahid* represents the final vestige of authority and stability in society after the collapse of the imamate, and undermining it would open the way to further problems. As a general principle, then, scholars who have not reached the status of a *muftī-mujtahid* as well as laypeople should follow the primary *muftī-mujtahid* in their location, regardless of their personal knowledge of the Sharīʿa or any perceived conflicts they identify.[12]

The stability fostered by the presence of *muftī-mujtahid*s lacks permanence, as individual *muftī-mujtahid*s are themselves impermanent and thus may leave the members of the community without legal guidance and a defined social structure.[13] In the event of the absence of *muftī-mujtahid*s,

[10] Al-Juwaynī, *al-Ghiyāthī*, 414–15.

[11] Al-Juwaynī's belief that both jurists are correct relates to his commitment to *taswīb* (admission of soundness or infallibility) – the position, discussed in Chapter 8, that jurists are correct to the extent that they follow a sound methodology and process of reasoning, even if they do not arrive at the ontologically correct answer.

[12] Al-Juwaynī, *al-Ghiyāthī*, 414–15.

[13] Al-Juwaynī was by no means the only scholar to theorize the absence of *mujtahid*s in society. Wael Hallaq notes that at the end of the sixth/twelfth and the beginning of the seventh/thirteenth century, texts on *uṣūl al-fiqh* began to include a section on the possibility of the complete absence of *mujtahids*. Hallaq emphasizes that this discussion was independent of the discussion on the putative closure of the gate of *ijtihād*, although there was some overlap. He observes that the Ḥanbalīs and many prominent Shāfiʿīs believed that *mujtahid*s must exist at all times, whereas the Ḥanafīs and other Shāfiʿīs argued that the extinction of the *mujtahid*s was a very real possibility. However, even though the discussion was undertaken in legal treatises and debated among jurists, Hallaq argues that it was actually a response to theological concerns regarding the end of the world and the Day of Judgment. In the declining political situation of the fourth/tenth and fifth/eleventh centuries, jurists increasingly felt that legal scholars would soon be the only leaders left for the Muslim community. By al-Juwaynī's lifetime in the middle of the fifth/eleventh century, the weakened state of the ʿAbbasid caliphate further stoked these fears, which were reflected in texts written in this period. The disappearance of knowledge

al-Juwaynī asserts that their position will be taken over by the jurist (*al-faqīh al-nāqil*), who will continue to transmit their legal works and verdicts. Such jurists, lauded for their memory, act as reservoirs of the knowledge of past scholars, which equips them to answer legal queries. However, al-Juwaynī does not ignore the intellectual shortcomings of these scholars. He considers a case similar to that encountered earlier in which the *muftī-mujtahid* departed from al-Shāfiʿī's precedent on a legal matter. In that case, al-Juwaynī granted priority to the *muftī-mujtahid*'s interpretation. However, when a jurist who is not himself capable of independent *ijtihād* identifies a conflict between a ruling issued by al-Shāfiʿī or another legal eponym and a ruling from a later *muftī-mujtahid* on the same issue, al-Juwaynī requires the jurist to grant priority to the ruling of the eponym.[14] Through this rule, al-Juwaynī seeks to provide the transmitting jurist with a singular pole of authority to avoid a situation in which the jurist, lacking a clear methodology for selecting among the multitude of opinions, would issue inconsistent rulings and thus create legal confusion and contradiction.

To further illustrate the scope of the transmitting jurist's jurisdiction, al-Juwaynī proposes a second case, one without a clear ruling from al-Shāfiʿī or another *muftī-mujtahid*. In such a situation, there are two possibilities: either there is a textual indicator that can resolve the legal query at hand without extensive reflection or the transmitting jurist, though not a full-fledged *muftī-mujtahid*, is astute enough to be able to engage in legal reasoning. In the first scenario, the transmitting jurist can provide a ruling with relative confidence thanks to the presence of a textual source whose meaning is clear. The permissibility of this kind of minimal interpretation by a jurist not qualified to engage in *ijtihād* likely

being one of the signs of the Day of Judgment, it is natural that apocalyptic fears provoked discussion of the possible absence of the carriers and preservers of knowledge – the scholars. See Wael Hallaq, "On the Origins of the Controversy about the Existence of Mujtahids and the Gate of Ijtihād," *Studia Islamica*, no. 63 (1986): 129–41. Ann Lambton also makes note of this increasing worry among jurists in the fifth/eleventh century; Lambton, *State and Government*, 109–16. The most comprehensive recent treatment of this issue is by Ahmad Ahmad, who looks at the larger theological debate on the fatigue of the Sharīʿa (*futūr al-sharīʿa*). Ahmad argues that there were three main positions on the question of decline: (1) the fatigue of the Sharīʿa has already occurred because the revelations of certain prophets have already become irrelevant; (2) the fatigue of the Sharīʿa has not occurred, but it can occur in the future; and (3) the fatigue will never occur because God's guidance will never cease. Ahmad correlates these positions with the Muʿtazila, the Ashʿarīs, and the Ḥanbalīs, respectively. See Ahmad Atif Ahmad, *The Fatigue of the Sharīʿa* (New York: Palgrave Macmillan, 2012).

14 Al-Juwaynī, *al-Ghiyāthī*, 417–28.

reflects the first type of *naẓar sharʿī* (reasoning in revelatory matters) that al-Juwaynī discusses in the *Burhān* before turning to *qiyās* proper. Al-Juwaynī describes this type of reasoning as "the application (*ilḥāq*) of a thing not covered by the text (*al-maskūt*) to a [thing] enunciated explicitly in the text (*manṭūq*)."[15] When an original ruling is apparent (*jalī*) and can easily be transferred to a new case, only minimal reasoning, not reaching the level of *qiyās*, is required, and this is the kind of reasoning that al-Juwaynī permits for the transmitting jurist.

In the second situation, in which there is no transmitted ruling but the transmitting jurist has attained a high level of legal knowledge, al-Juwaynī allows the jurist to act as a *muftī-mujtahid* and derive rulings as necessary. But the jurist must possess a robust understanding of *qiyās*; without it, no legal derivation is permissible. Al-Juwaynī's objective in permitting a transmitting jurist to function in the capacity of a *muftī-mujtahid* is to ensure that the law is not forgotten or abandoned because of novel legal situations that have no established answer. Given al-Juwaynī's commitment to legal continuity through legal universality, if he were to foreclose any possibility of legal derivation in the absence of *muftī-mujtahids*, he would willfully undermine his own commitments. By granting a narrow platform to the transmitting jurist, al-Juwaynī ensures the continuity of the law, albeit in a restricted form. However, since the scope of action he affords to transmitting jurists is limited, they are not a panacea for the sociopolitical difficulties of their context, and their longevity, like that of the *muftī-mujtahid*s, is finite. Their eventual expiration marks the definitive end of individuals with juristic knowledge, and this prospect forces al-Juwaynī to rely on the last mechanism for social and religious continuity: society itself, along with the individual.

THE LOSS OF ALL *ʿULAMĀʾ*

In considering a situation in which no scholars remain, al-Juwaynī faces the seemingly insurmountable task of guaranteeing legal guidance for people without any recourse to scholars or the texts they transmit. Before proposing a solution, he reiterates his concept of legal universality,[16] noting that even in the absence of formal legal guidance, people will continue to deduce the law, as all human actions have corresponding legal rulings. What facilitates the continuity of the law in this manner is

[15] Al-Juwaynī, *al-Burhān*, 2:782–84. [16] Al-Juwaynī, *al-Ghiyāthī*, 436, 522.

fundamental principles (*al-umūr al-kullī/al-marāsim al-kulliyya*) of the Sharīʿa, which people internalize and apply within their lives through habitual practice, thus insuring them against the possibility of loss. To illustrate this process of legal self-governance, al-Juwaynī lists central legal matters, such as the laws of prayer, fasting, and menstruation,[17] and identifies the fundamental legal principles that form the basis of the rulings in each area of *fiqh* (positive law). These fundamental principles then serve as legal signposts for individuals in search of legal guidance.

Al-Juwaynī's conceptualization of the role of fundamental legal principles is predicated on his epistemological framework, in which epistemically certain knowledge cannot be lost. As described in Chapter 4, al-Juwaynī constructs a fluid epistemology that enables the attainment of *practical* certainty by elevating acquired knowledge (*ʿilm naẓarī*), which is epistemically probable, to the status of necessary knowledge (*ʿilm ḍarūrī*). The deconstruction of the epistemic barrier between these two categories of knowledge occurs either through a process of exhaustive reasoning or through habitual repetition. The second method, the most pertinent to this discussion, is based on the idea that if a certain action is repeated over an extended period of time, the initially probabilistic nature of the knowledge embodied in the action evolves through habituation to reach certainty.[18] Once this knowledge is epistemically certain, it is incorporated into the knowledge reservoir of the individual and is unlikely to fall prey to doubt or forgetting. Applied to the realm of legal knowledge, this principle means that an individual's habitual practice will attain epistemic certainty and become a permanent part of that individual's knowledge reservoir irrespective of shifting religious and political contexts and the formal epistemic value of the ruling as issued by jurists. Such ingrained legal practices, nested within the individual, are what al-Juwaynī terms *al-umūr al-kullī* or *al-marāsim al-kulliyya*; in the *Burhān*, he defines them as "what the intellect penetrates at points at which details are forgotten."[19] Law, as a precise and particular discipline, is replete with details; however, there are fundamental elements within the law that encapsulate the

[17] Generally, *fiqh* books divided legal issues into matters of worship (*fiqh al-ʿibādāt*) and matters of transaction (*fiqh al-muʿāmalāt*). In the *Ghiyāthī*, al-Juwaynī focuses primarily on the first category, though he does not completely disregard the latter. Even in the first category, he addresses only matters that occur with high frequency in people's lives.

[18] For a full exposition of the two methods of transforming *ʿilm naẓarī* into *ʿilm ḍarūrī*, see Chapter 4.

[19] Al-Juwaynī, *al-Burhān*, 2:937. Al-Juwaynī states that he will discuss this concept in full in his *Ghiyāthī*, conceptually linking the two books.

core objective of the detailed rulings and promote people's general welfare (*maṣlaḥa*). These foundational matters of the law are, therefore, a reflection of the purpose of the law itself and are preserved in society through continuous individual repetition. Though al-Juwaynī does not explicate these foundational matters to any great extent in his *Burhān*, they occupy center stage in the final section of the *Ghiyāthī*, where they become the cornerstone for legal guidance.

THE CONTINUITY OF LEGAL GUIDANCE

The absence of *muftī-mujtahid*s thus does not decrease the need for legal guidance, nor does it leave people legally unbound. Instead, in the absence of legal scholars, individuals must rely on their independent reservoirs of knowledge, which are based on practice and buttressed by the society's custom and thus imbued with the ethos of the Sharīʿa. For al-Juwaynī, this ever-present Sharīʿa ethos emerges most prominently with the collapse of the imamate and the re-formation of society around local *muftī-mujtahid*s, and it is created and sustained in two ways. The first relates to al-Juwaynī's earlier justification of *ijmāʿ* with the argument that some norms appear uniformly in social practice without any specific textual source sanctioning them.[20] Such norms, he argues, are most likely based on a definitive source text in the form of a *mutawātir ḥadīth* that once existed but was not conveyed continuously across the generations to the present. However, the perpetuation of action in accordance with the now-lost text signals its complete integration into communal practice, which therefore embodies epistemically certain knowledge of the Sharīʿa despite the apparent absence of textual support. Applying this logic to al-Juwaynī's arguments in the *Ghiyāthī*, we see why, in his view, uniform communal practice of certain norms, even in the absence of *muftī-mujtahid*s and their texts, is able to represent certain knowledge once conveyed in texts.

The second mechanism for creating and, more importantly, maintaining Sharīʿa-based custom is the actions of *muftī-mujtahids* who, in providing legal guidance, promote a degree of legal uniformity in each location. This legally uniform practice shapes the custom of the location.[21] The resulting custom, once habituated by individuals, is thus inherently Sharīʿa-based and serves as a means for ongoing legal

[20] For this argument, see Chapter 6.

[21] The terms al-Juwaynī uses to refer to custom in this part of the *Ghiyāthī* are *ʿurf* and *ʿāda*. For a detailed discussion of these terms, see Chapter 6.

understanding in the absence of *muftī-mujtahids*. Like the fundamental principles of the Sharīʿa, Sharīʿa-based custom is originally rooted in revelatory texts. This means that they neither reflect nor contain the minutiae of the law, as al-Juwaynī himself indicates when he states that the fundamentals of the law are what remains once the details have been forgotten. Instead, they represent the core foundational principles of the Sharīʿa and the laws germane to daily life.[22]

The concepts of Sharīʿa-based custom and the fundamentals of the law serve as a precursor to al-Juwaynī's detailed discussion of the foundations of the law in the various areas of *fiqh* that remain after the demise of the imamate. This section of the *Ghiyāthī* gives shape to a form of "legal minimalism"[23] in which the core elements of each legal topic remain as guidance for the believers but all unnecessary details are lost. The legal rulings that al-Juwaynī addresses pertain to the areas of purification, prayer, almsgiving, fasting, inheritance, and contractual affairs (marriage, rental agreements, etc.). The selected matters occur with such frequency in the lives of ordinary people that, even in the absence of *muftī-mujtahids*, their practice constitutes a site of basic legal guidance. Moreover, because of the explicit nature of the rulings on many of these matters within the scriptural sources, they amount to epistemically certain legal norms manifested in the knowledge reservoirs of individuals and their social customs.

I will begin with a few general observations on al-Juwaynī's discussion of *fiqh*. Certain guiding principles and concerns that are not explicitly stated but become apparent through recurrent emphasis govern the various legal discussions at the end of the *Ghiyāthī*. The three main assumptions underpinning al-Juwaynī's legal discussion are the following: (1) obligations and prohibitions can be established only with adequate proofs, (2) individual needs (*ḥājāt*) can quickly rise to the level of general necessities (*ḍarūriyyāt*) and thus should be treated as a matter of expediency,[24] and (3) all parties' individual satisfaction (*riḍā*) must be sought in any affair involving more than one party. These recurrent principles exemplify al-Juwaynī's awareness of individual needs and the necessity of the law's responsiveness to them beyond the overall preservation of the law. Al-Juwaynī conceives of the law not as a mechanism to restrict and

[22] See note 17.

[23] I am adopting this term from Intisar Rabb. See Rabb, "Islamic Legal Minimalism: Legal Maxims and Lawmaking When Jurists Disappear," in *Law and Tradition in Classical Islamic Thought: Studies in Honor of Professor Hossein Modarressi*, ed. Michael Cook et al. (New York: Palgrave Macmillan, 2014), 145–66.

[24] Al-Juwaynī, *al-Ghiyāthī*, 473.

redirect individual action but as a framework to order action for the overall benefit of the individual and society. The result is a move away from the formalistic rules and regulations normally filling books of law toward the establishment of parameters for human interaction in the absence of the institutions that otherwise play this role. The Sharīʿa, in this light, is not only a reservoir of legal knowledge or a process for attaining legal knowledge but also a governing force in society, regulating and ordering human activity to facilitate harmony among people and obedience to God. Al-Juwaynī's expansive understanding of the Sharīʿa as a governing force becomes evident as he proceeds through each chapter of *fiqh*, outlining its most salient elements.

Turning now to the actual legal matters covered in the *Ghiyāthī*, I will highlight instances that demonstrate al-Juwaynī's three principles along with his understanding of the Sharīʿa. Starting with the first principle, one of the central elements of al-Juwaynī's legal discussion is his restriction of obligation and prohibition to matters that can be established decisively through proof and are considered epistemically certain. What type of proof, then, does he require to establish a legal ruling definitively? Within the Shāfiʿī school, the dominant position is that in order to claim that a legal ruling is certain (*qaṭʿī*), both the signification of the relevant source text and the means of the text's transmission must be certain.[25] Rulings that do not satisfy this requirement are considered probable (*ẓannī*) and can easily become subject to disagreement. In a social situation of curtailed access to legal knowledge, the high bar for the definitive establishment of legal rulings remains in place, but the mechanism to establishing the rulings is altered. Without recourse to texts or scholars, decisive legal rulings can be based only on the continuity of custom or communal practice (*ḥukm iṭṭirād al-iʿtiyād*). As noted earlier, this communal practice reflects the prior presence of a definitive textual source that is no longer transmitted. The underlying assumption is that no practice would receive such widespread approval unless it is related to some definitive source text. Over time, as people become complacent about transmitting the original source text and its transmission lapses, their actions continue to testify to its prior existence.

In the hypothetical situation in which no scholars or source texts exist to confirm the prohibition or obligation of a specific action, the only available means to ascertain the status of the action is custom. As a result,

[25] A text decisive in its signification and transmission is referred to as *qaṭʿī al-wurūd* and *qaṭʿī al-dalāla*.

the range of potentially obligatory and prohibited actions is severely curtailed. As an example, al-Juwaynī states that prayer remains an obligation because its necessity is established by continuous practice and because the Sharīʿa custom bolsters this understanding – effectively making it impossible for people to neglect or forget it as a duty.[26] But beyond the basic obligation of prayer, the details of its execution remain nebulous, and it is possible that individuals enact the minutiae of the prayer in conflicting and sometimes invalid ways. Offering the example of the prostration of forgetfulness (*sajdat al-sahw*), al-Juwaynī notes that a person may not recall when the prostration is necessary or what the consequences of its omission for the validity of prayer are; therefore, if the person incorrectly omits it or, alternatively, performs it unnecessarily, there is no legal consequence and the person's prayer is still considered valid.[27] In this example, then, the legal obligation to pray remains in force, but the subsidiary elements of the prayer are not obligatory to the same degree and minor deviations are thus overlooked in terms of legal consequences. This two-pronged approach to the law unites the knowledge necessary to the individual with widespread custom; together, they serve as the primary mechanism to maintain legal obligations. Actions that cannot be explicitly identified as either prohibited or obligatory on the basis of these two sources are assumed to be permissible (*mubāḥ*), as it is not possible to generate obligations without prior practice or custom.[28]

The second governing principle of al-Juwaynī's legal minimalism is that individual needs (*ḥājāt*) can easily become general necessities (*ḍarūriyyāt*) and should be considered a matter of expediency. Earlier, in the context of general welfare (*maṣlaḥa*), al-Juwaynī lists five categories of "general good," the first being necessities (*ḍarūriyyāt*) and the second being needs (*ḥājāt*).[29] He conceptualizes the former as things necessary for basic survival and the latter as things that are important requirements for human beings without survival itself being contingent on them. In the absence of the imamate and given the division of society into smaller

[26] Al-Juwaynī, *al-Ghiyāthī*, 468–69. [27] Ibid., 471–72.

[28] Within the Shāfiʿī school, the principle of the basic permissibility of any action in the absence of proof to the contrary (*al-aṣl fī al-ashyāʾ al-ibāḥa ḥattā yadullu al-dalīl ʿalā al-taḥrīm*) was applied predominantly to matters other than worship. For matters related to worship, the Shāfiʿīs took the position of suspension of judgment (*tawaqquf*). See al-Suyūṭī, *al-Ashbāh wa-l-naẓāʾir* (Cairo: Maʿhad al-Makhṭūṭāt al-ʿArabiyya, 1998), 1:166. See also al-Juwaynī, *al-Ghiyāthī*, 489–91.

[29] For more on al-Juwaynī's assessment of *maṣlaḥa* and its application in jurisprudence, see Chapter 8.

principalities, al-Juwaynī contends that individual needs should be conceptualized as necessities and addressed accordingly. As a corollary, previously prohibited (*ḥarām*) things should be reevaluated in light of the new circumstances; thus, if refraining from something prohibited prevents the fulfillment of a need or a necessity, then the prohibition should be lifted. To illustrate this point, al-Juwaynī cites various examples, ranging from foodstuffs to clothing, shelter, and other basic building blocks of human life.[30] With respect to food, since, in al-Juwaynī's view, the purpose of food is to provide strength and sustenance to people, if permissible food is not readily available, he permits them to eat carrion or other ordinarily prohibited foods. Al-Juwaynī compares this scenario with the case of an individual who has no access to food aside from carrion and pork. In the latter case, jurists agreed that the individual is compelled to eat food that is ordinarily impermissible out of necessity (*ḍarūra*),[31] since insisting on the prohibition would result in death. The situation posed by al-Juwaynī is not identical, since in his scenario permissible meat is not *readily* available but is available nonetheless, but he argues that limiting people to permissible meat only will lead to either inadequate satiation or depletion of the permissible foodstuffs, which will eventually force people to eat carrion or pork after all. Given the seriousness of malnutrition and resource depletion, al-Juwaynī asserts that a food shortage should be considered a dire enough situation that people facing it are permitted to eat carrion or pork, though only as much as they need to be minimally satiated. In this case, despite the unlikelihood of imminent starvation, the individual need for food is conceived as a necessity, making the consumption of ordinarily impermissible foods permissible.

Al-Juwaynī's third and final principle underpinning the functioning of the law in the absence of the imam is that the contentment (*riḍā*) of all affected parties must be sought in any affair involving multiple parties, be it personal or commercial. This principle applies, inter alia, to financial matters, which require regulation even in the smaller communities remaining after the collapse of the imamate. Among the various financial

[30] For the discussion of shelter, clothing, and other related matters, see al-Juwaynī, *al-Ghiyāthī*, 483–503.

[31] The broad idea of *ḍarūra* is invoked for a state of necessity that compels an individual either to do something otherwise impermissible or to omit something that is obligatory. For a more robust explication of *ḍarūra* in theory and practice, see Yasmin Safian, "Necessity (*ḍarūra*) in Islamic Law: A Study with Special Reference to the Harm Reduction Programme in Malaysia" (PhD diss., University of Exeter, 2010), chapters 1–4.

affairs that al-Juwaynī addresses, the most interesting is inheritance (*mīrāth*).[32] Inheritance is one of the few issues addressed extensively in the Quran,[33] which makes it decisive both in terms of its transmission (*qaṭʿī al-wurūd*) and in terms of its signification (*qaṭʿī al-dalāla*). Therefore, it could be argued that its details remain preserved in memory even in the absence of scholars and transmitted texts. However, al-Juwaynī's discussion nonetheless presumes a lack of knowledge regarding the specific rules governing the division of inheritances, because the subject does not come up with sufficient frequency in the course of everyday life to allow people to have internalized the laws of inheritance the way they have the laws regarding prayer and fasting. Thus, even though the laws in their transmitted form are considered certain, they, like the details of the forgetfulness prostration discussed earlier, have not been incorporated into customary practice and are thus not preserved. If the heirs in a particular instance are familiar with the laws of inheritance, al-Juwaynī says, they should by all means act accordingly; but in case of uncertainty regarding the exact share due to each heir, the goal should be securing everyone's satisfaction with the distribution, which is most likely achieved through equality (*taswiyya*) among the inheritors. Al-Juwaynī provides the example of two individuals, one certain of his or her right to inherit half of the deceased's assets, the other unsure whether he or she has a claim, and to how much. In this situation, according to al-Juwaynī, the heir with the definite claim should take his or her lawful portion and then share the remainder equitably with the unsure claimant.[34] In another scenario, with multiple heirs of whom some are certain of their inheritance and all are ignorant of the correct division, the inheritance should, in al-Juwaynī's view, be divided equally among all of the claimants. The guiding objective in both situations is the lawful division of an inheritance among legitimate parties and the satisfaction of each party, even if that entails giving some part of the inheritance to heirs who are not in fact legally entitled to it or

[32] For the full discussion, see al-Juwaynī, *al-Ghiyāthī*, 503–11.

[33] The principal Quranic verses regarding inheritance and its division are 4:11–12 and 176. In these verses, the division of inheritance between heirs is based on the number of potential heirs, their relationship to the deceased, and their gender. Al-Juwaynī's principle of equality in inheritance bypasses all of these concerns and focuses primarily on conferring the inheritance to the rightful recipients and ensuring that all parties are equally satisfied. The most comprehensive treatment of the laws of inheritance found in the Quran and *ḥadīth* is David S. Powers, *Studies in the Qurʾān and Ḥadīth: The Formation of the Islamic Law of Inheritance* (Berkeley: University of California Press, 1986). The book should be read in tandem with its numerous reviews.

[34] Al-Juwaynī, *al-Ghiyāthī*, 505–7.

allocating to some heirs a greater share than is lawfully theirs. Al-Juwaynī enshrines the element of securing individual satisfaction as the basis of all transactional and financial affairs and as the only mechanism capable of curtailing the spread of negative sentiments in society.[35]

The three principles that underpin al-Juwaynī's legal minimalism are not discrete and disconnected from one another; rather, they operate together to facilitate the orderly and harmonious functioning of society on the basis of knowledge of the Sharīʿa, thus allowing people to discharge their religious obligations and attain satisfaction. Moreover, in al-Juwaynī's doctrine of legal minimalism, the continuity of society is contingent on the preservation of an understanding of foundational legal matters in the memory of individuals alongside a living Sharīʿa-based custom that is the object of collective adherence. In spite of these mechanisms for continuity, legal knowledge remains susceptible to loss, since custom is not permanently fixed in society and knowledge of the Sharīʿa as preserved by individuals can diminish as knowledgeable individuals pass away. The worst-case scenario in which even custom and individual memory of the Sharīʿa have evaporated is the subject of al-Juwaynī's final discussion in the *Ghiyāthī*.

THE LOSS OF THE SHARĪʿA

Al-Juwaynī's primary objective throughout the *Ghiyāthī* is to ensure the continuity of society and of the Sharīʿa, regardless of the truncated form either is forced to take. One of the bulwarks he posits against loss, as we have seen, is the continuity of custom (*istiqrār al-ʿadā/iṭṭirād al-ʿurf*). However, given the impermanence of the people in whose practice Sharīʿa-based custom and memory of the Sharīʿa reside, he is forced to accept the possibility of the loss of the Sharīʿa altogether.[36] Such loss would leave society entirely bereft of religious guidance and void the legal obligation to follow this guidance (*taklīf*):

> If the derived and principal matters of the Sharīʿa (*furūʿ al-sharīʿa wa-uṣūluhā*) are effaced, and there is no one who preserves them to whom one can turn or on whom one can rely, the legal responsibility (*taklīf*) of worshippers is suspended and their condition has reached the state of those who have not received the invitation [to faith], and the Sharīʿa is not incumbent on them.[37]

[35] Ibid., 508–11. Al-Juwaynī argues that beyond financial affairs, the securing of individual contentment is also the basis of marriage. See ibid., 512–13.

[36] On this issue, see note 13. [37] Al-Juwaynī, *al-Ghiyāthī*, 526.

People living in the complete absence of the Sharīʿa are, in al-Juwaynī's view, comparable to those living in a time in which there is no prophecy or divine connection (*ahl al-fatra*)[38] – they are entirely unregulated by religious law. It is on this somber note that al-Juwaynī concludes the *Ghiyāthī*: the imamate, *muftī-mujtahid*s, transmitting jurists, and foundational rulings of the Sharīʿa can all be effaced, leaving people legally unbound by any religious dictates.[39]

Al-Juwaynī's argument for the continuity of law and society even in the absence of the imam and scholars is a direct outgrowth of his epistemological framework, in which epistemically necessary legal knowledge and custom preclude complete loss. However, since al-Juwaynī eventually concedes the possibility of the loss of all religious knowledge, this final

38 The question regarding the moral responsibility of *ahl al-fatra* ("people of the interval") was addressed by theologians and involved a great deal of disagreement. Reinhart's *Before Revelation* demonstrates the centrality of this discussion and its ramifications for rationality, ethics, and morality. The basic question at issue is the status of human actions before the receipt of divine legislation. Can such acts be categorized as permissible or prohibited, or should all judgment be withheld until God reveals His law? Questions related to the nature of the human intellect and its ability to reason independently of legislation naturally arose as corollaries. Reinhart describes three distinct positions on the basic question – proscription, permission, and no assessment. The first position considered most acts blameworthy until they were explicitly permitted by revelation. Reinhart found a single Ḥanbalī source attesting to this position. Adherents of the second position, by stark contrast, held that in the absence of revelation all actions were permitted. Finally, those holding the third position, that of no assessment, argued that since revelation is the exclusive yardstick of human action, there can be no assessment whatsoever of actions undertaken in its absence. According to Reinhart, this view eventually prevailed within theological circles and became the official position of the Ashʿarīs as well as the majority of the Ḥanbalīs. Despite the seemingly neat division between these three positions, Reinhart notes that there was a great deal of fluidity and change over time even within theological schools. Al-Juwaynī, like other Ashʿarīs, adopted the position of no assessment. There have been numerous reviews of Reinhart's book, both favorable and unfavorable. Among the latter, see those by Eric Ormsby in *Islamic Law and Society* 5, no. 1 (1998): 118–23, and Wilfred Madelung in *Bulletin of the School of Oriental and African Studies* 60, no. 1 (1997): 127–28. A more favorable review is Bernard Weiss's in *Journal of the American Oriental Society* 119, no. 2 (1999): 317–18. It is possible that the reviewers' differences reflect the fact that both Ormsby and Madelung are specialists in *kalam*, whereas Weiss specializes in *uṣūl al-fiqh*; therefore, the latter focuses on theoretical questions regarding the law that Western academic discussions have largely ignored, whereas the former focus on the more nuanced and technical matters that Reinhart does not fully address.

39 This last discussion is the shortest in the *Ghiyāthī*, comprising only four pages and naturally leaving the reader with many lingering questions. Al-Juwaynī states that he addresses the remaining issues in greater detail in his *Madārik al-ʿuqūl*, but unfortunately no manuscript of this text is extant, nor are there any commentaries or abridgments that can be consulted.

state in his thought experiment would seem to exceed the scope of his epistemology, which conceptualizes necessary knowledge (*ʿilm ḍarūrī*) as invulnerable to loss. Al-Juwaynī envisions the loss of knowledge of the Sharīʿa as a slowly unfolding phenomenon rather than as a sudden state brought about by the disappearance of *muftī-mujtahid*s. Legal knowledge is lost not because epistemically necessary legal matters suddenly become epistemically probable but because lapses in the transmission or practice of that knowledge leave it insufficiently relayed or preserved in custom. Therefore, the gradual disappearance of knowledge in this manner does not contradict al-Juwaynī's overall epistemology, since it results from external factors leading to the depletion and eventual extinction of knowledge as opposed to an internal epistemic shift in the knowledge itself. The continuity of epistemically necessary knowledge is supported by custom and practice, with which it stands in a dialectical relationship, both custom and knowledge continuously informing, reinforcing, and reacting to each other. This is why the complete eclipse of the Sharīʿa is marked by people's incapacity to recall and enact the fundamentals of the Sharīʿa.[40] Recognizing the dialectical relationship between custom and knowledge of the Sharīʿa, al-Juwaynī demonstrates that the dialectic between the two exists in moments of abundant knowledge as much as it does in moments of complete loss.

The end of the *Ghiyāthī* inextricably fuses al-Juwaynī's concern for continuity with his preoccupation with certainty. In his theological writings, al-Juwaynī's primary concern with the attainment of certainty, even if just *practical* certainty, is clear, but in his legal works his emphasis on certainty is tempered by his desire for continuity, especially legal continuity. Instead of prioritizing certainty and restricting the realm of legislation to epistemically certain matters only, al-Juwaynī draws on his belief in legal universality to endorse sources that produce merely probable rules as legitimate sources of norm generation. Throughout the *Burhān*, legal continuity and universality form the cornerstones of his arguments; it is only in the *Ghiyāthī* that he accepts that continuity, too, has its limits. Remarkably, though, in the *Ghiyāthī* the continuity of legal knowledge is contingent on the presence of legal certainty. This means that although al-Juwaynī forgoes certainty for the sake of continuity in the *Burhān*, continuity in the *Ghiyāthī* is only possible to the extent that legal certainty remains. Once legal certainty is completely lost, the

40 Al-Juwaynī, *al-Ghiyāthī*, 523–26.

continuity of the Muslim community slowly retreats into the distant past. The picture that al-Juwaynī paints is a bleak one, steeped in the threat of loss without the possibility of restoration. Grim as this view is, al-Juwaynī's apocalyptic predictions and adaptive genius nonetheless unearth avenues for reformulating our conception of the imamate, the Sharīʿa, and, most importantly, the individual.

THE SHARĪʿA AND CUSTOM AS GOVERNANCE

In Western academia, Islamic political thought has frequently been seen as an intellectually underdeveloped discipline that, instead of aiming at theorizing an authentic and ideal form of government on the basis of the Prophetic model, simply responds to historical circumstances and legitimizes arrangements that appear illegitimate in comparison to Prophetic rule. As Malcolm Kerr has put it,

> the failure of the constitutional theory of the Caliphate to provide a sufficiently positive allocation of procedural sovereignty disqualified it from serving as a practical constitutional instrument. It can perhaps be better understood as an apologia for the cumulative historical record of the institution and a defense of Sunnite practice against Shīʿite criticism, than as a reliable expression of what its exponents actually believed was the structure of rights, duties, procedures, and functions that they could normally expect to be observed.[41]

Kerr is not alone in holding this view of Islamic political thought. Hamilton Gibb previously argued much the same. "The Islamic ideology never found its proper and articulated expression in the political institutions of the Islamic states," Gibb writes, adding that the institution of the caliphate, instead of reflecting an authentically Islamic ideology, was merely a "cult of the Sassanid tradition," especially during the ʿAbbasid period. The jurists, who carried the responsibility of articulating an authentic and coherent political theory, were "rationalizing the history of the community" with a theory that was "merely the *post eventum* justification of the precedents which have been ratified by *ijmāʿ*."[42] Both Gibb and Kerr presume the existence of an early political ideal in the model of the Prophet and a growing gulf between this early ideal and the political reality that jurists faced under Umayyad and ʿAbbasid dynastic rule. Instead of articulating a political theory that was both true to the early

[41] Malcolm Kerr, *Islamic Reform* (Berkeley: University of California Press, 1966), 12–13.
[42] Gibb, *Studies on the Civilization of Islam*, 44–45, 162.

ideal and responsive to the changing political needs of their contexts, the jurists simply justified the political arrangements they found before them.

Ovamir Anjum classifies the various assessments of Islamic political thought produced by Western scholarship into two types: those asserting that the early ideal was too cumbersome to maintain despite sustained efforts and those that view Islamic political thought as doomed to failure from the outset.[43] But both generally agree that works of political thought penned by jurists[44] were predominately written in response to political realities and shrouded in a thick fog of compromise. This description is not without merit, as jurists did use their writings to negotiate their intellectual territory vis-à-vis the ruling elite. Al-Juwaynī himself was writing at a time when the ʿAbbasids had been reduced to titular power holders and the Seljuk vizier, Niẓām al-Mulk, wielded political, social, and intellectual control over Khurasan.[45] Priding himself on his bestowal of scholarly patronage, Niẓām al-Mulk exerted indirect influence over al-Juwaynī's scholarship, especially with regard to the latter's position on the legitimacy of Seljuk rule. This influence is epitomized in the *Ghiyāthī*, which is riddled with explicit praise of Niẓām al-Mulk and contains a section dedicated to legitimizing his rule.[46]

Wael Hallaq, in the hitherto only article dedicated to explicating the contents of the *Ghiyāthī*, notes this influence and describes the text as an expression of the political and intellectual environment al-Juwaynī inhabited. "Like other juridico-political treatises," Hallaq argues, "*Ghiyāth al-Umam* cannot be properly understood unless situated in its historical context."[47] In this sense, al-Juwaynī is as politically constrained as his predecessors were. However, what kindles Hallaq's fascination with al-Juwaynī is the latter's willingness to dismiss the sacrosanct institution of the imamate:

[43] In the first camp, Anjum places H. A. R. Gibb; in the second, he names Ann Lambton, Ira Lapidus, and Patricia Crone. See Anjum, *Politics, Law, and Community*, 1–32.

[44] This genre is distinct from Islamic political writings composed under the influence of the Hellenistic tradition, in which notions of eudaemonistic politics were more prevalent. The work of thinkers such as al-Kindī and al-Fārābī fall in this latter category.

[45] See Chapter 1 for a sketch of the political milieu al-Juwaynī inhabited and his relationship to Niẓām al-Mulk.

[46] In the *Ghiyāthī*, al-Juwaynī specifically refers to Niẓām al-Mulk in his discussion of a weak caliph overthrown by a strong ruler who discharges the duties of the imamate. He goes into great detail regarding the role of this leader, even discussing when it is permissible for the leader to lead the yearly pilgrimage. See al-Juwaynī, *al-Ghiyāthī*, 338–54, 364–70.

[47] Wael Hallaq, "Caliphs, Jurists and the Saljūqs in the Political Thought of Juwaynī," *Muslim World* 74 (1984): 26–41.

> Juwaynī leaves the readers of the *Ghiyāthī* with little doubt that he is ready to dispose of the ʿAbbasid imamate altogether in favor of a powerful sultan who will efficiently manage the affairs of the community. In order to bring the rule of such a sultan within the domain of the political theory of the Sharīʿa, Juwaynī had to first undermine Māwardī's theory which had gained acceptance by that time.[48]

Al-Juwaynī's willingness to accept a ruling sultan over and above a designated imam was, for Hallaq, a direct outcome of political contingencies and of al-Juwaynī's personal affiliation with Niẓām al-Mulk. Therefore, to separate al-Juwaynī's unique contributions from his particular political situation would result in only a partial understanding of his project. Although Hallaq recognizes the imprint of al-Juwaynī's political context on certain concessions he makes in the *Ghiyāthī*, I argue that the impact was even more far-reaching. The historical situation in which he lived not only affected his political thought but gave rise to his twin desires for certainty and continuity, which formed the basis of his entire thought. Thus, although his divergences from his predecessors are a noteworthy manifestation of the political concerns he harbored during his lifetime, the implications of his context on his thought were pervasive.

Secondary scholarship on Islamic political thought has chiefly focused on the theorization of the institution of the imamate and its development over time, treating it, and the related question of legitimacy, as the essential element of political writings. This is not unfounded, as the bulk of the juristic discourse on politics has indeed centered on the imam. The effect of this focus has been to make the continuity of society, the security of the Muslim community, and the proper functioning of quotidian affairs contingent on the imam. Although al-Juwaynī does not object to the superior efficacy of the imamate in the management of everyday political affairs, he identifies the social mechanisms of *governance* that underpin the imamate and transcend the formal confines of political institutions if and when formal institutions cannot be sustained.[49]

The distinction between government, in this case the imamate, and governance in political science is a rudimentary one. Government refers to the formal institutions of the imamate that are seen as legitimate and that hold sole jurisdiction over the political affairs of the Islamic empire.[50] The

[48] Ibid., 30.

[49] I have made a version of this argument elsewhere. See Sohaira Siddiqui, "Power vs. Authority: Al-Juwaynī's Intervention in Pragmatic Political Thought," *Journal of Islamic Studies* 28, no. 2 (2017): 193–220.

[50] Gerry Stoker's article "Governance as Theory" has been useful for mapping the basic understanding of governance as used in political science and other social sciences. See

primary functions of formal government are promoting public order, securing the territory, and facilitating collective action. Governance, on the other hand, is a more nebulous concept with several layers, including "a change in the meaning of government, referring to a new process of governing or a changed condition of ordered rule; or the new method by which society is governed."[51] Like government, governance is concerned with public order, security, and action, but the primary difference concerns process: whereas the former relies on the formal apparatus of government externally imposed on individuals, the latter depends on a polyvalent network of multiple governing forces that work in tandem.[52] Gerry Stoker notes that providing a categorical definition of governance is difficult. He thus identifies five constitutive elements:

1. Governance refers to a set of institutions and actors that are drawn from but also beyond government.
2. Governance identifies the blurring of boundaries and responsibilities for tackling social and economic issues.
3. Governance identifies the power dependence involved in the relationships between institutions involved in collective action.
4. Governance is about autonomous self-governing networks of actors.
5. Governance recognizes the capacity to get things done which does not rest on the power of government to command or use its authority.[53]

Ultimately, Stoker sees governance as a means of organizing society beyond the formal apparatus of government on the basis of relationships and networks among individuals. This understanding resonates with al-Juwaynī's thought, in which governance, more than government, provides the foundational structure of society and is reinforced by relationships and networks formed through communal religious adherence to the Sharīʿa. It is this implicit reliance on the governing structure of the Sharīʿa that enables al-Juwaynī to envision the continuity of society despite the total incapacity of formal government.

Such a gap in government is not typically countenanced by political theorists, who assume that the vacuum generated by the absence of government will be filled with discord, eventually leading to the collapse

Stoker, "Governance as Theory: Five Propositions," *International Social Science Journal* 50 (1998): 17–28. See also Guy Peters, "Governance as Political Theory," *Jerusalem Papers in Regulation and Governance* 22 (2010): 1–23.

51 R. A. W. Rhodes, "The New Governance: Governing without Government," *Political Studies* 44 (1996): 652–53.

52 Stoker, "Governance as Theory," 17–18.

53 Ibid., 18.

of society itself. Yet in the *Ghiyāthī*, al-Juwaynī does not connect this loss to inevitable societal breakdown. His acceptance of the possibility of political disintegration reflects his confidence in a more deeply rooted apparatus of governance, which transcends formal political structures. This veiled structure of governance is illuminated at the moment of a governmental lacuna, when, al-Juwaynī contends, society and order do not disintegrate but rather endure through Sharīʿa norms and the scholars who convey them. Society begins to unravel only in the absence of the Sharīʿa, which entails not just the disappearance of the formal apparatus of government but the loss of the communal cohesion and stability granted by shared adherence to the Sharīʿa. Therefore, communal action and negotiation on the basis of shared norms transcends the imamate, and even though al-Juwaynī's narrative eventually culminates in complete loss, his ability to conceive of society without government shows his faith in social cohesion created and maintained by shared religious norms as opposed to shared political ideals or leaders. These shared norms in the form of the Sharīʿa appear not as a set of concretized and reified laws but as a framework able to adapt to and evolve with a changing context.

Perhaps no term has engendered more cacophonous debate than *Sharīʿa*, which is why I have deliberately left it unaddressed until now. Joseph Schacht, the early scholar of Islamic law, described it as the "canon law of Islam" and "the totality of Allah's commandments relating to the activities of man."[54] Schacht's definition of the Sharīʿa limits it to legal doctrine (*fiqh*) – a matter of simply applying rules to individual lives. Later scholars who reject Schacht's definition have sought to distinguish the Sharīʿa as an autonomous entity from *fiqh* as positive law. One such scholar, Khaled Abou El Fadl, recognizes the authority of the jurists as "the repositories of a literary, text-based legitimacy"[55] but differentiates the juristic expression of the law from the Sharīʿa:

> God's law as an abstraction is called the Sharīʿa (literally, the way), while the concrete understanding and implementation of this Will is called *fiqh* (literally, understanding) ... The conceptual distinction between Sharīʿa and *fiqh* was the product of a recognition of the inevitable failures of human efforts at understanding the purposes or intentions of God. Human beings, the jurists insisted, simply do not possess the ability to encompass the wisdom of God. Consequently, every understanding or implementation of God's Will is necessarily imperfect because ... perfection belongs only to God.[56]

[54] Schacht, *Introduction to Islamic Law*, 1–5.
[55] Abou El Fadl, *Speaking in God's Name*, 12. [56] Ibid., 32.

This distinction between the Sharīʿa and *fiqh* mirrors a more profound differentiation in terms of epistemology and authority which grants *fiqh* only limited authority as a result of human epistemic limitations, whereas the Sharīʿa is elevated to the status of law "as understood in the mind of God."[57] Defining the Sharīʿa in this manner instills it with epistemic authority and dislodges it from the realm of human deliberation, delineating it as a space only God can penetrate.

Resisting this definition of the Sharīʿa as the law as conceived by God, Anver Emon conceptualizes it instead as the "rule of law," drawing on the rule of law discourse in legal studies. He acknowledges that theorists define the rule of law in various ways,[58] making it an ambiguous concept to employ, but its utility for Emon derives from the fact that the Sharīʿa, when viewed from a rule of law perspective, is neither *fiqh* nor God's law but a discourse:

> To describe Sharīʿa as Rule of Law, therefore, is to appreciate Sharīʿa discourses as emanating from within a claim space, and thereby to prompt important questions about the constitutive features that both delimit the space and contribute to the intelligibility of claims of justice made herein. As a term of art that focuses on how claims of justice are justified and legitimized, Sharīʿa as Rule of Law offers a conceptual framework for analyzing the operation and imposition of the force of law.[59]

Emon's definition aims to remove Sharīʿa from the realm of juristic law while refusing to relegate it to an unintelligible realm in which human reason and juristic abilities cannot function. For Emon, identifying the Sharīʿa as the rule of law means seeing it as a "conceptual site" or a "claim space" in which the competing needs of jurists, individuals, the government, and institutions can be negotiated and matters beyond the law, involving concepts such as justice, can materialize. However, Emon stresses that Sharīʿa as a claim space is delineated by specific boundaries that serve

[57] See Emon, "To Most Likely Know the Law," 418.

[58] Emon engages with the definitions provided by Thomas Carothers, Joseph Raz, and Lon Fuller, arguing that although these definitions are useful, they all assume the existence of a formal governmental apparatus and therefore imply that envisioning the Sharīʿa as the "rule of law" in the absence of formal institutions would constitute a contradiction. For these definitions, see Brian Z. Tamanaha, *On the Rule of Law: History, Politics, Theory* (Cambridge: Cambridge University Press, 2004); Thomas Carothers, "The Rule of Law Revival," *Foreign Affairs* 77, no. 2 (1998): 95–106; Joseph Raz, "The Rule of Law and Its Virtues," *Law Quarterly Review* 93 (1977): 195–211; and Lon Fuller, *The Morality of Law* (New Haven, CT: Yale University Press, 1969).

[59] Anver Emon, *Religious Pluralism and Islamic Law: Dhimmīs and Others in the Empire of Law* (Oxford: Oxford University Press, 2012), 16.

to distinguish intelligible and legitimate arguments from others. By describing the Sharīʿa as the rule of law, Emon articulates a broader definition that is nonetheless limited by what is deemed legitimate and thus authoritative.

However, these definitions of the Sharīʿa, each useful in its own way, do not capture al-Juwaynī's vision of the Sharīʿa. Al-Juwaynī's Sharīʿa is not juristic law; neither is it the realm of God's unintelligible law nor a claim space in which topics ranging from law to justice can be actualized. The Sharīʿa, for al-Juwaynī, facilitates the ordering and preservation of society and can best be encapsulated in Robert Cover's idea of the *nomos*, or normative universe. Instead of falling prey to defining law along the lines of rules and regulations, or of order, Cover argues that "we inhabit a *nomos* – a normative universe. We constantly create and maintain a world of right and wrong, of lawful and unlawful, of valid and void."[60] For Cover, the law, beyond providing rules for society, structures an entire normative world that individuals inhabit and within which they construct meaning through law. This understanding thus removes law from the realm of power and places it in the realm of meaning. If one refers to "normative behavior" in this context, one is referring not merely to what is legally valid or invalid but also to what is given significance within the *nomos*. Given the expansive nature of *nomos* as a "world of law," Cover argues that it must have two essential features. First, "the intelligibility of normative behavior inheres in the communal character of the narratives that provide the context of the behavior."[61] This means that a *nomos* cannot exist without a communally identifiable narrative that makes it significant. This narrative is not just a history of the law; it is also the narrative of the law through the lens of those who create it and those who practice it. The second requirement of the *nomos* is "commitments on the part of communities that affirm legal meaning."[62] Although the narrative imparts a sense of significance to the *nomos*, that significance becomes valid only through the collective commitment of a community. Putting these elements together, a *nomos*, or a legal world, is an "integrated world of obligation and reality from which the rest of the world is perceived,"[63] and it rests on a shared narrative and communal commitment. It is within this *nomos* that *jurisgenesis*, or the creation of legal meaning, takes place.[64] Importantly, Cover recognizes that multiple *nomoi* can exist in a single society and that *nomoi*

[60] Cover, "Nomos and Narrative," 4. [61] Ibid., 10. [62] Ibid. [63] Ibid., 31.

[64] Ibid., 11. See also Franklin Snyder, "Nomos, Narrative and Adjudication: Toward a Jurisgenetic Theory of Law," *William and Mary Law Review* 40, no. 5 (1999): 1623–729.

are not contingent on the state.[65] In fact, for Cover, even if the state imposes a certain *nomos* on society, other *nomoi* can exist, providing alternative notions of meaning. While the *nomos* cannot exist without law, it is also far more than just a site of law – it is a site of meaning generation, communal narrative, and communal perception.

Al-Juwaynī's depiction of the Sharīʿa in the *Ghiyāthī* fits Cover's definition of a *nomos*: it gives rise to a mechanism of social governance whose strength and force stand in a dialectical relationship with the legal knowledge present in society. The Sharīʿa, like Cover's notion of *nomos*, is not contingent on government, institutions, or even the juristic class; rather, it relies on a communal commitment to narrative and practice, which for al-Juwaynī are intimately intertwined. This communal element is precisely why the Sharīʿa remains a recognizable structuring force in society after the collapse of the imamate and even in the absence of *muftī-mujtahid*s. Al-Juwaynī declares the Sharīʿa completely extinguished only when no ostensible practice or memory of it can be identified in society. In Cover's terminology, the *nomos* dies when its narrative does. From this perspective, the Sharīʿa is not merely constituted by the legal norms that prevail in society but also represents the centrifugal force of a narrative that connects individuals. Therefore, knowledge and practice of the Sharīʿa along with its narrative are the key elements for evaluating its vitality. If knowledge of the Sharīʿa is ubiquitous, if the community is committed to its narrative, and if it is providing meaning for its followers, then the Sharīʿa is functioning optimally as a *nomos*. If, on the other hand, knowledge of the Sharīʿa remains present in society but its narrative and ability to provide meaning are weakening, the Sharīʿa as a governing force is in danger of enervation. Defining the Sharīʿa in this manner emphasizes the roles of the individual and the community that are neglected by other definitions.

The Sharīʿa as a governing *nomos* predicated on knowledge of the Sharīʿa in society indicates a new relationship between individuals and the law. In previous conceptualizations of the Sharīʿa, the law is fashioned by a juristic class and subsequently accepted and implemented by individuals. The individuals in this framework may be agents enacting the law, but they are not creators of knowledge nor are they active participants in the process of lawmaking. However, in al-Juwaynī's vision of the Sharīʿa, individual believers are preservers, interpreters, agents, and sustainers.

[65] Cover, "Nomos and Narrative," 11.

The centrality of the individual in the domain of the Sharīʿa was previously asserted by Sherman Jackson, who argues that the individual "enjoys a much more direct relationship with the law, and though the state might be said to occupy an intermediate position, it would stand not directly but much more peripherally between the individual and the law."[66] Jackson holds that the individual's relationship with the law is direct and unmediated, and individuals are sui juris, having "both the right and the obligation to conduct their affairs autonomously, according to the provisions of the law."[67] If the Sharīʿa as *nomos* consists of jurisgenesis and relies directly on the commitment of individuals to its normative universe, then each individual must be sui juris. Al-Juwaynī echoes this concept, as for him the individual constitutes an independent agent supporting and preserving the Sharīʿa within society. Theorizing the individual in this way constructs a reciprocal and dialectical relationship between the individual and the Sharīʿa in which the Sharīʿa informs human action and human action in turn dictates the strength and vitality of the Sharīʿa. From this perspective, al-Juwaynī's Sharīʿa is more than a static body of doctrines or an unintelligible idea; it is a dialectical *nomos* responsive to both individual knowledge and communal commitment.

Conceiving of the Sharīʿa as a dialectical *nomos* reveals that for al-Juwaynī, the community is fundamentally an epistemic one and thus a legitimate source of knowledge. As argued throughout the course of this book, al-Juwaynī posited custom as a potential source of knowledge alongside the traditional sources of speculative reason (*naẓar*) and revelation. Though he qualified custom in various ways, at the most basic level he recognized that knowledge acquisition was not merely an internal process undergone by the individual but also an external one that was often socially supported. This "external" nature of knowledge creation has recently been explored in the field of epistemology under the rubric of social epistemology. Whereas epistemology has traditionally focused

[66] Jackson, *Islamic Law and the State*, 218.

[67] Ibid. It is important to note that although Jackson speaks about individuals as *sui juris* in order to illustrate that the law can function independently of the state, he does acknowledge that certain elements of the law are connected to the state. Therefore, "the concept of *sui juris* operates … only as a general principle. There are, on the other hand, circumstances under which confirmation or some other sanctionative action representative of officialdom will be required for a legal cause to activate its corresponding rule." Jackson, *Islamic Law and the State*, 220. Jackson's discussion, stemming from his reading of Shihāb al-Dīn al-Qarāfī (d. 684/1285), is intended to demonstrate the distance to government in premodern conceptions of the law, whereas al-Juwaynī's discussion expresses much more explicitly the vitality of the law outside a government structure.

narrowly on the "knowing subject" and the creation of knowledge through reason, consciousness, memory, and perception, social epistemologists argue that knowledge is not entirely self-referential. Rather, they contend, it is created, sustained, and affected by external factors. Social epistemologists thus shift the focus from the individual to collective doxastic agents who inhabit a similar context.[68] Coupling these insights with those of Cover, we can say that to understand the collective doxastic reasoning of a community, the *nomos* and the narrative of that community ought to serve as the starting point: the reasoning of individuals can be understood only by first apprehending the world that provides their reasoning with meaning.

In al-Juwaynī's world, the Sharīʿa as *nomos* provides the framework within which reasoning unfolds. Moreover, because of shared commitments, the individual reasons not as an independent agent but always as part of the collective. In al-Juwaynī's view, memory, one of the four main sources of knowledge traditionally identified by epistemologists,[69] is not merely internal to the individual but also collective, as shown by the continuity of the Sharīʿa beyond the disappearance of the *muftī-mujtahid*s. Though individual knowledge of the Sharīʿa is important, if it is not buttressed by collective practice and collective memory, it is severely weakened. Focusing solely on the individual as the locus of knowledge threatens to obscure this essential role of the community. And because continuity for al-Juwaynī is contigent on social memory, neglecting the external forms of knowledge in effect means denying that the Sharīʿa has a communal element in its creation of a *nomos*. Thus, even though al-Juwaynī emphasizes the practical certainty of the individual and the ability of the individual to act as a reservoir of knowledge, he also recognizes that knowledge must transcend the individual to take its place in the dialectical relationship with the inhabited *nomos*.

CONCLUSION

In the course of al-Juwaynī's writings, we have seen him sacrifice his desire for epistemic certainty to ensure continuity, most importantly legal continuity. He demonstrates the primacy of continuity in the opening

[68] Goldman, "Why Social Epistemology"; BonJour, "Recent Work"; and Vahid, "Externalism/Internalism."

[69] The other three are reason, consciousness, and perception. See Audi, "Sources of Knowledge."

section of the *Ghiyāthī*, where he addresses the ideal imam, political stability, and the preservation of a believing society. Though he describes the imamate as the optimal mechanism for safeguarding the community and ensuring continuity, in the second and third sections of the book he acknowledges other mechanisms that can also accomplish this task. These secondary mechanisms of continuity are brought to the fore when the imamate ceases and authority passes to *muftī-mujtahid*s in recognition of their legal acumen. However, once the *muftī-mujtahid*s, too, disappear, al-Juwaynī turns to the Sharīʿa itself as the guarantor of social order and continuity, drawing on his epistemological paradigm, which grants individuals the prospect of practical certainty in their legal norms. Through habitual practice, these legal norms become ingrained in society and facilitate the continuity of small communities in the event of the failure of formal political institutions. Conceptualized in this manner, the Sharīʿa is not defined by a body of static doctrines or even a fixed methodological process; rather, it constitutes a *nomos*, both a site of law and a site of meaning. As such, it regulates the most basic elements of society while evolving with, and responding to, the knowledge of it that is present in society. Knowledge of the Sharīʿa is ideally maintained by the *muftī-mujtahid*s, but even in their absence the Sharīʿa is preserved as a lived reality to the extent that commitment to its forms and narrative endures in society. In this way, the Sharīʿa is a dialectical mechanism of governance – influencing society through the production of legal norms and responding to sociopolitical conditions. This conceptualization endows the individual believer with a more active role in relation to the Sharīʿa as not just an enactor of the law but also its preserver. The Sharīʿa thus expands with the expansion of knowledge in the community and contracts with its contraction, and any evaluation of the vitality of the Sharīʿa is adequate only if it looks beyond the law's formal dictates to the individuals who practice it.

Conclusion

Al-Juwaynī was born into a fractured political order split between, on the one hand, the ruling sultans and the caliphate and, on the other, a robust but diverse intellectual environment in which competing ideologies, both theological (Ashʿarism and Muʿtazilism) and legal (Shāfiʿism and Ḥanafism), vied for dominance. Al-Juwaynī's trajectory was shaped directly by this context and its political-intellectual alliances, and his concern with certainty and continuity thus seems a natural result of his circumstances.

The foundation of his thought is an epistemological framework that demarcates for the individual believer a domain of theological and legal certainty. The legal certainty that the individual acquires is *practical* in nature; it cannot be universalized or equated with the ontological reality of knowledge as envisioned by the omnipotent God, but it does enable the believer to have confidence in his or her legal enactments, which would otherwise lie outside the realm of true knowledge. Al-Juwaynī accomplishes this expansion of the scope of certainty not by diminishing the omnipotence of God but by affirming the rational capabilities of human beings and recognizing the multiplicity of avenues of knowledge acquisition. More specifically, al-Juwaynī argues that practical certainty in one's knowledge can be achieved through exhaustive reasoning as well as, crucially, through habitual action repeated over a lengthy period of time, with the result that what initially appears equivocal to the intellect eventually becomes part and parcel of an individual's independent reservoir of knowledge. The ramifications of this epistemology are most obvious in al-Juwaynī's *uṣūl al-fiqh*, where he forges new mechanisms for the rational justification of *ijmāʿ* and *mutawātir ḥadīth* as cardinal sources of legal knowledge.

Instead of embracing the scriptural proofs advanced by his Shāfiʿī predecessors for these two sources, al-Juwaynī legitimizes them on rational grounds, utilizing his own epistemological framework. Ignoring the scriptural proof texts often invoked in defense of *ijmāʿ* and *mutawātir ḥadīth*, al-Juwaynī asserts that custom and juristic practice are more compelling indicators of the validity of these sources. Though this move away from scriptural support appears counterintuitive, it is consistent with al-Juwaynī's epistemology and broader intellectual project. Despite the centrality of revelation as a source of knowledge, he sees it as susceptible to criticism because of its linguistic ambiguity. Consequently, in his eyes, reliance on ambiguous scriptural proofs to justify *ijmāʿ* and *mutawātir ḥadīth* in fact undermines the legitimacy of the legal system. As an alternative, al-Juwaynī develops rational and customary proofs to establish the validity of the key sources of the law with epistemic certainty. But this formalistic manifestation of his epistemological framework faces practical limitations when it collides with his desire for continuity and the accompanying belief in legal universalism.

Notwithstanding al-Juwaynī's success in providing epistemically certain rational proofs for the sources of the law, the epistemic value of the sources cannot extend to the rulings generated from them without qualification. This limitation is due to the opaque nature of scriptural indicators and, more often, the absence of scriptural guidance altogether. This basic obstacle to the achievement of legal certainty is amplified by al-Juwaynī's adherence to legal universalism, which demands that every human action is covered by a corresponding legal ruling, even if the derived legal norm is only tangentially connected to scripture. Like scholars before him, al-Juwaynī advocates extending the law to novel cases through *qiyās* and related techniques in spite of the epistemically probable nature of the resultant rulings. Probability, then, becomes the pivot around which legal universality and the continuity of the law are balanced. Al-Juwaynī attempts to mitigate the vagaries of probability through his epistemology, postulating continuous customary practice as a remedy. He thus argues that probable rulings, if continually enacted, can become *practically certain* to an individual. The significance of the notion of rulings that are simultaneously objectively uncertain and subjectively certain to the individual is apparent in al-Juwaynī's political thought, where subjective knowledge of the Sharīʿa embodied by individuals becomes the key to societal continuity.

Indeed, unlike political thinkers before him, who focused on the institution and power of the imamate, often to the neglect of other inquiries, al-

Juwaynī envisions in his *Ghiyāthī* the continuity of society and religious communities even in the absence of the imam. For him, this continuity is predicated on epistemically certain principles of law ingrained in the minds of individuals through continual practice or exhaustive reflection. These certain legal principles compensate for the gaps caused by the absence of the imam and are upheld by the scholarly guards of religious knowledge. Even if these scholarly sentinels were to disappear, people in society would continue to be governed by their individual and collective preserved knowledge of the Sharīʿa. In al-Juwaynī's analysis, therefore, the continuity of the Sharīʿa rests on a dialectical relationship in which the Sharīʿa, by informing human behavior, acts as a governing force in society, and in turn the community and its individuals, through their collective adherence and memory, ensure the Sharīʿa's perpetuation. The Sharīʿa unveiled in the final section of the *Ghiyāthī*, where all formal political and legal structures have fallen away, is not simply a series of rules but rather an embedded *nomos* that provides individuals with both order and meaning. However, the dependence of the Sharīʿa on individuals also means that these individuals are integral to its vitality and strength. The individual enacting the Sharīʿa is therefore dialectically preserving it.

Though at first glance al-Juwaynī's conclusions in the *Ghiyāthī* seem stark, they are best understood in light of his sociopolitical context, in which the evident weakness of the caliphate forced him to contemplate its total collapse. This prospect prompted him to reconceptualize the roles of the imam and the *ʿulamāʾ*, the relationship between custom and the Sharīʿa, and the Sharīʿa itself. To insure society against collapse alongside the imamate, al-Juwaynī strives to place the Sharīʿa on a foundation that can withstand the absence of the institutions that traditionally guarantee its power. Al-Juwaynī's concern with the continuity of the Sharīʿa is therefore a political and legal project that helps explain his interest in epistemological certainty in both law and theology. The interconnectivity between al-Juwaynī's discourses in law, political thought, and theology reveals his syncretism and serves as an encouragement for scholars to adopt a wider methodological lens in analyzing the thought of seminal figures in Islamic intellectual history.

EXPANDING METHODOLOGICAL APPROACHES WITHIN THE ACADEMIC STUDY OF ISLAM

In this book, I have insisted on al-Juwaynī's centrality as an intellectual figure because of his impact on later developments, the implications of his thought for our conception of the fifth/eleventh century, and his contributions to important inquiries in the contemporary study of Islam. Focusing specifically on his contributions reveals three key issues in secondary scholarship with which al-Juwaynī engages directly. These three, as mentioned in the Introduction to this book, are reason and revelation, legal uncertainty, and the role of the caliph. These themes also correspond to three dominant disciplines within Islamic studies, namely, the study of speculative theology, the study of Islamic law and legal theory, and the study of Islamic political thought. These three disciplines are often approached separately, since contemporary scholarship often forces scholars to specialize in a particular intellectual field. Although specialization is necessary and often yields insightful results, it is imperative to be aware of the interdisciplinarity of any field of intellectual inquiry and its connections to other disciplines within Islamic thought. Al-Juwaynī provides a case in point: although focusing solely on his theological works, for example, would have been a worthy endeavor likely to generate important contributions to the field, detaching his theology from his ideas in other domains would have obscured his overall project and provided an incomplete portrait of his thought as a whole.

Al-Juwaynī's conception of the Sharīʿa provides a good example of the importance of interdisciplinarity to the analysis of Islamic intellectual history. His vision of the Sharīʿa as *nomos* cannot be appreciated through a singular and unidisciplinary examination of his legal thought; it emerges through consideration of a network of interconnected questions permeating his theological, legal, and political inquiries as a whole. Al-Juwaynī conceives of the Sharīʿa not as a static body of laws but as a legal system that is born out of, and sustained through, a dialectical relationship between it and the community/individual. The goal of the Sharīʿa is not merely to provide legal guidance but also to create a normative universe, *nomos*, that the individuals in a community both embody and influence. Yet although this view of the Sharīʿa may seem commonsensical, al-Juwaynī's formulation of it relies on his epistemology, which opens the door to practical certainty on the part of the individual. This, in turn, creates a more intimate connection between the individual and the law. Al-Juwaynī returns to the notion of the Sharīʿa as *nomos* in his political writings, in envisioning the continuity of society in the absence of the imam, where he sees the Sharīʿa as a source of stability and order for society. Again, al-Juwaynī's conceptualization of the Sharīʿa as *nomos* is predicated on his epistemology and subsequently forms the foundation for his political theory. A narrow investigation of his legal thought might perhaps reveal his basic understanding of the Sharīʿa, but the full implications of his legal doctrine would be lost.

For contemporary scholars such as Bernard Weiss and Aron Zysow, who first called for recognition of the interdisciplinary nature of Islamic law, Islamic law was not simply a field of arcane legal discussion; it was also one deeply embedded in a theological framework that scholars must properly understand lest they overlook nuances within legal discourse. In the realms of law and theology, scholars of Islamic law have come to assume interconnectivity – in part thanks to classical jurists themselves indicating their indebtedness to theological ideas – but scholars of Islamic political thought remain resistant to connecting their discipline to foundational inquiries in other domains. This state of affairs has begun to change with the work of Ovamir Anjum, who has illuminated the centrality of epistemology to political thought in general and its particular necessity to the political project of Ibn Taymiyya. In doing so, Anjum has not only provided a more insightful portrait of Ibn Taymiyya as a political thinker but also, more importantly, revealed that Ibn Taymiyya's foundational discourse was a theological one.

This, of course, is not to say that disciplinary boundaries are arbitrary or unnecessary. Al-Juwaynī himself accepts the demarcation of the various disciplines and writes within the parameters of each discipline with which he engages. But underpinning his works are thematic threads and intellectual implications that tie the seemingly distinct disciplines together, demonstrating that disciplinary barriers are porous in nature. Investigating al-Juwaynī's theological or legal texts in isolation would undoubtedly provide insight into al-Juwaynī as a theologian or a jurist, respectively, but it would overlook the connections between different types of works. In general, we should be open to the existence of such linkages and make their exploration integral to our inquiries.

CONCLUDING REMARKS

There are two ways in which I might conclude this study of al-Juwaynī. In the first, I would summarize him as a looming intellectual figure of the fifth/eleventh century, embroiled in some of the most salient debates of his time and leaving an indelible mark on Islamic intellectual history through a combination of his scholarly production and his influence on his students. This summary casts al-Juwaynī as an intellectual manifestation of a set of sociopolitical circumstances that cannot be replicated – a fifth-/eleventh-century thinker bound to the conditions of his time and providing scholars with insight into the milieu he inhabited and the intellectual inquiries he directly shaped.

But I could also offer another vision of al-Juwaynī, one that pushes aside the contingencies binding him to his time and recognizes that the fundamental questions he undertook to answer are reappearing, in slightly modified ways, in modern societies. Contemporary inquiries about the scope of human reason, the relationship of the law to ethics, the adaptability and reform of Islamic law, and the various possible configurations of future Muslim polities can easily be related to al-Juwaynī's investigations into the scope of human reason, the effects of legal uncertainty on the law, and the achievement of certainty and continuity. By ignoring the answers that al-Juwaynī provided and instead focusing on the questions he posed and the cross-disciplinary methods he employed, we can transcend the temporal constraints binding his thought to fifth-/eleventh-century Nishapur, allowing him to contribute to the increasingly prevalent contemporary conversations regarding the future of Muslim societies. Whichever vision of al-Juwaynī the reader chooses to adopt, it is undeniable that his work was and remains a tour de force within the intellectual history of Islam.

Bibliography

Primary Sources

ʿAbd al-Jabbār, Abū al-Ḥasan. *al-Mughnī fī Abwāb al-Tawḥīd wa-l-ʿadl*. Edited by Muḥammad Muṣṭafā Ḥilmī. Cairo: al-Dār al-Miṣriyya Li-l-Taʾlīf wa-l-Nashr, 1960–69.

Abyārī, ʿAlī b. Ismāʿīl. *al-Taḥqīq wa-l-bayān fī sharḥ al-burhān fī uṣūl al-fiqh*. Doha: Wizārat al-Awqāf wa-l-Shuʾūn al-Islāmiyya, 2013.

Āmidī, Sayf al-Dīn. *al-Iḥkām fī uṣūl al-aḥkām*. Cairo: Maṭbaʿat Muḥammad ʿAlī Ṣubayḥ, 1917.

Anṣārī, Abū al-Qāsim. *al-Ghunya fī ʿilm al-kalām*. Edited by Muṣṭafā Ḥasnayn ʿAbd al-Hādī. Cairo: Dār al-Salām, 2010.

Baghdādī, ʿAbd al-Qāhir b. Ṭāhir al-Tamīmī. *Uṣūl al-dīn*. Istanbul: Maṭbaʿat al-Dawla, 1928.

Al-Farq bayna al-Firak: Moslem Schisms and Sects. Translated by Kate C. Seelye. New York: Columbia University Press, 1966.

Baghdādī, al-Khaṭīb. *al-Faqīh wa-l-mutafaqqih*. Edited by ʿĀdil b. Yusūf al-ʿAzāzī. Mecca: Dār Ibn al-Jawzī, 1996.

Bākharzī, Abū al-Ḥasan ʿAlī b. al-Ḥasan b. ʿAlī. *Dumyat al-qaṣr wa-ʿuṣrat ahl al-ʿaṣr*. Kuwait: Dār al-ʿUrūba, 1985.

Bāqillānī, Abū Bakr Muḥammad b. al-Ṭayyib b. *Kitāb Tamhīd al-awāʾil wa-talkhīṣ al-dalāʾil*. Beirut: al-Maktaba al-Sharqiyya, 1957.

al-Tamhīd fī al-radd ʿalā al-mulḥida al-muʿaṭṭila wa-l-rāfiḍa wa-l-khawārij wa-l-muʿtazila. Edited by Richard J. McCarthy. Baghdad: Publications of al-Ḥikma University of Baghdad, 1958.

al-Taqrīb wa-l-irshād. Beirut: al-Risāla, 1993.

Baṣrī, Abū al-Ḥusayn. *al-Muʿtamad fī uṣūl al-fiqh*. Damascus: al-Maʿhad al-ʿIlmī al-Faransī li-l-Dirāsāt al-ʿArabiyya, 1964.

Dhahabī, Shams al-Dīn Muḥammad b. Aḥmad. *Tārīkh al-Islām wa-wafayāt al-mashāhīr wa-l-aʿlām*. Edited by ʿUmar ʿAbd al-Salām Tadmurī. Beirut: Dār al-Kitāb al-ʿArabī, 1990.

Siyar aʿlām al-nubalāʾ. Edited by Muḥibb al-Dīn Abū Saʿīd ʿUmar b. Gharāma al-ʿAmrawi. Beirut: Dār al-Fikr, 1997.

Ghazālī, Abū Ḥāmid. *Shifāʾ al-ghalīl*. Baghdad: Maṭbāʿa al-Irshād, 1971.

al-Mustaṣfā. Mecca: al-Jāmīʿa al-Islāmiyya, 2008.

Ḥājj, Ibn al-Amīr. *al-Kāmil fī ikhtiṣār al-Shāmil*. Edited by ʿAbd al-Nāṣir ʿAbd al-Munʿim. Cairo: Dār al-Salām, 2010.

Ibn al-Athīr, ʿIzz al-Dīn. *al-Kāmil fī al-tārīkh*. Edited by ʿUmar ʿAbd al-Salām Tadmurī. Beirut: Dār al-Kitāb al-ʿArabī, 1997.

Ibn ʿAsākir, ʿAlī b. al-Ḥasan. *Tabyīn kadhib al-muftarī fī-mā nusiba ilā al-imām Abī al-Ḥasan al-Ashʿarī*. Edited by Muḥammad Zāhid al-Kawtharī. Damascus: al-Qudsī, 1928.

Tārīkh madīnat Dimashq. Edited by ʿAlī Shīrī. Beirut: Dār al-Fikr, 1995.

Ibn al-ʿImād. *Shadharāt al-dhahab fī akhbār man dhahab*. Beirut: al-Maktab al-Tijārī li-l-Ṭibāʿa wa-l-Nashr wa-l-Tawzīʿ, 1966.

Ibn Kathīr, Ismāʿīl b. ʿUmar. *al-Bidāya wa-l-nihāya*. Edited by Aḥmad ʿAbd al-Wahhāb al-Futayḥ. Cairo: Dār al-Ḥadīth, 1992.

Ibn Khallikān. *Wafayāt al-aʿyān wa-anbāʾ abnāʾ al-zamān*. Edited by Iḥsān ʿAbbās, Wadād Qāḍī, and Mūsā ʿIzz al-Dīn ʿUmar Aḥmad. Beirut: Dār Ṣādir, 1977.

Ibn Mattawayh. *Kitāb al-majmūʿ fī al-muḥīṭ bi-l-taklīf*. Edited by J. J. Houben. Beirut: Imprimerie Catholique, 1965.

Ibn Taghrībardī, Abū al-Maḥāsin Yūsuf. *al-Nujūm al-zāhira fī mulūk Miṣr wa-l-Qāhira*. Cairo: al-Muʾassasa al-Miṣriyya al-ʿĀmma li-l-Taʾlīf wa-l-Ṭibāʿa wa-l-Nashr, 1963.

Ibn Taymiyya, Taqī al-Dīn Aḥmad b. *ʿAbd al-Ḥalīm. Kitāb al-Radd ʿalā al-manṭiqiyyīn*. Edited by ʿAbd al-Ṣamad Sharaf al-Dīn al-Kutubī. Bombay: Qayyimah Press, 1949.

ʿIyād, Al-Qāḍī. *Tartīb al-madārik wa-taqrīb al-masālik li-maʿrifat Aʿlām Madhhab Mālik*. Beirut: Dār al-Kutub al-ʿIlmiyya, 1998.

Jawzī, ʿAbd al-Raḥmān b. ʿAlī Ibn. *al-Muntaẓam fī tārīkh al-mulūk wa-l-umam*. Edited by Muḥammad ʿAbd al-Qādir ʿAṭā and Ibrāhīm Shams al-Dīn. Beirut: Dār al-Kutub al-ʿIlmiyya, 1992.

Juwaynī, Abū al-Maʿālī ʿAbd al-Malik. *Mughīth al-khalq fī tarjīḥ al-qawl al-ḥaqq*. Cairo: al-Maṭbaʿa al-Miṣriyya, 1934.

al-ʿAqīda al-Niẓāmiyya. Edited by Muḥammad Zāhid al-Kawtharī. Cairo: Maktabat al-Khānjī, 1948.

Irshād ilā qawāṭiʿ al-adilla fī uṣūl al-iʿtiqād. Edited by Muḥammad Yusūf Mūsā and Shaykh ʿAlī ʿAbd al-Munʿim ʿAbd al-Ḥamīd. Cairo: Maktabat al-Khānjī, 1950.

al-Shāmil fī uṣūl al-dīn. Edited by ʿAlī al-Nashshār, Fayṣal ʿAwn, and Suhayr Mukhtār. Alexandria: Munshaʾāt al-Maʿārif, 1969.

al-Burhān fī uṣūl al-fiqh. Edited by ʿAbd al-ʿAẓīm al-Dīb. Cairo: Dār al-Anṣār, 1979; reprint, Doha: Wizārat al-Awqāf wa-l-Shuʾūn al-Islāmiyya, 1997.

al-Kāfiya fī al-jadal. Edited by Fawqiyya Ḥusayn Maḥmūd. Cairo: ʿIsā al-Bābī al-Ḥalabī, 1979.

Ghiyāth al-umam fī iltiyāth al-ẓulam. Edited by ʿAbd al-ʿAẓīm al-Dīb. Qatar: Kulliyyat al-Sharīʿa, 1980.

al-Shāmil fī Uṣūl al-Dīn: The Exposition of al-Bāqillānī's Commentary on the Kitāb al-Luma'; Some Additional Portions of the Text. Edited by Richard Frank. Tehran: McGill University/Tehran University, 1981.
al-Talkhīṣ fī uṣūl al-fiqh. Edited by 'Abd Allāh al-Nībālī and Shubbayr al-'Amrī. Mecca: Maktabat Dār al-Bāz, 1996.
al-'Aqīda al-Niẓāmiyya. Edited by Muḥammad al-Zubaydī. Beirut: Dār al-Sabīl al-Rashād, 2003.
Nihāyat al-maṭlab fī dirāyat al-madhhab. Edited by 'Abd al-'Aẓīm al-Dīb. Doha: Dār al-Minhāj/Wizārat al-Awqāf al-Qaṭariyya, 2007.
Maḥallī, Jalāl al-Dīn. *Sharḥ al-Waraqāt fī 'ilm uṣūl al-fiqh 'alā Waraqāt Abī al-Ma'ālī Imām al-Ḥaramayn*. Mecca: Maktabat Nazār Muṣṭafā al-Bāz, 1996.
Malāḥimī, Rukn al-Dīn Ibn. *al-Fā'iq fi Uṣūl al-dīn*. Edited by Wilferd Madelung and Martin McDermott. Tehran and Berlin: Iranian Institute of Philosophy and Freie Universität Berlin, 2007.
Māwardī, Abū al-Ḥasan 'Ali b. Muḥammad b. Ḥabīb. *al-Aḥkām al-sulṭāniyya*. Kuwait: Maktaba Dār Ibn Qutayba, 1989.
Muqaddasī, Muḥammad b. Aḥmad Shams al-Dīn. *Aḥsan al-taqāsīm fī ma'rifat al-aqālīm*. Edited by M. J. de Goeje. Leiden: E. J. Brill, 1967.
Nadīm, Muḥammad Isḥāq Ibn. *Kitāb al-Fihrist*. Edited by Gustav Flügel. Beirut: Khayat, 1964.
Rāzī, Fakhr al-Dīn. *al-Maḥṣūl fī 'ilm uṣūl al-fiqh*. Edited by Ṭāhā Jābir al-'Alwānī. Riyadh: Imam Ibn Sa'ūd Islamic University, 1979.
Sarakhsī, Abū Bakr Muḥammad b. Aḥmad. *Uṣūl al-Sarakhsī*. Edited by Abū al-Wafā' al-Afghānī. Hyderabad: Lajnat Iḥyā' al-Ma'ārif al-Nu'māniyya, 1953.
Shāfi'ī, Muḥammad b. Idrīs. *Kitāb al-Umm*. Bulaq: al-Maṭba'a al-Kubrā al-Amīriyya, 1907–8.
Shahrastani, Muhammad B. 'Abd al-Karim. *Kitab al-milal wa-l-nihal: Book of Religious and Philosophical Sects*. Edited by William Cureton. London: Society for the Publication of Oriental Texts, 1842–46.
Shahrazūrī, Abū 'Amr 'Uthmān b. 'Abd al-Rahmān. *Muqaddimat Ibn al-Ṣalāḥ fī 'ulūm al-ḥadīth*. Cairo: Dār al-Ma'ārif, 1990.
Subkī, Tāj al-Dīn. *Ṭabaqāt al-Shāfi'iyya al-kubrā*. Edited by Maḥmūd Muḥammad al-Ṭaḥānī and 'Abd al-Fattāḥ Muḥammad al-Ḥilw. Cairo: 'Īsā al-Bābī al-Ḥalabī, 1965.
Suyūṭī, Abū al-Faḍl 'Abd al-Raḥmān ibn Abī Bakr ibn Muḥammad Jalāl al-Dīn al-Khuḍayrī. *al-Ashbāh wa-l-naẓā'ir*. Cairo: Ma'had al-Makhṭūṭāt al-'Arabiyya, 1998.
'Uthmān, 'Abd Al-Karīm, ed. *Sharḥ al-Uṣūl al-Khamsa*. Cairo: Maktabat Wahba, 1965.
Zarkashī, Badr al-Dīn Muḥammad b. Bahādur. *al-Baḥr al-muḥīṭ fī uṣūl al-fiqh*. Edited by 'Abd al-Qādir 'Abd Allāh al-'Ānī, 5:240. Kuwait: Dār al-Ṣafwa li-Wizārat al-Awqāf, 1992.

Secondary Sources

Abdullah, Ismail Haji. "The Influence of Imam al-Juwaynī on the Theology of Imam al-Ghazālī." PhD diss., University of St. Andrews, 1996.

Adang, Camilla. "Ibn Ḥazm on Homosexuality: A Case-Study of Ẓāhirī Legal Methodology." *Al-Qanṭara* 24, no. 1 (2003): 5–31.

"'This Day I Have Perfected Your Religion for You': A Ẓāhirī Conception of Religious Authority." In *Speaking for Islam: Religious Authority in Muslim Societies*, edited by Gudrun Krämer and Sabine Schmidtke. Leiden: Brill, 2006.

Ahmad, Ahmad Atif. *Structural Interrelations of Theory and Practice in Islamic Law*. Leiden: Brill, 2006.

The Fatigue of the Sharīʿa. New York: Palgrave Macmillan, 2012.

Ali, Kecia. *Sexual Ethics and Islam: Feminist Reflections on Quran, Hadith and Jurisprudence*. London: Oneworld, 2016.

Allard, Michel. *Le Problème des attributs divins dans la doctrine d'al-Ashari et ses premiers grands disciples*. Beirut: Imprimerie Catholique, 1965.

Textes apologetiques de Guwayni (m. 478/1085). Beirut: Dar el-Mashreq, 1968.

Anjum, Ovamir. *Politics, Law, and Community in Islamic Thought: The Taymiyyan Moment*. Cambridge: Cambridge University Press, 2012.

Arberry, A. J. *Revelation and Reason in Islam*. New York: Routledge, 1957.

Arjomand, Said. "Crisis of the Imamate and the Institution of Occultation in Twelver Shiʿism: A Sociohistorical Perspective." *International Journal of Middle East Studies* 28, no. 4 (1996): 491–515.

"The Law, Agency and Policy in Medieval Islamic Society: Development of the Institutions of Learning from the Tenth to the Fifteenth Century." *Comparative Studies in Society and History* 41, no. 2 (1999): 262–93

The Shadow of God and the Hidden Imam. Chicago: University of Chicago Press, 2010.

Audi, Robert. "The Sources of Knowledge." In *The Oxford Handbook of Epistemology*, edited by Paul K. Moser. Oxford: Oxford University Press, 2002.

Bedir, Murteza. "An Early Response to al-Shāfiʿī: ʿĪsā ibn Abān on the Prophetic Report." *Islamic Law and Society* 9, no. 3 (2002): 285–311.

Bennett, David. "The Muʿtazilite Movement (I): The Origins of the Muʿtazila." In *Oxford Handbook of Islamic Theology*, edited by Sabine Schmidtke, 142–58. Oxford: Oxford University Press, 2016.

Berkey, Jonathan. *The Formation of Islam: Religion and Society in the Near East, 600–1800*. Cambridge: Cambridge University Press, 2002.

BonJour, Lawrence. "Recent Work on the Internalism–Externalism Controversy." In *The Blackwell Companion to Epistemology*, edited by Jonathan Dancy, Ernest Sosa, and Matthias Setup, 33–42. Chichester: Wiley-Blackwell, 2010.

Brown, Daniel. "The Triumph of Scripturalism: The Doctrine of *Naskh* and Its Modern Critics." In *The Shaping of an American Islamic Discourse: A Memorial to Fazlur Rahman*, edited by Earle Waugh and Frederick Denny, 49–66. Atlanta: Scholars Press, 1997.

Brown, Jonathan. *The Canonization of al-Bukharī and Muslim: The Formation and Function of the Sunnī* Ḥadīth *Canon*. Leiden: Brill, 2007.

"Did the Prophet Say It or Not? The Literal, Historical and Effective Truth of Hadith." *Journal of the American Oriental Society* 129, no. 2 (2009): 259–85.

Hadith: Muhammad's Legacy in the Medieval and Modern World. London: Oneworld, 2009.
Burton, John. *The Sources of Islamic Law: Islamic Theories of Abrogation*. Edinburgh: Edinburgh University Press, 1990.
"Abrogation." In *Encyclopaedia of the Qur'ān*, edited by Jane Dammen McAuliffe, 11–19. Leiden: Brill, 2001.
Bosworth, Clifford. *The Ghaznavids*. Edinburgh: Edinburgh University Press, 1963.
"The Political and Dynastic History of the Iranian World, Vol. 5: The Saljuk and Mongol Periods." In *Cambridge History of Iran*, edited by J. A. Boyle. Cambridge: Cambridge University Press, 1968.
Islamic Dynasties. Edinburgh: Clark Constable, 1980.
Böwering, Gerhard. *Islamic Political Thought: An Introduction*. Princeton: Princeton University Press, 2015.
Bulliet, Richard. "A Quantitative Approach to Medieval Muslim Biographical Dictionaries." *Journal of the Economic and Social History of the Orient* 13 (1970): 195–211.
The Patricians of Nishapur. Cambridge: Cambridge University Press, 1972.
"The Political-Religious History of Nishapur in the Eleventh Century." In *Islamic Civilization 950–1150*, edited by D. S. Richards, 71–91. Oxford: Bruno Cassirer, 1973.
"Numismatic Evidence for the Relationship between Ṭughril Beg and Chaghrī Beg." In *Near Eastern Numismatics, Iconography, Epigraphy and History: Studies in Honor of George C. Miles*, edited by Dickran K. Kouymjian, 289–96. Beirut: American University of Beirut, 1974.
Butterworth, Charles. *The Political Aspects of Islamic Philosophy: Essays in Honor of Muhsin S. Mahdi*. Cambridge, MA: Harvard University Press, 1992.
Cahen, Claude. "The Historiography of the Seljuqid Period." In *Historians of the Middle East*, edited by Bernard Lewis and Peter Holt, 59–78. London: Oxford University Press, 1962.
Carothers, Thomas. "The Rule of Law Revival." *Foreign Affairs* 77, no. 2 (1998): 95–106.
Cook, David. *Studies in Muslim Apocalyptic*. Princeton: Darwin Press, 1966.
Coulson, Noel J. *A History of Islamic Law*. Edinburgh: Edinburgh University Press, 1964.
Cover, Robert. "The Supreme Court, 1982 Term – Foreword: Nomos and Narrative." *Harvard Law Review* 4, no. 28 (1983): 4–68.
Crone, Patricia. "*Shūrā* as an Elective Institution." *Quaderni di Studi Arabi* 19 (2001): 3–39.
God's Rule – Government and Islam: Six Centuries of Medieval Islamic Political Thought. New York: Columbia University Press, 2004.
al-Dīb, ʿAbd al-ʿAẓīm. *Imām al-Ḥaramayn*. Kuwait: Dār al-Qalam, 1981.
Dickinson, Eerik. *An Introduction to the Science of the Ḥadīth*. Reading: Garnet, 2006.
Dodge, Bayard. *Al-Azhar: A Millennium of Muslim Learning*. Washington, DC: Middle East Institute, 1974.

Donner, Fred. "The Historical Context of the Qur'an." In *The Cambridge Companion to the Qur'an*, edited by Jane D. McAuliffe, 21–39. Cambridge: Cambridge University Press, 2006.

"The Qurʾān in Recent Scholarship – Challenges and Desiderata." In *The Qurʾān in Its Historical Context*, edited by Gabriel S. Reynolds, 29–50. Abingdon: Routledge, 2008.

"The Historian, the Believers, and the Qurʾān." In *New Perspectives on the Qurʾān*, edited by Gabriel S. Reynolds, 25–37. London: Routledge, 2011.

Dutton, Yasin. "*ʿAmal v. Ḥadīth* in Islamic Law: The Case of *Sadl al-Yadayn* (Holding One's Hands by One's Sides) When Doing the Prayer." *Islamic Law and Society* 3, no. 1 (1996): 13–40.

The Origins of Islamic Law: The Quran, the Muwaṭṭaʾ and Madinan ʿAmal. London: Routledge, 2002.

Original Islam: Mālik and the Madhhab of Madina. London: Routledge, 2012.

El Fadl, Khaled Abou. *Speaking in God's Name: Islamic Law, Authority and Women*. Oxford: Oneworld, 2001.

El Omari, Racha. "Accommodation and Resistance: Classical Muʿtazilites on Ḥadīth." *Journal of Near Eastern Studies* 71, no. 2 (2012): 234–35.

"The Muʿtazilite Movement (I): The Origins of the Muʿtazila." In *Oxford Handbook of Islamic Theology*, edited by Sabine Schmidtke, 130–41. Oxford: Oxford University Press, 2016.

The Theology of Abū l-Qāsim al-Balkhī/al-Kaʿbī (d. 319/931). Leiden: Brill, 2016.

El Shamsy, Ahmed. "The Wisdom of God's Law: Two Theories." In *Islamic Law in Theory: Studies on Jurisprudence in Honor of Bernard Weiss*, edited by Robert Gleave and Kevin Reinhart, 19–37. Leiden: Brill, 2014.

The Canonization of Islamic Law: A Social and Intellectual History. Cambridge: Cambridge University Press, 2015.

"Bridging the Gap: Two Early Texts of Islamic Legal Theory," *Journal of the American Oriental Society* 137, no. 3 (2017): 505–36.

Emon, Anver. "The Most Likely to Know the Law: Objectivity, Authority and Interpretation in Islamic Law." *Hebraic Political Studies* 4, no. 4 (2009): 431–38.

Religious Pluralism and Islamic Law: Dhimmīs and Others in the Empire of Law. Oxford: Oxford University Press, 2012.

Fadel, Mohammad. "The Social Logic of *Taqlīd* and the Rise of the *Mukhtaṣar*." *Islamic Law and Society* 3, no. 2 (1996): 193–233.

Fasāʾī, Ḥasan-i. *History of Persia under Qajar Rule*. Translated by Heribert Busse. New York: Columbia University Press, 1972.

Frank, Richard. "Remarks on the Early Development of Kalām." In Congresso di studi arabi e islamici, *Atti del terzo Congresso di studi arabi e islamici. Ravello, 1–6 settembre 1966*. Napoli: Istituto universitario orientale, 1967.

"Several Fundamental Assumptions of the Baṣran School of the Muʿtazila." *Studia Islamica*, no. 3 (1971): 5–18.

"Reason and Revealed Law: A Sample of Parallels and Divergences in Kalām and Falsafa." In *Recherches d'Islamologie: Recueil d'articles offerts à Georges C. Anawati et Louis Gardet*, edited by Georges C. Anawati and Louis Gardet, 123–38. Louvain: Peeters, 1978.

"Two Islamic Views of Agency," In *La Notion de liberté au Moyen Âge: Islam, Byzance, Occident*, edited by George Makdisi, Dominique Sourdel, and Janine Sourdel-Thomine, 37–49. Paris: Les Belles Lettres, 1985.

"Knowledge and *Taqlīd*: The Foundations of Religious Belief in Classical Ash'arism." *Journal of the American Oriental Society* 109, no. 1 (1989): 37–62.

Creation and the Cosmic System: Al-Ghazālī and Avicenna. Heidelberg: Winter, 1992.

Al-Ghazālī and the Ash'arite School. Durham, NC: Duke University Press, 1994.

"Currents and Countercurrents in the Mu'tazila, Ash'arites and al-Ghazālī." In *Islam: Essays on Scripture, Thought and Society: A Festschrift in Honour of Anthony H. Johns*, edited by Peter G. Riddell and Tony Street, 113–34. Leiden: Brill, 1997.

"The Non-Existent and the Possible in Classical Ash'arite Thinking." *Mélanges de l'Institut dominicain d'études orientales*, 24 (2000): 1–37.

Early Islamic Theology: The Mu'tazilites and al-Ash'arī. Vol. 2 of *Texts and Studies on the Development and History of Kalām*, edited by Dimitri Gutas. London: Routledge, 2007.

Classical Islamic Theology: The Ash'arites. Vol. 3 of *Texts and Studies on the Development and History of Kalām*, edited by Dimitri Gutas. Aldershot: Ashgate, 2008.

Fricker, Miranda. "Skepticism and the Genealogy of Knowledge: Situating Epistemology in Time." In *Social Epistemology*, edited by Adrian Haddock, Alan Millar, and Duncan Pritchard, 51–68. Oxford: Oxford University Press, 2010.

Frye, Richard, ed. *Histories of Nishapur*. Cambridge, MA: Harvard University Press, 1965.

Fuller, Lon. *The Morality of Law*. New Haven, CT: Yale University Press, 1969.

Geertz, Clifford. *Local Knowledge: Further Essays in Interpretive Anthropology*. New York: Basic Books Classics, 1985.

Gibb, Hamilton. "Al-Māwardī's Theory of the Caliphate." In *Studies on Islamic Civilization*, edited by Stanford Shaw and William Polk, 291–302. Boston: Beacon Press, 1968.

"The Heritage of Islam in the Modern World (1)." *International Journal of Middle East Studies* 1, no. 1 (1970): 3–17.

Studies on the Civilization of Islam. Princeton: Princeton University Press, 1982.

Gimaret, Daniel. "Pour servir à la lecture des Masā'il d'Abū Rašīd al-Nīsābūrī." *Bulletin d'études orientales*, no. 60 (2011): 11–38.

Gilliot, Claude. "Quand la théologie s'allié à l'histoire: Triomphe et échec du rationalisme musulman à travers l'oeuvre d'al-Juwaynī." *Arabica* 39, no. 2 (1992): 241–60.

Gleave, Robert. *Islam and Literalism: Literal Meaning and Interpretation in Islamic Legal Theory*. Edinburgh: Edinburgh University Press, 2013.

Goldman, Alvin. "Why Social Epistemology Is Real Epistemology." In *Social Epistemology*, edited by Adrian Haddock, Alan Millar, and Duncan Pritchard, 1–28. Oxford: Oxford University Press, 2010.

Goldziher, Ignaz. *The Ẓāhirīs: Their Doctrine and Their History*. Leiden: Brill, 2007.

Griffel, Frank. *Al-Ghazalī's Philosophical Theology*. Oxford: Oxford University Press, 2009.

Gutas, Dimitri. *Greek Thought, Arabic Culture: The Graeco-Arabic Translation Movement in Baghdad and Early ʿAbbasid Society*. London: Routledge, 1998.

Gwynne, Rosalind. "Al-Jubbāʾī, al-Ashʿarī and the Three Brothers: The Uses of Fiction." *Muslim World* 75, nos. 3–4 (2007): 132–61.

Hallaq, Wael. "Caliphs, Jurists and the Saljūqs in the Political Thought of Juwaynī." *Muslim World* 74 (1984): 26–41.

"Was the Gate of Ijtihad Closed?" *International Journal of Middle East Studies* 16, no. 1 (1984): 3–41.

"On the Authoritativeness of Sunni Consensus." *International Journal of Middle Eastern Studies* 18 (1986): 427–54.

"On the Origins of the Controversy about the Existence of Mujtahids and the Gate of Ijtihād." *Studia Islamica*, no. 63 (1986): 129–41.

"The Development of Logical Structure in Sunni Legal Theory." *Der Islam* 64 (1987): 42–67.

"Non-Analogical Arguments in Sunnī Juridical *Qiyās*." *Arabica* 36 (1989): 286–306.

"Logic, Formal Arguments and Formalization of Arguments in Sunnī Legal Thought." In *Islamic Law and Jurisprudence*, edited by Nicholas Heer, 3–31. Seattle: University of Washington Press, 1990.

"Was al-Shafiʿi the Master Architect of Islamic Jurisprudence?" *International Journal of Middle East Studies* 25, no. 4 (1993): 587–605.

"Iftaʾ and Ijtihad in Sunni Legal Theory: A Developmental Account." In *Islamic Legal Interpretation: Muftis and Their Fatwas*, edited by Muhammad Khalid Masud, Brinkley Messick, and David S. Powers, 33–44. Cambridge, MA: Harvard University Press, 1996.

A History of Islamic Legal Theories: An Introduction to Sunnī Uṣūl al-Fiqh. Cambridge: Cambridge University Press, 1997.

"The Authenticity of Prophetic Ḥadîth: A Pseudo-Problem." *Studia Islamica*, no. 89 (1999): 75–90.

"From Regional to Personal Schools of Law? A Reevaluation." *Islamic Law and Society* 8, no. 1 (2001): 1–26.

The Origins and Evolution of Islamic Law. Cambridge: Cambridge University Press, 2005.

Halm, Heinz. "Der Wesir al-Kunduri und die Fitna von Nishapur." *Die Welt des Orients* 6, 1971: 205–33.

Shiʿism. Edinburgh: Edinburgh University Press, 2004.

Hasan, Ahmad. "The Argument for the Authority of Ijmāʿ." *Islamic Studies* 10, no. 1 (1971): 39–52.

"The Justification of Qiyās." *Islamic Studies* 20, no. 3 (1981): 201–26.

Heck, Paul. "Jovayni, Emām-al-Ḥaramayn." In *Encyclopaedia Iranica* (New York, 1996–), www.iranicaonline.org/articles/jovayni-emam-al-haramayn.

Skepticism in Classical Islam. London: Routledge, 2013.

Heemskerk, Margaretha T. *Suffering in Mu'tazilite Theology*. Leiden: Brill, 2000.
"'Abd al-Jabbār b. Aḥmad al-Hamadhānī." In *Encyclopedia of Islam*, 3rd edition, edited by Kate Fleet, Gudrun Krämer, Denis Matringe, John Nawas, and Everett Rowson. Leiden: Brill, 2007.
Hess, Andrew. "Islamic Civilization and the Legend of Political Failure." *Journal of Near Eastern Studies* 44, no. 1 (1985): 27–39.
Hītū, Ḥasan, *al-Imām al-Shīrāzī*. Damascus: Dār al-Fikr, 1980.
Hourani, George. "Two Theories of Value in Medieval Islam." *Muslim World* 50, no. 4 (1969): 269.
Islamic Rationalism: The Ethics of 'Abd al-Jabbār. Oxford: Clarendon Press, 1971.
Reason and Tradition in Islamic Ethics. Cambridge: Cambridge University Press, 2007.
Hurvitz, Nimrod. "Schools of Law and Historical Context: Re-Examining the Formation of the Ḥanbalī Madhhab." *Islamic Law and Society* 7, no. 1 (2000): 37–64.
"From Scholarly Circles to Mass Movements: The Formation of Legal Communities in Islamic Societies." *American Historical Review* 108, no. 4 (2003): 985–1008.
Competing Texts: The Relationship between al-Māwardī's and Abū Ya'lā's "al-Aḥkām al-Sulṭāniyya." Cambridge, MA: Islamic Legal Studies Program, Harvard Law School, 2007.
Ibish, Yusuf. "Life and Works of al-Bāqillānī." *Islamic Studies* 4, no. 3 (1965): 225–36.
The Political Doctrine of al-Bāqillānī. Beirut: American University of Beirut, 1966.
Ibrahim, Ahmed Fekry. *Pragmatism in Islamic Law: A Social and Intellectual History*. Syracuse, NY: Syracuse University Press, 2015.
Jackson, Sherman. *Islamic Law and the State: The Constitutional Jurisprudence of Shihāb al-Dīn al-Qarāfī*. Leiden: Brill, 1996.
"Taqlīd, Legal Scaffolding and the Scope of Legal Injunctions in Post-Formative Theory." *Islamic Law and Society* 3, no. 2 (1996): 165–92.
"The Alchemy of Domination: Some Ash'arite Responses to Mu'tazilite Ethics." *International Journal of Middle East Studies* 21, no. 2 (1999): 185–201.
"Literalism, Empiricism and Induction: Apprehending and Concretizing Islamic Law's Maqāsid al-Sharī'a in the Modern World." *Michigan State Law Review* (2006): 1469–86.
Johansen, Baber. *Contingency in a Sacred Law: Legal and Ethical Norms in the Muslim Fiqh*. Leiden: Brill, 1999.
Jurgen, Paul. "The Seljuk Conquest(s) of Nishapur: A Reappraisal." *Iranian Studies* 38, no. 4 (2005): 575–77.
Ka Ka Khel, Muhammad Nazeer. "The Conceptual and Institutional Development of Shura in Early Islam." *Islamic Studies* 19, no. 4 (1980): 271–82.
Kennedy, Hugh. *The Prophet and the Age of the Caliphates*. London: Longman, 1986.
When Baghdad Ruled the Muslim World: The Rise and Fall of Islam's Greatest Dynasty. Boston: De Capo Press, 2006.

Kerr, Malcolm. *Islamic Reform*. Berkeley: University of California Press, 1966.
Khadduri, Majid, trans. *Al-Shāfiʿī's Risāla*. Cambridge: Islamic Texts Society, 1987.
Klopfer, Helmut. *Das Dogma des Imam al-Haramain al-Juwayni und sein Werk al-Aqidat an-Nizamiya*. Wiesbaden: Harrassowitz, 1958.
Klopfer, Helmut. ed. *al-Shāmil Fī Uṣūl al-dīn*. Cairo: Dār al-ʿArab, 1959.
Laher, Suheil Ismail. "Twisted Threads: Genesis, Development and Application of the Term and Concept of Tawātur in Islamic Thought." PhD diss., Harvard University, 2014.
Lambton, Ann. *State and Government in Medieval Islam*. Oxford: Oxford University Press, 1981.
"The Dilemma of Government in Islamic Persia: The *Siyāsat-nāma* of Niẓām al-Mulk." *Iran* 22 (1984): 55–66.
Lowry, Joseph. *Early Islamic Legal Theory: The Risāla of Muḥammad ibn Idrīs al-Shāfiʿī*. Leiden: Brill, 2007.
"Some Preliminary Observations on al-Šāfiʿī and Later *Uṣūl al-Fiqh*: The Case of the Term *Bayān*." *Arabica* 55, nos. 5–6 (2008): 505–27.
"The Prophet as Lawgiver and Legal Authority." In *The Cambridge Companion to Muḥammad*, edited by Jonathan Brockopp, 83–102. Cambridge: Cambridge University Press, 2010.
trans. *The Epistle on Legal Theory: A Translation of al-Shāfiʿī's Risālah*. New York: New York University Press, 2013.
Lucas, Scott. "Where Are All the Legal *Ḥadīth*?" *Islamic Law and Society* 8, no. 3 (2001): 408–31.
"Principles of Traditionist Jurisprudence Reconsidered." *Muslim World* 100, no. 1 (2010): 145–56.
McCarthy, Richard. *The Theology of al-Ashʿarī*. Beirut: Imprimerie Catholique, 1953.
Macdonald, Duncan B. *Development of Muslim Theology, Jurisprudence, and Constitutional Theory*. New York: Charles Scribner's Sons, 1903.
Madelung, Wilferd. "Abū l-Ḥusayn al-Baṣrī." In *The Encyclopedia of Islam*, 2nd edition, edited by P. Bearman, Th. Bianquis, C. E. Bosworth, E. Van Donzel, and W. P. Heinrichs. Leiden: Brill, 1960–2005.
"The Spread of Maturidism and the Turks." In *Religious Schools and Sects in Medieval Islam*, 109–68. London: Valorium Reprints, 1985.
Religious Trends in Early Iran. Albany: State University of New York Press, 1988.
Review of *Before Revelation*, by Kevin Reinhart. *Bulletin of the School of Oriental and African Studies* 60, no. 1 (1997): 127–28.
Al-Ṣāḥib Ibn ʿAbbād: Promoter of Rational Theology: Two Mutazili Kalam Texts from the Cairo Geniza. Edited by Wilferd Madelung and Sabine Schmidtke. Leiden: Brill, 2016.
Makdisi, George. "Muslim Institutions of Learning in Eleventh Century Baghdād." *Bulletin of the School of Oriental and African Studies* 24 (1960): 1–56.
"Ashʿarī and the Ashʿarites in Islamic Religious History, Part 1." *Studia Islamica*, no. 17 (1962): 37–80;
"Ashʿarī and the Ashʿarites in Islamic Religious History, Part 2." *Studia Islamica*, no. 18 (1963): 19–39.

"Madrasa and University in the Middle Ages." *Studia Islamica*, no. 32 (1970): 255–64.
"The Marriage of Tughril Beg." *International Journal of Middle East Studies* 1 (1970): 259–75.
The Rise of Colleges: Institutions of Learning in Islam and the West. Edinburgh: Edinburgh University Press, 1981.
"The Juridical Theology of Shāfiʿī: Origins and Significance of *Uṣūl al-Fiqh*." *Studia Islamica*, no. 59 (1984): 40–43.
Mahdi, Muhsin. *Al-Farābī and the Foundations of Islamic Political Thought*. Chicago: University of Chicago Press, 2001.
Maḥmūd, Fawqiyya. *al-Juwaynī: Imām al-Ḥaramayn*. Cairo: al-Dār al-Miṣriyya, 1964.
Malamud, Margaret. "The Politics of Heresy in Medieval Khurasan: The Karramiyya in Nishapur." *Iranian Studies* 27, nos. 1–4 (1994): 37–51.
"Sufi Organizations and Structures of Authority in Medieval Nishapur." *International Journal of Middle East Studies* 26, no. 3 (1994): 427–42.
Massignon, Loius. *The Passion of al-Hallāj*. Princeton: Princeton University Press, 1982.
Masud, Muhammad Khalid, Brinkley Messick, and David Powers. "Muftīs, Fatwas and Islamic Legal Interpretation." In *Islamic Legal Interpretation: Muftis and Their Fatwas*, edited by Muhammad Khalid Masud, Brinkley Messick, and David Powers, 3–32. Cambridge, MA: Harvard University Press, 1996.
Melchert, Christopher. *The Formation of the Sunni Schools of Law, 9th–10th Centuries C.E.* Leiden: Brill, 1997.
"The Traditionist-Jurisprudents and the Framing of Islamic Law." *Islamic Law and Society* 8, no. 3 (2001): 383–406.
"Qur'anic Abrogation across the Ninth Century: Shāfiʿī, Abū ʿUbaid, Muḥāsibī, and Ibn Qutaibah." In *Studies in Islamic Legal Theory*, edited by Bernard G. Weiss, 75–98. Leiden: Brill, 2002.
"Aḥmad ibn Ḥanbal and the Qur'an." *Journal of Qur'anic Studies*, 6, no. 2 (2004): 22–34.
Mikhail, Hanna. *Politics and Revelation: Māwardī and After*. Edinburgh: Edinburgh University Press, 1995.
Mitter, Ulrike. "Unconditional Manumission of Slaves in Early Islamic Law: A Ḥadīth Analysis." *Der Islam* 78, no. 1 (2001): 35–72.
Nagel, Tilman. *History of Islamic Theology*. Princeton: Markus Wiener, 2009.
Nasser, Shady Hekmat. *The Transmission of the Variant Readings of the Qurʾān: The Problem of Tawātur and the Emergence of Shawādhdh*. Leiden: Brill, 2013.
Nguyen, Martin. "The Confluence and Construction of Traditions: Al-Qushayrī and the Intersection of Qurʾānic Exegesis, Theology and Sufism." PhD diss., Harvard University, 2009.
Opwis, Felicitas. *Maṣlaḥa and the Purpose of the Law*. Leiden: Brill, 2010.
Ormsby, Eric. Review of *Before Revelation*, by Kevin Reinhart. *Islamic Law and Society* 5, no. 1 (1998): 118–23.
Osman, Amr. *The Ẓāhirī Madhhab: A Textualist Theory of Islamic Law*. Leiden: Brill, 2014.

Peters, Guy, "Governance as Political Theory." *Jerusalem Papers in Regulation and Governance* 22 (2010): 1–23.

Peters, Johannes Maria. *God's Created Speech: A Study in the Speculative Theology of ʿAbd al-Jabbār*. Leiden: E. J. Brill, 1976.

Peters, Rudolph. *Crime and Punishment in Islamic Law*. Cambridge: Cambridge University Press, 2005.

Powers, David. *Studies in the Qurʾān and Ḥadīth: The Formation of the Islamic Law of Inheritance*. Berkeley: University of California Press, 1986.

"The Exegetical Genre *Nāsikh al-Qurʾān wa Mansūkhuhu*." In *Approaches to the History of the Interpretation of the Qurʾān*, edited by Andrew Rippin, 117–38. New York: Oxford University Press, 1988.

Qadhi, Yasir. "Salafī-Ashʿarī Polemics of the 3rd and 4th Islamic Centuries." *Muslim World* 106, no. 3 (2016): 433–47.

Rabb, Intisar. "Islamic Legal Minimalism: Legal Maxims and Lawmaking When Jurists Disappear." In *Law and Tradition in Classical Islamic Thought: Studies in Honor of Professor Hossein Modarressi*, edited by Asma Sayeed, Najam Haider, Michael Cook, and Intisar Rabb, 145–66. New York: Palgrave Macmillan, 2014.

Ramic, Sukri. *Language and the Interpretation of Islamic Law*. Cambridge: Islamic Texts Society, 2005.

Reinhart, Kevin. *Before Revelation: The Boundaries of Muslim Moral Thought*. Albany: State University of New York Press, 1995.

Raz, Joseph. "The Rule of Law and Its Virtues." *Law Quarterly Review* 93 (1977): 195–211.

Rhodes, R. A. W. "The New Governance: Governing without Government." *Political Studies* 44 (1996): 652–53.

Richards, D. S. *The Annals of the Saljuk Turks: Selections from al-Kāmil fi'l Tārīkh of ʿIzz al-Dīn b. al-Athīr*. New York: Routledge, 2002.

Rippin, Andrew. "Al-Zuhrī, *Naskh al-Qurʾān* and the Problem of Early *Tafsīr* Texts." *Bulletin of the School of Oriental and African Studies* 47, no. 1 (1984): 22–43.

"The Exegetical Literature of Abrogation: Form and Content." In *Studies in Islamic and Middle Eastern Texts and Traditions in Memory of Norman Calder*, edited by G. R. Hawting, J. A. Mojaddedi, and Alexander Samely, 213–31. Oxford: Oxford University Press, 2000.

"Revelation and Canon." In *Quranic Studies: Sources and Methods of Scriptural Interpretation*, edited by John Wansbrough. Amherst, NY: Prometheus Books, 2002.

Rizvi, Sajid. *Niẓām al-Mulk: His Contribution to Statecraft, Political Theory and the Art of Government*. Lahore: Sheikh Muhammad Ashraf, 1978.

Rosenthal, Erwin. *Political Thought in Medieval Islam*. Cambridge: Cambridge University Press, 1958.

Rosenthal, Franz. *Knowledge Triumphant*. Leiden: Brill, 2007.

Sabra, Adam. "Ibn Ḥazm's Literalism: A Critique of Islamic Legal Theory – Part 1." *Al-Qanṭara* 28, no. 1 (2007): 7–40.

"Ibn Ḥazm's Literalism: A Critique of Islamic Legal Theory – Part 2." *Al-Qanṭara* 28, no. 2 (2007): 307–48.

Saflo, Mohammad. *Al-Juwaynī's Thought and Methodology, with a Translation and Commentary on "Luma' al-Adilla."* Berlin: Schwarz, 2000.
Safian, Yasmin. "Necessity (ḍarūra) in Islamic Law: A Study with Special Reference to the Harm Reduction Programme in Malaysia." PhD diss., University of Exeter, 2010.
Schacht, Joseph. *Introduction to Islamic Law*. Oxford: Clarendon Press, 1964.
The Origins of Muhammadan Jurisprudence. N.p.: American Council of Learned Societies, 2008.
Schmitdke, Sabine. "Early Ash'arī Theology: Abū Bakr al-Bāqillānī (d. 403/1013) and His *Hidayāt al-Mustarshidīn*." *Bulletin d'études orientales* 60 (2011): 39–71.
"The Mu'tazilite Movement (III): The Scholastic Phase." In *Oxford Handbook of Islamic Theology*, edited by Sabine Schmidtke. Oxford: Oxford University Press, 2016.
Shabana, Ayman. *Custom in Islamic Law and Legal Theory: The Development of the Concepts of 'Urf and 'Ādah in the Islamic Legal Tradition*. New York: Palgrave Macmillan, 2010.
Shafiq, Muhammad. "The Role and Place of Shura in the Islamic Polity." *Islamic Studies* 23, no 4 (1984): 419–41.
Shihadeh, Ayman. *The Teleological Ethics of Fakhr al-Dīn al-Rāzī*. Leiden: Brill, 2006.
"The Argument from Ignorance and Its Critics in Medieval Arabic Thought." *Arabic Sciences and Philosophy* 23 (2013): 175–76.
"From al-Ghazālī to al-Rāzī: 6th/12th Century Developments in Muslim Philosophical Theology." *Arabic Sciences and Philosophy* 15 (2015): 144–79.
"Theories of Ethical Value in Kalām: A New Interpretation." In *Oxford Handbook of Islamic Theology*, edited by Sabine Schmidtke. Oxford: Oxford University Press, 2016.
Siddiqi, Muhammad Zubayr. *Hadith Literature: Its Origin, Development and Special Features*. Cambridge: Islamic Texts Society, 1993.
Siddiqui, Sohaira. "Power vs. Authority: Al-Juwaynī's Intervention in Pragmatic Political Thought." *Journal of Islamic Studies* 28, no. 2 (2017): 193–220.
Snyder, Franklin. "Nomos, Narrative and Adjudication: Toward a Jurisgenetic Theory of Law." *William and Mary Law Review* 40, no. 5 (1999): 1623–729.
Sobers-Khan, Nur. *Slaves without Shackles: Forced Labor and Manumission in the Galata Court Registers, 1560–1572*. Berlin: Klaus Schwarz, 2014.
Spectorsky, Susan A. "Aḥmad Ibn Ḥanbal's *Fiqh*." *Journal of the American Oriental Society* 102, no. 3 (1982): 461–65.
Stewart, Devin. "Muḥammad Dāwūd al-Ẓāhirī's Manual of Jurisprudence." In *Studies in Islamic Legal Theory*, edited Bernard Weiss, 99–158. Leiden: Brill, 2002.
Stoker, Gerry. "Governance as Theory: Five Propositions." *International Social Science Journal* 50 (1998): 17–28.
Tamanaha, Brian Z. *On the Rule of Law: History, Politics, Theory*. Cambridge: Cambridge University Press, 2004.
Thiele, Jan. "Between Cordoba and Nīsābūr: The Emergence and Consolidation of Ash'arism (Fourth–Fifth/Tenth–Eleventh Century)." In *Oxford Handbook*

of Islamic Theology, edited by Sabine Schmitdke, 225–41. Oxford: Oxford University Press.

Tucker, Judith. *In the House of the Law: Gender and Islamic Law*. Berkeley: University of California Press, 2000.

Vahid, Hamid. "Externalism/Internalism." In *The Routledge Companion to Epistemology*, edited by Sven Bernecker and Duncan Pritchard, 144–55. London: Routledge, 2011.

van Ess, Josef. "Ḳadariyya." In *The Encyclopedia of Islam*, 2nd edition, edited by P. Bearman, Th. Bianquis, C. E. Bosworth, E. Van Donzel, and W. P. Heinrichs. Leiden: Brill, 1960–2005.

"Ein unbekanntes Fragment des Naẓẓām." In *Der Orient in der Forschung: Festschrift fur Otto Spies zum 65. Geburtstag*, edited by Wilhelm Hoenerbach, 171–201. Wiesbaden: Harrassowitz, 1967.

"Early Islamic Theologians on the Existence of God." In *Islam and the Medieval West*, edited by Khalil I. Semaan, 64–81. Albany: State University of New York Press, 1980.

"Sufism and Its Opponents: Reflections on Topoi, Tribulations and Transformations." In *Islamic Mysticism Contested: Thirteen Centuries of Controversies and Polemics*, edited by Frederick de Jong and Bernd Radtke, 22–44. Leiden: Brill, 1999.

Vasalou, Sophia. *Moral Agents and Their Deserts: The Character of Muʿtazilite Ethics*. Princeton: Princeton University Press, 2008.

Vishanoff, David. *The Formation of Islamic Hermeneutics: How Sunnī Legal Theorists Imagined a Revealed Law*. New Haven, CT: American Oriental Society, 2011.

Walker, Paul. "Faṭimid Institutions of Learning." *Journal of the American Research Center in Egypt* 34 (1997): 179–200.

Watt, Montgomery. *Free Will and Predestination in Early Islam*. London: Luzac, 1948.

Islamic Philosophy and Theology. Edinburgh: Edinburgh University Press, 1979.

"Suffering in Sunnite Islam." *Studia Islamica*, no. 50 (1979): 5–19.

Weiss, Bernard. Review of *Before Revelation*, by Kevin Reinhart. *Journal of the American Oriental Society* 119, no. 2 (1999): 317–18.

The Spirit of Islamic Law. Atlanta: University of Georgia Press, 2006.

The Search for God's Law: Islamic Jurisprudence in the Writings of Sayf al-Dīn al-Āmidī. Salt Lake City: University of Utah Press, 2010.

Wensinck, A. J. *The Muslim Creed*. New York: Routledge, 2013.

Wisnovsky, Robert. "Avicenna and the Avicennian Tradition." In *The Cambridge Companion to Arabic Philosophy*, edited by Peter Adamson and Richard C. Taylor, 92–136. Cambridge: Cambridge University Press, 2004.

"One Aspect of the Avicennian Turn." *Arabic Sciences and Philosophy* 14 (2004): 65–100.

Wymann-Landgraf, Umar Abd-Allah. *Mālik and Medina*. Leiden: Brill, 2013.

Young, Walter. *The Dialectical Forge: Juridical Disputation and the Evolution of Islamic Law*. Cham: Springer, 2017.

Zaman, Muhammad Qasim. "Ahl al-ḥall wa-l-ʿaqd." In *Encyclopedia of Islam*, 3rd edition, edited by Kate Fleet, Gudrun Krämer, Denis Matringe, John Nawas, and Everett Rowson. Leiden: Brill, 2007.

al-Zuḥaylī, Muḥammad. *al-Imām al-Juwaynī: Imām al-Ḥaramayn*. Damascus: Dār al-Qalam, 1992.

Zysow, Aron. *The Economy of Certainty: An Introduction to the Typology of Islamic Legal Theory*. Atlanta: Lockwood Press, 2013.

Index

Other titles in the series:

Agricultural Innovation in the Early Islamic World: The Diffusion of Crops and Farming Techniques, 700–1100, Andrew M. Watson
Muslim Tradition: Studies in Chronology, Provenance and Authorship of Early Hadith, G. H. A. Juynboll
Social History of Timbuktu: The Role of Muslim Scholars and Notables 1400–1900, Elias N. Saad
Sex and Society in Islam: Birth Control before the Nineteenth Century, B.F. Musallam
Towns and Townsmen of Ottoman Anatolia: Trade, Crafts and Food Production in an Urban Setting 1520-1650, Suraiya Faroqhi
Unlawful Gain and Legitimate Profit in Islamic Law: Riba, Gharar and Islamic Banking, Nabil A. Saleh
Men of Modest Substance: House Owners and House Property in Seventeenth-Century Ankara and Kayseri, Suraiya Faroqhi
Roman, Provincial and Islamic Law: The Origins of the Islamic Patronate, Patricia Crone
Economic Life in Ottoman Jerusalem, Amnon Cohen
Mannerism in Arabic Poetry: A Structural Analysis of Selected Texts (3rd Century AH/9th Century AD–5th Century AH/11th Century AD), Stefan Sperl
The Rise and Rule of Tamerlane, Beatrice Forbes Manz
Popular Culture in Medieval Cairo, Boaz Shoshan
Early Philosophical Shiism: The Ismaili Neoplatonism of Abu Yaʿqub Al-Sijistani, Paul E. Walker
Indian Merchants and Eurasian Trade, 1600–1750, Stephen Frederic Dale
Palestinian Peasants and Ottoman Officials: Rural Administration around Sixteenth-Century Jerusalem, Amy Singer
Arabic Historical Thought in the Classical Period, Tarif Khalidi
Mongols and Mamluks: The Mamluk-Ilkhanid War, 1260–1281, Reuven Amitai-Preiss
Knowledge and Social Practice in Medieval Damascus, 1190–1350, Michael Chamberlain
The Politics of Households in Ottoman Egypt: The Rise of the Qazdağlis, Jane Hathaway
Hierarchy and Egalitarianism in Islamic Thought, Louise Marlow
Commodity and Exchange in the Mongol Empire: A Cultural History of Islamic Textiles, Thomas T. Allsen
State and Provincial Society in the Ottoman Empire: Mosul, 1540–1834, Dina Rizk Khoury
The Mamluks in Egyptian Politics and Society, Thomas Philipp and Ulrich Haarmann (eds.)
The Delhi Sultanate: A Political and Military History, Peter Jackson
European and Islamic Trade in the Early Ottoman State: The Merchants of Genoa and Turkey, Kate Fleet
The Ottoman City between East and West: Aleppo, Izmir, and Istanbul, Edhem Eldem, Daniel Goffman, and Bruce Masters

The Politics of Trade in Safavid Iran: Silk for Silver, 1600–1730, Rudolph P. Matthee
The Idea of Idolatry and the Emergence of Islam: From Polemic to History, G. R. Hawting
A Monetary History of the Ottoman Empire, Şevket Pamuk
Classical Arabic Biography: The Heirs of the Prophets in the Age of al-Ma'mun, Michael Cooperson
Empire and Elites after the Muslim Conquest: The Transformation of Northern Mesopotamia, Chase F. Robinson
Poverty and Charity in Medieval Islam: Mamluk Egypt, 1250–1517, Adam Sabra
Culture and Conquest in Mongol Eurasia, Thomas T. Allsen
Christians and Jews in the Ottoman Arab World: The Roots of Sectarianism, Bruce Masters
Arabic Administration in Norman Sicily: The Royal Diwan, Jeremy Johns
Law, Society and Culture in the Maghrib, 1300–1500, David S. Powers
Revival and Reform in Islam: The Legacy of Muhammad al-Shawkani, Bernard Haykel
Tolerance and Coercion in Islam: Interfaith Relations in the Muslim Tradition, Yohanan Friedmann
Guns for the Sultan: Military Power and the Weapons Industry in the Ottoman Empire, Gábor Ágoston
Marriage, Money and Divorce in Medieval Islamic Society, Yossef Rapoport
The Empire of the Qara Khitai in Eurasian History: Between China and the Islamic World, Michal Biran
Domesticity and Power in the Early Mughal World, Ruby Lal
Power, Politics and Religion in Timurid Iran, Beatrice Forbes Manz
Postal Systems in the Pre-Modern Islamic World, Adam J. Silverstein
Kingship and Ideology in the Islamic and Mongol Worlds, Anne F. Broadbridge
Justice, Punishment and the Medieval Muslim Imagination, Christian Lange
The Shiites of Lebanon under Ottoman Rule, 1516–1788, Stefan Winter
Women and Slavery in the Late Ottoman Empire, Madeline Zilfi
The Second Ottoman Empire: Political and Social Transformation in the Early Modern World, Baki Tezcan
The Legendary Biographies of Tamerlane: Islam and Heroic Apocrypha in Central Asia, Ron Sela
Non-Muslims in the Early Islamic Empire: From Surrender to Coexistence, Milka Levy-Rubin
The Origins of the Shi'a: Identity, Ritual, and Sacred Space in Eighth-Century Kufa, Najam Haider
Politics, Law, and Community in Islamic Thought: The Taymiyyan Moment, Ovamir Anjum
The Power of Oratory in the Medieval Muslim World, Linda G. Jones
Animals in the Qur'an, Sarra Tlili
The Logic of Law Making in Islam: Women and Prayer in the Legal Tradition, Behnam Sadeghi
Empire and Power in the Reign of Süleyman: Narrating the Sixteenth-Century Ottoman World, Kaya Şahin
Law and Piety in Medieval Islam, Megan H. Reid

Women and the Transmission of Religious Knowledge in Islam, Asma Sayeed
The New Muslims of Post-Conquest Iran: Tradition, Memory, and Conversion, Sarah Bowen Savant
The Mamluk City in the Middle East: History, Culture, and the Urban Landscape, Nimrod Luz
Disability in the Ottoman Arab World, 1500–1800, Sara Scalenghe
The Holy City of Medina: Sacred Space in Early Islamic Arabia, Harry Munt
Muslim Midwives: The Craft of Birthing in the Premodern Middle East, Avner Giladi
Doubt in Islamic Law: A History of Legal Maxims, Interpretation, and Islamic Criminal Law, Intisar A. Rabb
The Second Formation of Islamic Law: The Hanafi School in the Early Modern Ottoman Empire, Guy Burak
Sexual Violation in Islamic Law: Substance, Evidence, and Procedure, Hina Azam
Gender Hierarchy in the Qur'an: Medieval Interpretations, Modern Responses, Karen Bauer
Intellectual Networks in Timurid Iran: Sharaf al-Din 'Ali Yazdi and the Islamicate Republic of Letters, Ilker Evrim Binbaş
Authority and Identity in Medieval Islamic Historiography: Persian Histories from the Peripheries, Mimi Hanaoka
The Economics of Ottoman Justice: Settlement and Trial in the Sharia Courts, Top of Form Metin Coşgel and Boğaç Ergene
The Mystics of al-Andalus: Ibn Barrajan and Islamic Thought in the Twelfth Century, Yousef Casewit
Muhammad's Heirs: The Rise of Muslim Scholarly Communities, 622–950, Jonathan E. Brockopp
The First of the Modern Ottomans: The Intellectual History of Ahmed Vasif, Ethan Menchinger
Non-Muslim Provinces under Early Islam: Islamic Rule and Iranian Legitimacy in Armenia and Caucasian Albania, Alison Vacca
Women and the Making of the Mongol Empire, Anne F. Broadbridge
Slavery and Empire in Central Asia, Jeff Eden
Christianity in Fifteenth-Century Iraq, Thomas A. Carlson
Child Custody in Islamic Law: Theory and Practice in Egypt since the Sixteenth Century, Ahmed Fekry Ibrahim
Ibadi Muslims of North Africa: Manuscripts, Mobilization, and the Making of a Written Tradition, Paul M. Love Jr.